Conflict in Organizational Groups

Conflict in Organizational Groups

New Directions in Theory and Practice

EDITED BY

Kristin J. Behfar and Leigh L. Thompson

Northwestern
University Press
Evanston, Illinois

Evanston, Illinois

Northwestern University Press
Evanston, Illinois 60208-4170
ISBN-13: 978-0-8101-2457-8
ISBN-10: 0-8101-2457-2

Printed in the United States of America

10 9 8 7 6 5 4 3 2 1

Library of Congress Cataloging-in-Publication Data

Conflict in organizational groups : new directions in theory and practice / edited by Kristin J. Behfar and Leigh L. Thompson.
    p. cm.
  "The chapters in this book were presented at a conference held at the Kellogg School of Management in June 2005 entitled Conflict in Organizational Groups : New Directions in Theory and Practice."
  Includes bibliographical references and index.
  ISBN-13: 978-0-8101-2457-8 (cloth : alk. paper)
  ISBN-10: 0-8101-2457-2 (cloth : alk. paper)
  1. Conflict management—Congresses. 2. Teams in the workplace—Congresses. 3. Interpersonal conflict—Congresses. I. Behfar, Kristin J. II. Thompson, Leigh L.
  HD42.C648 2007
  302.3'5—dc22
                         2007006131
The paper used in this publication meets the minimum requirements of the American National Standard for Information Sciences—Permanence of Paper for Printed Library Materials, ANSI Z39.48-1992.

CONTENTS

TABLES AND FIGURES

TABLES

FIGURES

PREFACE

The chapters in this book were presented at a conference held at the Kellogg School of Management in June 2005 entitled Conflict in Organizational Groups: New Directions in Theory and Practice. The goal of the conference was to bring together both junior and senior scholars from a variety of disciplines to discuss their newest ideas and current trends in group conflict research. The chapters in this book represent perspectives from the fields of business, political science, sociology, and psychology.

The Kellogg Team and Group Research Center (KTAG) and the Kellogg School of Management cosponsored the conference. We are grateful for the generous support of the KTAG center and the Kellogg school on this project and the subsequent development of this book.

Assistance with the coordination of the conference and preparation of this volume was provided by Aarthi Kuppuswamy, who planned and ran the conference beautifully. Subsequent administrative and editorial assistance was spearheaded by Silva Kurtisa.

This book is the second in a series of topical themes related to groups and teams. Every two years, the KTAG center at Kellogg hires a postdoctoral fellow in the area of groups and teams. The conference and the corresponding book are a testament to their achievements at Kellogg and beyond.

CONTRIBUTORS

Holly Arrow
Department of
    Psychology
University of Oregon
Eugene, Oregon

Kristin J. Behfar
Merage School of
    Business
University of California
Irvine, California

Katerina Bezrukova
Department of
    Psychology
Rutgers University
Camden, New Jersey

Matthew A. Cronin
School of Management
George Mason University
Fairfax, Virginia

Julie Davidson
London Business School
London, England

Ashley Donnenfeld
Tuck School of Business
Dartmouth College
Hanover, New
    Hampshire

Vanessa Urch Druskat
Whittemore School of
    Business and
    Economics
University of New
    Hampshire
Durham, New
    Hampshire

Karen A. Jehn
Social and Organizational
    Psychology
Leiden University
Leiden
The Netherlands

Douglas Kennett
Department of
    Anthropology
University of Oregon
Eugene, Oregon

Claus Langfred
John M. Olin School of
    Business
Washington University
St. Louis, Missouri

Lisa M. Moynihan
London Business School
London, England

Gerardo A. Okhuysen
David Eccles School of
    Business
University of Utah
Salt Lake City, Utah

John Orbell
Institute of Cognitive and
    Decision Sciences
University of Oregon
Eugene, Oregon

Randall S. Peterson
London Business School
London, England

Katherine W. Phillips
Kellogg School of
    Management
Northwestern University
Evanston, Illinois

Hettie A. Richardson
William and Catherine
    Rucks Department of
    Management
Louisiana State University
Baton Rouge, Louisiana

Oleg Smirnov
Department of Political
    Science
School of Business
University of Miami
Coral Gables, Florida

Sherry M. B. Thatcher
Management Information
    Systems Department
University of Arizona
Tucson, Arizona

Melissa C. Thomas-Hunt
Johnson School of
    Management
Cornell University
Ithaca, New York

Leigh Thompson
Kellogg School of
    Management
Northwestern University
Evanston, Illinois

Ruth Wageman
Tuck School of Business
Dartmouth College
Hanover, New
    Hampshire

Laurie R. Weingart
Tepper School of Business
Carnegie Mellon
    University
Pittsburgh, Pennsylvania

Steven B. Wolff
McClelland Center for
    Research
Hay Group
Boston, Massachusetts

INTRODUCTION

The idea to organize a conference about conflict in organizational groups arose from three interrelated and exciting opportunities for theory and practice. First, both the academic and business press have focused growing attention on the management challenges of organizational groups. In the past two years, many top business and academic publications have dedicated articles or special issues to the impact of conflict on groups and their organizations. Although this increased attention has convinced many business students and managers that conflict management and interpersonal skills are worth developing, it has also made clear how many unanswered questions there are about conflict. For example: Does diversity create more or less conflict in groups? Can we select team members with certain traits in order to reduce the potential for conflict? Why do self-managing teams have so much conflict when they have complete control over their work? How can management and engineering stop having conflict?

Scholars have studied these questions from various disciplinary perspectives. Recently the academic community has begun to integrate these perspectives, as evidenced by a growing number of cross-disciplinary coauthorships and thematic conferences. This convergence has produced several important research results to serve as a scientific basis for guiding practice. However, it has also created an enormous number of variables with which scholars must grapple in their efforts to understand the causes and consequences of conflict. In short, it has left the area wide open for exciting new ideas and theories about conflict in organizational teams.

In parallel, several statistical and methodological advances have allowed scholars to better model variables across levels of analysis. This development has allowed improved precision in measurement and the capability to specify models that recognize the dynamic nature of conflict.

Taken together, these three reasons inspired the assembling of the interdisciplinary mix of seasoned and newly minted authors who in this volume tackle important and complex questions about group conflict. Their chapters represent cutting-edge advances in theory, methodology, and challenges to dominant perspectives.

The introductory chapter by Kristin Behfar and Leigh Thompson provides an overview of how the current literature addresses the common question: Is conflict functional or dysfunctional for organizational groups? They propose a "quasifunc-tional" view for understanding the impact of conflict both within and between orga-nizational groups and identify promising research streams that align with this per-spective and combine scholarly research with managerial recommendations that pass the scientific litmus test and are accessible to the business community.

The rest of the book represents work in this tradition and is organized into two parts. Part 1 presents new advancements in measuring and theorizing about the rela-tionship between individual members and group conflict. Katherine Phillips and Melissa Thomas-Hunt (chapter 2) discuss how social-category diversity and status distance among team members influence the process of information elaboration (or task conflict). They develop four propositions to reconcile conflicting findings in the literature about the benefits of diversity on information elaboration in teams. They argue that status differences among team members can suppress the confidence or assertiveness of lower-status members as well as the exchange and integration of their unique knowledge, perspectives, and information. This effect creates misattributions for members' behaviors that can create harmful relationship conflict among mem-bers, reduce information elaboration, and ultimately reduce performance outcomes. They propose that by understanding partitions between low-status and high-status members, managers and leaders of organizational groups can help overcome these negative impacts of status differences.

Katerina Bezrukova, Sherry Thatcher, and Karen Jehn (chapter 3) use longitu-dinal field data to contrast the accuracy of two competing theoretical perspectives about the impact of group diversity on process and performance. Like Williams and Thomas-Hunt, they are interested in reconciling why there are conflicting results about the benefits of diversity. In their comparison of alignment and dispersion approaches, they argue and provide empirical evidence that the alignment approach provides a more fine-grained and consistent measurement of the impact of demo-graphic differences on conflict and group outcomes. They argue that assessing the strength of faultline measures, which account for cumulative proportions of variance across demographic variables, is one possible explanation for missing variance in pre-vious diversity studies.

Randall Peterson, Julie Davidson, and Lisa Moynihan (chapter 4) make a com-pelling case for more frequently including personality variables, particularly neuroti-cism, in the study of how team diversity influences conflict. They argue that although most of the team diversity research focuses on visible differences among members (for example, age, race, and gender), these differences become less salient over time as members interact and get to know each other. In contrast, personality differences can become more salient if they are the basis for conflict or disruptive behavior. The authors take this notion one step further by demonstrating why a lack of measure-ment specificity (for example, using factor-level rather than facet-level scores) in pre-vious studies has suppressed evidence of important differences and their significant effects on team conflict. They present evidence, for example, that the anger facet of neuroticism in particular causes harmful relationship conflict and decreases team cohesion. They propose a configuration approach to theorizing about team personality differences, suggesting that a team should be aware of its configuration to most effectively use the strengths of its members.

Holly Arrow, Oleg Smirnov, John Orbell, and Douglas Kennett (chapter 5) identify how conflict between groups influences the way individuals choose to serve the future interests of their groups and the effect of their actions on the groups' survival. The authors answer the intriguing question: When is self-sacrificing behavior worth the price? They examine how war shapes the evolution of two types of altruism (defined as an individual behaving in a way that benefits his or her group at a cost to himself or herself). One such behavior is communitarianism, which is nonmilitary assistance to the group at a cost to oneself. The other is heroism, which is military assistance to the group with the risk of death or injury. The authors find that when war is infrequent, heroism behaviors evolve. When war is extreme or perpetual and the group is small, communitarianism behaviors evolve. They conclude by extending these results to underlying mechanisms that lead to evolutionary altruism behaviors in organizations, such as overcoming reduced capacity to reason realistically, the reclassification of out-group members, the impact of resource threats and impending attacks (for example, hostile takeovers), and loyalties and politics. They make a persuasive case that conflict between groups is a powerful and socially motivating activity.

Part 2 of the volume addresses several variables that affect the nature of group process and performance. The opening chapter by Gerardo Okhuysen and Hettie Richardson (chapter 6) makes an extremely important contribution to explicating the meaning and measurement of conflict variables over time. The authors provide a compelling framework for incorporating the dynamic properties of conflict constructs into group models. Specifically, they articulate four conceptual and empirical properties of dynamic constructs: stability of meaning, variability over time, predictive ability, and variation in consensus. Their longitudinal study empirically demonstrates how conflict measures exhibit different characteristics over time; their results suggest that conflict should be conceptualized as an emergent state. They offer recommendations for improving cross-sectional design and cross-level analysis and for developing more dynamic theoretical models.

Claus Langfred (chapter 7) examines the relationship between team design and conflict. He poses the important question: What is the dynamic relationship between conflict and autonomy as self-managing teams try to manage their own conflict? He integrates the literature on team process and team design by outlining how different types of autonomous teams may be more or less prone to different types of conflict. In guiding theory, he suggests several moderators to help a team strike the correct balance between individual-level and team-level autonomy. This balance is an important predictor not only of what types of conflict a team will experience but also of how well the team can manage that conflict and meet performance goals.

Matthew Cronin and Laurie Weingart (chapter 8) examine how interpersonal trust and respect influence the type of conflict teams have. They demonstrate that trust (the willingness to rely on another) and respect (level of esteem for another) have very different effects on conflict. For example, respect increases task conflict and decreases relationship conflict, but trust decreases process conflict. The authors make a forceful argument about the fidelity and predictive power of attitude measures. They conclude with important advice for managing harmful conflicts: When a team experiences relationship conflict, the solution is to build respect, but when a team experiences process conflict, building trust is more important.

Vanessa Druskat and Steven Wolff (chapter 9) address the problem of how a team should deal with conflict caused by disruptive team members. They answer the intriguing question: What kind of confrontation is effective? Results of a longitudinal study demonstrate that when members exhibit problem behavior, teams that have norms for confronting this behavior were as effective as teams whose members used less disruptive and conflict-provoking forms of disagreement. The authors also found that individual skills consistent with emotional intelligence (empathy, self-control, persuasiveness, and developing others) moderated the link between confrontation and team effectiveness. They conclude with several recommendations for building theory about emergent and dynamic process norms.

Ruth Wageman and Ashley Donnenfeld (chapter 10) conclude the volume with an important framework for understanding how and when members of organizations should intervene in group conflict. They outline the aspects of team design that correlate with functional versus dysfunctional conflict; distinguish among intervention practices that address relational, cognitive, and process conflicts; and identify conditions that enable individuals to effectively intervene in team conflict. Taking this one step further, they identify individual qualities that increase capacity to effectively intervene—among them conceptualization and diagnostic skills, fluency with a repertoire of interventions, and a good sense of timing. They develop five propositions and make a compelling argument that their framework will improve the development activities of organizational team members trying to successfully intervene in group conflict.

Each chapter in this volume offers exciting insights into measuring, managing, and theorizing about conflict in organizational groups. We hope you enjoy reading them as much as we have.

Kristin J. Behfar
Leigh L. Thompson

Part 1

Conflict and the Individual Group Member

Chapter 1

CONFLICT WITHIN AND BETWEEN ORGANIZATIONAL GROUPS: FUNCTIONAL, DYSFUNCTIONAL, AND QUASIFUNCTIONAL PERSPECTIVES

Kristin J. Behfar and Leigh L. Thompson

ABSTRACT

This chapter identifies and critiques commonly held assumptions in theory and research on group conflict in organizations. We first review recent literature investigating within-group and between-group conflict and the generalized belief that within-group conflict is largely functional whereas between-group conflict is largely dysfunctional. We argue, however, that classifying conflict as functional or dysfunctional is an oversimplification. In doing so, we argue that a quasifunctional framework—one that recognizes boundary conditions and the temporal or contextual aspects of group functioning—is useful for understanding when conflict is functional and when it is dysfunctional.

INTRODUCTION

One of the most commonly raised questions about group conflict is whether it furthers or threatens group goals. Thus, the question of functional versus dysfunctional conflict is a key distinction for both scholars and practitioners. Organizational researchers as well as practitioners have bifurcated the literature into within-group and between-group categories of conflict, and we rely on this categorization to organize our discussion. A common stereotype in the conflict literature has been that intragroup conflict can be functional (for example, for stimulating varied perspectives during group decision making), whereas between-group conflict is primarily dysfunctional (for example, having consequences that often manifest in hostility and operational interruptions). We argue, however, that classifying conflict as functional or dysfunctional is an oversimplification in most cases. We propose a more "quasifunctional" view of conflict—that the impact of conflict on group processes and outcomes depends on several conditions, actions, and reactions in the group context. Specifically, we highlight a growing amount of research identifying prescriptive recommendations, interventions, or processes that implicitly or explicitly recognize the temporal and contextual aspects of group functioning in relation to conflict. A quasifunctional perspective suggests that, although generalizations can be made across contexts about the impact of conflict, conditions exist that can transform the impact of conflict from negative to positive and vice versa. This chapter critiques current perspectives on group conflict and posits that using a "quasi" perspective—one that sees conflict as being somewhere between functional and dysfunctional—is a more realistic way to organize the literature, make prescriptive recommendations, and understand conflict.

CONFLICT: FUNCTIONAL OR DYSFUNCTIONAL?

One reason for the common stereotype that intragroup conflict can be functional, whereas between-group conflict is primarily dysfunctional, is that academic research produced from various disciplinary perspectives (for example, organizational behavior, psychology, sociology, and communications) can be loosely organized to support this distinction (for example, see Argyris and Schon, 1996; Jehn and Bendersky, 2003; Pondy, 1992; Putnam and Poole, 1987; Smith and Berg, 1987). Although this stereotype is useful in simplifying a somewhat complex and occasionally contradictory literature, a limitation is highlighted by a seeming disconnect between academic and practitioner perspectives about the causes and consequences of conflict. That is, for primarily methodological purposes, academicians tend to understate the contextual impact of conflict in cause/effect relationships, investigating one cause in isolation from other causes; often, they do not take temporal effects or group operating context into consideration (Arrow, McGrath, and Berdahl, 2000; McGrath, 1991). The business world focuses more on the ripple effect and/or lingering residue that conflict has on relationships, office politics, and operations (Gowing, Kraft, and Campbell-Quick, 1998; Lubit, 2003; Senge, 1990). As a result, the academic literature has successfully explained many of the more micro processes and psychological mechanisms that underlie conflict behavior within and between groups. The business literature has focused more on the costs and consequences of coordination losses often associated with conflict. The question that still remains largely unanswered in the groups literature is primarily about the consequences of conflict: When is conflict functional or dysfunctional?

Earlier reviews have addressed this question by summarizing the mechanisms, processes, and outcomes associated with functional versus dysfunctional conflict. Levine and Thompson (1996) focused on informational influence and scarce resource competition as sources of conflict within groups. Using Kelley and Thibaut's (1969) model of conflict as either information based or outcome based, Levine and Thompson identified several psychological mechanisms that foster three main consequences: conflict avoidance (inaction, withdrawal, and preemptive action), conflict reduction (individualistic action, voting, and group negotiation), and conflict creation in and between groups (highlighting and exaggerating differences in interests and goals). Jehn and Bendersky (2003) also reviewed the empirical research about within-group conflict literature and focused on moderators (for example, task type, diversity, emotion) that ameliorate, exacerbate, amplify, or suppress conflict within groups.

We have a different focus on the functional versus dysfunctional perspectives on group conflict by identifying recent research developments that expose forces or conditions that draw a line between functional and dysfunctional conflict. Whereas our overarching purpose is to identify functional and dysfunctional aspects of group conflict, we propose regarding conflict from a quasifunctional perspective to integrate research and theoretical arguments across business perspectives, academic disciplines, and varying research streams. For purposes of exposition, we attempt to organize the group conflict literature into a 2x3 analysis summarized in Table 1.1: level of conflict (that is, within-group or between-group conflict) and valence (functional, that is, beneficial for group process and performance; dysfunctional, detrimental for group process and performance; or quasifunctional, suggesting conditions for encouraging or preventing conflict). We define conflict as the existence of, or perception of the existence of, resource competition, opposing interests, differences of opinion, and/or incompatible values (Guetzkow and Gyr, 1954; Wall and Callister, 1995). We first discuss conflict within groups and then turn the discussion to conflict between groups.

WITHIN-GROUP CONFLICT

The literature on within-group conflict typically suggests that some conflicts can be constructive or healthy, whereas other types of conflict can be destructive or counterproductive in achieving desirable group outcomes. Past research[1] often categorizes intragroup conflict into three types—relationship conflict, task conflict, and process conflict (Amason and Sapienza, 1997; Cosier and Rose, 1977; Guetzkow and Gyr, 1954; Jehn, 1997; Pelled, 1996; Pinkley, 1990; Wall and Nolan, 1986). Task or cognitive conflict is disagreement over differences in ideas, viewpoints, and opinions regarding the group's task (Jehn, 1995). Relationship conflict is conflict resulting from interpersonal incompatibilities, which includes affective components such as feeling tension and friction (Jehn, 1995). Process conflict is conflict about dividing

Table 1.1

Contrasting Traditional Views with the Quasifunctional View

	Conflict Is Dysfunctional	Conflict Is Functional	Quasifunctional
Within-group	**Concept:** Emotional tension distracts team from task work and encourages interpersonal animosity. **Causes:** • Poor team design • Lack of alignment on goals, values, and mental models **Consequences:** • Decreased performance • Decreased member satisfaction • Breakdown in process coordination and receptivity to feedback	**Concept:** Task-oriented disagreement that increases member awareness of alternatives and reduces conformity. **Causes:** • Good team design • Alignment on goals, values, and mental models **Consequences:** • Novel problem solving • Consideration of minority viewpoints • Increased motivation • Idea synergy	**Concept:** The impact of conflict depends on actions, reactions, and team context. **Examples:** • Conditions that aid in separating cognitive and emotional conflict • Explication of process conflict construct • Conflict resolution over time • Decision-making procedures to guide the manifestation of conflict • The role of team leaders
Between-group	**Concept:** Scarce resource competition and need to derive identity by comparison encourages stereotyping and in-group bias. **Examples:** • Resistance to change • Failed mergers and acquisitions • Interdepartmental blaming	**Concept:** Healthy competition between groups encourages innovation and productivity within groups. **Examples:** • Increased within-group cohesion and innovation • Increased creativity • Increase learning and vigilance in information monitoring	**Concept:** The impact of conflict depends on how organizations structure and manage policies to address conflict. **Examples:** • Alignment of organizational structure, operations, goals, and incentive programs • Managing the expression of conflict • Affirmative action policies

and delegating responsibility and deciding how to get work done (Jehn, 1997, p. 540). Using this tripartite distinction as a starting point, we first discuss the dysfunctional aspects of conflict. We then discuss the functional view of conflict (that is, its benefits).

WITHIN-GROUP CONFLICT: THE DYSFUNCTIONAL PERSPECTIVE

The dysfunctional perspective of within-group conflict primarily focuses on the tension, imbalance, and distraction that conflict can cause in teams (Guetzkow and Gyr, 1954; Heider, 1958). Within-group conflict that is most commonly viewed as causing dysfunction is referred to as emotional or interpersonal conflict (Guetzkow and Gyr, 1954; Jehn, 1995). It is considered dysfunctional because it consistently predicts a negative impact on team performance and individual member satisfaction (Amason, 1996; De Dreu and Weingart, 2003; Jehn, 1995; Simons and Peterson, 2000). It also has a negative impact on group process variables that are associated with favorable team outcomes. Team cohesion, for example, is the opposite of emotional conflict—members of a cohesive team feel interpersonal attraction (rather than tension), feel that the group has personal value to them (rather than creating accusatory attributions), and are more likely to contribute their resources to the team task (rather than focusing on behaviors of other members) (Stokes, 1983).

This type of conflict is dysfunctional for three main reasons: (1) It limits the information processing ability of the group because group members spend their time and energy focusing on each other rather than on the group problems (Amason, 1996; Evan, 1965; Jehn and Mannix, 2001); (2) it limits group members' cognitive functioning by increasing their stress and anxiety levels (Jehn and Mannix, 2001; Barry Staw, Sandelands, and Dutton, 1981); and (3) it encourages antagonistic or accusatory attributions for other group members' behavior, which can create a self-fulfilling prophecy of mutual hostility and conflict escalation (Baron, 1991; Janssen, Van De Vliert, and Veenstra, 1999; Torrance, 1957; Walton, 1969; compare Peterson and Behfar, 2003). We first discuss the conditions that precipitate this kind of dysfunctional conflict and then discuss the consequences of dysfunctional conflict.

Causes of Dysfunctional Conflict (Conflict as a Dependent Variable)
Because of the robust empirical findings that support the idea that emotional conflict is dysfunctional, it is natural that a line of research has emerged to examine what can cause and prevent this type of conflict. Conditions that precipitate dysfunctional conflict tend to stem from team design issues, perceived inequity, and lack of communication or understanding among members.

Team design is commonly treated as a precursor to successful teamwork (see chapters 7 and 10). This includes decisions about the degree of management control over the team, how the team is compensated, who is on the team, and the goal clarity for the team task. These are decisions that shape group process, are supposed to decrease resource competition, and give information to team members about what to expect from one another. General guidelines for good team design include assignment to a nonroutine task, a clear and challenging goal, clear role assignments, and high task interdependence among members—conditions that reduce uncertainty and competition among members (Gladstein, 1984; Locke and Latham, 1990; Wageman, 1995; see Ancona, Bresman, and Kaeufer [2002] and Jehn and Bezrukova [2004] for important variants of these general guidelines). However, simply assigning a group an interdependent, nonroutine task with a clear goal may be a necessary, but not a sufficient, condition for determining whether conflict is functional or dysfunctional.

Tension among members escalates when team design is either not clearly specified or breaks down. For example, if a team is designed to be self-managing but reports to a manager who constantly interferes with group process, conflict and confusion among members over roles and resources will distract the team's attention away from accomplishing the task (for example, see Druskat and Wheeler, 2003; Hackman, 1990). If team members are exclusively rewarded for their individual work rather than having joint responsibility for a successful team outcome, competition over team resources tends to increase and cooperation decreases (Deutsch and Coleman, 2000). Alternatively, if team members are exclusively rewarded for their joint outcome without individual accountability, potential social loafing or free-riding create tension surrounding inequity of work distribution (Hackman and Morris, 1975). Compensation structures, referred to as hybrid structures because they combine individual and group milestones, are effective in helping groups avoid emotional competition and declining motivation (Katz, 2001). Clearly defining what team members are responsible for and what they will receive for contributing to the team helps to reduce uncertainty, perceptions of unfairness, and competition over resources, all of which are associated with dysfunctional conflict.

Clear goals have long been considered a bedrock ingredient for effective teamwork and an essential element of good team design (Hackman, 1990; Locke and Latham, 1990). Groups with well-defined goals have an easier time focusing on the task at hand and are less prone to get bogged down in interpersonal and process problems (Jehn and Mannix, 2001). Lack of goal clarity creates conflict: Group members may either become invested in arguing their perspective on the goal or they may continue to contribute effort toward the goal but remain unaware that they are actually contributing ineffectively. Members who are punished, usually through poor performance outcomes, for their well-intended effort may feel undervalued, resentful, or confused (Lind and Tyler, 1988; Lind and Earley, 1992). Members can interpret this as unfair and may decrease their motivation to cooperate toward the group goal (Campion and Lord, 1982; Katz and Kahn, 1978; Locke, 1991). Resentment and confusion can lead to misplaced blaming, animosity, and mistrust—or emotional conflict. As task difficulty increases and resource scarcity increases, goal clarity becomes more important in reducing stress, anxiety, and dysfunctional conflict (Austin and Vancouver, 1996; Locke and Latham, 1990; Locke, Shaw, Saari, and Latham, 1981).

Team composition (who is on the team) has also been recognized as an important conflict-related variable (see chapter 2). Demographic differences among members in characteristics such as age, culture, work values, and functional background bring different social perspectives and preferences for work styles that can cause interpersonal tension to arise and escalate over time (Jehn, Northcraft, and Neale, 1999; Williams and O'Reilly, 1988). It is more difficult for heterogeneous groups to communicate and develop work norms, and they are more prone to dysfunctional conflict (Bettenhausen and Murnighan, 1985; Jehn and Mannix, 2001; Jehn et al., 1999; Steiner, 1972; Williams and O'Reilly, 1988). Research on faultlines (see chapter 3) has shown that different demographic divides and their salience can escalate a group's conflict experience (Thatcher, Jehn, and Zanutto, 2003). A response to this problem has been to better understand how groups narrow gaps in understanding caused by individual differences. A recent study, for example, demonstrates that teams with more variance in organizational values among members are more prone to dysfunctional conflict (Jehn and Mannix, 2001).

A parallel line of research that addresses how to align the values and expectations of team members focuses on mental models and shared cognition in teams (Peterson, Mitchell, Thompson, and Burr, 2000). Socially shared cognition or shared mental models represent alignment between individual-level expectations and group-level expectations for how to operate and manage teamwork (Thompson and Fine, 1999). To the extent that group members' mental models fail to align, there are conflicts— often resulting in tension between members (Jackson, 2003). This research highlights the importance of aligning priorities or preferences at the individual level in order to decrease dysfunctional interpersonal tension and differences at the group level.

Finally, disruptive personalities and aggressive or passive/aggressive behaviors (both verbal and nonverbal) can escalate interpersonal tension (Wall and Callister, 1995). It has been suggested that carefully matching personality traits with tasks (for example, put a worrier in charge of planning; put a detail person in charge of integration) is a successful way to minimize personality disruptions that escalate interpersonal tension (for example, Moynihan and Peterson, 2000; see chapter 4).

Dysfunctional Conflict as a Causal (Independent) Variable

A recent meta-analysis confirms the negative relationship between emotional conflict and both team performance and individual members' satisfaction with their team (De Dreu and Weingart, 2003). Interpersonal tension has a negative impact on group process because it counteracts the potentially positive forces of group synergy. For the three reasons mentioned previously, emotional conflict increases the salience of one's own interests rather than creating a group-level identity characterized by cooperation and cohesiveness among members (Deutsch, 1968). Emotional conflict also decreases member satisfaction with the group experience. A key outcome of sustaining group performance over time is a group's ability to make members feel that the efforts they put into the group are matched by what they get out of belonging to the group (Hackman and Morris, 1975). Low member satisfaction is associated with higher turnover, declining motivation, and lower productivity (Hackman and Morris, 1975)—all of which cause performance challenges as group members continue to work together and attempt to integrate their individual contributions. In addition, emotional conflict decreases a group's receptivity to performance feedback—especially after a group failure (Klein, 1989; Peterson and Behfar, 2003). A group's viability over time depends on its ability to adapt work processes and meet performance goals (Hackman and Morris, 1975). Performance feedback is one source of information that helps a group gauge how effective its processes are at achieving goals (Kluger and DeNisi, 1996). If members are making accusatory attributions and blaming one another for failures, the group's attention is distracted from getting work done, and performance suffers (Baron, 1991; Janssen et al., 1999; Jehn and Mannix, 2001; Torrance, 1957; Walton, 1969).

WITHIN-GROUP CONFLICT: THE FUNCTIONAL PERSPECTIVE

The type of within-group conflict that is typically treated as functional pertains to mainly cognitive group tasks, such as group decision making or problem solving. This type of functional conflict—commonly operationalized and measured as "task conflict," "fierce conversations," "constructive controversy," or "how management teams can have a good fight" (Eisenhardt, Kahwajy, and Bourgeois, 1997; Jehn, 1995; Scott, 2004; Tjosvold and Tjosvold, 1994)—will be referred to from this point on as cognitive conflict. Cognitive conflict is task-oriented disagreement: discussing pros and cons, considering alternative courses of action, or discussing how conflicting evidence fits into group decisions (Amason, 1996; Jehn, 1995). Generally, cognitive conflict is considered to have a functional or positive impact on performance and satisfaction because it increases members' awareness about problem-solving alternatives and encourages them to consider controversial evidence and viewpoints. Because so much of the academic and business literature has stereotyped cognitive conflict as a driver of positive outcomes, we first review the literature examining conditions that create functional conflict (that is, conflict as a dependent variable). We then review literature that treats conflict as a cause or independent variable of group performance.

Causes of Functional Conflict (Conflict as a Dependent Variable)

The literature very loosely theorizes about the antecedents of conflict; it commonly identifies causes of functional conflict to be the opposite of the causes of dysfunctional conflict discussed previously. For example, poor team design causes dysfunctional conflict, whereas good team design frees a team from emotional conflict and fosters functional conflict. If members feel that they are collectively responsible for accomplishing a goal, they should develop a more collaborative approach to discussing differences of opinion (Alper, Tjosvold, and Law, 1998; Campion, Papper, and Medsker, 1996; Wageman, 1995). Theoretically, following these principles engages groups in a collective effort to generate novel solutions, to engage in nonroutine problem-solving processes, and to encourage and motivate members to engage each other in information exchange. A similar argument is made regarding team composition. Theoretically, a more diverse team will generate valuable cognitive conflict based on the fact that team members bring multiple viewpoints and opinions to the team's discussions. However, as discussed previously, this heterogeneity can also cause dysfunctional interpersonal friction. We argue that this tight coupling of theoretical arguments about the causes of emotional and cognitive conflict is reflected in empirical evidence (for example, De Dreu and Weingart, 2003) that the stereotype of cognitive conflict as functional is not as clear-cut as it seems—a problem we will discuss in more detail in the following section about quasifunctional conflict (see p. 13).

A line of research that is somewhat related to identifying causes of functional cognitive conflict is the literature on structured debate techniques (see Katzenstein, 1996). These techniques (for example, brainstorming, dialectical inquiry, and devil's advocacy) are designed to focus discussion solely on the task at hand and provide structure in extracting expertise and alternative viewpoints of group members. However, the empirical evidence supporting the effectiveness of these techniques has been mixed. We will discuss this, too, in more detail.

Functional Conflict as a Causal (Independent) Variable
Cognitive conflict is regarded as functional when it generates constructive debate among team members (for example, Alper et al., 1998). The fundamental idea is that task-related disagreement during group decision making is functional because it slows the process of reaching consensus, thereby reducing pressures toward conformity that diminish group members' inclination and ability to discuss issues that are central to problem solving or conflict resolution. Within this perspective, there are two interrelated streams of research: (1) research focusing on how cognitive disagreements benefit group decision making or problem solving and (2) research highlighting errors and shortcomings in group decision making as a result of a lack of cognitive conflict. Both lines of research concentrate on the strong social/psychological group tendency toward conformity (Asch, 1952; Cartwright and Zander, 1968), treating cognitive conflict as the underlying mechanism that helps groups avoid conformity-based biases in decision making and problem solving.

One stream of research theorizes that cognitive conflict is functional because it stimulates consideration of decision alternatives and the pooling of resources (Eisenhardt et al., 1997; Hirokawa, 1988; Mason, 1981; Schweiger and Sandberg, 1989; Schwenk, 1990) and encourages consideration of minority viewpoints (Gruenfeld, 1995; Nemeth, 1992; Nemeth, Connell, Rogers, and Brown, 2001).

This task-focused exchange among team members is the vehicle that extracts the viewpoints and expertise of members as well, which in turn generates solutions superior to those the group and/or individual members first used to approach a task or problem (Amason, 1996; Jehn, 1995, 1997). In addition, groups that carefully consider options and diagnose problems prior to beginning work are more successful than those that do not engage in this type of cognitive appraisal (Hirokawa, 1983; Moreland and Levine, 1992).

A parallel line of research describes group decision-making biases and shortcomings that result from a lack of cognitive conflict. A lack of cognitive conflict is associated with several group biases caused by conformity. Each of these problems either explicitly recognizes or implies that this conformity is a symptom of a *lack of* cognitive conflict. Groupthink (Janis, 1972) is a widely cited decision-making bias that stems from an incomplete survey of alternatives and often results in disastrous outcomes (Janis, 1972). A lack of cognitive conflict is cited as the main mechanism that causes this conformity, with symptoms including a team that protects or insulates itself from outside or contrasting opinions or develops norms that suppress disagreements. This strong tendency stems either from an overly strong need to protect relationships, fear of disagreeing (that is, cognitive conflict) with a leader, fear of risk taking or loss of face in front of peers, and/or "self-appointed mind guards." In a similar vein, the Abilene paradox (Harvey, 1996) is a management consulting vignette about the "mismanagement of disagreement" or "pluralistic ignorance" in which group conformity occurs because of an avoidance of cognitive conflict stemming from a fear of disrupting the harmony of the group and relationships among group members. In this case, groups tend to embark on ill-fated courses of action on a suggestion by one member rather than to consider multiple points of view or possible alternatives. The common-information effect (Stasser, 1992; Stasser and Stewart, 1992) is another example of how group conformity or a lack of cognitive conflict, in the form of suppressing the voice of the minority, leads to biased decision making. This robust finding in the groups literature suggests that members not only discuss information that they have in common more often, but that they also give it more weight in arriving at a final decision (Wittenbaum, Hubbell, and Zuckerman, 1999). True cognitive conflict involves discussing new alternatives and weighing evidence, and the common-information effect and the associated tendency toward conformity are symptoms, or outcomes, of a lack of this cognitive conflict. Group polarization (Isenberg, 1986) is another decision-making bias that produces a decision or outcome that is more extreme than the original opinion or preference of any given individual member. Because the group does not carefully consider its courses of action, its decisions lead it to a more extreme, or polar, opinion. Again, this is an outcome from a lack of cognitive conflict.

The first research stream touts the positive benefits of cognitive conflict for catalyzing idea-related synergies. The second research stream reinforces this theoretical argument by illustrating how a lack of functional cognitive conflict is associated with more-negative outcomes. In both streams, however, there is an implicit recognition of the close relationship between task-based or cognitive conflict and task discussions becoming intertwined with emotion. This is demonstrated in the first stream of literature by its emphasis on the importance of *constructive* task- or fact-focused discussion (with recognition that there may be emotional spillover: Scott, 2004; Simons and Peterson, 2000) and is demonstrated in the second stream of literature with its emphasis on how the need for a group to preserve harmony and relationships makes groups more prone to conformity or to avoiding engaging in functional cognitive conflict. The theoretical explication and validity of the cognitive-conflict construct as a functional type of conflict is heavily dependent on task discussion not commingling with negative emotion in practice or experience.

WITHIN-GROUP CONFLICT: THE QUASIFUNCTIONAL PERSPECTIVE

While the research discussed previously has helped to explicate psychological processes and mechanisms that are associated with functional versus dysfunctional conflict, many of the underlying assumptions about cognitive conflict have recently been challenged. For example, the long-held assumption that cognitive conflict is functional has been called into serious question, as a recent meta-analysis demonstrates it has a negative impact on both performance and individual member satisfaction (De Dreu and Weingart, 2003). In addition, techniques for stimulating cognitive conflict, such as brainstorming and devil's advocacy, are ineffective if not managed correctly (Nemeth, Brown, and Rogers, 2001; Nemeth, Personnaz, Personnaz, and Goncalo, 2004). In response to these challenges to widely held assumptions, a growing body of research has begun to examine the boundary conditions and psychological mechanisms that underscore when task conflict, as well as relationship and process conflict, become functional or dysfunctional. This research considers three main characteristics: (1) the impact of time and evolving group dynamics on the conflict experience; (2) the impact of performance feedback and team context on conflict; and (3) group circumstances that prohibit conflict from escalating and/or becoming dysfunctional. This section identifies and discusses five examples of inter-related research streams that have developed in this tradition.

Example 1: As previously discussed, the perspective that cognitive conflict is exclusively functional is an oversimplification. In theory, moderate levels of cognitive conflict should improve group performance by stimulating discussion, increasing creativity, generating constructive criticism, and increasing awareness of issues and latent problems (Jehn, 1997; Wall and Callister, 1995). This argument, as well as the theoretical underpinnings of the construct, depend on task discussion remaining separate (that is, orthogonal) from emotional tension. In practice, it is not as easy for people to separate criticism of their ideas from criticism of their person (Eisenhardt et al., 1997). In support of this notion, research suggests that high levels of cognitive conflict can distract the group from reaching a consensus or accomplishing the task (Porter and Lilly, 1996), and too little cognitive conflict can lead to frustration due to a perceived lack of reciprocal commitment or disbelief that other members are contributing (Jehn, 1997). Cognitive and emotional conflicts are often highly correlated in experience and practice (see Simons and Peterson, 2000), and there is very little evidence to support the fact that the existence of cognitive conflict alone will predict better outcomes (De Dreu and Weingart, 2003). This suggests, therefore, that cognitive conflict is quasifunctional: It has the potential to be functional by increasing consideration of alternatives, but this depends on task debate remaining constructive and occurring under circumstances of low emotional conflict.

Several scholars have investigated conditions that help group members maintain the separation between cognitive and emotional conflict. For example, teams with a high level of trust are better able to have "fierce conversations" (Scott, 2004) while sustaining a boundary between cognitive and relationship conflict (Simons and Peterson, 2000; see chapter 8). This finding was replicated under conditions of negative performance feedback (Peterson and Behfar, 2003), which tends to increase the escalation of interpersonal tension among members as they attribute the group's performance failures to individual contributions (Guzzo, Wagner, MacGuire, Herr, and Hawley, 1986; Staw, 1975). In a similar vein, several scholars have found that deliberately fostered norms for comfort with risk taking predict a positive relationship between conflict of ideas and group outcomes. For example, teams characterized by strong psychological safety (Edmondson, 1999), norms for enforcing constructive controversy (Tjosvold and Tjosvold, 1994), and carefully articulated "temporary" norms for disagreement (Nemeth, Brown, and Rogers, 2001) have more positive group outcomes. Finally, individual skills such as emotional intelligence (Wolff, Pescosolido, and Druskat, 2002; see chapter 9) and cultural intelligence in multicultural teams (Earley and Mosakowski, 2004) have also been identified as skills that make people better at separating disagreement about ideas from personal affronts. How well individuals manage disagreement and the strength of group norms for managing disagreement determine whether cognitive conflict will be functional or dysfunctional.

Example 2: A second and related problem is that much of the literature on group decision making argues that there is evidence for the functional effects of cognitive conflict because *a lack of* this type of conflict produces poor group decisions (for example, too much conformity in the interest of preserving relationships). This is an analogous line of reasoning to confirming the null hypothesis (Greenwald, 1975). In spite of this flaw, we argue that this literature has inadvertently acknowledged why cognitive conflict can be quasifunctional with the prescriptive recommendations it offers for overcoming conformity biases. That is, the prescriptive advice has implicitly identified a boundary condition for determining how functional or dysfunctional cognitive conflict will be. This condition is how team *process is structured to manage cognitive conflict.* Recommendations for overcoming decision-making biases such as groupthink, the common-information effect, and the Abilene paradox all include procedures or processes designed to stimulate cognitive conflict. For example, this literature recommends that groups engage in rank ordering or conducting private votes as temporary process interventions to increase awareness and integration of unique information (Wittenbaum et al., 1999). When a group is under political or social pressure to produce a decision, the process interventions of bringing in outsiders, using subgroups or devil's advocates, and holding second-chance meetings have been suggested to reduce conformity (Janis, 1972). These procedures or processes serve several functions: (1) They help to align individual expectations—for example, they create temporary structures or mental models (Okhuysen and Eisenhardt, 2002; Thompson and Fine, 1999). (2) They help to separate emotional and cognitive conflict by reducing individual-level evaluation apprehension and the tendency to social loaf. (3) They reduce conformity pressures that suppress expression and integration of minority viewpoints (compare Nemeth et al., 2004). Such structured processes are designed to counteract pressures in the group context toward conformity by increasing consideration of alternatives, increasing processing of information by reducing biases in what information is attended to, and aiding in pooling resources—all predicted effects of functional cognitive conflict as outlined previously. These prescriptions to match process interventions with team context are often contrasted with less successful tactics that do not add structure to a team's process, such as increasing the amount of information a group has or increasing group size (Richard Guzzo and Shea, 1992; Latane, Williams, and Harkins, 1979; Taggar, 2002).

We argue that these procedural prescriptions highlight the quasifunctional nature of cognitive conflict because they account for the contextual and temporal pressures on groups. In a way, they are analogous to a timed-release medication—at different points during a group's decision-making process, these structures are imposed to introduce antidotes to group pressures that cause conflict to be dysfunctional rather than functional. The team-creativity literature, for example, is consistent with this. At different stages of the creative process, different types of team processes foster cognitive engagement that is linked to idea generation, uniqueness of ideas, and feasibility of new ideas. One of the most widely cited procedures for stimulating divergent thinking early in the creative process is to apply Osborn's rules, which are intended to prevent groups from too quickly judging and evaluating ideas (Osborn, 1957; Paulus, 1983). According to this logic, during the early stages of the creative process cognitive conflict suppresses creativity by elevating evaluation apprehension, and therefore conformity pressures, creating a dysfunctional "production-blocking" effect (compare Nemeth et al., 2004). The nominal group technique takes a slightly different view, first assigning individuals to brainstorm on their own and then bringing group members together to evaluate and criticize (that is, engage in cognitive conflict about) the ideas (Delbecq, Van de Ven, and Gustafson, 1974). As a group approaches a final solution, team members appreciate team leaders who, rather than allowing unlimited expression of opinions, intervene in a way that leads group members to converge on a decision (Peterson, 1999).

Structured procedures, however, are not a panacea. Recent research indicates that merely intervening with this type of structure does not guarantee that cognitive conflict will be functional. For example, assigning a devil's advocate for the sake of argument rather than representing a sincere alternative viewpoint can actually encourage group members to converge and defend the group's original position rather than integrate alternative proposals into their thought processes (Nemeth, Brown, and Rogers, 2001; Nemeth, Connell, Rogers, and Brown, 2001). An appropriate match between process structure and the temporal and contextual operations of a group is an important boundary condition of determining the impact of conflict.

Example 3: Whereas the literature discussed previously describes the impact of temporary process interventions on the functional or dysfunctional nature of conflict, the literature investigating a third type of conflict, process conflict, is aimed at investigating the impact of more *normative and ongoing* disagreements among members about the way a team should operate. Process conflict is defined as an awareness of controversies about aspects of how task accomplishment should proceed, how to delegate work assignments, and who has responsibility for various group tasks (Jehn, 1997). Teams scholars have long argued that process issues such as agreeing on a common approach, developing work plans, and dividing responsibility are essential to a group being able to perform well and avoid dysfunctional conflict (Pondy, 1967; Porter and Lilly, 1996).

Despite its theoretical importance, process conflict is the least well examined and understood of the three types of conflict (task, relationship, and process conflict). One problem has been that the process-conflict construct is often omitted from studies because process conflict does not reliably factor as distinct from cognitive conflict (compare Jehn, 1997; Jehn and Mannix, 2001). A primary problem with process conflict as a construct may be one of construct validity. Recent research, for example, identified three main process conflict–related issues that cause disagreements in teams: (1) work-pace timing and scheduling conflicts, (2) contribution and workload-distribution conflicts, and (3) disparate priorities and styles for deciding on a work method and approach (Behfar, Mannix, Peterson, and Trochim, 2002). Of these three types of process-related conflict, only the third is represented in the most commonly used process-conflict scale (Shah and Jehn, 1993). Compounding this problem, neither team members nor academic experts were able to distinguish this category of conflict from cognitive conflict—suggesting that the construct validity of the process conflict may be less of a theoretical problem and more an issue of criterion validity and measurement (see chapter 6 for additional measurement considerations).

This measurement issue may explain why the empirical findings regarding process conflict and its functional or dysfunctional impact on performance are limited and somewhat contradictory. In a small number of cross-sectional studies, high levels of process conflict have been negatively related to performance and satisfaction (Jehn, 1997; Jehn et al., 1999; Porter and Lilly, 1996). However, in a recent study of conflict patterns over time, high-performing teams had significantly higher levels of process conflict toward the end of the group interaction (but not at the beginning or middle) than low-performing teams (Jehn and Mannix, 2001). Research using scales that reflect a more distinct set of process issues (Behfar, Mannix, Peterson, and Trochim, 2002) suggests that high levels of process conflict reduce functional cognitive conflict and increase dysfunctional emotional conflict—such that as process conflict increases, cognitive conflict becomes less functional and emotional conflict becomes more dysfunctional (Behfar, Mannix, Peterson, and Trochim, 2002). There is also evidence that teams with higher levels of process conflict are not as good at identifying and using the expertise of team members (Behfar, Burris, and Thomas-Hunt, 2004). These findings are consistent with the logic that task strategies, team design, clear roles, and so on are key drivers of performance (Hackman, 1987). So, although much of the literature suggests that process interventions and procedural planning (for example, goal setting or role clarification) are useful in structuring group work, a growing amount of evidence suggests that conflict over fundamental procedural decisions is a condition that can blur the line between functional and dysfunctional conflict.

Example 4: A fourth and related line of emerging research suggests that the way groups *resolve* conflict determines whether conflict will have a functional or dysfunctional impact on group process and outcomes over time. Several researchers have previously proposed that conflict management is an important force in shaping group norms and a team's orientation toward working together—including the amount of concern team members show for other members versus themselves, how cooperative or competitive members are, and how avoidant or confrontational members are willing to be (Blake and Mouton, 1964; Deutsch, 1949; Pruitt and Rubin, 1986; Putnam and Poole, 1987; Rahim, 1983, 2002; Tjosvold and Tjosvold, 1994; Wall and Callister, 1995). These orientations elucidate how the three types of conflict (task, relationship, and process) can become entangled over time and blur members' vision toward an objective and task-focused work orientation. More recently, scholars have begun building theory about how specific group behaviors, norms, and strategies change in response to evolving team dynamics and external feedback (for example, Arrow et al., 2000; Arrow, Poole, Henry, Wheelan, and Moreland, 2004; Behfar, Kern, and Brett, 2006; Behfar, Peterson, Mannix, and Trochim, 2002; Poole, Siebold, and McPhee, 1996). Building on long-held theoretical foundations of the groups literature (for example, Homans, 1950), this research traces how conflict experiences influence how members interact, behave, and contribute to group process over time (Arrow et al., 2004; Bettenhausen and Murnighan, 1985; Guzzo and Shea, 1992; Peterson and Behfar, 2003; Zander, 1977). For example, a growing amount of evidence suggests that if members do not create group-level understandings to govern their processes (as opposed to "easy way out" strategies that increase individual-level comfort, such as divide and conquer or using voting as a default), they become prone to escalating emotional conflict over time (De Dreu, 1997) and less likely to engage in functional cognitive conflict (Behfar, Peterson, Mannix, and Trochim, 2002; DeChurch and Marks, 2001; Lovelace, Shapiro, and Weingart, 2001). Groups that are able to learn from high levels of process and emotional conflict early on in their life and that are able to restructure to prevent conflict from escalating in future tasks are able to recover performance and individual member satisfaction over time (Behfar, Peterson, Mannix, and Trochim, 2002). This highlights the quasifunctional nature of conflict. Through managing conflict, teams can learn from their mistakes (for example, how to prevent conflicts from escalating in the future), can better identify how best to leverage the strengths of individual members (for example, how to match work assignments with personality quirks and motivation of individual members), and can understand how to incorporate and seek out external feedback to increase process flexibility and foresee potential problems. Consistent with the research on quasifunctional conflict described previously, this line of research highlights the importance of group context (for example, history, external feedback, time pressures, evolving dynamics, and members' motivations) and procedures in determining how functional or dysfunctional conflict is over time.

Example 5: A fifth line of emerging research highlights the role that team leaders play in determining the impact of conflict. Much of the research into quasifunctional conflict that we have identified recognizes that minimizing dysfunctional conflict requires a team to monitor and match group process needs, performance goals, and group operating context. This is not surprising, considering that the literature classifies decisions about creating such a "match" as key elements for decreasing dysfunctional conflict, including delegating tasks and responsibilities, setting goals and deadlines, creating schedules, and monitoring progress toward goals (Edelmann, 1993; Pondy, 1967; Wall and Callister, 1995). However, these conflict-reducing functions in group life are rarely investigated; they are only hinted at through prescriptive recommendations and are typically relegated to the theoretical role that leaders and managers play (Gladstein, 1984; Hackman and Baetz, 1990).

A growing amount of evidence indicates that intervention by a leader into various stages of group functioning to create "boundary rules" (Sell, Lovaglia, Mannix, Samuelson, and Wilson, 2004) or "semi-structures" (Okhuysen and Eisenhardt, 2002) guides the manifestation of functional conflict (Peterson and Behfar, 2005). Team coaching theory is an important example of this research (Hackman and Wageman, 2005; also see Kim and Mauborgne, 2003, for a similar perspective). This theory outlines the role of a leader as one who both keeps track of a team's final goal and coaches the team to use appropriate processes to achieve that goal. This includes assessing the readiness of a team to receive an intervention as well as choosing the appropriate time in group process to intervene. Previous research suggests that groups are most ready to accept external interventions at the midpoint of their work cycles (Gersick, 1988). Team coaching theory expands this notion to include additional contextual and temporal strains on groups, including at the early stages of planning, when problem definition (that is, functional cognitive conflict) is key; after receiving feedback indicating that problem diagnosis and resource reorganization might be necessary (that is, reducing dysfunctional conflict); and after finishing a work cycle, when critical self-reflection by groups is important so they can learn about improving their processes.

Team coaching theory recognizes the quasifunctional nature of conflict by outlining the role of a formal authority in teaching the team how to work through, rather than get distracted by, challenges over time. Specifically, it recognizes the often delicate balance groups need to strike between managing task-related work and the interpersonal interaction among members (Homans, 1950). This type of approach, wherein a leader sets procedural structure and then steps back to let the team develop norms and work processes around that structure, is a very effective way to manage and contain natural conflicts (Wageman, 2001). In support of this notion, the group value model of team functioning has also suggested that a two-step intervention by a leader (first step, eliminate emotional tension; second step, restructure procedures) to increase group members' perceptions that operating procedures are fair is an effective way of stopping the escalation of emotional tension (Thibaut and Kelley, 1991; Thibaut and Walker, 1975). The literature on self-managing work teams also suggests that carefully timed interventions are helpful in keeping a team from experiencing dysfunctional conflict (Druskat and Wolff, 2001) and that appropriate leader interventions do not undermine the purpose of self-management, but rather make it easier to sustain. The role of formal and informal leaders in managing conflict is an underinvestigated area in the literature, and it holds important promise for helping managers understand how to maximize the benefits and minimize the injury of conflict.

In sum, these five streams of research into quasifunctional conflict that we have identified are a departure from previous theorizing about the more static functional-versus-dysfunctional effects of conflict, and they offer interesting theoretical advances toward understanding the more multidimensional *experiences* of the function and dysfunction of conflict. Although our review is not exhaustive, it does suggest that these new lines of research can be well integrated with and can build on previous theorizing about conflict, while incorporating temporal and contextual elements of group dynamics that are more consistent with business practices and management demands.

BETWEEN-GROUP CONFLICT

The previous section introduced the causes and consequences of intragroup conflict. Organizational groups, however, do not operate in a vacuum. They often must interact, share members, and integrate their outcomes with other organizational groups. We now turn our discussion to the functional and dysfunctional effects of conflict between groups.

BETWEEN-GROUP CONFLICT: THE DYSFUNCTIONAL PERSPECTIVE

Probably the best-known and longest-running perspective on between-group conflict is the dysfunctional perspective. We will not attempt a comprehensive review of this vast literature (but see Brewer and Kramer, 1985; Messick and Mackie, 1989). The more commonly held view of conflict between groups is that it is dysfunctional because it increases the salience of differences and the competition over scarce resources and often manifests itself in overt conflict.

One of the earliest treatments of between-group conflict from a dysfunctional perspective is Levine and Campbell's (1972) theory of ethnocentrism. According to Levine and Campbell, the basis of all between-group conflict is rooted in competition for scarce resources. Because other groups represent a direct threat to a given group's ability to acquire resources, groups are motivated to attack and devalue other groups. The long tradition of research on prisoner's dilemma games and, more aptly, social dilemma situations between groups highlights examples of intergroup competition for scarce resources (compare Brewer and Kramer, 1985; for a review see Messick and Mackie, 1989; Kopelman, Weber, and Messick, 2002). Moreover, Insko, Schopler, Graetz, Drigotas, Currey, Smith, et al. (1994) suggest that groups playing against one other in a prisoner's dilemma game compete more viciously than do individuals playing against one other. According to Insko et al. (1994), groups compete more intensely because they do not trust the other party and because they become more self-interested (characterized by fear and greed).

A quite different view of dysfunctional between-group conflict does not hinge on resource competition at all. The core idea of most versions of social identity theory[2] is that the conflict groups engage in with one another stems from an inherent need within individuals to derive their identity and well-being via belonging to a group that compares favorably against other groups (compare Tajfel and Turner, 1986). The most notable departure of this perspective from the scarce-resource perspective is that the key measure of dysfunctionality centers on prejudice and stereotyping rather than task performance. Researchers in this perspective have explored the minimum conditions necessary for groups to engage in stereotyping and have found that the mere division of people into even arbitrary groups (for example, based on a purely random device such as the color of shirts people are wearing) is enough to trigger in-group favoritism. In these experiments, a direct parallel is drawn to the incidence of social problems and social unrest such as racism, sexism, and interracial and interreligious conflict. For example, Sears and colleagues theoretically distinguished realistic group conflict theory from conflict over values and found that the degree of competition between groups for scarce resources did not predict attitudes toward social issues such as busing (Sears and Henry, 2003; Sears, van Laar, Carrillo, and Kosterman, 1997). Another particularly dysfunctional effect of this type of comparison in conflict situations is when socially acceptable behaviors are redefined (or relaxed) in comparison with egregious behavior of an out-group. For example, one ethnographic study of conflict between English and Scottish soccer fans found that otherwise peaceful Scottish fans (who viewed the English tendency toward brawling as "illegitimate") were able to justify "hooligan" behavior by redefining their own standards in relation to bad English behavior (Stott, Hutchison, and Drury, 2001). This has implications for growing ethical scandals in the corporate United States (Gowing et al., 1998).

In an organizational context, these divisions and robust tendencies toward in-group favoritism can invoke financial and human resource losses. For example, culture clashes between merging organizations often result in decreased operational efficiencies and/or bankruptcy (Gowing et al., 1998; Nahavandi and Malekzadeh, 1993). In merger settings, groups often act to protect their boundaries (reinforcing in-group/out-group distinctions) rather than cooperating with the merging party (Gaertner and Dovidio, 2000; Tajfel and Turner, 1986). When mergers fail, groups also tend to blame the merging organization as the cause of the failure as opposed to blaming it on a culture clash, bad management, or other more likely situational conditions (Weber and Camerer, 2003). This effect has also been found at the group-to-group level, such that departments or teams working together on a joint task place blame on the other group for, rather than acknowledging their own part in, negative outcomes (Worchel, Andreoli, and Folger, 1977).

Groups in organizations also have the power to resist organizational change efforts. They often show a decreased willingness to share information and coordinate with other groups and resist accepting new values, policies, and procedures (Sundstrom, De Meuse, and Futrell, 1990; Susskind, Miller, and Johnson, 1998; Tyler, Brockner, Konovsky, Cooper-Schneider, Folger, Martin, et al., 1994; Van Maanen and Kunda, 1989). Resistance to change is especially strong by groups if the procedures used create and introduce the change are perceived as unfair (Haveman, 1992; Shapiro and Kirkman, 1999). This type of conflict and resistance is considered dysfunctional because of the financial, human resource, and material waste it causes.

BETWEEN-GROUP CONFLICT: THE FUNCTIONAL PERSPECTIVE

The functional view of between-group conflict has not been very common. Indeed, given the number of wars that have occurred between groups and the terrible tragedies suffered for so many centuries, it seems almost shameful to suggest that groups should engage in conflict. Perhaps this is one reason why academicians are careful to circumscribe between-group conflict in the language of business and healthy competition. Whereas researchers have indicated that social groups need have no economic threat to experience conflict, organizational researchers are quick to focus on threats ranging from economic threats to status-loss threats as the basis for conflict (see chapter 5). For example, early social exchange theorists investigated between-group resource competition from the angle of power or dependence relations (Emerson, 1962), satisfaction with exchange relationships (Lawler and Yoon, 1996; Molm, 1991), normative expectations governing reciprocity (Levi-Strauss, 1969), and the more strategic economic tactics of power and punishments than are typical of tactics associated with overt conflict or war (Blau, 1987; Chadwick-Jones, 1976; Emerson, 1987, 1992; Molm, 1990).

In this vein, the most common line of theorizing about the functional effects of between-group conflict in organizations has focused on learning and information exchange, primarily between distinct—and occasionally competing—organizational groups. One perspective has been that a healthy amount of competition (that is, conflict) between groups in the same organization encourages increased productivity and innovation within groups. For example, one investigation of franchises in a large company (Pizza Hut) revealed that franchises often were in competition with one another but that this led to greater innovation of best practices in the franchises (Darr, Argote, and Epple, 1995). Another study found that competition between military squadrons actually strengthened the relationships among soldiers and reduced potentially demoralizing effects of failure within the group (Fiedler, 1967). In a similar vein, Ancona's (1990) investigation of conflicts that befall boundary-spanning teams working in the chasms of their organizations suggests that to the extent these teams behave in a decidedly individualistic and competitive way toward other teams, this enhances organizational learning. More recently, Ancona and Bresman (2003) suggested outright that teams should "beg, borrow, and steal" best practices for the sake of organizational learning. Similarly, Hargadon (in press) suggests that conflict between organizational groups is not only inevitable, it is actually a sign that the essential innovation process is working as it should. Hargadon suggests that the conflict between insiders and outsiders is pivotal for creative breakthroughs:

> The ability to think differently and then to convince others to think the same requires different and sometimes conflicting attitudes and behaviors: The locals distrust the shallow experiences and noncommittal "nature" of outsiders; the outsiders distrust the parochial and intransigent "nature" of the locals. And perhaps this is why creativity remains so fascinating, reflecting as it does a momentary détente in the tension between the local and global, novel and familiar.

Menon and Pfeffer (2003) take a slightly different view of functional between-group conflict. Whereas the aforementioned perspective focused on how intraorganizational teams experiencing between-group conflict learn from one another, Menon and Pfeffer make the powerful argument that organizational actors are particularly threatened by in-group members and are less threatened by out-group members. In this sense, Menon and Pfeffer are working at the level of between-group conflict but focusing on the overarching implications for the actors involved. Menon and Pfeffer use the language of approach and avoidance to analyze between-group conflict. The underlying thesis of their research is that when it comes to between-group conflict, approach is an infinitely better tactic than avoidance. According to Menon and Pfeffer, direct conflict from out-groups, such as competing brands and competing companies, puts managers in a state of hypervigilance, which leads them to engage in fierce processing of the out-groups' best practices, and so on. In contrast, if the out-group member is an organizational insider, the same manager will seek to avoid or repress the experience, which paralyzes the learning process. In a similar vein, research on social networks has found that successful individuals tend to monitor structurally equivalent actors in an organization (actors who are often members of a group in competition for resources and recognition) for performance information more than they depend on members in their own group (Shah, 1998). It is important to note that the functional perspective primarily pertains to between-group competition for scarce resources rather than between-group competition concerning values or beliefs.

QUASIFUNCTIONAL BETWEEN-GROUP CONFLICT: BRIDGING FUNCTION AND DYSFUNCTION

In some sense, it is much more difficult to build a bridge spanning the chasm between functional and dysfunctional views of between-group conflict—especially because this literature spans a wide variety of disciplines with opposing dominant paradigms. Perhaps the obvious quasi-issue that should be pointed out is that whereas many organizations are meritocracies, many societies[3] are democracies. Therefore, the boundaries, rules, and outcomes of engaging in organization conflict are more discrete and structured. It is also imperative to wrestle with the issue of organizational measures of performance (such as resource allocation and learning) juxtaposed with social measures of between-group cohabilation (such as stereotypes and discrimination). Conflict in organizations quite frankly represents both, as organizations are concerned with stereotyping and discrimination as well as financial success: Conflict between organizational groups may seem to be healthy and a sign that free enterprise is working as it should; conflict among social groups is a call for alarm. In this sense, it is one thing to point out that investment bankers devalue traders (Auletta, 1986); it is quite another thing to point out that certain racial groups are devalued through hiring and promotion practices (compare Stein, Post, and Rinden, 2000). It is one thing to make *Business Week* history when an executive hurls a nasty comment across the table at a board meeting. It is quite another thing for a member of an ostracized social group to use firearms to gain respect. This section discusses four examples of literature that recognizes the "quasi" nature of conflict between groups. Similar to the discussion of "quasi" within-group conflict, these four examples also highlight the importance of procedures to manage conflict and the appropriateness of their match with operating context over time.

Example 1: Similar to the idea that careful team design reduces dysfunctional conflict within teams, the literature on macro-organizational behavior has long recognized that the deliberate design of between-group interaction can prevent dysfunctional intraorganizational conflict. This literature outlines the importance of aligning organizational structure and operations in a way that decreases subgroup or operational competition (Ibarra, 1992; Lawrence and Lorsch, 1967; March and Simon, 1959). For example, aligning production processes with resources and correctly matching task type (for example, serial, parallel) with authority structure are examples of pursuits to carefully define the causes and consequences of between-group conflict (March and Simon, 1959; Woodward, 1965). Properly aligning incentive systems with the longevity and goal of a task is also a key driver in sustaining motivation to achieve organizational goals (Kerr, 1975). In a similar vein, a common prescription for increasing between-group cooperation (that is, reducing between-group conflict) is for upper management to increase commitment and group identification with a superordinate goal (Hoegl, Weinkauf, and Gemuenden, 2004). The aim of this advice is to have subgroups create a superordinate identity, which will make them more committed to achieving a joint task (Kane, Argote, and Levine, 2005), thereby reducing the salience of in-group/out-group differences. This again highlights the "quasi" nature of conflict: If structure and operating procedures are designed to minimize competition and align incentives between groups, the dysfunctional elements of conflict can be minimized.

Example 2: Also central to the quasi-issues addressed here is the manner in which conflict is expressed. In the discussion of within-group conflict, we highlighted the importance of separating emotional and cognitive conflict. Translating this to the between-group context, several scholars have pointed out the need to reduce tension (often conceptualized as blaming or excessive stereotyping) and to increase commonalities in task focus and communication between groups. This is commonly tendered as prescriptive advice.

One suggestion for reducing the salience of group identity and well-being via favorable comparisons with other groups is, ironically, to point out marginal or intangible benefits to the in-group for accepting resources that are less than expected (Bies, 1987). For example, arguments that frame resource losses in favorable terms— "it could have been worse"; "other groups will suffer more"; or "by taking this pay cut you are ensuring the survival of the organization"—can provide groups with alternative criteria for comparisons with the out-group that more favorably focus attention back to the team goal.

Another technique for reducing differences between groups is to encourage perspective taking. For example, a common tension exists between engineering and management departments. This is partly due to differences in goals (for example, management has financial goals as a priority, and engineering has as its goal structural integrity and durability). A more fundamental problem is the "representational gaps" that arise from differences in the the language used to describe problems, perceptions of progress, and timelines for progressing (Cronin and Weingart, forthcoming). If groups structure and coordinate their work during critical information sharing and technical clarification stages of a project's life cycle and are made to understand the problem from the perspective of the other group, they are better able to meet their timelines and project goals (Ancona and Chong, 1999; Hoegl et al., 2004). The knowledge management literature rests heavily on the assumption that conflict is not interfering with identifying and adopting best practices (Argote, McEvily, and Reagans, 2003).

Example 3: Ironically, one of the best and most controversial organizational examples of competition over scarce resources between groups comes from the literature on between-group helping (helping is typically viewed as the opposite of conflict)—namely, the design and implementation of affirmative action programs. These programs are designed to eliminate past and present discrimination based on race, color, religion, sex, or national origin. Unfortunately, research has shown that a stigma is attached to securing employment through affirmative action and that affirmative action often hurts rather than furthers an individual's career path (Heilman, Battle, Keller, and Lee, 1998; Nadler, 2002). Some have suggested the reason for this is that when a member of a low-status group accepts the help of a high-status group, the person's low-status position is often solidified because of deepening dependency (for example, performance reviews) on the high-status group and an increase in the stigma or stereotype that he or she belongs to a group that needs "helping" (Nadler, 2002). Research suggests that it is very difficult to reverse these stigmas without specific and persistent organizational policies to explain selection procedures and ongoing communication that highlights the individual's merit (Heilman et al., 1998). This disconnect between the intended and actual consequences of policy highlights the "quasi" nature of affirmative action policies in resolving conflict effectively over time. Although rules and policies intended to reduce power differentials are effective, their effectiveness over time depends on continued merit-based advocacy by managers.

Example 4: Finally, research on third-party interventions and mediation is another area that suggests that the *management* of conflict expression between groups is a key to reducing dysfunctional effects of between-group conflict (for example, strikes, workplace violence). Procedures such as binding agreements or mediation reduce resource competition, provide people with a way to save face in escalating conflict situations, and serve to (at least temporarily) reduce a conflict stimulus between groups (Brett, 2000). Research on between-group negotiations (for a review see Bazerman, Curhan, and Moore, 2000) largely holds that conflicts between groups are inevitable and that they contain great potential for integrative (also known as win/win) agreements. Whereas the potential of between-group negotiation is highlighted theoretically, groups often fail behaviorally to fully realize their potential. The "quasi" nature of conflict again demands careful procedures and management to determine how the conflict will manifest between groups.

CONCLUSIONS: COMMON THEMES AND FUTURE DIRECTIONS

Our discussion of a quasifunctional perspective was intended to highlight that the relationship between the causes and consequences of conflict over time creates a need to better incorporate temporal and contextual variables into theorizing about the functional and dysfunctional effects of conflict. We point out three implications for future research in both the within-group and between-group literatures. First, while both literatures seem to overlook important theoretical considerations of time and contextual variables in predicting the impact of conflict, they do implicitly recognize these issues through the prescriptive recommendations they make. Second, both literatures suggest that the *management* of conflict, not necessarily the type or intensity of conflict, is a critical determinant of how functional or dysfunctional conflict will be. Third, conflict episodes may require different approaches depending on long-term or short-term goals, stages of a project's life cycle, or an organizational policy. Organizations may need to expand their training programs from being traditionally dominated by a technical knowledge/skills focus to include social skills necessary to manage conflict (Hoegl et al., 2004). The chapters in this volume address many of these issues to further push theorizing in these directions.

NOTES

1. This research is heavily dependent on Jehn's (1995, 1997) research.
2. There are several distinctions among self-identity theories, but it is not the purpose of this chapter to review them.
3. We are making the comparison to political philosophies of North American societies.

REFERENCES

Alper, S., Tjosvold, D., and Law, K. 1998. Interdependence and controversy in group decision making: Antecedents to effective self-managing teams. *Organizational Behavior and Human Decision Processes, 74*(1), 33–53.

Amason, A. 1996. Distinguishing the effects of functional and dysfunctional conflict on strategic decision making: Resolving a paradox for top management teams. *Academy of Management Journal, 39*(1), 123–148.

Amason, A., and Sapienza, H. 1997. The effects of top management team size and interaction norms on cognitive and affective conflict. *Journal of Management, 23*, 496–516.

Ancona, D. 1990. Outward bound: Strategies for team survival in an organization. *Academy of Management Journal, 33*(2), 334–365.

Ancona, D., and Bresman, H. 2003. *Begging, borrowing, and stealing from the outside to create innovation inside teams.* Paper presented at the meeting of the Creativity and Innovation in Organizations Conference at the Kellogg School of Management, Evanston, Ill.

Ancona, D., and Chong, C. 1999. Cycles and synchrony: The temporal role of context in team behavior. In E. Mannix, M. Neale, and R. Wageman (Eds.), *Research on managing groups and teams* (vol. 2, pp. 33–48). Greenwich, Conn.: JAI Press.

Ancona, D., Bresman, H., and Kaeufer, K. 2002. The comparative advantage of X-teams. *Sloan Management Review* (Spring), 33–39.

Argote, L., McEvily, B., and Reagans, R. 2003. Managing knowledge in organizations: An integrative framework and review of emerging themes. *Management Science, 49*(4), 571–582.

Argyris, C., and Schon, D. 1996. *Organizational learning II: Theory, method, and practice.* Reading, Mass.: Addison-Wesley.

Arrow, H., McGrath, J., and Berdahl, J. 2000. *Small groups as complex systems: Formation, coordination, development, and adaptation.* Newbury Park, Calif.: SAGE Publications.

Arrow, H., Poole, M. S., Henry, K. B., Wheelan, S., and Moreland, R. 2004. Time, change, and development: The temporal perspective on groups. *Small Group Research, 35*(1), 73–105.

Asch, S. 1952. Group forces in the modification and distortion of judgments. In *Social psychology* (pp. 450–473): New York: Prentice Hall.

Auletta, K. 1986. *Greed and glory on Wall Street: The fall of the house of Lehman.* New York: Random House.

Austin, J., and Vancouver, J. 1996. Goal constructs in psychology: Structure, process, and content. *Psychological Bulletin, 120*(3), 338–375.

Baron, R. 1991. Positive effects of conflict: A cognitive perspective. *Employee Responsibilities and Rights Journal, 2*, 225–236.

Bazerman, M. H., Curhan, J., and Moore, D. 2000. The death and rebirth of the social psychology of negotiations. In G. Fletcher and M. Clark (Eds.), *Blackwell handbook of social psychology: Interpersonal processes* (pp. 196–228). Malden, Mass.: Blackwell Publishers.

Behfar, K., Burris, E., and Thomas-Hunt, M. 2004, August 9–11. *Group conflict, expertise, and performance: How functional role behaviors mediate effective utilization of expertise.* Paper presented at the meeting of the Academy of Management, New Orleans, La.

Behfar, K., Kern, M., and Brett, J. 2006. Managing challenges in multicultural teams. In E. Mannix and Y. Chen (Eds.), *Research on managing groups and teams.* Oxford, UK: Elsevier Science Press.

Behfar, K., Mannix, E., Peterson, R., and Trochim, W. 2002. *A multi-faceted approach to intra-group conflict: Issues of theory and measurement.* Paper presented at the meeting of the International Association for Conflict Management, Salt Lake City, Utah.

Behfar, K., Peterson, R., Mannix, E., and Trochim, W. 2002. *Conflict resolution strategies in leaderless groups: An exploratory study of their impact.* Paper presented at the meeting of the Academy of Management, Denver, Colo.

Bettenhausen, K., and Murnighan, J. 1985. The emergence of norms in competitive decision-making groups. *Administrative Science Quarterly, 30*(3), 350–372.

Bies, R. 1987. The predicament of injustice: The management of moral outrage. In B. Staw and L. Cummings (Eds.), *Research in organizational behavior* (vol. 9, pp. 289–319). Greenwich, Conn.: JAI Press.

Blake, R., and Mouton, J. 1964. *The managerial grid.* Houston, Texas: Gulf.

Blau, P. 1987. Microprocess and macrostructure. In K. Cook (Ed.), *Social exchange theory* (pp. 83–100). Newbury Park, Calif.: SAGE Publications.

Brett, J. 2000. Culture and negotiation. *International Journal of Psychology, 35*(2), 97–104.

Brewer, M., and Kramer, R. 1985. The psychology of intergroup attitudes and behavior. *Annual Review of Psychology, 36*, 219–243.

Campion, M., and Lord, R. 1982. A control systems conceptualization of the goal-setting and changing process. *Organizational Behavior and Human Performance, 30*(2), 265–287.

Campion, M., Papper, E., and Medsker, G. 1996. Relations between work team characteristics and effectiveness: A replication and extension. *Personnel Psychology, 49*(2), 429–452.

Cartwright, D., and Zander, A. (Eds.). 1968. *Group dynamics: Research and theory,* 3rd ed. New York: Harper and Row.

Chadwick-Jones, J. K. 1976. *Social exchange theory: Its structure and influence in social psychology.* London: Academic Press.

Cosier, R., and Rose, G. 1977. Cognitive conflict and goal conflict effects on task performance. *Organizational Behavior and Human Performance, 19*, 378–391.

Cronin, M., and Weingart, L. Forthcoming. Representational gaps, information processing, and conflict in functionally diverse teams. *Academy of Management Review.*

Darr, E., Argote, L., and Epple, D. 1995. The acquisition, transfer, and depreciation of knowledge in service organizations: Productivity in franchises. *Management Science, 41*(11), 1750–1762.

DeChurch, L., and Marks, M. 2001. Maximizing the benefits of task conflict: The role of conflict management. *International Journal of Conflict Management, 12*(1), 4–22.

De Dreu, C. 1997. Productive conflict: The importance of conflict management and conflict issues. In C. De Dreu and E. Van De Vliert (Eds.), *Using conflict in organizations* (pp. 9–22). London: SAGE.

De Dreu, C., and Weingart, L. 2003. Task versus relationship conflict, team performance, and team member satisfaction. *Journal of Applied Psychology, 88*(4), 741–749.

Delbecq, A., Van de Ven, A., and Gustafson, D. 1974. *Group techniques for program planning: A guide to nominal group and Delphi processes.* Glenview, Ill.: Scott Foresman.

Deutsch, M. 1949. A theory of cooperation and competition. *Human Relations, 2*(2), 129–152.

Deutsch, M. 1968. The effects of cooperation and competition upon group process. In D. Cartwright and A. Zander (Eds.), *Group dynamics: Research and theory* (3rd ed., pp. 461–482). New York: Harper and Row.

Deutsch, M., and Coleman, P. (Eds.). 2000. *The handbook of conflict resolution.* San Francisco: Jossey-Bass.

Druskat, V., and Wheeler, J. 2003. Managing from the boundary: The effective leadership of self-managing work teams. *Academy of Management Journal, 46*(4), 435–457.

Druskat, V., and Wolff, S. 2001. Building the emotional intelligence of groups. *Harvard Business Review* (March), 80–90.

Earley, P., and Mosakowski, E. 2004. Cultural intelligence. *Harvard Business Review, 82*(10), 151–157.

Edelman, R. J. 1993. *Interpersonal conflicts at work.* Leicester, UK: British Psychological Society.

Edmondson, A. 1999. Psychological safety and learning behavior in work teams. *Administrative Science Quarterly, 44,* 350–383.

Eisenhardt, K., Kahwajy, J., and Bourgeois, L. 1997. How management teams can have a good fight. *Harvard Business Review, 75*(4).

Emerson, R. 1962. Power-dependence relations. *American Sociological Review, 27*(1), 31–41.

Emerson, R. 1987. Toward a theory of value in social exchange. In K. Cook (Ed.), *Social exchange Theory* (pp. 11–46). Newbury Park, Calif.: SAGE Publications.

Emerson, R. 1992. Social exchange theory. In M. Rosenberg and R. Turner (Eds.), *Social psychology: Sociological perspectives* (pp. 30–65). New Brunswick, N.J.: Transaction Publishers.

Evan, W. 1965. Conflict and performance in R and D organizations. *Industrial Management Review, 7,* 37–46.

Fiedler, F. 1967. The effect of inter-group competition on group member adjustment. *Personnel Psychology, 20*(1), 33–45.

Gaertner, S., and Dovidio, J. 2000. *Reducing intergroup bias: The common ingroup identity model.* Philadelphia, Pa.: Taylor and Francis.

Gersick, C. 1988. Time and transition in work teams: Toward a new model of group development. *Academy of Management Journal, 31*(1), 9–41.

Gladstein, D. 1984. Groups in context: A model of task group effectiveness. *Administrative Science Quarterly, 29,* 499–517.

Gowing, M., Kraft, J., and Campbell-Quick, J. (Eds.). 1998. *The new organizational reality: Downsizing, restructuring, and revitalization.* Washington, D.C.: American Psychological Association.

Greenwald, A. 1975. Consequences of prejudice against the null hypothesis. *Psychological Bulletin, 82*(1), 1–19.

Gruenfeld, D. 1995. Status, ideology, and integrative complexity on the United States Supreme Court: Rethinking the politics of political decision making. *Journal of Personality and Social Psychology, 68*(1), 5–20.

Guetzkow, H., and Gyr, J. 1954. An analysis of conflict in decision-making groups. *Human Relations, 7,* 367–381.

Guzzo, R., and Shea, G. 1992. Group performance and intergroup relations in organizations. In M. Dunnette and L. Hough (Eds.), *Handbook of industrial and organizational psychology* (2nd ed., vol. 3, pp. 269–313). Palo Alto, Calif.: Consulting Psychologists Press.

Guzzo, R., Wagner, D., MacGuire, E., Herr, B., and Hawley, C. 1986. Implicit theories and the evaluation of group processes and performance. *Organizational Behavior and Human Decision Processes, 36,* 279–295.

Hackman, J. R. 1987. The design of work teams. In J. Lorsch (Ed.), *Handbook of organizational behavior.* Englewood Cliffs, N.J.: Prentice-Hall.

Hackman, J. R. (Ed.). 1990. *Groups that work (and those that don't): Creating conditions for effective teamwork.* San Francisco: Jossey-Bass.

Hackman, J. R., and Baetz, M. 1990. Leading groups in organizations. In P. Goodman (Ed.), *Designing effective workgroups.* San Francisco: Jossey-Bass.

Hackman, J. R., and Morris, C. 1975. Group tasks, group interaction process, and group performance effectiveness: A review and proposed integration. In L. Berkowitz (Ed.), *Advances in experimental social psychology* (vol. 8, pp. 45–99). New York: Academic Press.

Hackman, J. R., and Wageman, R. 2005. A theory of team coaching. *Academy of Management Review,* *30*(2), 269–287.

Hargadon, A. In press. Creativity that works. In C. Ford (Ed.), *The handbook of organizational innovation*. Mahwah, N.J.: Lawrence Erlbaum Associates.

Harvey, J. 1996. *The Abilene Paradox and other meditations on management*. San Francisco: Jossey-Bass.

Haveman, H. 1992. Between a rock and a hard place: Organizational change and performance under conditions of fundamental environmental transformation. *Administrative Science Quarterly,* *37*(1), 48.

Heider, F. 1958. *The psychology of interpersonal relations*. Hillsdale, N.J.: Lawrence Erlbaum Associates.

Heilman, M., Battle, W., Keller, C., and Lee, R. 1998. Type of affirmative action policy: A determinant of reactions to sex-based preferential selection? *Journal of Applied Psychology, 83*(2), 190–205.

Hirokawa, R. 1983. Group communication and problem-solving effectiveness: An investigation of group phases. *Human Communication Research, 9*(4), 291–305.

Hirokawa, R. 1988. Group communication and decision-making performance: A continued test of the functional perspective. *Human Communication Research, 14*(4), 487–515.

Hoegl, M., Weinkauf, K., and Gemuenden, H. G. 2004. Interteam coordination, project commitment, and teamwork in multiteam R&D projects: A longitudinal study. *Organization Science, 15*(1), 38–55.

Homans, G. 1950. *The human group*. New York: Harcourt, Brace and Company.

Ibarra, H. 1992. Structural alignments, individual strategies, and managerial action: Elements toward a network theory of getting things done. In N. Nohria and R. Eccles (Eds.), *Networks and organizations* (pp. 165–188). Boston: Harvard Business School Press.

Insko, C., Schopler, J., Graetz, K., Drigotas, S., Currey, D., Smith, S., et al. 1994. Interindividual-intergroup discontinuity in the Prisoner's Dilemma Game. *Journal of Conflict Resolution, 38,* 87–116.

Isenberg, D. 1986. Group polarization: A critical review and meta-analysis. *Journal of Personality and Social Psychology, 50*(6), 1141–1151.

Jackson, K. 2003. *The team exchange contract in autonomous groups: Behavior and work strategies for sustainable performance*. Doctoral dissertation, Cornell University, Ithaca, N.Y.

Janis, I. 1972. *A psychological study of foreign-policy decisions and fiascoes*. Boston: Houghton Mifflin Company College Division.

Janssen, O., Van De Vliert, E., and Veenstra, C. 1999. How task and person conflict shape the role of positive interdependence in management teams. *Journal of Management, 25*(2), 117–142.

Jehn, K. 1995. A multimethod examination of the benefits and detriments of intragroup conflict. *Administrative Science Quarterly, 40,* 256–282.

Jehn, K. 1997. A qualitative analysis of conflict types and dimensions in organizational groups. *Administrative Science Quarterly, 42,* 530–557.

Jehn, K., and Bendersky, C. 2003. Intragroup conflict in organizations: A contingency perspective on the conflict-outcome relationship. *Research in Organizational Behavior, 24,* 187–242.

Jehn, K., and Bezrukova, K. 2004. A field study of group diversity, workgroup context, and performance. *Journal of Organizational Behavior, 25*(6), 703–729.

Jehn, K., and Mannix, E. 2001. The dynamic nature of conflict: A longitudinal study of intragroup conflict and group performance. *Academy of Management Journal, 44*(2), 238–251.

Jehn, K., Northcraft, G., and Neale, M. 1999. Why differences make a difference: A field study of diversity, conflict, and performance in workgroups. *Administrative Science Quarterly, 44*(4), 741–763.

Kane, A., Argote, L., and Levine, J. 2005. Knowledge transfer between groups via personnel rotation: Effects of social identity and knowledge quality. *Organizational Behavior and Human Decision Processes, 96*(1), 56–71.

Katz, D., and Kahn, R. 1978. *The social psychology of organizations* (2nd ed.). New York: John Wiley and Sons.

Katz, N. 2001. Getting the most out of your team. *Harvard Business Review, 79*(8), 22.

Katzenstein, G. 1996. The debate on structured debate: Toward a unified theory. *Organizational Behavior and Human Decision Processes, 66*(3), 316–332.

Kelley, H., and Thibaut, J. 1969. Group problem solving. In G. Lindzey and E. Aronson (Eds.), *The handbook of social psychology* (2nd ed., pp. 1–101). Reading, Mass.: Addison-Wesley.

Kerr, S. 1975. On the folly of rewarding A, while hoping for B. *Academy of Management Journal, 18*(4), 769–783.

Kim, C., and Mauborgne, R. 2003. Tipping point leadership. *Harvard Business Review, 81*(4), 60–69.

Klein, H. 1989. An integrated control theory model of work motivation. *Academy of Management Review, 14*(2), 150–172.

Kluger, A., and DeNisi, A. 1996. The effects of feedback interventions on performance: A historical review, a meta-analysis, and a preliminary feedback intervention theory. *Psychological Bulletin, 119*(2), 254–284.

Kopelman, S., Weber, J. M., and Messick, D. M. 2002. Factors influencing cooperation in commons dilemmas: A review of experimental psychological research. In E. Ostrom, T. Dietz, N. Dolsak, P. C. Stern, S. Stonich, and E. U. Weber (Eds.), *The drama of the commons* (pp. 113–156). Washington, D.C.: National Academy Press.

Latane, B., Williams, K., and Harkins, S. 1979. Many hands make light the work: The causes and consequences of social loafing. *Journal of Personality and Social Psychology, 37*(6), 822–832.

Lawler, E., and Yoon, J. 1996. Commitment in exchange relations: Test of a theory of relational cohesion. *American Sociological Review, 61*(1), 89–108.

Lawrence, P., and Lorsch, J. 1967. *Organization and environment: Managing differentiation and integration.* Boston: Harvard University Press.

Levine, J., and Thompson, L. 1996. Conflict in groups. In E. Higgins and A. Kruglanski (Eds.), *Social psychology: Handbook of basic principles* (pp. 745–776). New York: Guilford.

Levine, R., and Campbell, D. 1972. *Ethnocentrism: Theories of conflict, attitudes and group behavior.* New York: Wiley.

Levi-Strauss, C. 1969. *The elementary structures of kinship.* Boston: Beacon Press.

Lind, E. A., and Earley, P. C. 1992. Procedural justice and culture. *International Journal of Psychology, 27*(2), 227–242.

Lind, E. A., and Tyler, T. 1988. *The social psychology of procedural justice.* New York: Plenum Press.

Locke, E. 1991. Introduction to special issue on theories of cognitive self-regulation. *Organizational Behavior and Human Decision Processes, 50*, 151–153.

Locke, E., and Latham, G. 1990. *A theory of goal setting and task performance.* Upper Saddle River, N.J.: Prentice Hall.

Locke, E., Shaw, K., Saari, L., and Latham, G. 1981. Goal setting and task performance: 1969–1980. *Psychological Bulletin, 90*(1), 125–152.

Lovelace, K., Shapiro, D., and Weingart, L. 2001. Maximizing cross-functional new product teams' innovativeness and constraint adherence: A conflict communications perspective. *Academy of Management Journal, 44*(4), 779–783.

Lubit, R. 2003. *Coping with toxic managers, subordinates ... and other difficult people: Using emotional intelligence to survive and prosper.* Upper Saddle River, N.J.: Prentice Hall.

March, J., and Simon, H. 1959. *Organizations.* New York: John Wiley and Sons.

Mason, R. 1981. *Challenging strategic planning assumptions*. New York: John Wiley and Sons.

McGrath, J. 1991. Time, interaction, and performance (TIP): A theory of groups. *Small Group Research, 22*(2), 147–174.

Menon, T., and Pfeffer, J. 2003. Valuing internal vs. external knowledge: Explaining the preference for outsiders. *Management Science, 49*(4), 497–513.

Messick, D., and Mackie, D. 1989. Intergroup relations. *Annual Review of Psychology, 40*, 45–81.

Molm, L. 1990. Structure, action, and outcomes: The dynamics of power in social exchange. *American Sociological Review, 55* (June), 427–447.

Molm, L. 1991. Affect and social exchange: Satisfaction in power-dependence relations. *American Sociological Review, 56* (August), 475–493.

Moreland, R., and Levine, J. 1992. Problem identification by groups. In S. Worchel, W. Wood, and J. Simpson (Eds.), *Group process and productivity* (pp. 17–47). Newbury Park, Calif.: SAGE Publications.

Moynihan, L., and Peterson, R. 2000. The role of personality in group process. In B. Schneider and B. Smith (Eds.), *Personality in organizations*. Mahwah, N.J.: Lawrence Erlbaum Associates.

Nadler, A. 2002. Inter-group helping relations as power relations: Maintaining or challenging social dominance between groups through helping. *Journal of Social Issues, 58*(3), 487–502.

Nahavandi, A., and Malekzadeh, A. 1993. *Organizational culture in the management of mergers*. Westport, Conn.: Quarum Books.

Nemeth, C. 1992. Minority dissent as a stimulant to group performance. In S. Worchel, W. Wood, and J. Simpson (Eds.), *Group process and productivity* (pp. 95–111). Newbury Park, Calif.: SAGE Publications.

Nemeth, C., Brown, K., and Rogers, J. 2001. Devil's advocate versus authentic dissent: Stimulating quantity and quality. *European Journal of Social Psychology, 31*(6), 707–720.

Nemeth, C., Connell, J., Rogers, J., and Brown, K. 2001. Improving decision making by means of dissent. *Journal of Applied Psychology, 31*(1), 48–58.

Nemeth, C., Personnaz, B., Personnaz, M., and Goncalo, J. 2004. The liberating role of conflict in group creativity: A study in two countries. *European Journal of Social Psychology, 34*(4), 365–374.

Okhuysen, G., and Eisenhardt, K. 2002. Integrating knowledge in groups: How formal interventions enable flexibility. *Organization Science, 13*(4), 370–386.

Osborn, A. 1957. *Applied imagination*. New York: Scribner.

Paulus, P. (Ed.). 1983. *Basic group processes*. New York: Springer-Verlag.

Pelled, L. 1996. Demographic diversity, conflict, and work group outcomes: An intervening process theory. *Organization Science, 6*, 615–631.

Peterson, E., Mitchell, T., Thompson, L., and Burr, R. 2000. Collective efficacy and aspects of shared mental models as predictors of performance over time in work groups. *Group Processes and Intergroup Relations, 3*(3), 296–316.

Peterson, R. 1999. Can you have too much of a good thing? The limits of voice for improving satisfaction with leaders. *Personality and Social Psychology Bulletin, 25*(3), 313–324.

Peterson, R., and Behfar, K. 2003. The dynamic relationship between performance feedback, trust, and conflict in groups: A longitudinal study. *Organizational Behavior and Human Decision Processes, 92*, 102–112.

Peterson, R., and Behfar, K. 2005. The role of leadership in group regulation: An "open system" view. In D. Messick and R. Kramer (Eds.), *New thinking about the psychology of leadership* (pp. 143–162). Mahwah, N.J.: Lawrence Erlbaum Associates.

Pinkley, R. 1990. Dimensions of conflict frame: Disputant interpretations of conflict. *Journal of Applied Psychology, 75*(2), 117–126.

Pondy, L. 1967. Organizational conflict: Concepts and models. *Administrative Science Quarterly, 12*, 296–320.

Pondy, L. 1992. Reflections on organizational conflict. *Journal of Organizational Behavior, 13*, 257–261.

Poole, M. S., Siebold, D., and McPhee, R. 1996. The structuration of group decisions. In R. Hirokawa and M. S. Poole (Eds.), *Communication and group decision making* (pp. 114–146). Newbury Park, Calif.: SAGE Publications.

Porter, T., and Lilly, B. 1996. The effects of conflict, trust, and task commitment on project team performance. *International Journal of Conflict Management, 7*(4), 361–376.

Pruitt, D., and Rubin, J. 1986. *Social conflict: Escalation, stalemate, and settlement.* New York: Random House.

Putnam, L., and Poole, M. S. 1987. Conflict and negotiation. In F. Jablin, L. Putnam, K. Roberts, and L. Porter (Eds.), *Handbook of organizational communication: An interdisciplinary perspective* (pp. 549–599). Newbury Park, Calif.: SAGE Publications.

Rahim, M. A. 1983. A measure of styles of handling interpersonal conflict. *Academy of Management Journal, 26*(2), 368–376.

Rahim, M. A. 2002. Toward a theory of managing organizational conflict. *International Journal of Conflict Management, 13*(3), 206–235.

Schweiger, D., and Sandberg, W. 1989. The utilization of individual capabilities in group approaches to strategic decision making. *Strategic Management Journal, 10*, 31–43.

Schwenk, C. 1990. Conflict in organizational decision making: An exploratory study of its effects in for-profit and not-for-profit organizations. *Management Science, 36*, 436–448.

Scott, S. 2004. *Fierce conversations: Achieving success at work and in life, one conversation at a time.* New York: Penguin Group.

Stott, C., Hutchison, P., and Drury, J. 2001. "Hooligans" abroad? Inter-group dynamics, social identity and participation in collective "disorder" at the 1998 World Cup Finals. *British Journal of Social Psychology, 40*(3), 359–384.

Sears, D. O., and Henry, P. J. 2003. *The origins of symbolic racism. Journal of Personality and Social Psychology, 85*, 259–275.

Sears, D. O., van Laar, C., Carillo, M., and Kosterman, R. 1997. Is it really racism? The origins of white Americans' opposition to race-targeted policies. *Public Opinion Quarterly, 61*, 16–53.

Sell, J., Lovaglia, M., Mannix, E., Samuelson, C., and Wilson, R. 2004. Investigating conflict, power, and status within and among groups. *Small Group Research, 35*, 44–72.

Senge, P. 1990. *The fifth discipline: The art and practice of the learning organization.* New York: Currency Doubleday.

Shah, P. 1998. Who are employees' social referents? Using a network perspective to determine referent others. *Academy of Management Journal, 41*(3), 249–268.

Shah, P., and Jehn, K. 1993. Do friends perform better than acquaintances? The interaction of friendship, conflict, and task. *Group Decision and Negotiation, 2*, 149–166.

Shapiro, D., and Kirkman, B. 1999. Employees' reaction to the change to work teams. *Journal of Organizational Change, 12*(1), 51–66.

Simons, T., and Peterson, R. 2000. Task conflict and relationship conflict in top management teams: The pivotal role of intragroup trust. *Journal of Applied Psychology, 83*(1), 102–111.

Smith, K., and Berg, D. 1987. *Paradoxes of group life: Understanding conflict, paralysis, and movement in group dynamics.* San Francisco: Jossey-Bass.

Stasser, G. 1992. Pooling of unshared information during group discussions. In S. Worchel, W. Wood, and J. Simpson (Eds.), *Group process and productivity* (pp. 48–67). Newbury Park, Calif.: SAGE Publications.

Stasser, G., and Stewart, D. 1992. Discovery of hidden profiles by decision-making groups: Solving a problem versus making a judgment. *Journal of Personality and Social Psychology, 63*(3), 126–434.

Staw, B. 1975. Attributions of the "causes" of performance: An alternative interpretation of cross-sectional research on organizations. *Organizational Behavior and Human Performance, 13*, 414–432.

Staw, B., Sandelands, L., and Dutton, J. 1981. Threat-rigidity effects in organizational behavior: A multi-level analysis. *Administrative Science Quarterly, 26*, 501–524.

Stein, R., Post, S., and Rinden, A. 2000. Reconciling context and contact effects on racial attitudes. *Political Research Quarterly, 53*(2), 285–303.

Steiner, I. 1972. *Group process and productivity.* New York: Academic Press.

Stokes, J. 1983. Components of group cohesion: Intermember attraction, instrumental value, and risk taking. *Small Group Behavior, 14*(2), 163–173.

Sundstrom, E., De Meuse, K., and Futrell, D. 1990. Work teams: Applications and effectiveness. *American Psychologist, 45*(2), 120–133.

Susskind, A., Miller, V., and Johnson, J. 1998. Downsizing and structural holes: Their impact on lay-off survivors' perceptions of organizational chaos and openness to change. *Communication Research, 25*(1), 30–65.

Taggar, S. 2002. Individual creativity and group ability to utilize individual creative resources: A multilevel model. *Academy of Management Journal, 45*(2), 315–330.

Tajfel, H., and Turner, J. 1986. The social identity theory of intergroup behavior. In S. Worchel and W. Austin (Eds.), *Psychology of intergroup relations* (pp. 7–24). Chicago: Nelson-Hall.

Thatcher, S., Jehh, K., and Zanutto, E. 2003. Cracks in diversity research: The effects of diversity faultlines on conflict and performance. *Group Decision and Negotiation, 12*(3), 217–241.

Thibaut, J., and Kelley, H. 1991. *The social psychology of groups.* New Brunswick, N.J.: Transaction Publishers.

Thibaut, J., and Walker, L. 1975. *Procedural justice: A psychological analysis.* Hillsdale, N.J.: Lawrence Erlbaum Associates.

Thompson, L., and Fine, G. 1999. Socially shared cognition, affect and behavior: A review and integration. *Personality and Social Psychology Review, 3*(4), 278–302.

Tjosvold, D., and Tjosvold, M. 1994. Cooperation, competition, and constructive controversy. In M. Beyerlein and D. John (Eds.), *Advances in interdisciplinary studies of work teams: Theories of self-managing work teams* (vol. 1, pp. 119–144). Greenwich, Conn.: JAI Press.

Torrance, E. 1957. Group decision making and disagreement. *Social Forces, 35*, 314–318.

Tyler, T., Brockner, J., Konovsky, M., Cooper-Schneider, R., Folger, R., Martin, C., et al. 1994. Interactive effects of procedural justice and outcome negativity on victims and survivors of job loss. *Academy of Management Journal, 37*(2), 397–409.

Van Maanen, J., and Kunda, G. 1989. "Real feelings": Emotional expression and organizational culture. *Research in Organizational Behavior, 11*, 43–103.

Wageman, R. 1995. Interdependence and group effectiveness. *Administrative Science Quarterly, 40*, 145–180.

Wageman, R. 2001. How leaders foster self-managing effectiveness: Design choices vs. hands-on coaching. *Organization Science, 12*(5), 559–577.

Wall, J. A., and Callister, R. 1995. Conflict and its management. *Journal of Management, 21*(3), 515–558.

Wall, V. D., and Nolan, L. 1986. Perceptions of inequity, satisfaction, and conflict in task-oriented groups. *Human Relations, 39*(1), 1033–1052.

Walton, R. 1969. *Interpersonal peacemaking: Confrontations and third-party consultation.* Reading, Mass.: Addison-Wesley.

Weber, R. A., and Camerer, C. 2003. Cultural conflict and merger failure: An experimental approach. *Management Science, 49*(4), 400–415.

Williams, K., and O'Reilly, C. 1988. Demography and diversity in organizations: A review of 40 years of research. In B. Staw and L. Cummings (Eds.), *Research in organizational behavior* (vol. 20, pp. 77–140). Greenwich, Conn.: JAI Press.

Wittenbaum, G. M., Hubbell, A. P., and Zuckerman, C. 1999. Mutual enhancement: Toward an understanding of the collective preference for shared information. *Journal of Personality and Social Psychology, 77*(5), 967–978.

Wolff, S., Pescosolido, A., and Druskat, V. 2002. Emotional intelligence as the basis of leadership emergence in self-managing teams. *Leadership Quarterly, 13*(5), 505–522.

Woodward, J. 1965. *Industrial organization: Theory and practice.* New York: Oxford University Press.

Worchel, S., Andreoli, V., and Folger, R. 1977. Intergroup cooperation and intergroup attraction: The effect of previous interaction and outcome of combined effort. *Journal of Experimental Social Psychology, 13*, 131–140.

Zander, A. 1977. *Groups at work.* San Francisco: Jossey-Bass.

Chapter 2

Garnering the Benefits of Conflict: The Role of Diversity and Status Distance in Groups

*Katherine W. Phillips and
Melissa C. Thomas-Hunt*

Abstract

The ability of groups to benefit from cognitive conflict (that is, differences in information, knowledge, and opinions) can be a critical source of competitive advantage. In this chapter we focus on how diversity and status affect conflict in groups. Despite an evolution of more nuanced approaches to the study of the effects of diversity on conflict, there is still ambiguity in the literature. We first review some of the recent literature on diversity as it relates to conflict and the process of sharing unique information in groups. We then suggest that consideration of the status distance among group members may further clarify these investigations. We argue that the characteristics that contribute to diversity are often imbued with different status cues, leading group members to differentially value their members and their contributions. We discuss and consider the implications of status distance for leveraging the benefits of cognitive conflict and capturing the unique perspectives that any group member holds in a group.

Introduction

Increasingly, organizations use groups to bring together individuals who have differing knowledge, information, and perspectives (for example, Schneider and Northcraft, 1999). This effort is based on the belief that the sharing of unique perspectives creates the potential for groups to create new ideas and solutions that no one group member could have created on his or her own. However, the process of integrating this differing knowledge can result in increased disagreement and conflict. The conflict literature has recognized that not all types of conflict are created equal. Functional or cognitive conflict captures a group's willingness to discuss the pros and cons of alternatives, consider multiple viewpoints and perspectives, or question the evidence used to make decisions (Amason, 1996; Jehn, 1995). This cognitive conflict can be beneficial to group decision making on nonroutine tasks when it is distinguished from dysfunctional or relationship conflict, which can undermine group performance (see chapter 1, this volume).

In any given group, cognitive conflict can become intertwined with relationship conflict (Simons and Peterson, 2000) and prevent groups from benefiting from the unique perspectives present. The challenge that managers face is to create a context in which the explicit elaboration of unique information, knowledge, and opinions allows each group member's perspectives to be heard and integrated into the group discussion without jeopardizing the social integrity of the group (Van Knippenberg, De Dreu, and Homans, 2004). The presence of different information, opinions, and viewpoints in and of itself is not enough to engender benefits for group performance. For real benefits to accrue, group members must be willing to elaborate on the information and opinions they possess and integrate those varying viewpoints during the discussion. Throughout this chapter, as we discuss cognitive conflict, we couple it with the process of information elaboration (Van Knippenberg et al., 2004), and we believe cognitive conflict can only be functional when group members are willing to state, consider, and integrate the multiple perspectives present into the group discussion.

To get differing perspectives on the table in the first place, managers often begin by creating diverse groups. According to Williams and O'Reilly (1998), diversity exists in a group when individuals use any number of different attributes to tell themselves that another member is different (p. 81). Thus diversity can come in many different forms. There are major distinctions between informational diversity (which captures the extent to which a group is characterized by individuals who bring differing information, opinions, and perspectives to the group) and social-category diversity such as differences in race/ethnicity, gender, or country of origin (Jehn, Northcraft, and Neale, 1999). Social-category diversity is often used as a proxy for the informational diversity that is sought. This practice is based on the belief that people representing different social groups will bring differing information and perspectives to the table (Phillips, 2003) and thus again foster beneficial cognitive conflict for the group. Capturing these theoretical benefits of social-category diversity is easier said than done.

Traditionally, researchers have used social-categorization theory and the similarity/attraction paradigm to argue that in groups having social-category diversity, the knowledge exchange process is thwarted by intergroup rivalries (see Williams and O'Reilly, 1998, for review). Social-category diversity leads to greater relationship conflict in groups (Pelled, Eisenhardt, and Xin, 1999), decreased communication

(Zenger and Lawrence, 1989; Hoffman, 1985), greater stereotyping, and discrimination in some cases (Stephan and Stephan, 1985). We suggest that an additional layer of complexity permeates interactions in groups with social-category diversity—one in which the social categories represented diverge in the status they are afforded and consequently affect the way in which unique knowledge contributions are offered to and perceived by the group. We argue that imposing a status-distance lens in considering the interactions within groups with social-category diversity may be helpful for researchers and managers alike as we look for additional levers and tools that will allow for the management of these complex group task environments.

Here we use a diversity lens to review and integrate the research on information sharing and conflict. These three bodies of work—group diversity, information sharing, and conflict—have generally developed separately, yet important connections between them may lend unique insight into understanding the role of conflict in groups. We also introduce a missing factor, that of status, and develop the concept of status distance as one that is determined by group, organizational, and societal factors. We consider how status distance affects the amount of cognitive and relationship conflict in groups. In doing so, we limit our discussions to groups that are characterized by some level of social category and presumably informational diversity. We develop specific propositions about how the status distance between members of groups will affect the type and level of conflict experienced and how that is likely to affect subsequent performance and interactions within small decision-making groups.

RECENT INSIGHTS ON DIVERSITY, CONFLICT, AND INFORMATION SHARING IN GROUPS

In general, diversity research has often yielded inconsistent results. On the one hand, diversity tends to trigger these social categorization and similarity/attraction processes that can hinder communication, decrease group cohesiveness, and lead to higher levels of dysfunctional conflict, making it difficult for groups to benefit from their differences in perspective (for example, Ely and Thomas, 2001; Jackson, Joshi, and Erhardt, 2003; Pelled et al., 1999; for extensive reviews see Williams and O'Reilly, 1998; Milliken and Martins, 1996). On the other hand, diversity has the potential of benefiting group performance (especially when creativity or nonroutine tasks are involved) because of the breadth of knowledge and perspectives thought to accompany diversity. According to this perspective, called the information/decision-making perspective by Williams and O'Reilly (1998), diverse groups have a larger pool of resources, and because they need to reconcile conflicting viewpoints they may process task-relevant information more thoroughly and generate more creative and innovative ideas and solutions (Ancona and Caldwell, 1992; Bantel and Jackson, 1989; De Dreu and West, 2001; Sommers, 2006). Some studies have indeed found that informational diversity can increase cognitive conflict (Jehn et al., 1999; Pelled et al.,

1999) and improve performance and innovation (Bantel and Jackson, 1989; Cox, Lobel, and McLeod, 1991; Jehn et al., 1999; Pelled et al., 1999).

According to Williams and O'Reilly (1998) and other reviews of the literature (for example, Jackson et al., 2003; Milliken and Martins, 1996) the one source of diversity that has most often yielded positive effects on group performance outcomes is functional background, typically thought of as a form of informational diversity. The overall evidence suggests that although functional diversity, in which group members represent different functional groups in the organization, can lead to lower cohesion (Ancona and Caldwell, 1992), the knowledge, perspective, and informational differences that accompany functional-background diversity generally benefit the performance of such teams. In this case, the differences in functional background are often accompanied by the promise of task-relevant knowledge, perspectives, and informational differences that then benefit the group through the cognitive conflict that is generated (Jehn et al., 1999; Pelled et al., 1999). However, differences in functional background can also trigger social categorization effects with people responding negatively to members from other functional backgrounds. The terminology differences, differences in priorities, and differences in perspective in functionally diverse groups may make it difficult for their members to communicate and build cohesion, and these differences can lead to detrimental relationship conflict as well. In fact, for many groups the distinction between cognitive conflict and relationship conflict is difficult to isolate (De Dreu and Weingart, 2003), so functionally diverse groups could theoretically be even more prone to problems than groups whose diversity falls along other dimensions.

However, there are several reasons why functional background (which is also a social category) might more consistently lead to beneficial cognitive conflict for a group than other types of social-category diversity (that is, explicit differences in social-category membership such as race/ethnicity, gender, and country of origin) (Jehn et al., 1999; Pelled et al., 1999). In this chapter, we use these functionally diverse groups as a model to develop a better understanding of the moderators that might contribute to the success of teams that have social-category diversity. In other words, why are functionally diverse groups able to benefit from their informational differences even though functional diversity may also trigger social-categorization processes that can be detrimental for the group? What factors might allow groups that have other types of social-category diversity to benefit from the knowledge and perspective differences that they, too, might possess?

THE EXAMPLE OF FUNCTIONALLY DIVERSE GROUPS

First, functionally diverse groups often benefit from *congruence,* or an explicit alignment between their social-category distinctions and task-relevant information that other types of diversity may be less likely to engender. Congruence occurs when group members' expectations about who will agree with or support whom during the group discussion are actually met (Phillips, 2003; Phillips, Mannix, Neale, and Gruenfeld, 2004; Phillips and Loyd, 2006). Individuals expect socially similar others to agree with them more on task-relevant and task-irrelevant issues than socially dissimilar others (for example, Allen and Wilder, 1979; Chen and Kenrick, 2002; Phillips, 2003; Phillips and Loyd, 2006; Phillips et al., 2004). Because group members expect differences in knowledge or opinion to emerge from individuals who are socially dissimilar, they are more likely to give consideration to the unique perspectives put forth by such individuals than to those contributed by socially similar individuals (Phillips, 2003; Thomas-Hunt, Ogden, and Neale, 2003). For instance, in a group composed of two engineers and a marketing person, the two engineers are expected to agree with one another during the task discussion, and the marketing person is expected to have a different perspective. When the congruence is maintained—the engineers contribute similar information and the marketing person contributes different information—group members are best able to focus on the task and to benefit from their differences in perspective (Phillips, 2003; Phillips et al., 2004). Furthermore, group members are more likely to elaborate on other members' task-relevant information (Van Knippenberg et al., 2004) as they each understand the importance of their contribution to the group setting. Consequently, it is not surprising that functionally diverse groups most easily leverage their cognitive diversity, because there is an expectation that each member will contribute his or her particular identifiable area of expertise (Stasser, Stewart, and Wittenbaum, 1995).

These expectations of agreement are also relevant in groups in which the social-category differences appear to be irrelevant for the task at hand (Phillips, 2003). Phillips (2003) highlighted the social category of geographic location instead of functional background and found that even when this salient social category was irrelevant for the decision to be made, groups benefited more from different perspectives about the task (that is, different individual opinions about the best decision) when the unique perspectives came from people who were socially different from, instead of similar to, the others in the group (that is, when congruence was maintained). This work suggests that both functionally diverse groups and those characterized by less task-relevant social distinctions can benefit more from their underlying informational diversity when people who seem explicitly different from one another in social category actually fulfill expectations and express knowledge, perspectives, and information that are indeed different from the knowledge, perspectives, and information of others (also see Phillips et al., 2004, and Thomas-Hunt et al., 2003, for further evidence for the benefits of congruence).

BALANCE THEORY AND DIVERSITY

The theoretical basis of this empirical research is grounded in Heider's (1958) balance theory, which argues that people are motivated to maintain their social ties (common social identity) with similar others and feel the need to reconcile differences of opinion if socially similar others are in disagreement. Group members would rather agree than disagree with socially similar others, so they are likely to adjust their affective and behavioral responses to the group to restore balance between the social and task-relevant differences within the group (Crano and Cooper, 1973; Heider, 1958; Newcomb, 1961). Balance can be restored in a group in two ways. The first way is ultimately detrimental to group outcomes because it involves the suppression of information and opinions in an effort to restore balance and agree with similar others. Increased conformity to socially similar rather than dissimilar others (Asch, 1952; Abrams, Wetherell, Cochrane, Hogg, and Turner, 1990; Phillips and Loyd, 2006) is a robust effect and has been supported by other research on group dynamics such as the work on groupthink (Janis, 1982). In relation to our initial example, if one engineer disagrees with the other engineer in our three-person functionally diverse group, she or he may diminish the importance of the opinion, or question the strength of the opinion, or voice themselves less confidently in an effort to restore expectations and positive feelings toward the similar other (Phillips, 2003; Phillips et al., 2004).

Ironically, Phillips and Loyd (2006) and Phillips, Liljenquist, and Neale (2005) found that when task-relevant differences of opinion are present in a group—because of this same desire to restore balance and regenerate a positive tie with the socially similar other—groups that have some level of social-category diversity may actually outperform those that have no social-category diversity at all (that is, homogeneous groups). Group members are more likely to elaborate on their perspectives in the diverse environments and delve more into the task in an effort to understand the unexpected constellation of agreement and disagreement (Phillips and Loyd, 2006). Moreover, the engineer who experiences the most incongruence (that is, agreement with a dissimilar other and disagreement with a similar other) feels less supported and validated during the group discussion but helps the group work toward a solution that includes all members' information and perspectives (Phillips et al., 2005). This second way of restoring balance increases the discussion of differing information and knowledge instead of suppressing it and benefits group performance when the discussion of that information is critical. This work suggests that social-category diversity (even when it is not explicitly related to the task) can be beneficial for teams in which unique information and opinions need to be shared in the group (also see Antonio, Chang, Hakuta, Kenny, Levin, and Milem, 2004; Sommers, 2006). Recent research by Sommers (2006) shows that racial diversity in jury decision making can be beneficial, as it changes the behavior of those in the majority, allowing them to express perspectives and consider information and alternatives that they otherwise would readily dismiss or ignore in homogeneous settings. Social-category differences trigger expectations that informational and opinion differences may be present in groups and *legitimate* the expression of unique knowledge, perspectives, and information (Phillips, 2003; Phillips and Loyd, 2006; Phillips, Northcraft, and Neale, 2006; Thomas-Hunt et al., 2003; Van Knippenberg et al., 2004; Van Knippenberg

and Haslam, 2003). This work is consistent with past work on ways to remedy conformity pressure and groupthink—by introducing diversity that releases members'
loyalties to and need for support from the group members (for example, Turner and
Pratkanis, 1994; Turner, Pratkanis, Probasco, and Leve, 1992).

Moreover, this recent research on the effects of diversity on group process and
performance—especially considering situations in which group members clearly have
unique information and opinions to share with one another—leads to a very different conclusion than past work, which suggested that social-category differences can
only be harmful to the group process (for example, less communication and cohesion, more detrimental conflict) and performance. This recent research suggests that,
in fact, embracing social-category differences may actually help rather than hinder
the performance of groups. Further support of this phenomenon is derived from
work that finds that a team culture can reduce the relative consideration given to a
social outsider's unique information (Thomas-Hunt, Chow, and Neale, 2005).
When individuals are told to primarily see themselves as part of the team rather than
as unique contributors, unique contributions may be devalued and potentially even
generate disdain for the contributing member, particularly when the contributing
member is from a different social category. Ideally, groups will possess a clear common goal or purpose and a belief that the diversity among individual members will
be an asset in achieving the stated goal (Van Knippenberg and Haslam, 2003). For
functionally diverse groups, compared with groups characterized by other types of
social-category differences, this belief may be easier to develop given the nature of the
tasks that cross-functional teams work on. In many of these groups, the belief may
generally be held that each of the different functional groups is indeed needed to
achieve the overall goals of the group. Moreover, it may be easier in functionally
diverse groups to identify the nature of each group member's unique contribution
given the different functional expertise each member brings.

Thus, part of believing that diversity in the membership of a group will foster
beneficial cognitive conflict and be an advantage to group performance hinges on recognizing that individual members' possess unique knowledge that is useful to the
group. However, social-category distinctions frequently signal more than simply that
members are different from one another. They are frequently laden with expectations
that members from certain categories are better than others. So the challenge presented by most other types of social-category diversity in groups (for example, race, gender, age, tenure differences) is not solely driven by the fact that members are different.
Instead, it is critically important to consider the fact that many social-category differences, even including functional differences in organizational settings, are assigned
value, and members' performance expectations are calculated based on the social categories into which they are grouped. Consequently, the more distance there is between
the value imputed to any one group member A's social-category memberships and
other group members' social-category memberships, the lower the likelihood that
group members will expect and elaborate on useful contributions of knowledge from

member A. It is also likely that diminished expectations of A's contributions will result in fewer contributions from A, as we know that individuals' behavior in groups is largely driven by the expectations that others hold of them (Troyer and Yount, 1997). We refer to the difference in value assigned to members of a group as the level of *status distance* in the group (for similar construals of status distance, see Pearlin and Rosenberg, 1962; Poole, 1927) and argue that the status distance between members often obscures the unique contributions that individuals are poised to make.

A STATUS-DISTANCE LENS

The concept of status distance has its roots in work dating back to Simmel (1908) and Bogardus (1925), who argued that one could measure the social distance between subgroups in society. Social distance focused on the degree to which people were willing to interact with (for example, work with, live near, marry) members of different racial or ethnic groups. It has generally been used to understand whether people will voluntarily interact with individuals who are more distant from them in status (Blau, 1977; McPherson and Smith-Lovin, 1987). Its heavy emphasis on voluntary social interaction instead of instrumental interactions for the purpose of accomplishing a common goal makes it difficult to adopt the concept of status distance wholesale to the small work group setting. However, the concept of tolerated social closeness exacted by social distance has obvious implications for interactions in small groups in which there is social-category diversity.

According to status-characteristics theory, status reflects one's relative standing in a group and determines one's ability to contribute to and be listened to in a task group (Berger, Cohen, and Zelditch, 1972; Berger, Ridgeway, Fisek, and Norman, 1998). Status hierarchies naturally develop in small group settings, and some researchers (for example, Overbeck, Correll, and Park, 2005) have recently argued that a certain level of status sorting must occur in groups for individuals to successfully interact; not all group members can be high status. Most of this work has focused on the differences in value (for example, more or less value) associated with possession of particular characteristics (gender, race, motherhood, physical attractiveness), but it has not empirically considered how the magnitude of difference (that is, the degree of differentiation) in values imparted to members' characteristics affects the interaction pattern in the group. More recently, researchers have found that the degree of difference in value afforded to members' status characteristics affects the amount of influence members exert within groups (Foddy and Smithson, 1996). Therefore, we agree that group members are sorted into a status hierarchy that guides behavior. However, we contend that across diverse groups, the actual status distance between individuals in those groups may vary. That is, two groups that have the same diverse composition may have different levels of status distance. This difference in status distance has essentially been an omitted variable in past diversity studies.

The recent research that finds social-category diversity beneficial to group performance largely considers diversity derived from social categories that are afforded relatively equivalent levels of status in their environments (Phillips, 2003; Phillips et al., 2004, study 2). Those examining racial diversity have done so in jury or discussion contexts in which all persons' inputs and opinions about the decision are equally weighted, which may be one means of reducing status distance (Antonio et al., 2004; Sommers, 2006). When people see social-category diversity, they assume that informational diversity will accompany it. Based on this supposition, it follows that individuals in groups with social-category diversity will be more likely to expect informational differences to exist and will probe for such differences, integrate them into the discussion, and potentially make better decisions (Phillips et al., 2005). Whereas the work does not explicitly discuss status distance, the teams studied reflect the dynamics of those organizational groups (for example, cross-functional teams) that are often assembled with the implicit assumption that each representative possesses knowledge or expertise needed by the team to succeed in attaining its goal. In these instances, the level of status distance between members may be sufficiently low to allow them to share unique information and engage in the kind of cognitive conflict and elaboration of unique information that leads to improved group performance. At the same time, the level of status distance may minimize more detrimental forms of conflict that emerge from misunderstandings about individuals' intentions (Amason and Schweiger, 1994; De Dreu and Weingart, 2003; Jehn, 1995).

In many instances, groups are assembled and the skills, abilities, and knowledge base of the membership are not known. Furthermore, even when information is provided about members' areas of expertise, the value implicitly associated with their social categories often overshadows members' claims of expertise (Hollingshead and Fraidin, 2003). Consequently, the same social-category differences that diversity researchers hope will foster the elaboration of task-relevant information may also be accompanied by status differences that hinder the exchange and integration of unique knowledge, perspectives, and information in groups. Clearly these status differences may be so detrimental that the benefits of the diversity cannot be garnered.

The long history of work on status expectations in small groups has found that some social-category differences that are societally imbued with value, such as gender, may influence group knowledge integration processes by affecting the contribution of unique knowledge and the consideration it receives by other group members (for example, Berger, Fisek, Norman, and Zelditch, 1977; Ridgeway, 1987; Thomas-Hunt et al., 2003). Groups vary in the amount of status distance they afford to the same characteristics. Furthermore, the same characteristics may be assigned different status values in different contexts for the same group (Pearlin and Rosenberg, 1962). In most group contexts, men are generally perceived as having much higher status than women (that is, they are perceived as more competent) (Ridgeway, 2001), whereas in other contexts, men and women are perceived to be relatively equal in status (Heilman, Martell, and Simon, 1988; Nieva and Gutek,

1980). In an environment in which men and women are perceived to be equals, a lower status distance among the group members should result in more equal contributions and consideration of all group members' ideas and knowledge. As researchers try to study the influence of status distance on groups, the appropriate measurement tools must be developed. Since status distance is inherently a dynamic concept and is affected by interactions among individuals in groups, it may be important to assess the status distance at multiple times in the life stage of the groups.

DETERMINANTS OF STATUS DISTANCE

We now address the question of how some groups develop greater status distance among their group members than others. When individuals enter task groups, several factors may be used to help signal the status of each individual. We will consider three factors—one's social characteristics, to which societal or organizational worth is attributed; one's relative organizational position, such as manager or subordinate; and one's local task knowledge or well-known expertise about the task. A woman may have less status than a man because of societally conferred status, but there may be a decrease in the status distance between them if she is his boss in the organization. To the extent that organizational and local task sources of status reinforce the societal source of status, the status distance between individuals will increase. So in a group with a male who has superior status and has the expertise, the status distance between the male and female group members will be heightened. The ability of the female group member to contribute unique knowledge, perspectives, and information, thereby influencing the group, will be hindered by the greater status distance (Ridgeway, Johnson, and Diekema, 1994). In contrast, if the initially conferred societal status distinction is not reinforced by organizational and local task status, then the status distance among the groups' members will be diminished (Pugh and Wahrman, 1983). Ideally, when there are cross-cutting sources of status, the expectations held for each member will equalize, allowing the group to benefit from the unique knowledge, perspectives, and information of the full membership.

The status distance present in a group may also be affected by the broader organizational structure and context. For instance, the social-category membership of a group's leader may signal how much that particular characteristic is valued and afford greater status to other members who share that category membership. Organizations with more female leadership, for instance, may garner more valuable contributions from their lower-level female members (compare Ely, 1994). In this case, the status distance between men and women throughout the entire organization may be affected by the presence of women in the upper echelons (for example, Baron, Mittman, and Newman, 1991; Ridgeway, 1988).

We now turn to more explicitly discuss the effect of a group's status distance on its conflict, elaboration of information, and group performance.

STATUS DISTANCE, CONFLICT, AND PERFORMANCE

Our consideration of the impact of status distance on group functioning is largely informed by status characteristics theory. The premise of status characteristics theory is that power and prestige orders within interacting task groups are based on the performance expectations held of individuals (Berger et al., 1972; Berger et al., 1977; Berger, Rosenholtz, and Zelditch, 1980). Within such groups, individuals defer to those members for whom the highest performance expectations are held, giving such individuals more opportunities to participate and influence group decisions. Performance expectations are initiated based on the status of personal characteristics possessed by group members that over time in society have become associated with certain levels of task competence (Berger et al., 1977; Ridgeway, 2001). Status characteristics have been divided into two categories: those that provide *specific cues* (such as math aptitude) or information about task competence on a well-specified domain and those that provide *diffuse cues* (for example, race/ethnicity, age, physical attractiveness, gender) or more generalized information about potential ability or performance across a wide array of activities.

Much of the empirical work grounded in status characteristics theory has focused specifically on how gender affects the way in which individuals are treated within groups. This body of work has found that group members often hold lower performance expectations for women than men (Berger et al., 1980; Lockheed and Hall, 1976; Meeker and Weitzel-O'Neil, 1977) and give women fewer opportunities to participate than men (Meeker and Weitzel-O'Neil, 1985; Ridgeway and Berger, 1986). Furthermore, in our own work we found that both women and men held lower performance expectations for women than for men on a male-typed task and that women with expert knowledge were less influential within their groups than were other women and men (Thomas-Hunt and Phillips, 2004). The lack of influence of women with expert knowledge resulted in the lower performance of groups in which the most expert member was a woman relative to those in which the most expert person was a man.

More generally, when low expectations of performance are held for a collaboration partner, violations of behavioral expectations have a more detrimental effect on the consideration that a partner's ideas are given (Sheldon, Thomas-Hunt, and Proell, in press). Specifically, Sheldon et al. (in press) examined collaboration partners who were perceived to have delayed within a task-related exchange; the researchers found that those partners were only viewed less favorably and exerted less influence within their collaborations when they were perceived as having low status. High-status delayers were actually more influential than high-status nondelayers. These findings suggest that low- and high-status group members are treated differently within groups. When individuals are members of social categories for which low performance expectations are held, they are given fewer opportunities to deviate from the norms, express dissenting perspectives, and influence group outcomes. Consequently, the lower an individual's status is relative to other group members, the less consideration and elaboration that their contributions will be given. For cognitive conflict to be beneficial to group functioning, group members must be willing to elaborate on the task-relevant knowledge and insights that they possess (Van Knippenberg et al., 2004). This elaboration means engaging in discussion with and seriously considering the perspectives of others as a group decision is reached.

So, holding constant the absolute amount of diversity present in groups (that is, the capacity of all of the groups to have cognitive conflict or differences of opinion and perspective arise), it will be important to consider the impact of status distance.

The following propositions summarize the role of status distance in diverse groups.

> **Proposition 1: Diverse groups that have greater status distance among members will experience lower levels of cognitive conflict (that is, task information elaboration) relative to diverse groups that have lower status distance among members.**

Social-role theory posits that individuals adjust their own behaviors according to their understanding of what is expected from them based on their role in society, and status-characteristics theory focuses on the way group members are treated as a function of their status (Eagly, 1987). Bodies of work on both of these theories have focused on the effects of gender on individuals' experiences in task groups, concluding that women and men behave differently (Carli, 1991; Eagly, 1983; Eakins and Eakins, 1978) and are treated differently in interactions (Berger et al., 1977; Carli, 1991; Ridgeway and Diekema, 1989). These differences in behavior may contribute to misattributions of people's intentions and increase dysfunctional conflict in groups. For example, compared to men, women are less likely to interrupt (Argyle, Lalljee, and Cook, 1968; Eakins and Eakins, 1978; Mulac, Wiemann, Widenmann, and Gibson, 1988), are less likely to gain the floor after interrupting (Zimmerman and West, 1975), and are more likely to hedge (Crosby and Nyquist, 1977) and use disclaimers (for example, Hirschman, 1973). Finally, low-status individuals, unlike high-status individuals, do not take full advantage of the structural power that they possess (Proell and Thomas-Hunt, 2005). In an investigation of resource-allocation behavior, women paired with men and individuals who had less experience than their partners retained fewer resources for themselves than women paired with other women, men paired with anyone, or individuals who had more experience than their partners (Proell and Thomas-Hunt, 2005). All of this work suggests that differences in behavioral and interaction norms between high- and low-status members in groups may breed dysfunctional conflicts that detract from knowledge sharing and integration.

Furthermore, within groups in which the status distance is significant, the potential exists for low-status members to withhold contributions that may cause other group members to further question their usefulness to the group. Their lack of engagement and contributions may lead to the perception that lower-status individuals are social loafers and may further the negative attributions about their competence, increasing interpersonal tension within the group. Contributing knowledge, however, may not remedy the perceptions of low-status members, as the lower expectations held for them may lead other members to devalue or ignore their contributions altogether. This response again may frustrate the ignored members and increase all group members' perceptions of relationship conflict within the group. Relationship conflict, defined by Jehn (1995) as conflict in interpersonal relations that are not directly related to the task, is highly correlated with cognitive conflict, which is conflict related to the content of the task itself (De Dreu and Weingart, 2003). The genesis of relationship conflict in task groups may be rooted in this task-related process of knowledge contribution and integration. A lack of respect for the contributions of lower-status individuals is likely to contribute to this problem (see chapter 8 in this volume). This cycle may become a self-fulfilling prophecy that further diminishes the group's ability to benefit from the unique perspectives possessed by all group members. Furthermore, in groups that have higher status distance, the negative social categorization effects that accompany social-category diversity may be even stronger, creating an us-versus-them mentality that is detrimental for relationships among group members.

> **Proposition 2: Diverse groups that have greater status distance among members will experience higher levels of relationship conflict relative to diverse groups that have lower status distance among members.**

In summary, not only may a high status distance contribute to more harmful conflict within a group, but the more beneficial form of cognitive conflict that captures the elaboration of information discussed previously may never emerge. The diminished willingness of low-status members to contribute their knowledge and the dismissal of that which they do contribute reduces the likelihood that groups characterized by high status distance will be confronted with and will consider different perspectives and opinions. A lack of task information elaboration and increased relationship conflict should in turn negatively affect group performance.

> **Proposition 3: Diverse groups that have greater status distance among members will ultimately perform worse than diverse groups that have lower status distance among members. This status-distance/performance relationship will be mediated by cognitive and relationship conflict.**

Moreover, if societal, organizational, and local status expectations reinforce one another, increasing the status distance in the group, the barriers between subgroups are likely to widen (Lau and Murnighan, 1998, 2005). Work on faultlines in diverse groups may be particularly relevant for understanding this phenomenon. As fault-lines grow deeper in diverse groups, they constrain interaction across the subgroups, decrease trust, and make it more difficult for group members to work together. Moreover, group members are less likely to seek each other out for social support, and the benefits of being together in a group will become more and more elusive. Because of this, not only is the effectiveness of the group in jeopardy, but group members' satisfaction and desire to remain a part of the group may also be compromised. Thus, our final proposition is:

> **Proposition 4: Diverse groups that have greater status distance among members will report lower satisfaction and desire by members to remain in the group than will diverse groups that have lower status distance among members.**

CONCLUSION

Thus, the same social-category differences that diversity researchers hope will foster cognitive conflict and the elaboration of task-relevant information may also be accompanied by status differences that reduce the confidence and assertiveness of certain members and hinder the exchange and integration of unique knowledge, perspectives, and information in groups. Status distance captures the extent to which a status hierarchy exists that reinforces a lack of interaction, communication, and cohesion among members from different subgroups. Interaction is promoted by low status distance or by situations in which individuals have more proximate status, and teams should thus be more likely to benefit from the task-relevant differences that may accompany their heterogeneity. An examination of diversity without a consideration of status hierarchies within groups (for example, Berger, Conner, and Fisek, 1974; Blau, 1977; Ridgeway, 1982) inherently fails to capture the true dynamics of such contexts (for example, Chatman and O'Reilly, 2004). Recent research on diversity in groups, like that on self-verification (Polzer, Milton, and Swann, 2002; Swann, Milton, and Polzer, 2000) and the integration-and-learning perspective (Ely and Thomas, 2001), points to possible ways to diminish the status distance among members of diverse groups. The group and organizational contexts are going to be critically important in neutralizing the societally based status expectations that are slow to change. Thus, organizations and managers must work on developing a sense of respect for each individual contributor and the value that each brings to the group (see chapter 8, this volume). This will ultimately allow groups to garner the benefits of cognitive conflict and avoid the misattributions that lead to relationship conflict in groups.

REFERENCES

Abrams, D. M., Wetherell, M., Cochrane, S., Hogg, M. A., and Turner, J. C. 1990. Knowing what to think by knowing who you are: Self-categorization and the nature of norm formation, conformity and group polarization. *British Journal of Social Psychology, 29,* 97–119.

Allen, V. L., and Wilder, D. A. 1979. Group categorization and attribution of belief similarity. *Small Group Behavior, 10,* 73–80.

Amason, A. C. 1996. Distinguishing the effects of functional and dysfunctional conflict on strategic decision making: Resolving a paradox for top management teams. *Academy of Management Journal, 39,* 123–148.

Amason, A. C., and Schweiger, D. M. 1994. Resolving the paradox of conflict, strategic decision-making, and organizational performance. *International Journal of Conflict Management, 5,* 239–253.

Ancona, D., and Caldwell, D. 1992. Demography and design: Predictors of new product team performance. *Organization Science, 3,* 321–341.

Antonio, A. L., Chang, M. J., Hakuta, K., Kenny, D. A., Levin, S., and Milem, J. F. 2004. Effects of racial diversity on complex thinking in college students. *Psychological Science, 15*(8), 507–510.

Argyle, M., Lalljee, M., and Cook, M. 1968. The effects of visibility on interaction in a dyad. *Human Relations, 21,* 3–17.

Asch, S. E. 1952. *Social psychology.* Englewood Cliffs, N.J.: Prentice Hall.

Bantel, K. A., and Jackson, S. E. 1989. Top management and innovations in banking: Does the composition of the top team make a difference? *Strategic Management Journal, 10,* 107–124.

Baron, J. W., Mittman, B. S., and Newman, A. E. 1991. Targets of opportunity: Organizational and environmental determinants of gender integration within the California civil service, 1979–1985. *American Journal of Sociology, 96,* 1362–1401.

Berger, J., Cohen, B. P., and Zelditch, M., Jr. 1972. Status characteristics and social interaction. *American Sociological Review, 63,* 379–405.

Berger, J., Conner, T., and Fisek, M. H. (Eds.). 1974. *Expectation states theory: A theoretical research program.* Cambridge, Mass.: Winthrop.

Berger, J., Rosenholtz, S. J., and Zelditch, M., Jr. 1980. Status organizing processes. *Annual Review of Sociology, 6,* 479–508.

Berger, J., Fisek, M. H., Norman, R. Z., and Zelditch, M., Jr. 1977. *Status characteristics and social interaction.* New York: Elsevier.

Berger, J., Ridgeway, C. L., Fisek, M. H., and Norman, R. Z. 1998. The legitimation and delegitimation of power and prestige orders. *American Sociological Review, 63,* 379–405.

Blau, P. 1977. *Inequality and heterogeneity.* New York: Free Press.

Bogardus, E. S. 1925. Social distance and its origins. *Journal of Applied Sociology, 9,* 216–226.

Carli, L. L. 1991. Gender, status, and influence. In E. J. Lawler, B. Markovsky, C. Ridgeway, and H. A. Walker (Eds.), *Advances in group processes: Theory and research* (vol. 8, pp. 89–113). Greenwich, Conn.: JAI Press.

Chatman, J. A., and O'Reilly, C. A. 2004. Asymmetric reactions to work group sex diversity among men and women. *Academy of Management Journal, 47,* 193–208.

Chen, F. F., and Kenrick, D. T. 2002. Repulsion or attraction? Group membership and assumed attitude similarity. *Journal of Personality and Social Psychology, 83,* 111–125.

Cox, T., Lobel, S., and McLeod, P. 1991. Effects of ethnic group cultural differences on cooperative and competitive behavior on a group task. *Academy of Management Journal, 34,* 827–847.

Crano, W., and Cooper, R. 1973. Examination of Newcomb's extension of structural balance theory. *Journal of Personality and Social Psychology, 27*(3), 344–353.

Crosby, F., and Nyquist, L. 1977. The female register: An empirical study of Lakoff's hypothesis. *Language in Society, 6,* 313–322.

De Dreu, C. K. W., and Weingart, L. R. 2003. Task versus relationship conflict, team performance, and team member satisfaction: A meta-analysis. *Journal of Applied Psychology, 88* (4), 741–749.

De Dreu, C. K. W., and West, M. A. 2001. Minority dissent and team innovation: The importance of participation in decision making. *Journal of Applied Psychology, 86,* 1191–1201.

Eagly, A. H. 1983. Gender and social influence: A social psychological analysis. *American Psychologist, 38,* 971–981.

Eagly, A. H. 1987. *Sex differences in social behavior: A social-role analysis.* Hillsdale, N.J.: Lawrence Erlbaum.

Eakins, B., and Eakins, R. G. 1978. *Sex differences in human communication.* Boston: Houghton Mifflin.

Ely, R. 1994. The effects of organizational demographics and social identity on relationships among professional women. *Administrative Science Quarterly, 39,* 203–238.

Ely, R., and Thomas, D. 2001. Cultural diversity at work: The effects of diversity perspectives on work group processes and outcomes. *Administrative Science Quarterly, 46,* 229–273.

Foddy, M., and Smithson, M. 1996. Relative ability, paths of relevance, and influence in task-oriented groups. *Social Psychology Quarterly, 59* (2), 140–153.

Heider, F. 1958. *The psychology of interpersonal relations.* New York: Wiley.

Heilman, M. E., Martell, R. F., and Simon, M. 1988. The vagaries of bias: Conditions regulating the undervaluation, equivaluation, and overvaluation of female job applicants. *Organizational Behavior and Human Decision Processes, 41,* 98–110.

Hirschman, L. 1973. *Female-male differences in conversational interaction.* Paper presented at the meeting of the Linguistic Society of America, San Diego, Calif.

Hoffman, E. 1985. The effect of race-ratio composition on the frequency of organizational communication. *Social Psychology Quarterly, 48,* 17–26.

Hollingshead, A. B., and Fraidin, S. 2003. Gender stereotypes and assumptions about expertise in transactive memory. *Journal of Experimental Social Psychology, 39,* 355–363.

Jackson, S. E., Joshi, A., and Erhardt, N. L. 2003. Recent research on team and organizational diversity: SWOT analysis and implications. *Journal of Management, 29,* 801–830.

Janis, I. 1982. *Groupthink: Psychological studies of policy decisions and fiascoes,* 2nd edition. Boston: Houghton Mifflin.

Jehn, K. A. 1995. A multimethod examination of the benefits and detriments of intragroup conflict. *Administrative Science Quarterly, 40* (2), 256–282.

Jehn, K., Northcraft, G., and Neale, M. 1999. Why differences make a difference: A field study of diversity, conflict, and performance in work groups. *Administrative Science Quarterly, 44,* 741–763.

Lau, D., and Murnighan, K. 1998. Demographic diversity and faultlines: The compositional dynamics of organizational groups. *Academy of Management Review, 23,* 325–240.

Lau, D., and Murnighan, K. 2005. Interactions within groups and subgroups: The effects of demographic faultlines. *Academy of Management Journal, 48,* 645–659.

Lockheed, M. E., and Hall, K. P. 1976. Conceptualizing sex as a status characteristic: Application to leadership training strategies. *Journal of Social Issues, 32,* 111–124.

McPherson, J. M., and Smith-Lovin, L. 1987. Homophily in voluntary organizations: Status distance and the composition of face-to-face groups. *American Sociological Review, 52,* 370–379.

Meeker, B. F., and Weitzel-O'Neil, P. A. 1977. Sex roles and interpersonal behavior in task-oriented groups. *American Sociological Review, 42,* 91–105.

Meeker, B. F., and Weitzel-O'Neil, P. A. 1985. Sex roles and interpersonal behavior in task-oriented groups. In J. Berger and M. Zelditch, Jr. (Eds.), *Status, reward, and influence* (pp. 379–405). Washington, D.C.: Jossey-Bass.

Milliken, F. J., and Martins, L. 1996. Searching for common threads: Understanding the multiple effects of diversity in organizational groups. *Academy of Management Review, 21,* 402–433.

Mulac, A., Wiemann, J. M., Widenmann, S. J., and Gibson, T. W. 1988. Male/female language differences in same-sex and mixed-sex dyads: The gender-linked language effect. *Communication Monographs, 55,* 315–335.

Newcomb, T. M. 1961. *The acquaintance process.* New York: Holt, Rinehart and Winston.

Nieva, V., and Gutek, B. 1980. Sex effects on evaluation. *Academy of Management Journal, 5*(2), 267–276.

Overbeck, J., Correll, J., and Park, B. 2005. Internal status sorting in groups: The problem of too many stars. In M. Thomas-Hunt (Ed.), *Research on managing groups and teams* (vol. 7, Status and Groups, pp. 169–201). Greenwich, Conn.: JAI Press.

Pearlin, L. I., and Rosenberg, M. 1962. Nurse-patient social distance and the social context of a mental hospital. *American Sociological Review, 27,* 56–65.

Pelled, L. H., Eisenhardt, K. M., and Xin, K. R. 1999. Exploring the black box: An analysis of work group diversity, conflict, and performance. *Administrative Science Quarterly, 44,* 1–28.

Phillips, K. W. 2003. The effects of categorically based expectations on minority influence: The importance of congruence. *Personality and Social Psychology Bulletin, 29,* 3–13.

Phillips, K. W., and Loyd, D. L. 2006. When surface and deep-level diversity collide: The effects on dissenting group members. *Organizational Behavior and Human Decision Processes, 99,* 143–160.

Phillips, K. W., Liljenquist, K., and Neale, M. A. 2005. *Is the pain worth the gain? The advantages and liabilities of agreeing with socially distinct newcomers.* Working paper, Northwestern University.

Phillips, K. W., Northcraft, G., and Neale, M. A. 2006. Surface-level diversity and information sharing: When does deep-level similarity help? *Group Processes and Intergroup Relations, 9*(4), 467–482.

Phillips, K. W., Mannix, E., Neale, M., and Gruenfeld, D. 2004. Diverse groups and information sharing: The effects of congruent ties. *Journal of Experimental Social Psychology, 40,* 498–510.

Polzer, J. T., Milton, L. P., and Swann, W. B., Jr. 2002. Capitalizing on diversity: Interpersonal congruence in small work groups. *Administrative Science Quarterly, 47,* 296–324.

Poole, W. C. 1927. Distance in sociology. *American Journal of Sociology, 33*(1), 99–104.

Proell, C. A., and Thomas-Hunt, M. C. 2005. *As powers collide: The interactive effects of status and structural power on resource allocations.* Working paper, Cornell University.

Pugh, M. D., and Wahrman, R. 1983. Neutralizing sexism in mixed-sex groups: Do women have to be better than men? *American Journal of Sociology, 88*(4), 746–762.

Ridgeway, C. L. 1982. Status in groups: The importance of motivation. *American Sociological Review, 47,* 76–88.

Ridgeway, C. L. 1987. Nonverbal behavior, dominance, and the basis of status in task groups. *American Sociological Review, 52,* 683–694.

Ridgeway, C. L. 1988. Gender differences in task groups: A status and legitimacy account. In M. Webster and M. Foschi (Eds.), *Status generalization: New theory and research* (pp. 188–206). Stanford, Calif.: Stanford University Press.

Ridgeway, C. L. 2001. Gender, status, and leadership. *Journal of Social Issues, 57,* 637–655.

Ridgeway, C. L., and Berger, J. 1986. Expectations, legitimation, and dominance behavior in task groups. *American Sociological Review, 51,* 603–617.

Ridgeway, C. L., and Diekema, D. 1989. Dominance and collective hierarchy formation in male and female task groups. *American Sociological Review, 54,* 79–93.

Ridgeway, C. L., Johnson, C., and Diekema, D. 1994. External status, legitimacy, and compliance in male and female groups. *Social Forces, 72,* 1051–1077.

Schneider, S. K., and Northcraft, G. B. 1999. Three social dilemmas of workforce diversity in organizations: A social identity perspective. *Human Relations, 52,* 1445–1467.

Sheldon, O. J., Thomas-Hunt, M. C., and Proell, C. A. In press. When timeliness matters: The moderating effect of status on behavioral reactions to perceived time delay within distributed work interactions. *Journal of Applied Psychology.*

Simmel, G. 1908. The stranger. In Kurt Wolff (Trans.), *The sociology of Georg Simmel* (pp. 402–408). New York: Free Press, 1950.

Simons, T., and Peterson, R. 2000. Task conflict and relationship conflict in top management teams: The pivotal role of intragroup trust. *Journal of Applied Psychology, 83,* 102–111.

Sommers, S. R. 2006. On racial diversity and group decision making: Identifying multiple effects of racial composition on jury deliberations. *Journal of Personality and Social Psychology, 90,* 597–612.

Stasser, G., Stewart, D. D., and Wittenbaum, G. M. 1995. Expert roles and information exchange during discussion: The importance of knowing who knows what. *Journal of Experimental Social Psychology, 31,* 244–265.

Stephan, W., and Stephan, C. 1985. Intergroup anxiety. *Journal of Social Issues, 41,* 157–175.

Swann, W. B., Jr., Milton, L. P., and Polzer, J. T. 2000. Should we create a niche or fall in line? Identity negotiation and small group effectiveness. *Journal of Personality and Social Psychology, 79,* 238–250.

Thomas-Hunt, M. C., and Phillips, K. W. 2004. When what you know is not enough: Expertise and gender dynamics in task groups. *Personality and Social Psychology Bulletin, 30,* 1585–1598.

Thomas-Hunt, M. C., Chow, R., and Neale, M. A. 2005. *When expertise doesn't count: The effects of organizational culture and expert status on knowledge consideration within groups.* Working paper, Cornell University.

Thomas-Hunt, M. C., Ogden, T. Y., and Neale, M. A. 2003. Who's really sharing? Effects of social and expert status on knowledge exchange within groups. *Management Science, 49,* 464–477.

Troyer, L., and Yount, C. W. 1997. Whose expectations matter? The relative power of first- and second-order expectations in determining social influence. *American Journal of Sociology, 103,* 692–732.

Turner, M. E., and Pratkanis, A. R. 1994. Social identity maintenance prescriptions for preventing groupthink: Reducing identity protection and enhancing intellectual conflict. *International Journal of Conflict Management, 5,* 254–270.

Turner, M. E., Pratkanis, A. R., Probasco, P., and Leve, C. 1992. Threat, cohesion, and group effectiveness: Testing a social identity maintenance perspective on groupthink. *Journal of Personality and Social Psychology, 63,* 781–796.

Van Knippenberg, D., and Haslam, S. A. 2003. Realizing the diversity dividend: Exploring the subtle interplay between identity, ideology and reality. In S. A. Haslam, D. van Knippenberg, M. Platow, and N. Ellemers (Eds.), *Social identity at work: Developing theory for organizational practice* (pp. 61–77). New York: Taylor and Francis.

Van Knippenberg, D., De Dreu, C. K. W., and Homan, A. C. 2004. Work group diversity and group performance: An integrative model and research agenda. *Journal of Applied Psychology, 89,* 1008–1022.

Williams, K., and O'Reilly, C. 1998. Demography and diversity in organizations: A review of 40 years of research. In B. M. Staw and R. Sutton (Eds.), *Research in organizational behavior* (vol. 21, pp. 77–140). Greenwich, Conn.: JAI Press.

Zenger, T., and Lawrence, B. 1989. Organizational demography: The differential effects of age and tenure distributions on technical communications. *Academy of Management Journal, 32,* 353–376.

Zimmerman, D. H., and West, C. 1975. Sex roles, interruptions, and silences in conversation. In B. Thorne and N. Henley (Eds.), *Language and sex: Difference and dominance* (pp. 105–129). Rowley, Mass.: Newbury House Publishers.

Chapter 3

GROUP HETEROGENEITY AND FAULTLINES: COMPARING ALIGNMENT AND DISPERSION THEORIES OF GROUP COMPOSITION

Katerina Bezrukova, Sherry M. B. Thatcher,
and Karen A. Jehn

ABSTRACT

This field study examines group diversity from two theoretical viewpoints: dispersion approach (heterogeneity) and alignment approach (faultlines). We argue that the alignment approach provides an additional explanatory tool to that of the dispersion approach in understanding the effects of group composition on process and outcomes. Data from 60 work groups show that whereas groups with strong faultlines had higher levels of intragroup conflict and lower levels of performance and satisfaction, groups that were heterogeneous in tenure and functional background had higher levels of performance. Task conflict and process conflict mediated the relationship between faultlines and satisfaction. Our findings suggest that whereas both views of diversity contribute to our understanding of the relationship among

This research was supported by the SEI Center for Advanced Studies in Management of the Wharton School and the George Harvey Program on Redefining Diversity: Value Creation through Diversity. We are very grateful to Elaine Zanutto for the guidance in statistical analysis and to Madhan Gounder, Hina A. Kharbey, Isaac O. Choi, Andre Kursancew, and Poonam Maharjan for the assistance in data analysis.

group-level diversity, group processes, and performance, the rationale underlying group faultlines (the alignment approach) provides, in general, a more comprehensive explanation of group processes and performance than does a group heterogeneity model alone.

Introduction

As the trend continues toward greater economic globalization and societal diversity, companies are recognizing the need to leverage the various backgrounds of their employees to sustain their competitive advantage in a global marketplace (Jehn and Bezrukova, 2004; Thomas and Ely, 1996). This trend is paralleled by the realization, reinforced with empirical evidence, that well-managed work groups can serve as catalysts to multiply the contributions of individual employees (Bishop, Scott, and Burroughs, 2000; Donnellon, 1996). Unfortunately, it appears that these two trends frequently fail to intersect and produce synergistic benefits for companies (Kochan, Bezrukova, Ely, Jackson, Joshi, Jehn, Leonard, Levine, and Thomas, 2003). This may be attributed to potential challenges that managers face regarding how to properly translate the diversity of work groups into higher profits.

In response, many researchers have tackled the issues related to diversity in teams. However, the results of the studies have been rather contradictory and thus inconclusive; diversity seems as likely to hinder performance as it is to improve it (compare Riordan, 2000; Williams and O'Reilly, 1998). According to the recent reviews of diversity and relational demography research, one reason for these contradictory findings is the lack of theoretical guidance for understanding diversity in teams (Jackson, Joshi, and Erhardt, 2003; Webber and Donahue, 2001).

The most recent response to this claim of theoretical inadequacy has been to focus on the issue of demographic alignment as put forth in the group faultline theory introduced by Lau and Murnighan (1998). Previous diversity research has mainly drawn on heterogeneity, or the dispersion view of group composition. Group diversity has been explained either through changes in information processing (for example, introducing a broader array of information) or through a social categorization process (for example, favoring in-groups and derogating out-groups to enhance self-construals) (Williams and O'Reilly, 1998). From a methodological standpoint, this line of research emphasizes the degree of distribution among group members along relevant dimensions of attributes (Alexander, Nuchols, Bloom, and Lee, 1995). This work has been criticized because it is based on the assumption that these demographic attributes are independent. For instance, when examining race, gender has been ignored, leading to the assumption that the experiences of African American men in a group would be similar to that of African American women in an otherwise identical group (for example, Roth, Huffcutt, and Bobko, 2003).

The alignment approach, in turn, argues that the compositional dynamics of interacting multiple attributes affects group processes more than separate demographic characteristics (for example, Lau and Murnighan, 1998). Members who share several similar attributes are likely to align and coalesce into subgroups, reinforcing one another and differentiating themselves from other subgroups in a team (Earley and Mosakowski, 2000; Cramton and Hinds, 2005). Although some theorizing about interacting or overlapping demographic dissimilarities has been done in the past (for example, see the literature on multiform heterogeneity: Blau, 1977, and Kanter, 1977; also see more recent studies: Lau and Murnighan, 2005; Li and Hambrick, 2005; Roccas and Brewer, 2002), research examining the alignment properties of such overlaps and the resulting splits within a group has remained scarce.

Moreover, previous studies have shown significant effects for various demographic heterogeneity factors (for example, age, race, gender, tenure) on group processes and performance. Although these findings are important, a weakness of this previous research is that none of the studies has contrasted group faultline models (that is, alignment) with group heterogeneity models (that is, dispersion). Therefore, the main purpose of our study is to examine the relative importance of group faultlines and group heterogeneity on group processes and performance. We hope to explain the missing variance inherent in the studies that examined only group heterogeneity. For several reasons, we believe that the rationale underlying group faultlines provides a better explanation of group processes and performance than does the rationale underlying group heterogeneity alone. Our central argument is that the presence (or absence) of certain demographic differences within a group may (or may not) influence members' behaviors, but the particular alignment of group members based on these differences will influence behavior. Alignment explains how evolving subgroups may become polarized around certain viewpoints because of conformity pressure arising within subgroups and competition across them (Lau and Murnighan, 1998; Thatcher, Jehn, and Zanutto, 2003; Wit and Kerr, 2002); therefore, "faultlines may have more potential for performance losses owing to increased conflict" (Lau and Murnighan, 1998, p. 327). Thus, our second theoretical contribution is to extend conflict literature by examining how group composition based on alignment enables us to better explain how group composition acts as an antecedent of conflict. Our methodological contribution to existing research on group composition and faultlines comes in the form of examining the predictive power of both heterogeneity variables and faultline variables on group processes and outcomes. Understanding how forms of group composition affect group processes and outcomes will provide valuable information to managers as they form and supervise teams.

DISPERSION VERSUS ALIGNMENT

We classify approaches to group composition into two types, the dispersion approach and the alignment approach. Group composition research based on the dispersion approach[1] examines how members' attributes are distributed within a group and how this dispersion may influence a number of group outcomes (McGrath, 1998; Milliken and Martins, 1996; Moreland and Levine, 1992). The concept of heterogeneity has been often used to reflect dispersion in this line of research. Social-categorization theory, the similarity/attraction paradigm, and the cognitive-resource perspective have been used to explain the theoretical mechanisms underlying the relationship among heterogeneity, group process, and performance. Social-categorization theory posits that individuals classify themselves and others into in-group and out-group categories. Classification occurs to enhance positive self-construal and to make predictions about subsequent interactions (Tajfel and Turner, 1986). These categorization processes tend to give rise to stereotypes, prejudice, and out-group discrimination that may result in conflict and lead to substandard performance (Jehn, Northcraft, and Neale, 1999; Pelled, Eisenhardt, and Xin, 1999). Byrne (1971) proposed the similarity/attraction paradigm to explain why people are attracted to similar others and why they apply negative assumptions to those who are dissimilar (Byrne, 1971). The similarity/attraction paradigm suggests that demographic characteristics serve as a method for determining similarity, leading to more frequent communication and a desire to remain in the group (Lincoln and Miller, 1979). Finally, a cognitive-resource perspective suggests that the dispersion of member attributes supplies a large amount of information and facilitates a complex problem-solving process. That is, decision making of high quality may arise from different experiences and perspectives that diverse group members bring to their team (Dahlin, Weingart, and Hinds, 2005; Gruenfeld, Mannix, Williams, and Neale, 1996).

Although much empirical work has been conducted under the dispersion framework, there is still no consensus around the relationship between diversity and performance (Williams and O'Reilly, 1998). Some studies have shown that diversity leads to decreased levels of performance (Michel and Hambrick, 1992; Thatcher, 1999; Zajac, Golden, and Shortell, 1991) due to social-categorization and similarity/attraction effects (Byrne, 1971; Tajfel and Turner, 1986). Other studies have shown that diversity can improve group performance (Bantel and Jackson, 1989; Hambrick, Cho, and Chen, 1996; Eisenhardt, Kahwajy, and Bourgeois, 1997) by increasing cognitive-resource diversity (Ancona and Caldwell, 1992; Gruenfeld et al., 1996). Still other studies have shown no relationship between diversity and performance (O'Reilly, Snyder, and Boothe, 1993; Wiersema and Bantel, 1992).

An alignment approach to group composition suggests that whereas the social-categorization processes may be similar for heterogeneous and faultline-based groups, there will be additional perceptual categorizations and behavioral outcomes due to the creation of subgroups based on overlapping similarities in faultline-based groups. An overlap of social categories sharpens the boundaries around subgroups and results in salient subgroup identities. The added effect of this overlap is that strong subgroups emerging from faultlines may be less fluid and more stable, especially as more characteristics align. Thus, alignment models predict group processes and performance as a function of simultaneous alignment across members based on multiple characteristics. This differs from the dispersion models of group composition, which do not take into account the interdependence among multiple forms of diversity. The heterogeneity concept, for example, captures the degree to which a group differs on only one demographic characteristic (for example, gender; see Table 3.1 for comparison between faultlines and diversity scores) while often ignoring other demographic characteristics (for example, race) (McGrath, 1998). Even when dispersion researchers take into account more than one demographic characteristic by examining overall demographic diversity (for example, Schippers, Den Hartog, Koopman, and Wienk, 2003), they use an additive model and aggregate the effects of the single-characteristic dispersion model (for an exception, see Alexander et al., 1995). Although these aggregate dispersion models explain the degree to which a group is demographically different on age *and* gender *and* tenure, for instance, they inadequately reflect the degree of interdependence among these characteristics. For example, we are unable to tell if all the Caucasians in a group are also men. This limitation is overcome in alignment-based research.

Three areas of work inform the theoretical mechanisms underlying the alignment perspective: multiform heterogeneity (Blau, 1977; Kanter, 1977), group faultlines (Lau and Murnighan, 1998), and factional groups (Hambrick, Li, Xin, and Tsui, 2001; Li and Hambrick, 2005). The literature on multiform heterogeneity has stressed the importance of focusing on the multiple parameters of social structure (for example, sex, race). Multiform heterogeneity refers to overlapping groups and subgroups generated by the differences in sex, race, national background, religion, and so on (Blau, 1977). Consolidated or highly correlated parameters strengthen in-group bonds and reinforce group barriers, whereas low correlation among them indicates the intersection of parameters that promotes group integration.

Faultline theory reasons that the compositional dynamics of multiple attributes (for example, alignment) have a greater effect on group processes and performance than separate demographic characteristics (e.g., Lau and Murnighan, 1998; 2005; Thatcher et al., 2003). Faultline theory defines group faultlines as hypothetical dividing lines that split a group into relatively homogeneous subgroups based on the group members' demographic alignment along one or more attributes (adapted from Lau and Murnighan, 1998). For instance, Cramton and Hinds (2005) have theorized about how the alignment of compositional diversity and geographic distribution creates tension between subgroups emerging from faultlines. In a study of the formation

Table 3.1

Examples of Groups with Strong and Weak Faultlines and Diversity Scores

Group Number	Member A	Member B	Member C	Member D	L&M Faultline Strength*†	Race Diversity	Sex Diversity	Age Diversity	TJ,&Z Fau Strength Score‡
1	White male 21	White male 21	Black female 50	Black female 50	Very strong (3 align, 1 way)	.5 (medium diversity score)	.5 (medium diversity score)	.472 (medium diversity score)	1.00
2	Asian female 21	White male 21	Black female 25	Asian male 35	Weak (1 align, 3 ways)	.625 (high diversity score)	.5 (medium diversity score)	.259 (low diversity score)	.51
3	White male 21	White male 21	Black female 30	Black female 30	Very strong (3 align, 1 way)	.5 (medium diversity score)	.5 (medium diversity score)	.204 (very low diversity score)	1.00

*With the number of identified attributes fixed at three, faultline strength, as defined by Lau and Murnighan (L&M) (1998), is determined here by the number of demographic attributes that align (denoted as "align") and the possible ways to subdivide the group on the basis of these attributes (denoted as "ways").

†We use the following classification of faultline strength, based on the maximum number of characteristics that align: 1 = weak, 2 = medium, 3 = strong, 4 = very strong.

‡This is the faultline score as measured by the Fau algorithm in Thatcher, Jehn, and Zanutto (TJ,&Z) (2003). Race and gender are categorical variables. The data are rescaled so that all of these are equivalent: twenty-year difference in age, difference in gender, difference in race. Age is continuous.

of breakaway organizations, Dyck and Starke (1999) found that competition between the breakaway group and supporters of the status quo became evident when there was increased alignment of subgroup members.

Finally, Hambrick and his colleagues argue that in international joint ventures (IJVs), "compositional gaps" that occur along multiple demographic dimensions (for example, culture, age) in factional groups may accentuate managerial coalitions and influence group functioning and effectiveness (Hambrick et al., 2001; Li and Hambrick, 2005). A compositional gap is the difference between managerial coalitions on one or more dimensions that are of potential importance to the group's functioning. This gap separates a group into two distinctly different factions, where a faction is relatively homogeneous or is tightly clustered around its own central tendency (Hambrick et al., 2001; Li and Hambrick, 2005). Studies of IJV management groups have shown that the formation of subgroups based on demographics is inherently coalitional and is likely to reduce identification with the whole team and negatively affect group functioning and IJV effectiveness (Earley and Mosakowski, 2000; Hambrick et al., 2001).

In sum, the alignment approach to group composition takes into account the facts that (1) individuals have multiple identities simultaneously (for example, Asian, male) rather than one identity at a time (Asian), (2) these identities are interdependent, and (3) they interact with one another. Thus, the alignment approach accounts for the interdependence among multiple demographic characteristics that the dispersion approach often neglects.

COMPOSITIONAL EFFECTS ON CONFLICT AND PERFORMANCE

Theorizing on group diversity suggests that group composition influences patterns of interaction in a group (for example, conflict) and affects outcomes (for example, performance, satisfaction) (Williams and O'Reilly, 1998). In this study, we focus on three types of conflict—relationship conflict, task conflict, and process conflict—that have been identified in working groups, bicultural teams, and other organizing entities (Amason, 1996; Jehn, 1997; Jehn et al., 1999; Pelled, 1996). Since most dispersion studies in the literature on group diversity are concerned with the effects of diversity on conflict and group performance, we develop our rationale predicting first, the effects of heterogeneity and second, the effects of faultlines on group-level conflict and performance. In general, we believe that faultlines will be better predictors of performance due to the effects of additional social categorization (the particular subgroup within the larger group).

The dispersion approach is based on theories of social identity and social categorization (Tajfel and Turner, 1986), which assert that individuals classify themselves and others into social categories based on demographic characteristics (for example, race, gender, function). Group members confirm their affiliation with a certain category by showing in-group favoritism and out-group hostility (Tajfel and Turner, 1986). As a result of these negative categorization processes, individuals in groups with high levels of heterogeneity may experience frustration, discomfort, hostility, and anxiety resulting in high levels of relationship conflict (disagreements and incompatibilities about personal issues unrelated to the task) and low levels of satisfaction (Jehn, 1997). For example, heterogeneity on the dimensions of gender and ethnicity is related to interpersonal tension, low levels of friendliness, and low levels of satisfaction (Jehn et al., 1999; O'Reilly, Caldwell, and Barnett, 1989; Pelled, Xin, and Weiss, 2001).

Likewise, the alignment approach also predicts conflict based on similarity/attraction and social categorization, but there are additional perceptual and behavioral phenomena due to the creation of subgroups based on overlapping similarities. Members' perception of distinct subgroups and their engagement in coalition formation as a result of an alignment are examples of such phenomena. Alignment perspective suggests that these strong subgroupings resulting from faultlines can lead to political issues and covert relationship conflict in the group (Lau and Murnighan, 1998). Members of one subgroup may develop negative stereotypes toward members of another subgroup while simultaneously cultivating homegrown stereotypes (overly positive generalizations that groups develop about their own characteristics) to support their own subgroup (Prentice and Miller, 2002). This us-versus-them mentality in subgroups may incite antagonism from members of one subgroup toward members of another subgroup (Labianca, Brass, and Gray, 1998). We argue that as a result, members of such groups will perceive that the overall work group is filled with tension and anger, resulting in high levels of intragroup relationship conflict and low levels of satisfaction.

Groups with high levels of heterogeneity and groups with strong faultlines are both predicted to experience high levels of relationship conflict and low levels of satisfaction; we now explain why we expect faultlines to have a stronger effect than heterogeneity. Literature based on the cross-categorization perspective (for example, Brewer, 2000; Hewstone, Rubin, and Willis, 2002; Vanbeselaere, 2000) suggests that members of groups with faultlines may exhibit stronger intergroup bias and animosity toward members of another subgroup than do individuals in heterogeneous groups due to an additional social categorization (the particular subgroup within the larger group). Members of heterogeneous groups may possess crosscutting social identities that contribute to cooperative contact by reducing bias toward out-group members (Brewer, 2000; Ensari and Miller, 2001). For example, two women in a group may consider the male members to be an out-group; however, if the female members and some of the male members are white, the category of race will crosscut that of gender. This crosscutting will dilute the out-group bias based on gender. Therefore, we propose that intergroup bias based on the alignment of multiple characteristics (faultlines) may result in more negative stereotyping and animosity than that occurring in heterogeneous groups. Thus, we posit the following hypothesis:

Hypothesis 1 (H1): **Whereas groups with high levels of heterogeneity and groups with strong faultlines will both experience high levels of intragroup relationship conflict and low levels of satisfaction, faultlines will have a stronger effect on relationship conflict and satisfaction than will heterogeneity.**

The dispersion approach suggests that members of heterogeneous groups are likely to have different training and socialization experiences (Lovelace, Shapiro, and Weingart, 2001; Mortensen and Hinds, 2001). Although these differences may reflect a variety of ideas and perspectives in a team (Milliken and Martins, 1996), they may also be the cause of debates and disagreements about group tasks (Tziner and Eden, 1985; Wittenbaum and Stasser, 1996). The presence of differing perspectives is likely to manifest itself as intragroup task conflict (Pelled et al., 1999). Task conflicts are disagreements among group members' ideas and opinions about the task being performed, such as disagreements regarding an organization's current strategic position (Jehn, 1997). Empirical studies have demonstrated that employees in groups that were heterogeneous in terms of the members' functional backgrounds and education experienced high levels of task-related conflicts (Jehn, Chadwick, and Thatcher, 1997; Pelled et al., 1999).

On the other hand, the alignment perspective would suggest that when groups have faultlines, members of emerging subgroups may freely express divergent opinions as they feel support from their subgroup members due to mutual liking and perceived similarity of aligned members (Lau and Murnighan, 1998; Phillips, 2003; Phillips, Mannix, Neale, and Gruenfeld, 2004). They may also have a tendency toward conformity to the opinion or perspectives favored by their own subgroup (Baron, Kerr, and Miller, 1993) and a need to distinguish their views from those of the other subgroup (Brewer, 2000; Hogg, Turner, and Davidson, 1990). The result—with each subgroup intensely polarized around its ideas and thoughts (Ancona, 1990) and exhibiting strong vocal support for its particular position—is a high level of intragroup task conflict.

We expect faultlines to be a better predictor of intragroup task conflict than heterogeneity. On the basis of research into interindividual/intergroup discontinuity (Schopler, Insko, Graetz, Drigotas, and Smith, 1991; Wildschut, Insko, and Gaertner, 2002), we argue that members of groups with faultlines may disagree over various ideas or perspectives in a more convincing way than do individuals in heterogeneous groups. Interindividual/intergroup discontinuity refers to the tendency for intergroup relations to be more competitive and less cooperative than interindividual relations (Schopler et al., 1991). One of the proposed explanations for this tendency is that mutual social support for the competitive pursuit of self-interested behavior is available to subgroup members but absent for individuals (Wildschut et al., 2002). Although the potential exists that divergent viewpoints will emerge from heterogeneous groups, individuals in these groups may not actively share their points of view if they are not supported by others (Wit and Kerr, 2002). Groups with strong faultlines are likely to have intense conflicts over tasks because each subgroup rallies around one particular point of view (Lau and Murnighan, 2005). Thus, we propose the following hypothesis:

Hypothesis 2 (H2): **Whereas groups with high levels of heterogeneity and groups with strong faultlines will both experience high levels of intragroup task conflict, faultlines will have a stronger effect on task conflict than will heterogeneity.**

The dispersion perspective suggests that members of heterogeneous groups tend to rely on approaches to work that are particular to their backgrounds (Bantel and Jackson, 1989; Gruenfeld et al., 1996), and they display differing views about how one should approach a task (Jehn et al., 1999). These differences of opinion about how to do the work affects a group's ability to coordinate task progress (Behfar, Mannix, Peterson, and Trochin, 2005) and often results in disagreements over procedural issues (Jehn et al., 1999). Process conflict refers to disagreements about the process of doing a task or dealing with logistical problems—how task accomplishment should proceed in the work unit, who is responsible for what, and how things should be delegated (Jehn, 1997). For instance, research has demonstrated that heterogeneous groups experienced more difficulty defining how to proceed with their task than did homogeneous groups (Jehn, 1997; Watson, Kumar, and Michaelson, 1993).

The alignment approach proposes that members across subgroups formed by faultlines might have different "thought worlds" (Dougherty, 1987) and different understandings about how work should be done in a group. Members of such groups may feel that their priorities and work approaches are not aligned within a group, and so they may spend more time staking out territory and viciously arguing who does what, when, and how (Behfar et al., 2005). A faultline that breaks a group into subgroups may also inhibit boundary-spanning activities, leading to less coordination of interdependent but differentiated subgroups within a group (for example, Edmondson, 1999; Miles and Perreault, 1976). Under these circumstances, developing a shared approach to task accomplishment in groups with strong faultlines will be difficult, and process conflict will be more likely to surface.

Groups with high levels of heterogeneity and groups with strong faultlines are both predicted to experience high levels of process conflict; however, we expect faultlines to be a better predictor than heterogeneity. For example, a group with two homogeneous subgroups whose respective members are aligned along two differing characteristics of age and tenure will be likely to have two very diverse approaches to a task. Assuming that each subgroup has several supporters, there is likely to be a strong degree of competitiveness between the two subgroups. Members of groups with strong faultlines may support certain ways of doing work favored by their respective subgroups, at the same time displaying prejudice and intolerance toward opinions of members of another subgroup. Heterogeneous groups, in turn, may have several divergent viewpoints, but without support from others, individuals may not vigorously compete and argue their points of view. Thus, whereas heterogeneous groups and groups with strong faultlines will both experience challenges in coordinating accomplishment of a task, groups with strong faultlines will disagree over process-related issues in a more competitive way than will heterogeneous groups. This leads us to the third hypothesis:

Hypothesis 3 (H3): **Whereas groups with high levels of heterogeneity and groups with strong faultlines will both experience high levels of intragroup process conflict, faultlines will have a stronger effect on process conflict than will heterogeneity.**

We further predict that heterogeneity and faultlines will have differing effects on a group's performance. The dispersion approach, which is grounded in the well-respected perspective of value in diversity, expects heterogeneous groups to outperform homogeneous groups because people who are different from one another are able to bring new knowledge, skills, and perspectives to the group (Cox, Lobel, and McLeod, 1991; Watson et al., 1993; Williams and O'Reilly, 1998). Whereas the value-in-diversity perspective acknowledges the fact that greater heterogeneity makes it more difficult for people to cooperate, it also predicts that heterogeneity greatly enhances the potential for a wider array of views and information, novel solutions, creative synthesis, and overall group performance (Gruenfeld et al., 1996; Phillips et al., 2004). Furthermore, in management groups with high levels of heterogeneity, out-group discrimination is less likely to occur because there are few common bases for subgroup formation (Early and Mosakowski, 2000). Due to the number of out-group contacts that heterogeneous group members are likely to have, they may not be seriously inhibited by social identity and categorization processes and may, instead, greatly benefit from their diverse pool of resources (Richard, Barnett, Dwyer, and Chadwick, 2004). For example, groups with heterogeneous backgrounds performed better than homogenous groups even though their responses were slower (Hambrick et al., 1996). Jehn et al. (1999) also found that heterogeneous groups had higher levels of group performance than homogeneous groups, and Bantel and Jackson (1989) found higher levels of innovation in groups that were heterogeneous than in groups that were homogenous. Thus,

Hypothesis 4a (H4a): **Groups with high levels of heterogeneity will have high levels of performance.**

The alignment perspective predicts that faulty group processes emerging from negative categorizations across subgroups formed by faultlines may lead to severe losses in group performance. Due to additional subgroup identification, group members may be less supportive across different subgroups (Kramer, Hanna, Su, and Wei, 2001) and thus may not disclose accurate data needed to complete the task (Putnam and Jones, 1982). For example, faultline theory describes how conformity pressures arise in subgroups, causing polarization around different viewpoints and competition across them (Lau and Murnighan, 1998; Wit and Kerr, 2002). This polarization can interfere with subgroup members' willingness to make choices that benefit all group members, thus resulting in productivity losses (Polzer, Mannix, and Neale, 1998). As Lau and Murnighan note, "Although turmoil among a number of internal subgroups may be debilitating, it may not generate as much intensity as two competing subgroups that can foment diametric opposition to one another" (1998, p. 331). Therefore, we propose this hypothesis:

Hypothesis 4b (H4b): **Groups with strong faultlines will have low levels of performance.**

MEDIATORS OF HETEROGENEITY AND FAULTLINES EFFECTS

Finally, because we have hypothesized that group heterogeneity and faultlines promote conflict and also affect team members' satisfaction and performance, we further hypothesize that the effects of both group heterogeneity and faultlines will be mediated by conflict. Organizational research has reported the negative consequences of relationship conflict for satisfaction with a team (Amason, 1996; De Dreu and Van De Vliert, 1997; Jehn, 1995, 1997). Researchers propose that the anxiety and threats produced by relationship conflict detract a group from task accomplishment (Jehn, 1997) and cause dissatisfaction among group members (Amason and Schweiger, 1994; Jehn, 1994). Moreover, when a group argues about who does what, the resulting process conflict may shift focus to irrelevant discussions of members' abilities and set off tension and personal attacks (Jehn, 1997). For example, groups with high levels of process conflict were unable to define priorities, agree on a common approach, or divide responsibility, and members were generally dissatisfied with the group (Jehn et al., 1999). Task conflict also negatively relates to team member satisfaction (Amason, 1996; Jehn, 1997; Schwenk and Cosier, 1993). Ross (1989) argues that a person's first reaction to disagreement and questioning of one's opinion is dissatisfaction, and, as such, task conflict can cause tension, anxiety, and discomfort among group members. Given our previous arguments that faultlines will have a stronger effect on conflict and satisfaction than heterogeneity, we think there will be stronger mediated relationships with faultlines than with heterogeneity. Thus,

> **Hypothesis 5 (H5):** **All types of conflict (relationship, task, and process) will mediate the effects of group heterogeneity and group faultlines on group satisfaction; in addition, groups with strong faultlines will have stronger mediated relationships.**

There has been a growing tendency in the literature to assume that task conflict can, under certain circumstances, be a positive force and improve group performance (Jehn, 1995; Jehn and Bendersky, 2003). For example, research has demonstrated that minorities who argued consistently and flexibly promoted a thorough, intensive elaboration of the problem (De Dreu and West, 2001; Moscovici, 1980; Phillips, 2003). Task conflict also counteracts the biased information seeking of consensus-based subgroups (Schultz-Hardt, Jochims, and Frey, 2002) and leads to problem solutions characterized by high levels of creativity and quality (Ancona and Caldwell, 1992; De Dreu and Van De Vliert, 1997; Nemeth and Kwan, 1987). Although the disagreements related to the task appear to stimulate the quality of group decision making and are good for performance, this positive effect breaks down quickly when task conflict is intense. A recent meta-analysis has indicated that task conflict may not always be beneficial for group performance and can, indeed, be negatively associated with performance (De Dreu and Weingart, 2003). As conflict intensifies, cognitive load increases and interferes with creative thinking and cognitive flexibility, information processing slows down, and group performance suffers. Task conflict generated by heterogeneous groups may be qualitatively different than the task conflict generated by aligned subgroups. Groups with high levels of heterogeneity will be more likely to benefit from task conflict because these groups are characterized by less competition and a more open environment. Thus, conflict generated by heterogeneity will be less intense than the conflict generated by faultlines. Because we have argued for different effects of group faultlines and heterogeneity on performance, we likewise argue for different mediating effects of task conflict. Therefore, we propose the following hypothesis:

> **Hypothesis 6a (H6a):** **Task conflict will mediate the effects of group heterogeneity on group performance; that is, the more heterogeneous the group is, the higher the level of task conflict within the group, which leads to higher levels of group performance.**

> **Hypothesis 6b (H6b):** **Task conflict will mediate the effects of group faultlines on group performance; that is, the stronger the group faultlines, the higher the level of task conflict within the group, which leads to lower levels of group performance.**

METHOD

RESEARCH SITE AND SAMPLE

Our sample includes 60 colocated groups from a Fortune 500 corporation in the information processing industry. We identified the work groups using a reporting system developed by the company and information about the structure of the departments provided by key senior staff members. By interview and observation, we verified that these were actual working groups (that is, they interacted frequently and were task interdependent, individual members identified each other as group members, and groups were seen by other members of the organization as work groups) in existence for, on average, more than a year. They included employees in production, sales, marketing, and distribution departments. These were all management groups involved in solving complex cognitive tasks, and the type of work they did was relatively similar across all groups. Key senior staff believed that "groups" of 1 or 2 employees or groups with more than 16 employees were not actual working groups. This is consistent with our definition of a group and with group process theories regarding group size (Goodman, Ravlin, and Argote, 1986). We also eliminated all 3-person groups since it was impossible not to have "token" splits (that is, having a "subgroup" consisting of only 1 member). Thus, we have a sample of 60 groups and 455 individuals with complete demographic and performance data. The age of employees ranged from 27 to 68 years with a mean of 47 years. Seventy-two percent of the employees were male. Most employees (88 percent) were white, 7 percent were African American, 2.7 percent were Asian, and 2.3 percent were Hispanic. The level of education ranged from grade school to the Ph.D. level; the modal level was a bachelor's degree. Tenure with the company ranged from 1 year to 44 years with a mean of 14 years. Work functions included four distinct categories (administrative, customer service, finance, and marketing).

MEASURES

Heterogeneity
We used Blau's (1977) heterogeneity index to measure group heterogeneity for categorical variables (that is, race, gender, function) calculated as $H = -\Sigma Pi^2$, where P represents the fractional share of team members assigned to a particular grouping within a given characteristic and i is the number of different categories represented on a team. We used the coefficient of variation to measure group diversity for continuous variables (for example, age, level of education) (Allison, 1978), as is common in diversity research that compares diversity across groups of different sizes (O'Reilly, Williams, and Barsade, 1998; Pelled et al., 1999; Polzer, Milton, and Swann, 2002).

Faultlines

The development of our faultline measure was motivated by Lau and Murnighan's (1998) original faultline theory suggesting that the alignment of multiple demographic attributes can potentially subdivide a group. Our faultline measure hence takes into account cumulative proportions of variance across demographic variables. This makes our measure different from a simple aggregate measure, in that it estimates how well the variability within the group can be explained by the presence of different clusters within the group (for more details see Thatcher et al., 2003; Zanutto, Bezrukova, and Jehn, 2005). We measure the *strength* of faultline splits using a multivariate measure of group similarities over several variables taken from the literature on statistical cluster analysis (Jobson 1992, p. 549). This statistic essentially measures the degree of alignment or correlation of attributes in the resulting subgroups. Faultline strength can take on values between 0 and 1, with larger values indicating greater strength. Possible values of faultline strength ranged from .318 (weak faultline strength) to .782 (very strong faultline strength) in our data set. We also measure the degree of difference between two subgroups using a multivariate distance score taken from the multivariate statistical cluster analysis (for example, Morrison, 1967; Jobson, 1992; Sharma, 1996) that is calculated as the *distance* between subgroup centroids (the Euclidean distance between the two sets of average). Faultline distance can take on values between 0 and ∞ with larger values indicating a larger distance between the subgroups. Possible values of faultline distance in our data set ranged from 1.308 (weak faultline distance) to 3.645 (very strong faultline distance). To account for the joint effect of faultline strength and distance, we multiplied the two standardized scores and used this overall group faultline score in our analyses (range: −.59 to 7.87). We measure group faultlines along six demographic characteristics (age, race, tenure, education, function, and gender).

Performance

Our measures of group performance were bonuses and performance ratings from the organization's archival data. Bonus amounts are the actual bonus amounts paid out for the year to an employee; these amounts are to some extent calculated on the basis of group performance. Performance ratings are the codes indicating whether the productive output of a group member meets or surpasses specific performance goals; these codes are associated with an employee's performance review (for example, 5 refers to outstanding performance, and 1 refers to unsatisfactory). Both types of performance measures indirectly reflect how well employees or groups capitalize on multiple perspectives being brought to bear on a problem. We averaged our data across groups to produce group scores of the factors and conducted all analyses at the group level. This was done to ensure that we can effectively compare our results of the effects of heterogeneity and group faultlines to the effects found in other studies. We collected evidence regarding the validity of the group-level constructs, following the suggestions of Bliese (2000). We first conducted one-way analysis of variance and found between-group variance for all of these variables significant at either the .01 or the .001 level. To justify aggregation, we performed intraclass correlation coefficients (ICC[1]s) that estimate the proportion of variance in the variables between groups over the sum of between- and within-group variance. We obtained the following values of ICC(1)s for bonuses and performance ratings: .487 and .133, respectively. On the basis of these results, we concluded that aggregation was justified and created our group-level performance variables.

Controls

We included mean member gender (percentage of men), mean member race (percentage of white employees), and mean member age as group-level control variables. An extensive body of literature has identified the effect of gender on patterns of interaction and status (Eagly, Diekman, Johannesen-Schmidt, and Koenig, 2004; Ferdi and Wheelan, 1992; Ng and Van Dyne, 2001; Ridgeway and Smith-Lovin, 1999) and indicated its substantial impact on various performance outcomes. We expected our race and gender controls to be associated with performance and satisfaction such that males and whites were likely to have higher levels of performance and to be more satisfied than females and more satisfied than both genders of other races (Cordero, DiTomaso, and Farris, 1996; Fenwick and Neal, 2001). For instance, men's competitive orientation and their tendencies toward more-analytical decision making explained the superior performance of mixed groups in Fenwick and Neal's (2001) study. Although the majority of our groups were predominantly white, we followed Richard et al.'s (2004) suggestion and included a proportional control variable for race; this enabled us to interpret the results of our heterogeneity variables with more confidence. Since age has an effect on strategic planning formality and often serves as a proxy for formal status that influences members' attitudes regarding performance in groups (Bantel, 1993; Bunderson, 2003), we also controlled for the mean group age. We expected mean group age to be negatively associated with group performance and positively related to satisfaction (Bantel, 1993). Other demographic variables were not correlated with our variables and were thus not included in the analyses. All controls were obtained from the company's archival files.

QUALITATIVE DATA ANALYSIS

To generate measures of conflict and satisfaction, we analyzed the content of 300 pages of company documents that were part of a program sponsored by the human resources department. As part of this program, which was designed to help managers and supervisors of work groups in their planning, employees completed "development reports" regarding their work groups. They were asked to identify the key issues for their groups in dealing with performance gaps and to set action priorities. Since this company's program is ongoing, employees are comfortable with reporting on these issues and openly express their opinions in this common forum without retaliation or criticism. Thus, the reports capture the dominant group processes in work groups, particularly including how much conflict members have and how satisfied they are with their group experience and performance. Employees submit their information directly over the corporate intranet or via the Internet. This information is confidential and available only to the employee, his or her direct manager, and a selected group of human resources personnel in aggregate form.

We employed a content-analysis procedure that allowed us to make direct quantitative comparisons of groups using established computer-aided text analysis techniques (for example, Abrahamson and Hambrick, 1997; Jehn and Werner, 1993). Following the method of Jehn and Werner (1993), two independent raters reviewed all individual responses and coded the text for each variable of interest as defined by theory (see appendix 3.A for coding procedure and guidelines). In particular, the raters jointly went through the first few individual responses to develop the coding guidelines. (These raters, students working for credit, were unfamiliar with faultline theory and were blind to the hypotheses.) They coded the rest of the responses individually following guiding questions to evaluate each variable of interest for each individual response on 7-point Likert scales (for scale anchors, see specific variables in the following two sections). The agreements between the raters were 92, 89, 93, 97, and 90 percent on relationship conflict, task conflict, process conflict, satisfaction with group experience, and satisfaction with group performance, respectively, and were determined by checking the number of times that the raters agreed on their scores. When raters rated a response farther than 1 point apart, they discussed the response until they reached agreement and then refined their coding rules. We have further aggregated the coded individual statements to the group level and checked for within-group agreement. We obtained the following values of ICC(1)s for relationship conflict, task conflict, process conflict, satisfaction with group experience, and group performance: .861, .700, .871, .887, and .712, respectively.

Conflict

Three types of conflict (task, process, and relationship) were operationalized by content coding the company's textual data. The raters defined the extent of each type of conflict indicated by the employee on a scale from 1 (no conflict) to 7 (extreme amount of conflict). Following is an example from the data demonstrating task conflict:

> *Objectives need to be aligned* . . . Strategic has limited input in how to achieve the revenue. Strategic does not find out what the plans or marketing programs are for achieving revenue. Everyone has their self interest and *no one has an interest in a*

combined goal. Lack of direction as a business unit. Not achieving our objective as a business unit.

Satisfaction

We operationalized satisfaction as satisfaction with group experience and satisfaction with group performance. Satisfaction with group experience is the extent to which individuals express a positive affective orientation toward their group (adapted from Schippers et al., 2003). Satisfaction with group performance refers to how well a member of a group believes the group as a whole does in accomplishing group tasks (Jehn et al., 1997). The raters coded both variables using a 7-point Likert scale (1 = extremely dissatisfied/negative performance; 7 = extremely satisfied/positive performance). This is an example of satisfaction with group experience:

> What I like most about XXX [group's name] is all *the nice people* that work for this company. . . . I feel wanted and appreciated. *The positive people all want to help you* and get a good product out with out concern for "hidden agendas." *It lets me be myself.*

RESULTS

Because most group diversity studies have linked the effects of diversity to group performance, we employed a group level of analysis to provide a fair comparison of the two theoretical perspectives. We use multiple hierarchical regression analysis and compare the relative strength of the heterogeneity and faultlines effects using the adjusted R^2 statistic—a version of R^2 that has been adjusted for the number of predictors in a model.

Table 3.2 displays the means, standard deviations, and correlations among all variables. Race heterogeneity was negatively and significantly associated with satisfaction with group performance, whereas tenure heterogeneity was positively and significantly correlated with performance ratings and bonuses. Group faultlines were positively and significantly associated with group-level relationship conflict and were negatively and significantly correlated with bonuses and satisfaction with group experience. Relationship conflict was negatively and significantly associated with satisfaction with group performance. Task conflict was positively and significantly related to bonuses but was negatively and significantly correlated with satisfaction with group performance. Finally, process conflict was negatively associated with satisfaction with group experience and performance. We further examined the relationships among faultlines, heterogeneity, conflict, and performance using multiple hierarchical regression analyses.

Table 3.2
Means, Standard Deviations, and Zero-Order Correlations among Variables

Correlations	Mean (n=60)	SD (n=60)	1	2	3	4	5	6	7	8	9	10	11	12	13	14	15	16
1. Race (% of white)	.887	.124																
2. Gender (% of men)	.694	.235	.078															
3. Mean group age	47.189	3.648	−.199	.278*														
4. Group faultlines	.661	1.351	.068	−.041	−.078													
5. Age heterogeneity	.148	.056	.083	.079	−.102	.422†												
6. Race heterogeneity	.176	.176	−.986†	−.010	.229	−.075	−.092											
7. Gender heterogeneity	.315	.165	.043	−.427†	−.022	.082	.068	−.089										
8. Tenure heterogeneity	.574	.222	.103	−.008	−.010	−.041	.089	−.110	.173									
9. Education heterogeneity	.247	.112	.143	−.004	−.276*	−.048	−.096	−.124	−.301*	−.272*								
10. Function heterogeneity	.153	.194	.134	.182	−.194	.130	−.020	−.124	−.154	−.119	.193							
11. Relationship conflict	1.735	.564	−.104	.031	.023	.439†	.074	.085	−.107	−.097	−.033	−.009						
12. Task conflict	2.190	1.103	−.080	.048	.142	.228	.131	.076	.060	.166	−.219	−.133	.293					
13. Process conflict	3.257	1.447	−.086	−.174	−.040	.239	.066	.099	.043	.028	−.182	−.033	.553†	.420†				
14. Performance ratings	3.892	.363	.085	.192	.095	−.243	−.128	−.083	−.020	.312*	−.123	.231	−.224	−.077	−.087			
15. Bonuses	27.715	27.376	−.096	.223	−.441†	−.273*	−.190	.105	−.021	.322*	−.213	−.036	−.082	.341†	−.014	.434†		
16. Satisfaction with group experience	3.378	.955	.065	.122	.157	−.308*	−.110	−.068	.028	.007	.041	−.056	−.294	−.122	−.461†	.225	.146	
17. Satisfaction with group performance	2.900	.947	.311†	.050	−.084	−.226	−.011	−.299*	.053	−.095	−.019	.239	−.295*	−.307*	−.361†	.199	.054	.436†

* p < .05

† p < .01

MAIN EFFECTS HYPOTHESIS TESTING

We first tested the main effects of group heterogeneity and faultlines on conflict, performance, and satisfaction (see Tables 3.3 and 3.4). Step 1 of the hierarchical regression contains controls including mean member gender, mean member race, and mean member age. Step 2 includes the main effects of either separate group heterogeneity variables (heterogeneity model) or group faultlines (faultline model). Hypothesis 1 predicted that whereas groups with high levels of heterogeneity and groups with strong faultlines will both experience high levels of intragroup relationship conflict and low levels of satisfaction, faultlines will have a stronger effect on relationship conflict and satisfaction than will heterogeneity. There were no statistically significant relationships between our heterogeneity variables and relationship conflict or satisfaction; however, group faultlines were positively and significantly related to relationship conflict ($\beta = .436$, $p = .003$) and significantly and negatively related to satisfaction with group experience ($\beta = -.295$, $p = .037$) and satisfaction with group performance ($\beta = -.250$, $p = .049$) as predicted. The change in R^2 from step 1 to step 2 for the faultline model indicated a significant increase above and beyond the control variables. In general, faultlines accounted for 12 percent of the variance in relationship conflict, 5 percent of the variance in satisfaction with group experience, and almost 10 percent of the variance in satisfaction with group performance.

Hypothesis 2 predicted that whereas groups with high levels of heterogeneity and groups with strong faultlines will both experience high levels of intragroup task conflict, faultlines will have a stronger effect on task conflict than will heterogeneity. Again, we found that although there were no statistically significant relationships between our heterogeneity variables and task conflict, group faultlines were positively and marginally significantly related to task conflict ($\beta = .245$, $p = .069$). The change in R^2 from step 1 to step 2 for the faultline model indicated an increase in variance explained by faultlines above and beyond the control variables at $p < .1$.

Hypothesis 3 predicted that whereas groups with high levels of heterogeneity and groups with strong faultlines will both experience high levels of intragroup process conflict, faultlines will have a stronger effect on process conflict than will heterogeneity. Our results show that there were no statistically significant relationships between our heterogeneity variables and process conflict; however, group faultlines were positively and marginally significantly associated with this type of conflict ($\beta = .239$, $p = .069$). The change in R^2 from step 1 to step 2 for the faultline model indicated an increase above and beyond the control variables at $p < .1$.

In support of hypothesis 4a predicting that groups with high levels of heterogeneity will have high levels of performance, we found that tenure heterogeneity was significantly and positively associated with both group bonuses and performance ratings ($\beta = .348$, $p = .006$ and $\beta = .332$, $p = .014$, respectively), and functional

Table 3.3

Hierarchical Multiple Regressions Predicting Group-Level Conflict

	Relationship Conflict		Task Conflict		Process Conflict	
	Faultline Model	Heterogeneity Model	Faultline Model	Heterogeneity Model	Faultline Model	Heterogeneity Model
Step 1: Controls						
Race	-.110		-.055		-.075	
Gender	.040		.018		-.166	
Mean age	-.013		.125		-.009	
R^2	.012		.023		.036	
Adjusted R^2	-.058		-.031		-.016	
F	.117		.425		.692	
Step 2: Main effects						
Group faultlines	.436‡		.245†		.239†	
Gender heterogeneity		-.328		-.024		-.092
Age heterogeneity		.102		.122		.084
Race heterogeneity		-.989		-.216		1.305
Education heterogeneity		-.133		-.125		-.247
Tenure heterogeneity		-.126		.122		-.014
Function heterogeneity		.043		-.063		.037

(continues)

Table 3.3 (continued)

Hierarchical Multiple Regressions Predicting Group-Level Conflict

	Faultline Model	Heterogeneity Model	Faultline Model	Heterogeneity Model	Faultline Model	Heterogeneity Model
Step 2: Main effects (cont.)						
Change in R^2	.188	.066	.059	.068	.057	.084
F change	9.623‡	.429	3.436†	.600	3.433†	.800
R^2	.200	.078	.083	.091	.092	.120
Adjusted R^2	.122	-.152	.013	-.079	.026	-.038
F	2.566†	.340	1.192	.535	1.400	.759

* $p < .05$
† $p < .1$
‡ $p < .01$

Table 3.4

Hierarchical Multiple Regressions Predicting Group-Level Outcomes

	Group Performance (bonuses)	Group Performance Ratings	Satisfaction with Group Experience	Satisfaction with Group Performance
Step 1: Controls				
Race	-.024	.085	.096	.302*
Gender	.113	.167	.086	.036
Mean age	.405‡	.065	.168	-.033
R^2	.206	.045	.043	.098
Adjusted R^2	.163	-.006	-.017	.050
F	4.842‡	.889	.720	2.038

(continues)

Table 3.4 *(continued)*

Hierarchical Multiple Regressions Predicting Group-Level Outcomes

	Faultline Model	Heterogeneity Model	Faultline Model	Heterogeneity Model	Faultline Model	Heterogeneity Model	Faultline Model	Heterogeneity Model
Step 2: Main effects								
Group faultlines	−.237*		−.239†		−.295*		−.250*	
Gender heterogeneity		−.013		.000		.188		.012
Age heterogeneity		−.193†		−.172		−.095		−.041
Race heterogeneity		−.434		−.465		−.783		.411
Education heterogeneity		−.030		−.074		.128		−.111
Tenure heterogeneity		.348‡		.332*		.038		.024
Function heterogeneity		.065		.267*		−.091		.222
Change in R^2	.056	.153	.057	.194	.086	.057	.062	.054
F change	4.161*	1.994†	3.462†	2.124†	4.629*	.447	4.059*	.534
R^2	.262	.359	.102	.239	.129	.100	.160	.153
Adjusted R^2	.208	.244	.037	.102	.055	−.092	.099	.000
F	4.877‡	3.115‡	1.562	1.748	1.738	.521	2.627*	1.002

* $p < .05$
† $p < .1$
‡ $p < .01$

heterogeneity was again positively related to performance ratings (β = .267, p = .049). In contrast, age heterogeneity was marginally significantly and negatively associated with group bonuses (β = −.193, p = .100). Supporting hypothesis 4b, groups with strong faultlines had low levels of bonuses and performance ratings. This difference was statistically significant for bonuses (β = −.237, p = .046) and for performance ratings at $p < .1$ (β = −.239, p = .068). Whereas the changes in R^2 from step 1 to step 2 for the faultline model indicated a significant increase above and beyond controls in both group bonuses and performance ratings, the changes in R^2 for the heterogeneity model were only significant at $p < .1$. In general, heterogeneity accounted for 24.4 percent of the variance in group bonuses and 10.2 percent of the variance in performance ratings, and faultlines accounted for 20.8 percent of the variance in bonuses and 3.7 percent of the variance in performance ratings.

To examine the relative importance of group faultlines and group heterogeneity simultaneously on group processes and performance, as well as to compare the utility of the heterogeneity model in addition to the faultline model, we performed two sets of additional analyses (not included in the tables). First, we included our faultline variable together with all heterogeneity variables in the regression equation and reran the analyses. Second, we conducted a series of hierarchical regression analyses comparing the baseline models with heterogeneity variables and *without* faultlines, with the models including both heterogeneity and faultline variables. The results were virtually identical to those we reported previously, except that faultlines explained 20, 4.9, 4.6, 2.8, 4.5, 7.8, and 8.8 percent of the variance in relationship conflict, task conflict, process conflict, bonuses, performance ratings, satisfaction with group experience, and satisfaction with group performance, respectively, *above and beyond* the heterogeneity variables. Following the procedure suggested by Jehn et al. (1999) and widely used in recent demography research (Schippers et al., 2003), we also averaged age, race, tenure, level of education, functional background, and gender heterogeneity variables to arrive at our overall group heterogeneity measure. The effect of this variable was significant with performance ratings at $p < .1$ (β = .238, p = .090).

TESTING THE MEDIATING EFFECTS OF CONFLICT

Hypothesis 5 predicted that all conflict types (relationship, task, process) would mediate the effects of group heterogeneity and faultlines on group satisfaction; in addition, groups with strong faultlines would have a stronger mediated relationship. Using the procedure suggested by Baron and Kenny (1986), we found that heterogeneity variables were not significantly related to any of our conflict variables, and thus the mediating role of relationship, task, and process conflict between heterogeneity and satisfaction variables was not confirmed. Group faultlines, in turn, were significantly associated at $p < .01$, $p < .5$, or $p < .1$ with all types of conflict and both satisfaction variables. Whereas the mediating role of relationship conflict between group faultlines and satisfaction was not confirmed for any of the satisfaction variables, the mediating role of process conflict was confirmed for both satisfaction variables, and the partial mediating role of task conflict was confirmed for satisfaction with group performance. When controlling for process conflict, we found that the significant effect of group faultlines on satisfaction with group experience and group performance became non-significant (n.s.) (β = .120 [n.s.] and β = .151 [n.s.], respectively), and the effect of the mediator remained strong (β = $-$.406, p = .004 and β = $-$.299, p = .020, respectively). When controlling for task conflict, we found that the significant effect of group fault-lines on satisfaction with group performance became nonsignificant (β = .119 [n.s.]) and the effect of the mediator remained (β = $-$.258, p =.041).

Hypotheses 6a and 6b predicted that task conflict would mediate the effects of group heterogeneity and group faultlines on group performance in the opposite directions. Because heterogeneity variables were not significantly related to task con-flict, the mediating role of task conflict between heterogeneity and outcome variables was not confirmed. Group faultlines, in turn, were associated with task conflict and performance outcomes at p < .05 or p < .1. However, Baron and Kenny's (1986) test of mediation failed to confirm the mediating role of task conflict between faultlines and performance.

DISCUSSION

The objective of this research was to compare dispersion and alignment theoretical approaches to group composition and to examine group faultlines and heterogeneity. We undertook this effort to explain missing variance inherent in past diversity stud-ies that only considered group heterogeneity. We tested Lau and Murnighan's (1998) arguments regarding faultlines using 60 groups from a Fortune 500 company. In the following paragraphs, we discuss our results and summarize how our study extends prior research on diversity and conflict.

DISCUSSION OF RESULTS AND CONTRIBUTIONS

In this study, we hypothesized that because faultlines highlight the presence of clear subgroup distinctions across demographic variables within the larger group, they would be a better predictor of processes and performance than heterogeneity. Our results show relationships between faultlines and conflict (significant with relation-ship conflict at p < .01 and with task and process conflicts at p < .1) but no statisti-cally significant relationships between heterogeneity and conflict variables. These findings support the original faultline model (Lau and Murnighan, 1998), which suggested that subgroups resulting from group faultlines lead to more salient conflict-ual relationships. For example, differences in heterogeneous groups may lead to per-ceptions of certain types of conflict, but because there may be crosscutting characteristics, the polarization and conflict escalation that occur in groups with faultlines may not emerge. Previous diversity research has also shown that differences alone may not strongly influence conflict in ongoing work groups (for example, Ely and Thomas, 2001; Watson et al., 1993). The reason is that differences in some characteristics can be offset by similarities in others, thereby mitigating potential conflicts. This may be the case in our work groups and consequently may be one reason for the effects we observed. In fact, our follow-up analyses demonstrated that group faultlines explained 20, 4.9, and 4.6 percent of the variance in relationship conflict, task conflict, and process conflict, respectively, above and beyond heterogeneity variables.

We were surprised by the fact that group heterogeneity did not have any significant effects with any of our satisfaction variables. One would envision that each dimension of heterogeneity may in principle elicit social-categorization processes and predictable reactions with affective outcomes. However, consistent with Knippenberg, De Dreu, and Homan's (2004) assertion that there are more-complex relationships between heterogeneity and categorization, one explanation for this observed effect is that perhaps the salience of social categorization may not be fully realized in our heterogeneous groups. Heterogeneity does not take into account an overlap among individuals and group membership (for example, person 1 is similar to person 2 on age but is also similar to person 3 on gender) as do faultlines. Unlike the heterogeneity effects and as we predicted, our results indicate statistically significant relationships between faultlines and satisfaction variables. In such groups, individuals must truly feel that the us versus them distinction negatively colors their group experience.

In line with reviews on group diversity (Jackson et al., 2003; Webber and Donahue, 2001; Williams and O'Reilly, 1998), our analyses showed somewhat mixed and inconsistent effects of heterogeneity with objective performance. We found that members of groups heterogeneous in age had lower levels of group performance, whereas members of groups heterogeneous in functional background and tenure had higher levels of group performance. These findings closely align with and support two theoretical arguments currently prevailing in the diversity literature. Problems that arise from perceived differences amongst members of groups heterogeneous in age may interfere with performance (for example, Pelled, 1996), whereas the breadth of perspectives that functionally diverse group members embrace may enhance performance (for example, Gruenfeld et al., 1996).

Our results regarding performance and faultlines are more consistent. Groups with strong demographic alignments had low levels of group bonuses and performance ratings, supporting our predictions that group faultlines lead to performance losses. Members of such groups are more likely to affiliate themselves with their respective subgroups and thus be less concerned with the success of the larger group (Workman, 2001). We argue that this is due to the added polarization of the subgroups as more attributes are aligned. One interesting observation is that our results showed only significant at $p < .1$ effects of group faultlines on performance ratings compared with bonuses; thus, we realize that our performance measures may be differently affected by antecedent predictors, some more strongly than others. One reason for this, for example, is that group bonuses are based on hard performance numbers, whereas performance ratings indicate a subjective perception of a group's performance by its supervisor, who may conform to certain types of norms and values. Thus, bonuses more accurately reflect how group composition and process influence actual behavior than do performance ratings, which are more subjective. Unfortunately, we do not have detailed information on the nature of our performance ratings to provide a more elaborate discussion of the effects we observed.

To compare the utility of the heterogeneity model in addition to the faultline model, we performed follow-up analyses and found that faultlines explained 2.8 and 4.5 percent of the variance in bonuses and performance ratings, respectively, above and beyond all heterogeneity variables. One might argue that statistical power is an issue and that a fair comparison test should include an equal number of variables; thus, we explored this possibility by aggregating our heterogeneity variables (Jehn et al., 1999; Schippers et al., 2003) and rerunning the analyses. When we tested the two models simultaneously, the effect of the heterogeneity variable was not significant with bonuses and was only significant at $p < .1$ with performance ratings ($\beta = .238$, $p = .090$), whereas the effects of faultlines were statistically significant for both performance variables ($p < .05$). In additional analyses, faultlines explained 6.8 and 8.1 percent of the variance in bonuses and performance ratings, respectively, above and beyond the aggregated heterogeneity variable. Our general proposition predicting that group faultlines will be a better predictor of performance than group heterogeneity was thus supported. These results indicate that it is the alignment, and not only the dispersion, of demographic characteristics that strongly influences group processes and performance.

Whereas no mediation was confirmed for any of our heterogeneity variables, we found some empirical support for mediation among group faultlines, task and process conflict, and satisfaction. In general, our results showed that strong faultlines intensify task and process conflict in a group, which then decreases satisfaction. These findings are particularly interesting in their relevance to process conflict. Despite its theoretical importance, process conflict has been the least understood and examined of the three types of conflict (Behfar et al., 2005; chapter 1, this volume). The majority of diversity research has focused on the relationship/task distinction of conflict (for an exception, see Jehn et al., 1999). We believe it is critical to examine task and process conflict as separate constructs to improve the explanatory power of models of group diversity. We hence contribute to conflict literature not only by looking at how demographic alignment explains conflict but also by considering process conflict separately from task conflict.

Our methodological contribution to existing research on group composition and faultlines is in comparing the predictive power of heterogeneity variables with faultline variables on group processes and performance. We conceptualize diversity in two ways: group heterogeneity (the degree of dispersion of demographic attributes) (Blau, 1977) and group faultlines (the alignment of demographic attributes) (Lau and Murnighan, 1998). We demonstrate that using two different conceptualizations of diversity on the same data set provides different patterns of results, and we explain these differences theoretically. Lastly, to our knowledge, this study provides one of the first empirical tests of group faultline theory using organizational data, and it validates predictions about the effects of demographic faultlines on conflict and performance.

LIMITATIONS

The strengths of the current research (data collected from an actual workplace setting) are accompanied by potential weaknesses. Some limitations of this study are common to demography studies that use archival file data. First, whereas we were able to construct reliable measures of group process variables using content analysis of company documents, no direct measures of process variables were available. Second, one may raise the question of the objectivity of employees' comments as they were going to be used by managers and supervisors in future planning. Although this question is reasonable, we believe that these comments are a relatively objective reflection of dominant group processes. As part of an ongoing and supportive planning process program, employees were asked to identify the key issues and problems in their groups, and their responses reveal that they were quite comfortable reporting their opinions regarding these issues. Furthermore, employees who were more proactive in reporting on the intranet may also have a stronger influence on the computation of the measure than those who were less proactive. However, we believe our study has an advantage over many archival studies because we had relevant text data on team processes, something often missing in large archival data sets.

Next, there were limitations in the data regarding control variables. For instance, an important control variable would be how long a team has been together. Although we do not have any specific data on the life span of these groups, we do have some evidence from a company contact that these groups are not newly formed and they all have been in existence for at least one year. Task interdependence is another important control variable. From a company source and interviews with a few key managers, we verified that the groups in our sample interacted on a regular basis and were task interdependent. However, we could not obtain any specific survey data, for example, regarding how frequently (for example, number of interactions per day) and in what capacities these groups interacted. In addition, the effects of diversity on performance may be positive or negative depending on the type of task. Despite the fact that no specific data were available regarding the task type, we reexamined our text files and found that all teams were management groups that had certain nonroutine task characteristics and showed no significant variation on task type across groups.

In a recent meta-analytical study, De Dreu and Weingart (2003) demonstrated that the positive effects of task conflict break down quickly when conflict becomes intense. Our findings support the argument that task conflict may interfere with group processes and result in less satisfaction with group performance. Much debate has taken place about whether task conflict is beneficial (for example Jehn, 1995; Schultz-Hardt et al., 2002) or detrimental for performance and satisfaction (cf., De Dreu and Weingart, 2003). Our study provides some insight into this important question.

PRACTICAL IMPLICATIONS

It is often assumed that well-managed diverse work groups can serve as a catalyst to enhance the contributions of individual employees. This research attempts to deconstruct such generalities as "good diversity management" and specifically examine when and how diverse teams produce either beneficial or poor results. Our findings show that an alignment across group members and the resulting demographically motivated subgroups may be more important than just the heterogeneity of demographic characteristics in predicting group processes and performance of organizational work groups. We hope this knowledge will assist managers and group leaders in day-to-day supervision of diverse organizational work groups and will better equip them to effectively handle the dynamics of diverse groups by minimizing the chances that subgroups are demographically motivated.

On the basis of our results, we recommend that managers strive to be aware of nuances of group composition and the potentially harmful effects of faultlines that divide groups into homogenous subgroups along demographic lines. One way to accomplish this is to encourage employees in diverse groups to participate in boundary-spanning activities across potential faultlines. By exercising project management or job rotation, managers can promote the creation of temporary teams for particular tasks that cut across groups and departments and thus potentially break down demographically aligned subgroups. Similar effects can be achieved through encouraging task-related networks that provide meaningful functions a group can perform (for example, setting up a recruitment or orientation task force). This is in contrast to a popular organizational practice of promoting more-peripheral social clubs, which may reinforce stereotypes. Another positive managerial practice would be to force conflict resolution when needed. For example, managers of groups with strong faultlines may want to initially promote task conflict and process conflict so as to generate high-quality ideas. Managers should then be active in bringing resolution to these conflicts and introducing ways the group can create boundary spanning across the subgroups. Thus, it is possible to manage some of the potential benefits and problems of faultlines if one is aware of the effect of group composition on group process and performance. Taking these steps will help managers maximize the productivity of their increasingly diverse workforce without being fearful of diversity.

NOTES

1. We would like to note that whereas relational demography research may also fall under the framework of dispersion, we focus our discussion on group-level theories.

REFERENCES

Abrahamson, E., and Hambrick, D. C. 1997. Attentional homogeneity in industries: The effect of discretion. *Journal of Organizational Behavior, 18,* 513–532.

Alexander, J., Nuchols, B., Bloom, J., and Lee, S. Y. 1995. Organizational demography and turnover: An examination of multiform and nonlinear heterogeneity. *Human Relations, 48,* 1455–1480.

Allison, P. D. 1978. Measures of inequality. *American Sociological Review, 43,* 865–880.

Amason, A. C. 1996. Distinguishing the effects of functional and dysfunctional conflict on strategic decision making: Resolving a paradox for the top management teams. *Academy of Management Journal, 39,* 123–148.

Amason, A. C., and Schweiger, D. M. 1994. Resolving the paradox of conflict, strategic decision making, and organizational performance. *International Journal of Conflict Management, 5,* 239–253.

Ancona, D. G. 1990. Outward bound: Strategies for team survival in the organization. *Academy of Management Journal, 33,* 334–365.

Ancona, D. G., and Caldwell, D. 1992. Bridging the boundary: External activity and performance in organizational teams. *Administrative Science Quarterly, 37,* 634–665.

Bantel, K. A. 1993. Top team, environment, and performance effects on strategic planning formality. *Group and Organization Management, 18,* 436–458.

Bantel, K. A., and Jackson, S. E. 1989. Top management and innovation in banking: Does the composition of the top team make a difference? *Strategic Management Journal, 10,* 107–124.

Baron, R. M., and Kenny, D. A. 1986. The moderator-mediator variable distinction in social psychological research: Conceptual, strategic, and statistical considerations. *Journal of Personality and Social Psychology, 51*(6), 1173–1182.

Baron, R. M., Kerr, N., and Miller, N. 1993. *Group process, group decision, group action.* Buckingham, UK: Open University Press.

Behfar, K. J., Mannix, E. A., Peterson, R. S., and Trochin, W. M. K. 2005. *A multi-faceted approach to intra-group conflict: Issues of theory and measurement.* Working paper, Northwestern University.

Bishop, J., Scott, K., and Burroughs, S. 2000. Support, commitment, and employee outcomes in a team environment. *Journal of Management, 26,* 1113–1132.

Blau, P. 1977. *Inequality and composition: A primitive theory of social structure.* New York: Free Press.

Bliese, P. D. 2000. Within-group agreement, non-independence, and reliability: Implication for data aggregation and analysis. In K. J. Klein and S. W. J. Kozlowski (Eds.), *Multilevel theory, research, and methods in organizations: Foundations, extensions, and new directions* (pp. 349–381). San Francisco: Jossey-Bass.

Brewer, M. B. 2000. Reducing prejudice through cross-categorization: Effects of multiple social identities. In S. Oskamp (Ed.), *Reducing prejudice and discrimination* (pp. 165–183). Mahwah, N.J.: Erlbaum.

Bunderson, S. J. 2003. Recognizing and utilizing expertise in work groups: A status characteristic perspective. *Administrative Science Quarterly, 48,* 557–591.

Byrne, D. 1971. *The attraction paradigm.* New York: Academic Press.

Cordero, R., DiTomaso, N., and Farris, G. F. 1996. Gender and race/ethnic composition of technical work groups: Relationship to creative productivity and morale. *Journal of Engineering and Technology Management, 13,* 205–221.

Cox, T., Lobel, S., and McLeod, P. 1991. Effects of ethnic group cultural differences on cooperative and competitive behavior on a group task. *Academy of Management Journal, 34,* 827–847.

Cramton, C. D., and Hinds, P. J. 2005. Subgroups dynamics in internationally distributed teams: Ethnocentrism or cross-national learning? In B. Staw and R. Kramer (Eds.), *Research in Organizational Behavior* (vol. 26, pp. 231–263). Oxford, UK: Elsevier Science.

Dahlin, K. B., Weingart, L. R., and Hinds, P. J. 2005. Team diversity and information use. *Academy of Management Journal, 48,* 1107–1123.

De Dreu, C. K. W., and Van De Vliert, E. 1997. Affective and cognitive conflict in work groups: Increasing performance through value-based intragroup conflict, in benefits of conflict in groups and organizations. In C. K. W. De Dreu and E. Van De Vliert (Eds.), *Using conflict in organizations.* London: SAGE Publications.

De Dreu, C. K. W., and Weingart, L. R. 2003. Task versus relationship conflict, team performance, and team member satisfaction: A meta-analysis. *Journal of Applied Psychology, 88,* 741–749.

De Dreu, C. K. W., and West, M. A. 2001. Minority dissent and team innovation: The importance of participation in decision making. *Journal of Applied Psychology, 86,* 1191–1201.

Donnellon, A. 1996. *Team talk: The power of language in team dynamics.* Boston: Harvard Business School Press.

Dougherty, D. 1987. *New products in old organizations: The myth of the better mousetrap in search of the beaten path.* Doctoral dissertation, Sloan School of Management, Massachusetts Institute of Technology, Cambridge.

Dyck, B., and Starke, F. A. 1999. The formation of breakaway organizations: Observations and a process model. *Administrative Science Quarterly, 44,* 792–822.

Eagly, A. H., Diekman, A. B., Johannesen-Schmidt, M. C., and Koenig, A. M. 2004. Gender gaps in sociopolitical attitudes: A social psychological analysis. *Journal of Personality and Social Psychology, 87*(6), 796–816.

Earley, P. C., and Mosakowski, E. 2000. Creating hybrid team cultures: An empirical test of transnational team functioning. *Academy of Management Journal, 43*(1), 26–49.

Edmondson, A. 1999. A safe harbor: Social psychological conditions enabling boundary spanning in work teams. In R. Wageman (Ed.), *Research on managing groups and teams* (vol. 2, pp. 179–199). Greenwich, Conn.: JAI Press.

Eisenhardt, K., Kahwajy, J., and Bourgeois, L. 1997. Conflict and strategic choice: How top management teams disagree. *California Management Review, 39,* 42–62.

Ely, R. J., and Thomas, D. A. 2001. Cultural diversity at work: The effects of diversity perspectives on work group processes and outcomes. *Administrative Science Quarterly, 46*(2), 229–273.

Ensari, N., and Miller, N. 2001. The out-group must not be so bad after all: The effects of disclosure, typicality, and salience on intergroup bias. *Journal of Personality and Social Psychology, 83*(2), 313–329.

Fenwick, G. D., and Neal, D. J. 2001. Effect of gender composition on group performance. *Gender, Work and Organization, 8,* 205–225.

Ferdi, A. F., and Wheelan, S. A. 1992. Developmental patterns in same-sex and mixed-sex groups. *Small Group Research, 23*(3), 356–378.

Goodman, P. S., Ravlin, E. C., and Argote, L. 1986. Current thinking about groups: Setting the stage for new ideas. In P. Goodman (Ed.), *Designing effective work groups* (pp. 1–33). San Francisco: Jossey-Bass.

Gruenfeld, D. H., Mannix, E. A., Williams, K. Y., and Neale, M. A. 1996. Group composition and decision making: How member familiarity and information distribution affect process and performance. *Organizational Behavior and Human Decision Processes, 67,* 1–15.

Hambrick, D., Cho, T., and Chen, M. 1996. The influence of top management team heterogeneity on firms' competitive moves. *Administrative Science Quarterly, 41,* 659–684.

Hambrick, D., Li, J. T., Xin, K., and Tsui, A. S. 2001. Compositional gaps and downward spirals in international joint venture management groups. *Strategic Management Journal, 22*(11), 1033–1053.

Hewstone, M., Rubin, M., and Willis, H. 2002. Intergroup bias. *Annual Review of Psychology, 53,* 575–604.

Hogg, M. A., Turner, J. C., and Davidson, B. 1990. Polarized norms and social frames of reference: A test of self-categorization theory of group polarization. *Basic and Applied Social Psychology, 11,* 77–100.

Jackson, S. E., Joshi, A., and Erhardt, N. L. 2003. Recent research on teams and organizational diversity: SWOT analysis and implications. *Journal of Management, 29*(6), 801–830.

Jehn, K. A. 1994. Enhancing effectiveness: An investigation of advantages and disadvantages of value-based intragroup conflict. *International Journal of Conflict Management, 5,* 223–238.

Jehn, K. A. 1995. A multimethod examination of the benefits and detriments of intragroup conflict. *Administrative Science Quarterly, 40,* 256–282.

Jehn, K. A. 1997. A qualitative analysis of conflict types and dimensions in organizational groups. *Administrative Science Quarterly, 42,* 520–557.

Jehn, K. A., and Bendersky, C. 2003. Intragroup conflict in organizations: A contingency perspective on the conflict-outcome relationship. In B. Staw and R. Kramer, (Eds.), *Research in organizational behavior* (vol. 25, pp. 187–242). Oxford, UK: Elsevier Science.

Jehn, K. A., and Bezrukova, K. 2004. A field study of group diversity, group context, and performance. *Journal of Organizational Behavior, 25,* 1–27.

Jehn, K. A., and Werner, O. 1993. Hapax Legomenon II: Theory, a thesaurus, and word frequency. *Cultural Anthropology Method, 5,* 8–10.

Jehn, K. A., Chadwick, C., and Thatcher, S. M. B. 1997. To agree or not to agree: The effects of value congruence, individual demographic dissimilarity and conflict on workgroup outcomes. *International Journal of Conflict Management, 8*(4), 287–306.

Jehn, K. A., Northcraft, G., and Neale, M. 1999. Why differences make a difference: A field study of diversity, conflict, and performance in workgroups. *Administrative Science Quarterly, 44,* 741–763.

Jobson, J. D. 1992. *Applied multivariate data analysis. Volume II: Categorical and multivariate methods.* New York: Springer–Verlag.

Kanter, R. M. 1977. *Men and women of the corporation.* New York: Basic Books.

Knippenberg, D., De Dreu, C. K. W., and Homan, A. C. 2004. Work group diversity and group performance: An integrative model and research agenda. *Journal of Applied Psychology, 89,* 1008–1022.

Kochan, T., Bezrukova, K., Ely, R., Jackson, S., Joshi, A., Jehn, K., Leonard, J., Levine, D., and Thomas, D. 2003. The effects of diversity on business performance: Report of a feasibility study of the diversity research network. *Human Resource Management Journal, 42*(1), 3–21.

Kramer, R. M., Hanna, B. A., Su, S., and Wei, J. 2001. Collective identity, collective trust, and social capital: Linking group identification and group cooperation. In M. Turner (Ed.), *Groups at work: Theory and research* (pp. 173–196). Mahwah, N.J.: Erlbaum, Applied Social Research Series.

Labianca, G., Brass, D. J., and Gray, B. 1998. Social networks and perceptions of intergroup conflict: The role of negative relationships and third parties. *Academy of Management Journal, 41*(1), 55–67.

Lau, D., and Murnighan, J. K. 1998. Demographic diversity and faultlines: The compositional dynamics of organizational groups. *Academy of Management Review, 23,* 325–340.

Lau, D., and Murnighan, J. K. 2005. Interactions within groups and subgroups: The dynamic effects of demographic faultlines. *Academy of Management Journal, 48*(4), 645–659.

Li, J., and Hambrick, D. C. 2005. Factional groups: A new vantage on demographic faultlines, conflict, and disintegration in work teams. *Academy of Management Journal, 48*(5), 794–813.

Lincoln, J., and Miller, J. 1979. Work and friendship ties in organizations: A comparative analysis of relational networks. *Administrative Science Quarterly, 24,* 181–199.

Lovelace, K., Shapiro, D. L., and Weingart, L. R. 2001. Maximizing cross-functional new product teams' innovativeness and constraint adherence: A conflict communications perspective. *Academy of Management Journal, 44,* 779–783.

McGrath, J. E. 1998. A view of group composition through a group-theoretic lens. In M. A. Neale, E. A. Mannix, and D. H. Gruenfeld (Eds.), *Research on managing groups and teams* (vol. 1, pp. 255–272). Greenwich, Conn.: JAI Press.

Michel, J., and Hambrick, D. 1992. Diversification posture and the characteristics of the top management team. *Academy of Management Journal, 35,* 9–37.

Miles, R. H., and Perreault, W. D. 1976. Organizational role conflict: Its antecedents and consequences. *Organizational Behavior and Human Performance, 17,* 19–44.

Milliken, F., and Martins, L. 1996. Searching for common threads: Understanding the multiple effects of diversity in organizational groups. *Academy of Management Review, 21,* 402–433.

Moreland, R. L., and Levine, J. M. 1992. The composition of small groups. In E. J. Lawler, B. Markovsky, C. Ridgeway, and H. A. Walker (Eds.), *Advances in group processes* (vol. 8, pp. 237–280). Greenwich, Conn.: JAI Press.

Morrison, D. G. 1967. Measurement problems in cluster analysis. *Management Science, 13*(2), B-775–B-780.

Mortensen, M., and Hinds, P. J. 2001. Conflict and shared identity in geographically distributed teams. *International Journal of Conflict Management, 12,* 212–238.

Moscovici, S. 1980. Toward a theory of conversion behaviour. In L. Beekowitz (Ed.), *Advances in experimental social psychology* (vol. 13, pp. 209–242). San Diego, Calif.: Academic Press.

Nemeth, C., and Kwan, J. 1987. Minority influence, divergent thinking, and detection of correct solutions. *Journal of Applied Social Psychology, 17,* 786–797.

Ng, K. Y., and Van Dyne, L. 2001. Individualism–collectivism as a boundary condition for effectiveness of minority influence in decision making. *Organizational Behavior and Human Decision Processes, 84,* 198–225.

O'Reilly, C. A., Caldwell, D., and Barnett, W. 1989. Work group demography, social integration, and turnover. *Administrative Science Quarterly, 34,* 21–37.

O'Reilly, C. A., Snyder, R., and Boothe, J. 1993. Effects of executive team demography on organizational change. In G. Huber and W. Glick (Eds.), *Organizational change and redesign* (pp. 147–175). New York: Oxford Press.

O'Reilly, C. A., Williams, K., and Barsade, S. 1998. Group demography and innovation: Does diversity help? In M. A. Neale, E. A. Mannix, and D. H. Gruenfeld (Eds.), *Research on managing groups and teams* (vol. 1, pp. 183–207). Greenwich, Conn.: JAI Press.

Pelled, L. H. 1996. Demographic diversity, conflict, work group outcomes: An intervening process theory. *Organization Science, 7,* 615–631.

Pelled, L. H., Eisenhardt, K. M., and Xin, K. R. 1999. Exploring the black box: An analysis of work group diversity, conflict and performance. *Administrative Science Quarterly, 44,* 1–28.

Pelled, L. H., Xin, K. R., and Weiss, A.M. 2001. No es como mi: Relational demography and conflict in a Mexican production facility. *Journal of Occupational and Organizational Psychology, 74,* 63–84.

Phillips, K. W. 2003. The effects of categorically based expectations on minority influence: The importance of congruence. *Personality and Social Psychology Bulletin, 29,* 3–13.

Phillips, K. W., Mannix, E. A., Neale, M. A., and Gruenfeld, D. H. 2004. Diverse groups and information sharing: The effects of congruent ties. *Journal of Experimental Social Psychology, 40,* 497–510.

Polzer, J. T., Mannix, E. A., and Neale, M. A. 1998. Interest alignment and coalitions in multiparty negotiation. *Academy of Management Journal, 41,* 42–54.

Polzer, J. T., Milton, L. P., and Swann, W. B. Jr. 2002. Capitalizing on diversity: Interpersonal congruence in small work groups. *Administrative Science Quarterly, 47*(2), 296–324.

Prentice, D. A., and Miller, D. T. 2002. The emergence of homegrown stereotypes. *American Psychologist, 57,* 352–359.

Putnam, L. L., and Jones, T. S. 1982. The role of communication in bargaining. *Human Communication Research, 8,* 262–280.

Richard, O. C., Barnett, T., Dwyer, S., and Chadwick, K. 2004. Cultural diversity in management, firm performance, and the moderating role of entrepreneurial orientation dimensions. *Academy of Management Journal, 47,* 255–266.

Ridgeway, C. L., and Smith-Lovin, L. 1999. The gender system and interaction. *Annual Review of Sociology, 25,* 191–216.

Riordan, C. M. 2000. Relational demography within groups: Past developments, contradictions, and new directions. In G. R. Ferris (Ed.), *Research in personnel and human resource management* (vol. 19, pp. 131–173). Oxford, UK: Elsevier Science.

Roccas, S., and Brewer M. B. 2002. Social identity complexity. *Personality and Social Review, 6,* 88–106.

Ross, R. 1989. Conflict. In R. Ross and J. Ross (Eds.), *Small groups in organizational settings* (pp. 139–178). Englewood Cliffs, N.J.: Prentice-Hall.

Roth, P. L., Huffcutt, A. I., and Bobko, P. 2003. Ethnic group differences in measures of job performance: A new meta-analysis. *Journal of Applied Psychology, 88,* 694–706.

Schippers, M. C., Den Hartog, D. N., Koopman, P. L., and Wienk, J. A. 2003. Diversity and team outcomes: The moderating effects of outcome interdependence and group longevity and the mediating effect of reflexivity. *Journal of Organizational Behavior, 24,* 779–802.

Schopler, J., Insko, C. A., Graetz, K. A., Drigotas, S. M., and Smith, V. A. 1991. The generality of the individual-group discontinuity effect: Variations in positivity-negativity of outcomes, players' relative power, and magnitude of outcomes. *Personality and Social Psychology Bulletin, 17,* 612–624.

Schultz-Hardt, S., Jochims, M., and Frey, D. 2002. Productive conflict in group decision making: Genuine and contrived dissent as strategies to counteract biased information seeking. *Organizational Behavior and Human Decision Processes, 88,* 563–586.

Schwenk, C. R., and Cosier, R. A. 1993. Effects of consensus and devil's advocacy on strategic decision-making. *Journal of Applied Social Psychology, 23,* 126–139.

Sharma, S. 1996. *Applied multivariate techniques.* New York: John Wiley and Sons.

Tajfel, H., and Turner, J. C. 1986. The social identity theory of intergroup behavior. In S. Worchel and W. G. Austin (Eds.), *Psychology of intergroup relations* (pp. 7–24). Chicago: Nelson-Hall.

Thatcher, S. M. B. 1999. The contextual importance of diversity: The impact of relational demography and team diversity on individual performance and satisfaction. *Performance Improvement Quarterly, 12,* 97–112.

Thatcher, S. M. B., Jehn, K. A., and Zanutto, E. 2003. Cracks in diversity research: The effects of faultlines on conflict and performance. *Group Decision and Negotiation, 12,* 217–241.

Thomas, D. A., and Ely, R. J. 1996. Making differences matter: A new paradigm for managing diversity. *Harvard Business Review, 74*(5), 79–91.

Tziner, A., and Eden, D. 1985. The effects of crew composition on crew performance: Does the whole equal the sum of its parts? *Journal of Applied Psychology, 70,* 85–93.

Vanbeselaere, N. 2000. The treatment of relevant and irrelevant outgroups in minimal group situations with crossed categorizations. *Journal of Social Psychology, 140,* 515–526.

Watson, W. E., Kumar, K., and Michaelson, L. K. 1993. Cultural diversity's impact on interaction process and performance: Comparing homogeneous and diverse task groups. *Academy of Management Journal, 38,* 590–602.

Webber, S., and Donahue, L. 2001. Impact of highly and less job-related diversity on work group cohesion and performance: A meta–analysis. *Journal of Management, 27,* 141–162.

Wiersema, M., and Bantel, K. 1992. Top management team demography and corporate strategic change. *Academy of Management Journal, 35,* 91–121.

Wildschut, T., Insko, C. A., and Gaertner, L. 2002. Intragroup social influence and intergroup competition. *Journal of Personality and Social Psychology, 82,* 975–992.

Williams, K., and O'Reilly, C. A. 1998. Demography and diversity in organizations: A review of 40 years of research. In B. M. Staw and L. L. Cummings (Eds.), *Research in organizational behavior* (vol. 20, pp. 77–140). Oxford, UK: Elsevier Science.

Wit, A. P., and Kerr, N. L. 2002. "Me versus just us versus us all" categorization and cooperation in nested social dilemmas. *Journal of Personality and Social Psychology, 83,* 616–637.

Wittenbaum, G. M., and Stasser, G. 1996. Management of information in small groups. In J. L. Nye and A. M. Brower (Eds.), *What's social about social cognition? Social cognition research in small groups* (pp. 3–28). Newbury Park, Calif.: SAGE Publications.

Workman, M. 2001. Collectivism, individualism, and cohesion in a team-based occupation. *Journal of Vocational Behavior, 58,* 82–97.

Zajac, E. B., Golden, R., and Shortell, S. 1991. New organizational forms for enhancing innovation: The case of internal corporate joint ventures. *Management Science, 37,* 170–184.

Zanutto, E., Bezrukova, K., and Jehn, K. A. 2005. *Measuring faultline strength and distance.* Working paper, University of Pennsylvania.

APPENDIX 3.A: CONTENT ANALYSIS RULES

I. Coding procedure
    1. Two raters were given the definitions of terms and guiding questions.
        a. Definitions: "Relationship conflict is defined as disagreement over personal issues not related to work." "Task conflict is defined as disagreement about task-related issues (for example, viewpoints, opin-

ions).” “Process conflict is defined as disagreement about process-related issues (for example, work approaches, methods, responsibilities).”

    b.   Questions for the raters: (i) What is the intensity of the relationship conflict? (ii) What is the intensity of the task conflict? (iii) What is the intensity of the process conflict? (iv) To what extent are group members satisfied with the group work? (v) To what extent are group members satisfied with their group performance?

  2.   Two raters coded the documents:

    a.   Two raters jointly went through the first 10 individual responses to develop the initial rules (see II. Guidelines for examples) and to clarify construct definitions.

    b.   They went through all the responses to find extreme examples of conflict, satisfaction with group experience, and satisfaction with group performance (both high and low ends) to indicate the scale range.

    c.   The raters individually rated these examples (on a scale from 1 = the least to 7 = the most) and then discussed their scores to sort out any discrepancies.

    d.   The raters independently rated the next 30 responses, compared their responses, and discussed responses that they scored farther than 1 point apart; if necessary, they refined their rules.

    e.   Finally, two raters scored the rest of the responses.

II.   Guidelines

  1.   The unit of analysis is the entire individual response; use all context available in the response to arrive at the score.

  2.   Base your decision on all relevant statements indicating the variable being scored; highlight the key sentences (example for task conflict: “. . . Objectives need to be aligned . . . Strategic has limited input in how to achieve the revenue. Strategic does not find out what the plans or marketing programs are for achieving revenue. . . .”).

  3.   Assign a missing value to a response that has an unusually low level of comprehensibility due to incomplete or poor sentence structure or grammar and spelling mistakes (for example, a rater cannot understand what the person is saying).

  4.   When scoring the response for the variable, first, place it within a range of low/extremely negative to moderate/neutral (scores from 1–4) or moderate/neutral to high/extremely positive (scores from 4–7). Second, compare the response to other responses with scores within the same range and choose the respective score based on the comparison.

Chapter 4

DOES ONE ROTTEN APPLE SPOIL THE BARREL? USING A CONFIGURATION APPROACH TO ASSESS THE CONFLICT-INDUCING EFFECTS OF A HIGH-NEUROTICISM TEAM MEMBER

Randall S. Peterson, Julie Davidson, and Lisa M. Moynihan

ABSTRACT

Scholars have become increasingly interested in recent years in the origins of conflict in groups. The bulk of the research on the issue of early group conflict centers on diversity among group members and tends to start from the assumption that visible demographic differences are a major source of conflict in groups. But increasingly, others are suggesting that we need to expand the field's view of diversity (Mannix and Neale, 2005). In this chapter, we make the case for why personality variables should be examined more frequently and in a more fine-grained way when studying conflict in groups. We discuss the importance of taking a configuration perspective on composition in groups and illustrate our argument with an empirical example investigating the relationship between the personality variable of neuroticism and conflict and cohesion in master's in business administration (MBA) student teams. In particular, we find that the anger facet of neuroticism increases relationship conflict and reduces cohesion amongst team members.

Introduction

Conflict amongst people working in groups is a natural and universal feature of group life. Some groups seem to be able to harness conflict and make it productive (Eisenhardt, Kahwajy, and Bourgeois, 1997; Nemeth, 1997), while other groups founder on it and self-destruct (Guetzkow and Gyr, 1954; Jehn and Mannix, 2001). As a result, conflict is one of the most widely studied areas in the groups literature as scholars seek to understand the differences that lead to such divergent outcomes (Levine and Moreland, 1998). A great deal of existing research literature looks at the effects of conflict on a range of group processes and performance (see De Dreu and Weingart, 2003, for a meta-analysis), ranging from information sharing to cohesion and decision making. Relatively less research has, however, looked at the origins of conflict (but see Peterson and Behfar, 2003). This seems surprising to us, given the potential importance of being able to predict the likely presence of conflict before it does any damage, or even to prevent dysfunctional conflict from arising in the first place.

One area in which research on the antecedents of conflict has been pursued vigorously is in the study of diversity, in which demographic differences are expected to be a major source of conflict in groups (see Williams and O'Reilly, 1998, for a review). We applaud this effort and the progress that has been made thus far by looking at demographic differences, but we also join with other scholars in recognizing the opportunity to broaden our understanding and application of the term "diversity" (Mannix and Neale, 2005) to look at how additional forms of diversity affect team-level processes such as conflict. Although the bulk of the research on diversity has focused on visible demographic attributes such as race, gender, and age, scholars are beginning to examine other less visible individual-level constructs that underlie group-level processes such as conflict (Mannix and Neale, 2005). For instance, Barsade and her colleagues examined how the trait of positive affect influenced conflict in top management teams (Barsade, Ward, Turner, and Sonnenfeld, 2000).

Another facet of diversity that has been examined to a much lesser extent than visible demographic attributes is personality. We argue that a great deal could be learned about the propensity and rationale for teams to engage in conflict by broadening the group diversity research to include the study of member personality, and in particular we think the neuroticism factor of personality is especially interesting. Deeper-level diversity measures such as attitudes or personality have stronger effects on group cohesion and performance than do more surface-level demographic diversity variables (Harrison, Price, and Bell, 1998). The lack of research on the effects of personality on conflict has led some scholars to conclude broadly that personality variables are more often positively related to performance, in that they can facilitate creativity or group problem solving (Mannix and Neale, 2005). However, we believe that the story is even more complex than that—we will argue here that personality diversity can negatively affect groups by inducing conflict, and we specifically focus on the personality trait of neuroticism, one of the "big five" personality factors (Wiggins, 1996).

Observing the effects of diversity variables on group processes relies on adequate measurement. As groups scholars recognize (Levine and Moreland, 1998; Mannix and Neale, 2005), it is usually insufficient to simply measure and aggregate members' attributes; rather, more sophisticated measures are required to uncover and truly assess the impact of key variables on group processes. We propose and demonstrate in this chapter that researchers may uncover additional interesting results by (1) using more refined and detailed measures of personality and (2) adopting more complex ways of theorizing about the effects of personality on conflict and other group processes.

Specifically, the aim of this chapter is to shed light on how neuroticism exhibited by group members affects the occurrence and amount of conflict in a group. Drawing on an empirical example of master's of business administration (MBA) student teams, we seek to contribute to the literature on conflict in groups by increasing understanding of the antecedents of conflict, in particular among deeper-level personality measures. By examining how diversity variables can be studied to capture their effects, we also seek to advance theorizing and methodology for studying group processes such as conflict. We argue that the current way in which many scholars include personality (and other) variables in groups studies is often too simplistic to yield interesting and robust findings (Moynihan and Peterson, 2001). Indeed, we hope that groups scholars will find other ways to apply the approach that we put forward in this chapter, beyond personality traits and conflict in groups.

GROUP CONFLICT: OVERVIEW OF ANTECEDENTS AND TYPES

Much of the literature on group conflict focuses on how it affects group performance (for example, Jehn and Mannix, 2001), team member satisfaction (for example, De Dreu and Weingart, 2003), and turnover (for example, Pelled, 1996), for instance. With the exception of a large body of work on diversity (see Mannix and Neale, 2005; Williams and O'Reilly, 1998) and some recent work on the role of performance feedback (Peterson and Behfar, 2003), little attention has been paid to elucidating the antecedents leading to conflict. In their review of the diversity literature, Williams and O'Reilly (1998) call for more research in a few particular areas, including the need "to understand in more detail how different types of diversity affect group process and performance" (p. 117) and to examine "the nature of the conflict generated by diversity" (p. 118). Our research in this chapter aims at beginning to answer both of these needs.

Diversity within a group of individuals is often defined quite broadly as, for instance, "variation based on any attribute that another person may use to detect individual differences" (Mannix and Neale, 2003, p. 35). Although this definition of diversity encompasses differences among group members' personality traits, personality differences have received less attention as antecedents of group conflict in part because they are less visible and more difficult to measure (Moynihan and Peterson, 2001). As a result, researchers have tended to use demographic variables such as gender, age, race, and functional background as proxies for individuals' values and orientations (Williams and O'Reilly, 1998). However, as more research is undertaken with organizational teams and groups, scholars are increasingly recognizing the importance of personality as a group variable for two key reasons. First, surface-level demographic characteristics are poor indicators of values and orientations. For example, significant variation has been found in the values and attitudes of individuals of the same race (Block, Roberson, and Neugen, 1993), and little variation has been found in studies of men versus women (Rowe and Snizek, 1995). Second, scholars have demonstrated that demographic characteristics within groups may become less salient over time, whereas personal characteristics such as personality traits appear to become more salient over time (Harrison et al., 1998; Levine and Moreland, 1998). Given that personality traits represent the essence of a person, they are closer antecedents of cognitive and affective orientations than are demographic variables, and they are therefore likely to be more powerful predictors of group processes such as intragroup conflict and performance (Moynihan and Peterson, 2001). Personality traits access "deep-level diversity" as opposed to "surface-level diversity" (Watson, Kumar, and Michaelson, 1993).

In examining the effect of personality—particularly neuroticism—on conflict, it is important to differentiate among the possible types of conflict in which group members may engage. Scholars have distinguished two main types of conflict: task conflict and relationship conflict. Task conflict exists when group members disagree and/or express different ideas and opinions about the content of their tasks; relationship conflict exists when group members have interpersonal incompatibilities leading to tension, animosity, and personal irritation (Jehn, 1995). There is some disagreement about the effects of each type of conflict on groups: Several scholars argue that task conflict may have beneficial outcomes in uncovering new perspectives and ideas, but recent meta-analysis evidence suggests that task conflict is mostly associated with poor performance and negative group processes (see De Dreu and Weingart, 2003). There is widespread agreement about relationship conflict, affirming that it is associated with solely negative outcomes (for example, De Dreu and Weingart, 2003; Jehn, 1995). We revisit how group members' degree of neuroticism may affect both task and relationship conflict after a brief overview of the neuroticism factor and its measurement.

A Focus on Neuroticism: Definitions and Measurement Considerations

A Brief Introduction to Personality Research

Personality is defined as the essence of a person or what is most representative of him or her (Allport, 1937; Hall and Lindzey, 1957). It is the pattern of relatively enduring ways in which a person thinks, feels, and behaves (Pervin, 1980). Scholars have demonstrated that personality influences a variety of individual behaviors including career choice (Holland, 1966), job satisfaction (Staw and Ross, 1985), and leadership style (Bass, 1990; Hogan and Kaiser, 2005; Peterson, Smith, Martorana, and Owens, 2003).

The history of personality psychology is a turbulent one. Many groups researchers will be familiar with the person/situation debate instigated by Mischel's (1968) review of the field, in which he claimed that the usefulness of broad dispositional personality variables had been grossly inflated. Mischel's review found that many personality variables did not show cross-situational consistency and did not explain high amounts of variance. However, since the time of that review, personality measurement has been greatly improved via the five-factor model of personality (neuroticism, extraversion, openness, agreeableness, and conscientiousness). In addition, researchers are more cognizant of focusing on narrower trait variables as well as on outcome variables, which results in greater amounts of variance explained. In fact, as we will demonstrate in this chapter, we believe there is great merit to considering personality at a narrower level than the five factors, subject to careful theorizing. In other words, researchers can use more restricted measures once they know precisely what results they expect to obtain. The challenge is being able to theorize carefully enough so that narrow measures of personality can reliably be used.

The five-factor model of personality is most widely used today to describe individuals' personality traits because it is a simple, robust, and comprehensive way of understanding basic personality differences (McCrae and Costa, 1987; Wiggins, 1996). The five-factor model provides a framework to organize the main personality traits and to identify the individual differences that affect behavior. Each of the five factors—neuroticism, extraversion, openness, agreeableness, and conscientiousness—is described briefly in Table 4.1 (Costa and McCrae, 1988).

The Neuroticism Personality Factor

Neuroticism is characterized by high scores on negative affect or negative emotionality, which create a tendency for an individual to be anxious, insecure, temperamental, and self-conscious (McCrae and Costa, 1987). The neuroticism factor comprises six

Table 4.1
Big Five Personality Factors

Factor	Description of High Scorers
Neuroticism	High scorers experience a great deal of negative emotion.
Extraversion	High scorers get energy from others but are also assertive and have strong positive emotion.
Openness	High scorers are interested in the new and different.
Agreeableness	High scorers are cooperative and trusting, get along with others, and have sympathy for others' problems.
Conscientiousness	High scorers want a structured and organized life.

Source: Costa and McCrae, 1988.

Table 4.2
Neuroticism Facets

Facet of the Factor Neuroticism	Description of High Scorers
Anxiety	High scorers are worrying, tense, and apprehensive.
Anger	High scorers are quick to anger and hot-blooded.
Discouragement	High scorers are self-blaming and pessimistic.
Self-consciousness	High scorers are sensitive to embarrassment.
Impulsiveness	High scorers are easily tempted.
Vulnerability	High scorers are sensitive to stress and pressure.

Source: Costa and McCrae, 1988.

subfactors or facets that delineate the factor in more detail (as for each of the four other dimensions). For neuroticism, the six facets are anxiety, anger, discouragement, self-consciousness, impulsiveness, and vulnerability. Table 4.2 briefly explains each facet.

Few scholars have examined the neuroticism factor on its own. However, where it has been studied, neuroticism has consistently been a detrimental trait for work group performance. Studies have demonstrated that low levels of emotional stability (that is, a high level of neuroticism) amongst group members, calculated as the mean of group members' individual scores, predict poor team performance (Heslin, 1964; Mann, 1959; Peterson et al., 2003), reduced team viability (Barrick, Stewart, Neubert, and Mount, 1998), and increased team rigidity and diminished cohesion (Peterson et al., 2003). Neuroticism also affects how group members accomplish tasks. For example, a study of Reserve Officer Training Corps (ROTC) cadets revealed a negative relationship between neuroticism and group productivity in the completion of tasks requiring syllogistic reasoning, mechanical assembly, and creative story composition (Haythorn, 1953). Given that neuroticism is rooted in negative affectivity, it is also not surprising that teams with a negative affective tone (higher on the neuroticism scale) experienced higher absenteeism and less prosocial behavior (George, 1990).

These negative outcomes of neuroticism suggest important potential influences on group processes, particularly group conflict. Although Hoffman (1959) found that groups whose members' personality traits differed tended to produce higher-quality outputs and more creative solutions, we are interested in isolating the impact of neuroticism on how members get along. We suspect that a high degree of neuroticism in a group has the potential to ignite tensions among individuals and thus lead to relationship conflict. In addition, contrary to Hoffman's findings of many years ago, we expect that individuals who convey a high degree of negative affect will also express a high degree of neuroticism about the task itself, leading to task conflict.

MEASUREMENT CONSIDERATIONS

Despite recent evidence that personality is an excellent predictor of things like social behavior in groups, there is still a relative paucity of research on the effects of personality on groups, particularly on group conflict. We suspect that two interrelated reasons having to do with theorizing and methodology are holding back research in this important domain. First, the measures of personality used by many scholars are sometimes too broad to be useful (that is, using a sledgehammer where a scalpel would be more effective). Second, theorizing about how individual members' personality traits affect the group and the task at hand is often too basic—looking for simple main effects rather than interactions, moderators, and so on. The consequence of these problems is that personality variables often do not contribute very interesting or instructive findings. Thus, personality is often not given serious consideration by scholars studying group composition effects. We address each of these problems in turn in our empirical study of neuroticism and conflict.

One of the basic problems faced by a scholar who is interested in tracking the effects of personality on intragroup conflict is what to measure and how. The advantage of the five-factor model is that it enables scholars to simplify their analysis of the impact of personality on other indicators by looking at five rather than thirty personality variables (that is, the six facets of each of the five factors). Although we are not suggesting that researchers abandon the five-factor model, we believe there is some merit to considering personality at a narrower level than the five factors if careful theorizing has been done. The challenge is to theorize carefully enough so that narrow measures of personality can reliably be used.

The second, closely related problem is how to more precisely theorize about the effects of group members' personalities. Most published studies of the effects of personality in groups, and indeed most group measures, assume that individual scores should be aggregated to the group level by using the mean of the scores for each trait (Moynihan and Peterson, 2001). This universal approach presumes that their personality traits affect individuals' own behavior, which in turn directly affects the interpersonal processes within the group and then the group's ultimate performance. The implicit assumption is that a group member who is low on a particular trait like neuroticism can compensate for a member who is high on neuroticism.

Not every study on personality in groups employs the universal approach, of course, but it is far and away the most widely used method. Once the assumptions behind it are digested, however, we see that the universal approach is more than just a convenient statistical treatment of group data—it imposes a way of theorizing about how each individual's personality affects what happens in the group. Before researchers who adopt the universal approach blindly apply this standard "statistical" treatment of group data, they should understand and agree with the assumptions behind how the group members' personality traits combine.

Although the universal approach is the most popular, there are other ways to theorize about personality effects in groups—such as a configuration approach (Moynihan and Peterson, 2001). The configuration approach is more complex than the universal approach because it considers how the *mix* of traits within the group affects processes and outcomes. This method is a truly group approach in that it examines how individuals fit with each other. As such, the configuration approach allows for a variety of ways to represent the group-level personality trait (for example, mean, variance, minimum, maximum), depending on the purpose of the group (Moynihan and Peterson, 2001). For instance, a researcher who believes that the distribution of a trait among members of a group may affect the way they interact would consider the variance of the trait. Bond and Shiu (1997), for example, examined the variance in the level of conscientiousness in groups and found that high-conscientious group members were likely irritated when working with low-conscientious members and excluded them from the conversation—thus affecting the group's performance.

Deciding among the different approaches depends on the theory one adopts after considering the task facing the group, the research question, and the specific traits being analyzed (Barrick et al., 1998). Although the universal method is the most widely employed, the configuration approach yields interesting and more complex findings for how group members' personalities affect group outcomes. In our example of how the neuroticism trait affects the level of conflict in a group, we consider group members' neuroticism scores configurationally.

AN EXAMPLE: APPLYING THE CONFIGURATION APPROACH TO THE STUDY OF NEUROTICISM AND INTRAGROUP CONFLICT

We have pointed out the need for further research on the antecedents of group conflict and on the potential for personality variables, particularly neuroticism, to shed some light on the likelihood that conflict will emerge. We have also outlined considerations that researchers should take into account when measuring the effects of different variables in a group context. We now illustrate our points with an empirical example focused on predicting and measuring the effects of neuroticism on conflict in MBA student teams.

Our key question is this: Can one high-neuroticism team member destroy the dynamics of a group with his or her high negative affect? We measure this by looking primarily at intragroup conflict, both task based and relationship based. We are most interested in conflict, but given the dearth of literature linking personality with conflict, we also turn to literature on cohesion, which is highly negatively related to relationship conflict (Pelled, 1996). Both cohesion and relationship conflict are rooted in affect, and when group members display frustration or anger with each other, it is likely that the motivation to remain together as a group (that is, cohesion) is weaker. Figure 4.1 summarizes the two hypotheses we introduce in the following sections on conflict and cohesion.

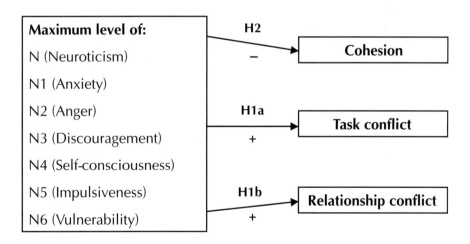

Figure 4.1
Impact of a High-Neuroticism Group Member: Hypotheses 1 and 2

THE CONFIGURATION APPROACH: NEUROTICISM AND CONFLICT

Although scholars have tested the effects of the mean level of neuroticism on team performance, viability, and cohesion, we have been unable to find any empirical studies of the relationship between mean level of neuroticism and conflict, let alone any studies looking at the effects of a particularly high-neuroticism individual group member. We expect, however, the presence of a particularly high-neuroticism team member (that is, where the score for the individual scoring highest on neuroticism, rather than the mean score, represents the group) to result in higher levels of relationship conflict. By expressing a high degree of negative emotionality—such as anger, vulnerability, or discouragement—a high-neuroticism group member is likely to be less compatible with his or her fellow members. This reduced compatibility is likely to raise the tension level within the group, leading to relationship conflict. We also expect task conflict to be elevated by the presence in a group of a particularly high scorer on neuroticism. An individual who is anxious or angry, for example, may be more likely to raise substantive issues about the task itself, since that individual is likely to be more anxious generally about the task. We expect this anxiety and raising of issues to lead to disagreement about the task and therefore to task conflict. Thus, we expect the following for hypothesis 1:

> *Hypothesis 1:* **The higher the maximum level of neuroticism in a group, the greater the level of (a) task conflict and (b) relationship conflict.**

Our "one bad apple" theory—that a single team member who expresses a high degree of negative emotion may disrupt the functioning of the entire group by increasing conflict—suggests a configuration approach to theory. This means that we will be looking only at the maximum level of neuroticism in the group rather than at the group mean. We are also interested in examining the neuroticism trait at both the factor level (neuroticism) and at the six facet levels (anxiety, anger, discouragement, self-consciousness, impulsiveness, and vulnerability), because it is possible that the facets could yield different outcomes and behaviors among group members.

THE CONFIGURATION APPROACH: NEUROTICISM AND COHESION

Cohesion refers to the collective motivation to remain together as a group (Korsgaard, Schweiger, and Sapienza, 1995). It reflects the "synergistic interactions between team members, including positive communication, conflict resolution, and effective workload sharing" (Barrick et al., 1998, p. 382). Understanding and measuring the construct are complex tasks, and as a result the nature and scope of cohesion remain uncertain (Levine and Moreland, 1998). Some factors that have been proposed as antecedents of cohesion include (1) the amount of contact between group members (the more time people spend together, the greater their cohesion); (2) the degree of attraction between members; (3) the nature of the rewards that are available within the group (the more rewarding the group is, in some way, the greater the cohesion); and (4) the potential for external threats, such as conflicts with other groups (Levine and Moreland, 1998). Cohesion appears to be tightly integrated with cooperation. Thus, group members are expected to exhibit more cooperative behavior when they are highly attached to their group (Deutsch, 1949)—in other words, when the group is more cohesive.

As was discussed earlier, low neuroticism (that is, high emotional stability) is a good predictor of team viability, which is a likely result of cohesion (Heslin, 1964). Barrick et al. (1998) expected that a higher average level of emotional stability within a group would result in a more relaxed and positive atmosphere that enables group members to cooperate. Barrick et al. (1998) tested two hypotheses around this idea. First, they examined the relationship between the mean level of individual scores on emotional stability and the work team's capability of continuing to work together. Second, they studied the relationship between the least emotionally stable member of each group and the group's capability to continue working together, expecting that the higher scores for the least emotionally stable member would be positively related to the team staying together (Barrick et al., 1998). They also specifically tested cohesiveness as a mediator between the emotional stability trait and team viability. Their findings revealed support (1) for a relationship between the mean level of emotional stability and team viability and (2) for a mediating role for cohesion between emotional stability and team viability. Surprisingly, results were not significant for the relationship between the minimum level of emotional stability in the group and team viability.

Given that neuroticism is the inverse of emotional stability, we expect higher levels of neuroticism to diminish cohesion within a group. We believe this to especially hold true in a group with a member who scores higher on the neuroticism trait than other group members. A high-neuroticism team member is not only different from the other group members, but he or she also disrupts the equilibrium of the group through excessive negative emotionality, such as the expression of anger or anxiety. We therefore revisit the proposition that failed to find support in Barrick et al. (1998) and outline hypothesis 2 as follows:

Hypothesis 2: **The higher the maximum level of neuroticism in a group, the lower the level of team cohesion.**

TESTING OUR CONFIGURATION HYPOTHESES

METHODOLOGY

This empirical study was conducted with data collected over two years from 95 core teams of first-year MBA students at London Business School. At the beginning of each academic program, first-year MBA students are divided into teams of five to seven students each; the students work in these teams for the duration of the academic year. Reflecting the international nature of the student body at the school, the teams are designed to be as diverse as possible, each team having members from four global regions (North America, Latin America, Europe, and Asia). These work teams form an important component of the assessment of these students: Group grades are given for most classes and projects, and even individual grades are obtained from work that builds on group work.

PERSONALITY VARIABLES

The Revised NEO Personality Inventory (NEO PI-R) (Costa and McCrae, 1992) personality test is administered to all students before they attend any part of the MBA program. We aggregated the neuroticism scores to the work group level according to both the mean and maximum levels of the factor and each of the six facets. When examining the relationship between the maximum level of neuroticism and our group process variables, we control for the mean level of neuroticism within the group and for age and gender diversity.

COHESION AND CONFLICT VARIABLES

At a few points during the first academic year, the MBA teams complete a "group health check" survey as part of the core MBA program. Each team member completes one survey in which he or she answers the questions for the group as a whole. Each question is assessed on a 7-point Likert scale. Six questions measure the team's cohesion (the third was reverse coded): (1) If I were to work in another team, I would want it to include people who are similar to those in my current team. (2) I wish I had more time for "socializing" with other team members. (3) There are not many people I like as individuals in this team. (4) This team has influenced me in a lot of positive ways. (5) I have learned a lot from participating in this team. (6) This team has been very helpful to me. Another four questions derived from Jehn's (1995) work relate to the level of relationship conflict evident in the team: (1) How much friction is there among members of your team? (2) How much emotional conflict is there among members of your team? (3) How much are personality conflicts evident in your team? (4) How much tension is there among members of your team? A further five questions assess the amount of task conflict within the team: (1) How often do members in your team challenge each other's viewpoints or opinions? (2) How frequently do members of your team engage in debate about different opinions or ideas? (3) To what extent does your team debate different ideas when solving a problem? (4) To what extent does your team argue the pros and cons of different opinions? (5) How often do your team members discuss evidence for alternative viewpoints? For each group process variable, we first checked to ensure that the individual questions factored to each of the cohesion and conflict variables, as expected. We then aggregated the individual team members' scores on each measure to the group level.

RESULTS OF CONFIGURATION TESTS

The analyses we present in this chapter are designed to illustrate how a more complex treatment of personality variables can lead to interesting findings, and we do so with quite straightforward analyses—correlations between neuroticism and our group outcomes of conflict and cohesion. In this section, we present the results of applying the configuration approach to study the relationship between neuroticism and group processes. First, we consider how the neuroticism factor is correlated with cohesion, relationship conflict, and task conflict. Throughout our analysis, we present our findings for the group process variables collected a few months after the teams are formed and begin their interaction (Table 4.3). As Table 4.3 demonstrates, we uncover very little that is interesting by examining the correlation between the maximum level of neuroticism in each group and the corresponding amount of cohesion and conflict reported by the team. Recall that the maximum level of neuroticism represents the score of the group member who exhibited the highest degree of the neuroticism personality trait. In this first analysis, the maximum level of neuroticism is not significantly related to cohesion or to either of the conflict variables. Not surprisingly, cohesion is significantly and negatively related to relationship conflict. In other words, the group reports being more cohesive as it experiences less relationship conflict. The lack of significant correlation between relationship and task conflict, however, is unexpected.

Given that the factor level of neuroticism did not exhibit very interesting results, we turn to the facet level. The neuroticism factor score consists of an aggregation of scores on six facets: anxiety, anger, discouragement, self-consciousness, impulsiveness, and vulnerability. Table 4.4 provides partial correlation results for the maximum level of each neuroticism facet with cohesion, relationship conflict, and task conflict, controlling for average level of neuroticism, age, and gender.

This more detailed look at the neuroticism personality trait helps to explain our lack of results at the factor level. At the factor level (Table 4.3), we found no significant relationships between personality and the group process variables. At the facet level, however (Table 4.4), we can see that the anger facet (N2) is related to group process. The maximum level of anger in the group is negatively related to cohesion ($r = -.21$, $p < .05$). Thus, these results indicate that a particularly high level

Table 4.3
Correlations at the Factor Level*

	Neuroticism (maximum)	Cohesion	Relationship Conflict	Task Conflict
Neuroticism (maximum)	1.00			
Cohesion	−0.08	1.00		
Relationship Conflict	0.01	−0.68	1.00	
Task Conflict	0.05	0.53	−0.26	1.00

* Includes controls for average-level neuroticism, age, and gender within each group.
⬭ Correlation is significant, $p < .05$.

Table 4.4
Correlations at the Facet Level*

	Cohesion	Relationship Conflict	Task Conflict
N1 (maximum): Anxiety	0.05	−0.06	0.08
N2 (maximum): Anger	−0.21	0.18	0.10
N3 (maximum): Discouragement	0.10	0.01	0.09
N4 (maximum): Self-consciousness	0.01	−0.06	−0.01
N5 (maximum): Impulsiveness	−0.05	0.06	0.04
N6 (maximum): Vulnerability	0.03	−0.11	−0.02

* Includes controls for average-level neuroticism, age, and gender within each group.
⬭ Correlation is significant, $p < .05$
⬭ Correlation is marginally significant, $p > .05$ and $< .10$.

of anger exhibited by one of the group members is related to the group as a whole being less cohesive, or getting along less well, as predicted at the factor level by our hypothesis 2.

Looking beyond the factor level to the facet level affords us two advantages. First, it pinpoints the particular behavior (in this case, anger) that results in less group cohesion. Second, it illustrates the reason why the neuroticism factor as a whole is not related to group cohesion: Although the anger facet is significantly related, the other five facets do not exhibit strong relationships with cohesion.

These advantages are also evident when we examine the relationship between the neuroticism facets and relationship conflict. At the facet level, we can see that anger ($r = .18$, $p < .10$) is marginally positively related to relationship conflict; this implies that groups with a particularly high scorer on anger are associated with a high degree of interpersonal conflict among their members. These findings are in line with our general hypothesis 1b that a maximum level of neuroticism is related to higher relationship conflict. Hypothesis 1a, however, receives no support at all, even at the facet level. We do not find any significant correlations between any of the neuroticism facets and task conflict (Table 4.4). While we expected negative emotionality to induce both types of conflict, it appears that it may be a primary driver of relationship conflict but not of task conflict. To explain task conflict in groups, we need to turn to other personality variables and/or to other variables altogether.

In summary, only by examining the facet level of the neuroticism trait did we uncover support for hypotheses 1b and 2. Analyzing the correlations between the neuroticism factor and the group process variables did not yield any significant results. It appears that the six facets captured by the neuroticism factor have different effects on the group; some, like anger, may decrease cohesion and amplify conflict, whereas others do not have a significant effect, at least at the maximum level of the facet. Given these findings, we can theorize about why each facet of neuroticism may affect group processes differently. Our results suggest that a group member who exhibits a higher degree of anger than other members would have a disruptive influence on the group as a whole. We expect that angry outbursts from such an individual would lead to animosity and tension with teammates—this is the very definition of relationship conflict.

This simple empirical example of how neuroticism influences the degree of cohesion and conflict in MBA student teams illustrates two important ways that awareness of personality variables can enhance our understanding of group interactions. First, by adopting a configuration approach, we assess how a particular distribution of the neuroticism trait among the teammates affects the likelihood for cohesion and conflict. Second, by probing beyond the neuroticism factor and examining the six facets of neuroticism, we are able to have a finer-grained analysis of the causes of conflict in groups. In doing these two things for the research reported here, we discovered that certain facets (in this case, anger) affect the group interaction, a finding that was masked at the factor level. Therefore, analyzing correlations at the facet level yielded results that were more precise and interesting than those discovered at the factor level.

DISCUSSION AND CONCLUSIONS

Our chief goal in this chapter was to examine how the neuroticism personality trait induces conflict in groups, depending on the configuration of the trait among group members. Our secondary goal was to make the case for why personality variables should be examined more frequently and in a more fine-grained way when studying group conflict. Many groups scholars overlook personality traits when studying group processes and conflict, often in favor of demographic variables such as gender, race, or age (Moynihan and Peterson, 2001; Williams and O'Reilly, 1998). Recent evidence suggests, however, that personality characteristics and values become even more salient over time, and demographic characteristics become less salient as group members get to know each other better (Harrison et al., 1998). Even when groups researchers do include personality variables in their studies, the variables are often measured only at a high level and aggregated by using the mean score of the group, muting results. We argue here that researchers are more likely to uncover additional interesting findings by (1) using finer-grained measures of personality (for example, using facet-level personality data) and (2) adopting more complex methods of theorizing about how personality affects group processes and conflict (for example, using a configuration approach).

To illustrate our point, we looked at how maximum neuroticism (negative emotionality) on the part of one high-scoring individual in a group may bring about conflict among group members. We examined how researchers can undertake a more fine-grained analysis of personality effects in groups by studying the neuroticism scores and group conflict and cohesion data from MBA core teams. We find, in short, that the anger facet, in particular, increases relationship conflict and reduces cohesion amongst team members. Had we simply studied the impact of the neuroticism factor as a whole, we would not have found any effects, because the neuroticism facets other than anger do not appear to be important determinants of group process.

THEORETICAL IMPLICATIONS

This chapter offers several implications for scholars interested in groups research, particularly those interested in intragroup conflict. First, we believe that groups scholars should consider personality effects in addition to the more traditional social and organizational effects as potential sources of team-level conflict. Researchers interested in diversity should also consider underlying attributes that become evident only after getting to know a person well (for example, personality and values) as well as those that can be readily detected on first meeting a person (age, sex, race). When investigating deep-level diversity, researchers must also consider the aspect of time, as deep-level diversity effects from personality only become apparent as group members learn about each other's traits through repeated interactions.

Second, personality effects may not be completely straightforward. Our results revealed that the neuroticism factor was not significantly associated with either of the conflict variables. However, once we examined neuroticism at the six facet levels, we found that one particular facet—anger—exhibited significant correlations with cohesion and relationship conflict. It is possible that facets of other personality variables may also have different and opposing effects on conflict or other group process variables that are masked at the factor level. For example, the trust and altruism facets of agreeableness may be negatively related to group conflict, whereas the facet of tender-mindedness may be positively related to conflict. The facets of extraversion may also show differential effects. The assertiveness facet of extraversion may be helpful to groups in small or moderate amounts, whereas the facet of positive emotion may be most helpful in large amounts.

Third, going beyond the simple universal approach to studying personality is necessary to gain a rich understanding of the influence of personality on group behavior. Scholars may need to explore the configuration of the group—how the personality traits interact—instead of simply averaging the personality traits of the group members (Moynihan and Peterson, 2001). In our example, we undertook a configurational approach to studying the effects of neuroticism on group conflict.

Although the focus of this chapter is on personality and group conflict, specifically neuroticism, we believe our ideas can apply more broadly to studies of other group phenomena. It may not be appropriate to aggregate individual data to the group level simply by averaging it if there are assumptions around how individuals in the group may be differently affected by the variables or if the task or context may moderate the relationship between variables. For example, group members may exhibit different levels of trust depending on their tenure with the organization or their functional background.

PRACTICAL IMPLICATIONS

Given that more and more work is accomplished by teams (Ilgen, 1999), organizations can also benefit from learning how team members' personality traits affect conflict, especially given that personality characteristics appear to become especially salient as team members spend more time together (Harrison et al., 1998). Managers would benefit from recognizing the disruptive or catalytic effects that a team member with a particularly high level of a certain personality trait may have on the rest of the team. For example, as we demonstrate in this chapter, a team member who is prone to expressing a high degree of anger may be responsible for decreasing the cohesiveness of the team and increasing the occurrence of relationship conflict among teammates. We are not suggesting that managers use personality traits to select individuals into or out of teams in organizations, but they may find it useful as a means of attenuating conflict to develop strategies to contain or control a team member who has a particularly high level of neuroticism. Also, organizations may wish to provide training for their managers on how to successfully manage this type of relationship conflict in their teams.

There does not seem to be a consensus on how to best manage relationship conflict arising from angry outbursts. One study found, for instance, that team members who are able to discuss anger incidents in an open-minded manner may actually enhance their relationships and productivity because they may be able to attribute their emotional reaction to either unintentional or justified actions. However, another study found that teams that engaged in avoiding responses to relationship conflict exhibited greater effectiveness than teams that engaged in either collaborating or contending responses (De Dreu and van Vianen, 2001).

In summary, it appears that only when a group is cognizant of its own configuration can it most effectively use the strengths of its members. Thus, if a group includes a member who has a high level of anger, a first step may be to make that individual aware of how his or her expressions of anger negatively affect the group's processes. Helping the group create routines and a language to address these outbursts can also help. Of course, there may be times when expressing anger in a productive manner could even be helpful for a group. A simple action such as phrasing anger in terms of a behavior rather than a personal attack may help to productively channel an angry outburst. However, we speculate that this may be the case only when a group is stuck on an issue. In such a situation, expressing anger or frustration could motivate a group to become unstuck and move forward with a decision. An assessment of successful methods of defusing tension and relationship conflict arising from high neuroticism or other variables may therefore provide a fruitful avenue for future research.

CONCLUSION

In sum, we find support for our suggestion that the presence of a particularly high-neuroticism group member predicts a decrease in group cohesion and an increase in group relationship conflict. In other words, it appears that a rotten apple may in fact spoil the barrel. However, we only find these effects by looking beyond the broad neuroticism factor to the facet level and by going beyond the universal approach to studying the effects of personality configurationally. If scholars are willing to spend a bit more time developing more complex approaches to studying personality in groups, we are confident that they may be rewarded for their efforts by gaining a richer understanding of the origins and effects of group conflict.

REFERENCES

Allport, G. W. 1937. *Personality: A psychological interpretation.* New York: Holt.

Barrick, M. R., Stewart, G. L., Neubert, M. J., and Mount, M. K. 1998. Relating member ability and personality to work-team processes and team effectiveness. *Journal of Applied Psychology, 83,* 377–391.

Barsade, S., Ward, A., Turner, J., and Sonnenfeld, J. 2000. To your heart's content: A model of affective diversity in top management teams. *Administrative Science Quarterly, 45,* 802–836.

Bass, B. M. 1990. *Bass and Stogdill's handbook of leadership,* 3rd edition. New York: Free Press.

Block, C. J., Roberson, L. A., and Neugen, D. A. 1993. Racial identity theory: A framework for understanding attitudes toward workforce diversity. Paper presented at the Eighth Annual Conference of the Society for Industrial/Organizational Psychology, San Francisco.

Bond, M. H., and Shiu, W. Y. 1997. The relationship between a group's personality resources and the two dimensions of its group process. *Small Group Research, 28,* 194–217.

Costa, P. T., and McCrae, R. R. 1988. Personality in adulthood: A six-year longitudinal study of self-reports and spouse ratings on the NEO Personality Inventory. *Journal of Personality and Social Psychology, 54,* 853–863.

Costa, P. T., and McCrae, R. R. 1992. *Revised NEO Personality Inventory manual.* Odessa, Fla.: Psychological Assessment Resources.

De Dreu, C. K. W., and van Vianen, A. E. M. 2001. Managing relationship conflict and the effectiveness of organizational teams. *Journal of Organizational Behavior, 22,* 309–328.

De Dreu, C. K. W., and Weingart, L. R. 2003. Task versus relationship conflict, team performance, and team member satisfaction: A meta-analysis. *Journal of Applied Psychology, 88,* 741–749.

Deutsch, M. 1949. An experimental study of the effects of cooperation and competition upon group process. *Human Relations, 2,* 199–231.

Eisenhardt, K. M., Kahwajy, J. L., and Bourgeois, L. J. III. 1997. Conflict and strategic choice: How top management teams disagree. *California Management Review, 39*(2), 42–62.

George, J. M. 1990. Personality, affect, and behavior in groups. *Journal of Applied Psychology, 75,* 107–116.

Guetzkow, H., and Gyr, J. 1954. An analysis of conflict in decision-making groups. *Human Relations, 7,* 367–381.

Hall, C. S., and Lindzey, G. 1957. *Theories of personality.* New York: John Wiley and Sons.

Harrison, D. A., Price, K. H., and Bell, M. P. 1998. Beyond relational demography: Time and the effects of surface- and deep-level diversity on work group cohesion. *Academy of Management Journal, 41,* 96–107.

Haythorn, W. 1953. The influence of individual members on the characteristics of small groups. *Journal of Abnormal and Social Psychology, 48,* 276–284.

Heslin, R. 1964. Predicting group task effectiveness from member characteristics. *Psychological Bulletin, 62,* 248–256.

Hoffman, L. 1959. Homogeneity and member personality and its effect on group problem solving. *Journal of Abnormal and Social Psychology, 58,* 27–32.

Hogan, R., and Kaiser, R. B. 2005. What we know about leadership. *Review of General Psychology, 9,* 169–180.

Holland, J. L. 1966. *The psychology of vocational choice.* Waltham, Mass.: Blaisdell.

Ilgen, D. R. 1999. Teams embedded in organizations: Some implications. *American Psychologist, 54*(2), 129–139.

Jehn, K. 1995. A multimethod examination of the benefits and detriments of intragroup conflict. *Administrative Science Quarterly, 40,* 256–282.

Jehn, K., and Mannix, E. 2001. The dynamic nature of conflict: A longitudinal study of intragroup conflict and group performance. *Academy of Management Journal, 44,* 238–251.

Korsgaard, M. A., Schweiger, D. M., and Sapienza, H. J. 1995. Building commitment, attachment, and trust in strategic decision-making teams: The role of procedural justice. *Academy of Management Journal, 38,* 60–84.

Levine, J. M., and Moreland, R. L. 1998. Small groups. In D. T. Gilbert, S. T. Fiske, and G. Lindzey (Eds.), *The handbook of social psychology,* 4th edition (pp. 415–469). New York: McGraw-Hill.

Mann, R. D. 1959. A review of the relationships between personality and performance in small groups. *Psychological Bulletin, 56,* 241–270.

Mannix, E., and Neale, M. A. 2005. What differences make a difference? The promise and reality of diverse teams in organizations. *Psychological Science in the Public Interest, 6,* 31–55.

McCrae, R. R., and Costa, P. T. 1987. Validation of the five-factor model of personality across instruments and observers. *Journal of Personality and Social Psychology, 52,* 81–90.

Mischel, W. 1968. *Personality and assessment.* New York: Wiley.

Moynihan, L. M., and Peterson, R. S. 2001. A contingent configuration approach to understanding the role of member personality in organizational groups. *Research in Organizational Behavior, 23,* 327–378.

Nemeth, C. J. 1997. Managing innovation: When less is more. *California Management Review, 40,* 59–67.

Pelled, L. H. 1996. Demographic diversity, conflict, and work group outcomes: An intervening process theory. *Organization Science, 7*(6), 615–631.

Pervin, L. A. 1980. *Personality theory and assessment.* New York: Wiley.

Peterson, R. S., and Behfar, K. J. 2003. The dynamic relationship between performance feedback, trust, and conflict in groups: A longitudinal study. *Organizational Behavior and Human Decision Processes, 92,* 102–112.

Peterson, R. S., Smith, D. B., Martorana, P. V., and Owens, P. D. 2003. The impact of CEO personality on top management team dynamics: One mechanism by which leadership affects organizational performance. *Journal of Applied Psychology, 88,* 795–808.

Rowe, R., and Snizek, W. E. 1995. Gender differences in work values: Perpetuating the myth. *Work and Occupations, 22,* 215–226.

Staw, B. M., and Ross, J. 1985. Stability in the midst of change: A dispositional approach to job attitudes. *Journal of Applied Psychology, 70,* 469–480.

Watson, W. E., Kumar, K., and Michaelson, L. K. 1993. Cultural diversity's impact on interaction process and performance: Comparing homogeneous and diverse task groups. *Academy of Management Journal, 36,* 590–602.

Wiggins, J. S. 1996. *The five-factor model of personality.* New York: Guilford.

Williams, K. Y., and O'Reilly, C. A. III. 1998. Demography and diversity in organizations: A review of 40 years of research. *Research in Organizational Behavior, 20,* 77–140.

Chapter 5

SELECTIVE CONSEQUENCES OF WAR

Holly Arrow, Oleg Smirnov, John Orbell, and Douglas Kennett

ABSTRACT

Deadly intergroup conflict—war—appears to have been a persistent characteristic of our ancestral past. Using a computational model, we explore how the selective pressures of warfare may have shaped the human propensity for behaviors that benefit one's own group at an individual cost. We distinguish between two types of altruistic behavior: heroism, the propensity to risk injury or death by fighting on behalf of one's group, and communitarianism, the propensity to provide nonmilitary assistance to fellow in-group members, again at some cost to oneself. Our model explores how the asymmetric consequences of war for winners and losers and the possible contributions of communitarianism and heroism toward winning wars may have shaped the evolution of both classes of behavior. Results suggest that even infrequent war can promote the evolution of heroism, but that communitarianism is promoted only in the context of constant war and when group size is small. We discuss how cognitive and behavioral adaptations to recurrent intergroup conflict over millennia may be relevant to group conflict in the twenty-first century.

INTRODUCTION

A group of seafaring people settle on a previously uninhabited volcanic island that provides all the resources needed for survival: fresh water, fertile land for crops, trees for fuel, and attractive sites for rock shelters near protected bays rich in marine life. The settlers build stone-walled terraces to improve the land for agriculture, and stone fish traps harness the tide to provide protein for a growing population.

113

Fast forward a few hundred years. The island is now densely populated by descendants of the original settlers, and the trees are gone. The rock shelters near the bays have been abandoned. The islanders now live in fortified settlements on the top of rocky peaks in communities numbering from around 25 to perhaps a few hundred people each. Although they are far from the fields and bays, exposed to the weather, and inconvenient in other ways, the new settlements provide a commanding view of the surrounding area. Ditches, walls, and high ground offer obvious military advantages over the seaside rock shelters, and archaeological evidence and ethnographic accounts indicate that some older communities have been completely exterminated. Settlement patterns have been reorganized to cope with deadly intergroup conflict.

Rapa, the island in this tale (Kennett, Anderson, Prebble, Conte, and Southon, 2006), is located in the South Pacific, a region that has inspired Western fantasies of earthly paradise from Gauguin to Margaret Mead. Paradise is a fleeting phenomenon, however, easily degraded by crowding, resource stress, and war. The pattern is evident throughout Polynesia, where warfare is rare among founding populations of islands but increases through time with demographic expansion and increased competition for resources (Kennett, Anderson, and Winterhalder, 2006; Kirch, 1984). Archaeological evidence suggests that this deadly pattern was a recurrent feature of our species' prehistory (Keeley, 1997; LeBlanc and Register, 2003; see Fry, 2006 for a contrasting perspective). In this chapter, we explore some possible consequences of resource conflicts and war in shaping how humans behave in groups.

Our species has a demonstrated ability to survive in a wide variety of habitats, from savannah to remote islands, from dense forest to arctic tundra, to cities and industrial organizations. One feature that has remained constant across space and time, however, is the context that humans take with them wherever they migrate and that shapes whatever institutions they devise: the human social group. Group living is likely the oldest and most stable feature of the changing environment in which humans and our hominid ancestors evolved and to which we are adapted, and groups are still the context for much of the activity that takes place in modern organizations. Like the inhabitants of Rapa, but on more compressed timescales, groups in organizations can also transition from periods of peaceful focus on productive work to periods of intense intergroup conflict. The transition back to a peaceful regime is much harder to achieve, whether in a modern organization or on a remote island. Why?

We believe that it is difficult to find a way out of intense intergroup conflict regimes in part because such conflict activates cognitive and behavioral propensities that were shaped by war, that are evoked by cues associated with war, and that have helped our ancestors—both recent and remote—adapt successfully to a social environment in which conflict with other groups can threaten the survival of the groups involved. In this chapter, we report on a project that uses a computational model to explore the possible role of warfare in shaping the evolution of two such behavioral propensities. Both are forms of evolutionary altruism (Sober and Wilson, 1998) that benefit one's in-group at some cost to oneself. We distinguish between *communitarianism*, which refers to costly actions that benefit other in-group members in the context of intragroup dynamics, and *heroism*, which refers to actions that expose oneself to danger to benefit the group as a whole in the context of intergroup conflict. By investigating different forms of altruistic behavior in the same model, we seek to investigate whether or not they may have evolved by the same route.

Note that we use these particular terms to refer only to those behaviors that come at an individual cost. Everyday behavior includes a wide array of prosocial actions that are not individually costly, and people may also benefit personally from attacking others who happen to be out-group members. Such actions do not pose a conflict of interest between individual and group, and they are not the focus of our chapter.

Group interaction does, however, routinely pose conflicts of interest between what is best for the group and what is best for the individual—between group-serving and self-serving courses of action. This tension among choices to cooperate or defect is familiar across the literature of the social sciences (for example, Axelrod, 1997; Weber, Kopelman, and Messick, 2004). People differ in how often and under what circumstances they act in a way that serves the collective interest, but without some willingness to curb one's immediate self-interest and do what is best for the group, human well-being and survival are threatened. Concern for the collective outcomes of others in such conflicts of interest typically stops short at the boundary of one's own in-group, however, and the same people who are willing to (with some frequency) put aside immediate self-interest to benefit fellow in-group members may seek to actively harm out-group members.

From the perspective of the in-group, these behaviors are not contradictory as long as they target in-group and out-group members respectively. Abundant evidence documents the sensitivity of humans to in-group and out-group membership cues (for example, Schaller and Conway, 2001; Stangor, Lynch, Duan, and Glass, 1992; Turner, 1987; Wilder, 1986). The tendency of intergroup relations to be much less cooperative than interpersonal relations is well established (Pemberton, Insko, and Schopler, 1996; Wildschut, Pinter, Vevea, Insko, and Schopler, 2003), and the discontinuity can go beyond simple failure to cooperate to active aggression (for example, Meier and Hinsz, 2004; Sherif, Harvey, White, Hood, and Sherif, 1961).

When group members are threatened with danger, people may act altruistically to protect the group *by* injuring or killing others. In contemporary state societies, this role is played by the police officer or soldier. In smaller-scale societies, it is the job of the warrior—a role that may be required of most or even all able-bodied adult males. From this perspective, helping to build a fish trap that will benefit everyone (in-group cooperation) rather than defecting by letting others build it and free-riding on their efforts, and fighting neighbors (intergroup hostility) rather than fleeing or hiding and letting others fight on one's behalf, can both be considered forms of altruism, although the behaviors themselves (helping, harming) look quite different and are likely based on different subsets of cognitive and motivational components.

Fighting for one's group at the risk of serious injury or death is thus conceptually equivalent to other altruistic behaviors that benefit others at a personal cost. Of course, societies can arrange for successful warriors to reap fitness benefits as compensation via, for example, higher status or access to women (for example, Chagnon, 1988; Junker, 1999; Patton, 2000). These rewards can adjust the cost/benefit ratio so that heroism is no longer altruistic in an evolutionary sense, regardless of the proximal individual motivations that drive behavior (Eibl-Eibesfeldt, 1979; Tooby and Cosmides, 1988). Warriors who die, of course, forego any fitness rewards, and warriors who manage to avoid the greatest dangers could presumably reap the benefits due to warriors while the more courageous perish. The rewards a given warrior does or does not reap depend on the outcome (live, die, sustain serious injury) for a particular conflict. Whatever the results for the individual, however, the group stands to benefit from a warrior's contribution.

Societies in which group-benefiting behaviors are rewarded are more likely to prosper than those that lack such reward systems, which can result in a form of cultural selection among groups known as equilibrium selection (Boone, 1998; Boyd and Richerson, 1990; Miller, 2000). Before these reinforcement systems are established, however, the behavior has to develop in the first place, and in advance of these cultural adjustments, we need to explain how behavior that is evolutionarily altruistic could initially emerge.

A growing literature studies contexts in which people negotiate simultaneous conflicts of interest within and between groups (for example, Bornstein, 1994; Bornstein, Kugler, and Zamir, 2005; Goren, 2001). We, too, are interested in the interplay between mixed-motive conflicts of interest between individuals and the groups to which they belong (Schelling, 1960) and in conflicts of interest among groups that seek to exploit the same finite resources.

We believe that recurrent intergroup violence—war—may promote the resolution of such conflicts of interest in favor of one's group. Whether such resolutions are viewed as having positive or negative effects depends on both temporal and contextual frames of reference. Behfar and Thompson (chapter 1, this volume) distinguish between within-group and between-group forms of conflict and among functional, dysfunctional, and quasifunctional perspectives depending on whether conflict is viewed as positive, negative, or mixed in its results. Like many scholars who study conflict, we are interested in the results of conflict. Our primary interest is on ultimate results over a long time frame (evolutionary history) rather than proximate results of particular conflicts, although proximate results (winning or losing a war) are part of the engine that drive the process of evolution in our model.

We believe that an evolutionary perspective may help check the common tendency of scholars to assume that intergroup conflict is necessarily dysfunctional, overlooking how it might (from the perspective of a group rather than a society or organization) serve the interests of those involved (in other words, how it might be functional or quasifunctional in the terms set out in chapter 1).

We proceed as follows. First, we consider the role of war in evolution. After reviewing evidence that war has exerted selective pressure on human groups, we explain the logic of multilevel selection and how it might apply to war and group-serving behavior. Second, we describe our computational model and present some results that show how group size and cost/benefit structures may affect the evolution of heroism and communitarianism. We conclude by discussing some possible implications of our thinking about human adaptation to war for understanding conflict-related cognition and behavior in contemporary groups.

THE ROLE OF WAR IN EVOLUTION

THE SELECTIVE PRESSURES OF WAR

Any major source of death can operate as an agent of selection, and war appears to fit this criterion. Archaeological (for example, Keeley, 1997; LeBlanc and Register, 2003) and anthropological (for example, Chagnon, 1974; Ross, 1984) evidence suggests that our ancestral past was characterized by persistent coalitional violence with significant mortality rates. Estimated death rates (Keeley, 1997, p. 196) from prehistoric data range from as high as 48 percent for males and 45 percent for females for a site in Nubia dating to 10,000 before the common era (BCE) to more modest rates such as 8 percent overall mortality (men, women, and children) from Brittany in 6,000 BCE (see, however, Fry, 2006). Going further back in prehistory, remains are too fragmentary to allow credible estimates of relative mortality or to distinguish between murder and war as causes of death. However, evidence of inter-personal violence and cannibalism dates as far back as the period during which the genus *Homo* was first emerging (see Walker, 2001, for a recent review of the bioar-chaeological evidence).

Contemporary hunter/gatherer societies, believed to provide the closest ana-logues for much of the evolutionary past of *Homo sapiens,* have death rates ranging from the relatively low (but nontrivial) 8.3 percent overall mortality for the Gebusi (Knauft, 1985) to highs of 59 percent male, 27 percent female mortality for the Jivaro (Ross, 1984) and 37 percent male, 4 percent female for the Yanomomo (Chagnon, 1974). Male/female asymmetries in death rates are also evident in geno-cidal conflicts playing out today. Refugees streaming out of the western Sudanese province of Darfur are being fed and sheltered in camps that are 90 percent women and children; the men and older boys in these families have almost all been killed or captured or are otherwise missing (Pelley, 2005).

Substantial male mortality rates from intergroup violence have also been docu-mented for some bands of common chimpanzees, Pan troglodytes (Wilson and

Wrangham, 2003), suggesting that acts of war (including raiding and opportunistic killing of out-group members) have plausibly been exerting selective pressure since before the branching off of hominids and chimpanzees from our common primate ancestor roughly five million years ago.

Along with a tendency for war to kill more males than females, the outcomes of war exhibit other important asymmetries. One is the advantage of attackers over defenders, especially for raids and ambushes, the most common form of combat in hunter/forager societies (LeBlanc and Register, 2003). This is also the form of coalitional violence practiced by common chimps (Wrangham and Peterson, 1996). Raids are designed to kill members of the enemy groups while minimizing the risk to attackers, and surprise helps to achieve this lopsided result. In other words, offense trumps defense. Successful raiders may also carry off resources such as food, animals, or women that will boost their own group's rate of reproduction and suppress population growth in the group they attacked.

In war, the odds of survival also strongly favor the victor. The asymmetry in casualty rates is most extreme for massacres, in which all or almost all of the losing group are killed. Among the Inuit, for example, ethnographic accounts document that the goal of warfare was annihilation of the enemy group (LeBlanc and Register, 2003, p. 118), and surprise dawn raids were the preferred tactic. Among tribal farming peoples, annihilation was also a typical goal in war, although men were the primary target and women might be integrated into the victor's society, which would take over the land of the defeated group. Even when the primary objective is winning rather than killing, losing increases casualties because people on the losing side tend to run away, presenting low-risk killing opportunities similar to those sought in surprise raids. Keegan (1976) notes that "the most dangerous course in war is to retreat when in close contact with the enemy . . . [which] appears to stimulate an almost uncontrollable urge to kill among those presented with a view of the enemy's backs" (p. 150). In summary, the selective pressures of war should favor any characteristic that promotes surprise attack and winning. Membership in a defeated group increases mortality, especially for males.

THE LOGIC OF MULTILEVEL SELECTION AND WAR

While individual behavior can certainly affect one's chances of survival in war, especially for those in the midst of a fight, the probability of being killed is also strongly influenced by what side one is on, winning or losing—in other words, on one's group membership. War kills not just individuals but members of groups. Hence evolutionary models of war should consider the possible role of group selection in addition to natural selection at the individual level.

Early group-selection models, which proposed an evolutionary advantage to groups that restricted population growth and hence did not degrade their resource base (Wynne-Edwards, 1962), suffered from both logical and practical flaws. Williams (1966) pointed out that natural selection against individuals who restricted their own fertility would systematically weaken such tendencies over time. On a population level, members of groups that grow more rapidly will also become more common over time than those that restrict growth. For group selection to work (which Williams acknowledged was possible), the trait being selected cannot restrain reproductive success at the group level—instead, it must enhance it.

Sober and Wilson (1998) set out specific criteria for multilevel selection for group-benefiting altruism. In a population of groups in which the incidence of altruism varies, groups with a higher incidence of altruism must reproduce at a higher rate. The progeny of these groups must either mix with one another or otherwise compete in the formation of new groups. We followed these criteria in constructing our computational model, with war as the form of explicit competition that determines the composition of new groups. In multilevel models, whether group selection operates as a meaningful force depends on the relative strength of (1) natural selection acting on individuals within a group and (2) group selection operating on differences between groups. This logic, which requires that an individual's fitness be partitioned into within-group and between-group components, can be represented mathematically via a rearrangement of terms in Hamilton's equation for inclusive fitness (kin selection), which is widely accepted among evolutionary theorists (see Reeve, 2000, for the mathematical details). A similar reinterpretation of terms has been used to track the evolutionary accounting for reciprocal altruism, applied by Patton to war among Amazonian tribes (Patton, 2000).

THE EVOLUTION OF COMMUNITARIANISM AND HEROISM: A COMPUTATIONAL MODEL

Our model has the following general structure: A population of individuals is divided into several groups. Each group occupies a territory that provides resources for survival, and each group member has some propensity (between 0 and 1, representing never and always) toward what we call communitarianism—nonmilitary altruistic behavior that benefits in-group members (via acts such as food sharing or care of the injured or wounded) and that comes at a cost to one's own reproductive fitness. Communitarianism increases the overall growth rate of the group (baseline fertility) at some cost to the sharing and caring members, who might otherwise choose to hoard food stocks or let weaker group members die, removing in-group competitors for food and other resources.

When a group's population exceeds the carrying capacity of its natural resources, it attacks another group at random. The outcome of the attack is determined by the number of individuals who participate in fighting in each group and by the propensity of each fighter for altruistic heroism. Heroism also ranges between 0 and 1, with 0 representing no participation in dangerous fighting/defense and 1 representing maximal heroism. Larger groups have an advantage, but a smaller group can plausibly win if its members are more heroic. Indeed, such victories by a smaller but heroically motivated force play an important role in collective mythology and history (for example, in the fourth act of Shakespeare's *Henry V*—"We few, we happy few, we band of brothers"). Once the outcome is determined, members of the losing group are annihilated (or otherwise vacate the territory and the simulation, perhaps becoming refugees), and the winning group fissions, with some members moving to the vacated territory.

At the end of each generation, each individual has some probability of reproducing, and offspring resemble their parents in communitarian and heroic propensities within a specified range of variation. In the current version of the model, our focus is on phenotypic behavior at the level of individuals and groups. Individuals who express these behaviors are the unit or object *of* natural selection, while what is selected *for* is the behavioral propensity (see Mayr, 2001, pp. 126–134, for a good discussion of objects of selection). We make the explicit assumption that behavioral tendencies are heritable, consistent with evidence from behavioral genetics (Loehlin, Willerman, and Horn, 1988), but genes per se are not modeled, and we do not presume that there is a particular gene for heroism or for any other complex social behavior. We do assume that offspring resemble their parents. The range of variation stands in for the more explicit genetic mixing of sexual reproduction and for the imperfect association of genotype and phenotype. In human societies, of course, broader cultural structures can reinforce or dampen the expression of any behavioral tendency, but we do not include culture in the current model, only direct transmission from parent to offspring. An individual's probability of offspring (reproductive success) is reduced both by communitarianism and (in the event of war) by heroism. In our model, the only cause of death is war.

By treating communitarianism and heroism as distinct sets of behaviors, we can investigate them separately as propensities that might plausibly have been selected by war but might also have developed in response to different sets of selective pressures. The model allows for individuals to be all-around citizens who are equally willing (or unwilling) to make sacrifices for the group in peace or war. It also allows for communitarian pacifists or heroic fighters who are not otherwise prone to peaceful altruistic acts.

The following parameters can be varied: number of groups, richness of natural resources in each group's territory (which effectively limits group size), baseline individual fertility (probability of offspring), extent to which communitarianism can improve fertility rates within a group, reproductive costs to individuals of communitarianism and heroism, number of generations, and mutation rate. For technical details including equations, see appendix 5.A.

PATTERNS OF EVOLUTION BASED ON GROUP SIZE AND COST/BENEFIT SETTINGS

To examine the selective pressure of war on communitarianism and heroism, we started by exploring the impact of two parameters: the maximum sustainable size of groups (which is constrained by the habitat resource base) and the relative costs and benefits of the two types of behavior. We chose group size to explore whether it has an impact separate from the proposed psychological effects often evoked to explain the robust finding that incidence and severity of social loafing and free-riding (selfish behaviors that damage group performance) increase in larger groups (for example, Latané, Williams, and Harkins, 1979; Seijts and Latham, 2000). The phenomenon has been attributed to the increasing difficulty of monitoring others' contributions and the corresponding decreased accountability of each member, coupled with a decreasing sense that one's contributions are critical (Kerr and Bruun, 1983). In our simulation, agents are unaffected by any feelings of responsibility or criticality—they simply act in accordance with their traitlike "propensities." The model allows us to investigate whether, absent these psychological effects, the evolution of such behavioral propensities could still be affected by differences in criticality for heroism and the dilution of benefits of communitarian action based on group size.

We chose a range of group sizes consistent with ethnographic and archaeological literature that suggests that the size of hunter/gatherer bands would be roughly 20–50 people (Caporael and Baron 1997; Dunbar, 1993), increasing to around 100–200 for "cultural lineage groups" and Neolithic villages (Dunbar, 1993). Applying three additional assumptions—that warriors are male, that they are adults, and that there are roughly equal numbers of males and females in each group—we used the age demographics given for a few contemporary hunter/gatherer peoples (Hill and Hurtado, 1991; Howell, 1979) to give a rough estimate that around 35 percent of a group would be in the right age and sex categories to be warriors. This yields numbers of eligible warriors from a minimum of 7 for groups of size 20 to a maximum of 70 for groups of size 200. Because, in our simulation, all members fight (and hence we are, in effect, modeling the warrior segment of groups), the group sizes we chose for our simulation were 10, 25, 50, and 75. We kept the number of groups fixed at four, and all four habitats had equal carrying capacities (either 10, 25, 50, or 75).

We varied the cost/benefit settings to explore the relative sensitivity of the two forms of altruistic behavior to costs and benefits and also to identify the range in which multilevel selection would actually occur. The logic of multilevel selection requires that the forces favoring groups that benefit from altruistic behavior over groups that do not are at least as strong as the selective forces favoring selfishness among individuals within groups. However, for both heroism and communitarianism, some of the benefits are affected by emergent properties of groups and wars and hence are not directly controlled by parameter choice. The benefits of war depend on winning, and winning depends on a combination of relative group size and heroism. The benefits of communitarianism that redound to an individual group member are also affected by the number of individuals contributing and by whether group size proves to be pivotal in particular wars. Since these are emergent factors, we could not directly calculate a priori when costs at the individual level would be balanced by benefits at the group level.

Focusing on the costs and benefits that are determined directly by parameter settings, we chose three cost/benefit levels for the experiment: a low-cost, high-benefit setting; a high-cost, low-benefit setting; and an intermediate setting. We subsequently refer to these as the low-, high-, and medium-cost conditions. The benefit was implemented as the maximum increase in group-level reproductive rate (probability of offspring) that could be achieved if all members of a group were 100 percent communitarian. The cost was how much communitarianism and heroism affects reproductive success (assuming survival to the reproductive phase). To facilitate direct comparisons, the cost of heroism and the cost of communitarianism were the same for each condition (for more details, see appendix 5.A). The two factors were crossed, and 10 runs of 2,000 generations each were completed for each of the 12 cells, for a total n of 120. Initial mean values of both communitarianism and heroism were .5 for all groups, a choice that allows for observation of both increases and decreases over time.

RESULTS

As expected, both communitarianism and heroism were sensitive to cost, evolving to higher levels when the cost/benefit setting was more favorable. However, communitarianism was more sensitive to cost than heroism and evolved to mean levels above the starting point of .5 only at the low-cost setting or when the sustainable group size was small (10 or 25) and the cost was moderate. Figure 5.1 shows the mean communitarianism values for the final 500 generations of the 2,000-generation runs for the 12 conditions. Heroism, in contrast, evolved to higher levels than the starting value under all conditions (Figure 5.2). The number of wars was clearly sensitive to the cost/benefit setting (Figure 5.3), which sets a limit on maximum baseline group fertility. The decrease in war frequency with larger group size for the low-cost and medium-cost conditions tracks the pattern for communitarianism, which makes sense given that mean group communitarianism is what increases fertility. When communitarianism is relatively "cheap" and yields substantial benefits to group fertility, population growth leads groups to outstrip the carrying capacity of their territories more quickly, triggering frequent wars (about one and a half per generation under the low-cost condition, which translates to a 75 percent likelihood of each group being in a war each generation).

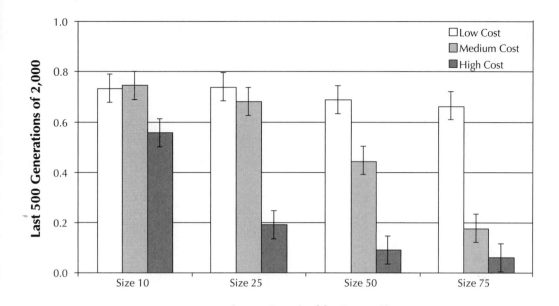

Figure 5.1
**Evolved Communitarianism for Different Cost and Size Settings: 120
Runs of 2,000 Generations Each (10 runs per cell)**

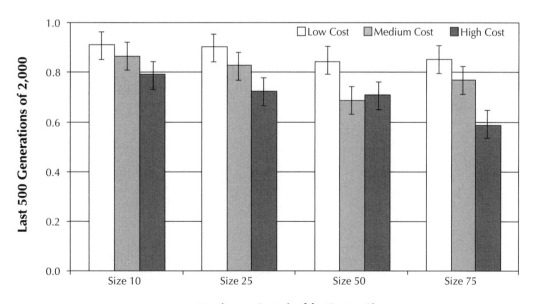

Figure 5.2
**Evolved Heroism for Different Cost and Size Settings: 120 Runs of 2,000
Generations Each (10 runs per cell)**

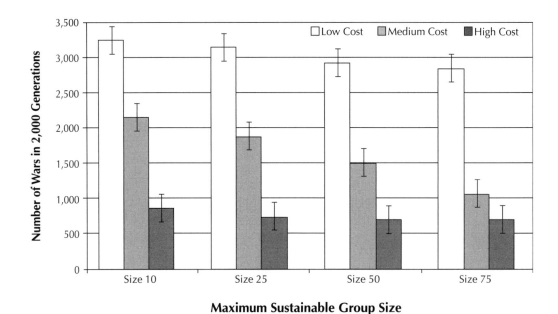

Figure 5.3
Total Number of Wars at Different Cost and Size Settings: 120 Runs of 2,000 Generations Each (10 runs per cell)

Heroism, in contrast, neither triggers nor requires frequent wars to evolve. Even in the high-cost, larger-group-size conditions in which communitarianism collapses and groups experience war on average only about once every six generations, heroism can still evolve to quite high levels. Although this might at first seem counterintuitive, since heroism only yields benefits during war, the cost of heroism is also paid per war rather than per generation. This makes sense because only in war does heroism expose a warrior to danger. In peacetime the behavior is not expressed, within-group natural selection against heroism does not operate, and any changes in heroism are simply genetic drift.

The relationship between number of wars and communitarianism (both emergent properties in the simulation) is bidirectional: While wars, fission, and migration provide a group-level selection mechanism for communitarianism in line with the logic of Sober and Wilson (1988), the resulting increase in fertility also promotes overpopulation, triggering wars. In our model, multilevel selection for communitarianism via warfare gains traction in an environment of runaway population growth and persistent intergroup violence. The evolution of heroism based on war is more robust, and a relatively small number of wars selects for heroism almost as strongly as do constant battles.

To test the statistical reliability of the patterns just described, two-factor analyses of variance (low, medium, and high cost crossed with maximum sustainable group size of 10, 25, 50, and 75) were conducted to investigate the impact of these predictors on the evolved values of communitarianism and heroism. For communitarianism, size, $F(3, 108) = 25.46$, cost $F(2, 108) = 74.35$, and the cost by size interaction $F(6, 108) = 6.34$, were all significant at the $p < .001$ level, with an adjusted R^2 of 0.68 for the model. The nature of the interaction is evident in Figure 5.1: The evolved level of communitarianism is more affected by group size when costs are medium or high than when costs are low. For heroism, size and cost had significant main effects, $F(3, 108) = 3.58$, $p < .02$, and $F(2, 108) = 10.59$, $p < .001$, respectively. The cost by size interaction term was nonsignificant, $F < 1$, with adjusted R^2 of 0.18 for the model.

Because of the impact of communitarianism on war via fertility and unsustainable population growth, the outcome variable for communitarianism (mean for the last 500 of the 2,000 generations) was entered as a covariate in a factorial analysis of covariance (ANCOVA) predicting the total number of wars from maximum sustainable group size and cost. As expected, the covariate accounted for a substantial amount of variance, $F(1, 107) = 63.98$, $p < .001$. Cost, $F(2, 107) = 149.21$, and the cost by size interaction term, $F(6, 107) = 4.64$, were significant at the $p < .001$ level. Size was nonsignificant ($F < 1$), and adjusted R^2 was 0.92 for the model.

Beneath the orderly pattern of means for the last 500 generations evident in Figures 5.1 and 5.2, substantial variability was apparent among the trajectories across time for multiple runs in many of the 12 conditions covered in the design. Fortunately, analyses of variance are robust against violations of the homoscedasticity assumption with the equal cell sizes provided by our design (Hays, 1988). This variation is not just a nuisance; it is interesting in its own right, showing the extent to which trajectories of evolution are consistent and predictable given a fixed starting point and specified group size and cost/benefit parameter values.

Figures 5.4a–5.4c illustrate some differences. With high cost and large group sizes, the evolution of communitarianism follows a consistent trajectory of sharp decline and persistently low values (Figure 5.4a). With medium cost and a sustainable group size of 25, however, considerably more variety is evident (Figure 5.4b). Although a dominant trajectory is apparent, with 6 of the 10 runs showing a steady increase ending at values between .8 and 1.0, one of the runs follows the trajectory of immediate decline we saw in Figure 5.4a, another decreases to low levels but recovers and ends up the same place as the steadily increasing trajectories, and the other two trajectories are eccentric and unstable, rising to high levels only to collapse precipitously. For high cost and sustainable group size of 10 (Figure 5.4c) all predictability vanishes; although all the runs start at the same initial value and unfold in identical environments as defined by simulation parameters, ending values span the full range of possibilities, and there is no central tendency. The three figures together illustrate a

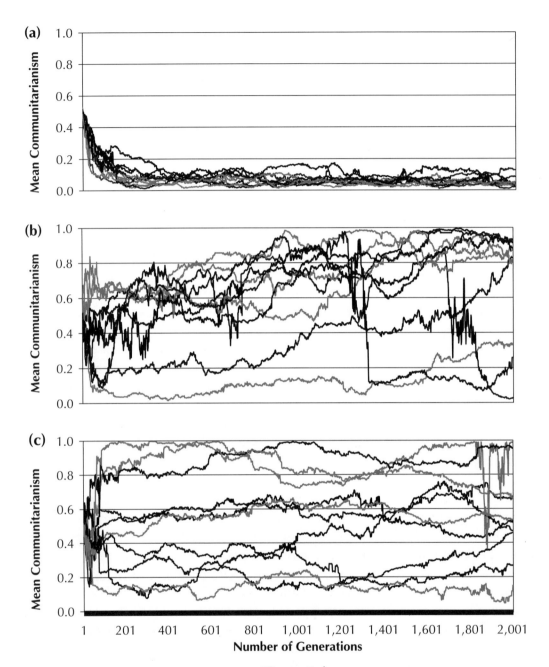

Figure 5.4
Communitarianism for Individual Runs across 2,000 Generations for
Three Parameter Settings: (a) High Cost, Sustainable Group Size of 75;
(b) Medium Cost, Sustainable Group Size of 25; (c) High Cost,
Sustainable Group Size of 10*

* Each group shows 10 runs with identical parameter settings. Sustainable group size is based on the fixed size of a group's resource base. See appendix 5.A for simulation details.

lesson common to studies of complex systems, which is that changes in control parameters can change not only the mean values of state (outcome) variables, but the degree of predictability in the system, from the inevitable result of a single strong attractor to the unpredictability of rapidly diverging trajectories (Arrow, 2005).

DISCUSSION

Group-Serving Behaviors in Intragroup and Intergroup Contexts

Our theorizing, as implemented in our computational model, suggests that a propensity for heroism—a human impulse to risk injury or death to protect, defend, and do battle on behalf of one's group—could have evolved in a setting in which heroism helped groups win wars, even if more heroic group members risked dying without issue and even if genocidal conflicts were relatively rare. Other forms of selection that deliver hidden benefits for such behavior—whether via reciprocal altruism (Patton, 2000), sexual selection (Miller, 2000), or kin selection—have likely contributed to stabilizing and reinforcing these tendencies. As Tooby and Cosmides (1996) propose in analyzing the evolution of friendship, once useful adaptations develop for delivering benefits to others, further evolution tends to reduce the costs and create compensations that make the delivery of benefits rewarding. Another contributing factor could be the Baldwin effect, whereby beneficial behaviors that are originally not tied to genes are reinforced by the selection of genetic determinants for such behavior (Mayr, 2001, p. 137).

In contrast to the robust results for heroism, warfare in our model only selected for intragroup communitarian tendencies under extreme conditions of perpetual war, high benefits to group fertility, and low costs to individuals. Inconsistent and variable results across multiple runs also leads us to believe that group selection for such behavior via warfare is quite unlikely to have occurred. This does not preclude selection for apparently self-sacrificing intragroup behavior by other mechanisms, of course, but it does suggest that pushing the intergroup conflict button should trigger a stronger and more reliable response than pushing the good-of-the-group button when there is no perception of threat from another group.

Anecdotal evidence that group-serving behavior is easier to evoke in the context of intergroup threat is abundant: The power of the "rally 'round the flag" effect provides a ready temptation for political leaders to evoke out-group enemies as a unifying strategy. Empirical results from studies using intergroup social dilemma paradigms also indicate that when a mixed-motive game is embedded in an intergroup context, people are less likely to free-ride (Bornstein, 1992), although the pattern of increased intragroup cooperation appears more reliably for males (Van Vugt, De Cremer, and Yuki, 2006). (Other studies have also shown different patterns of in-group favoring choices for men and women—for example, Gaertner and Insko, 2000.) The widespread use of war rhetoric as a strategy to inspire collective effort in endeavors as inconsistent with war as medical research (war on cancer) and economic development (war on poverty) may also express an implicit understanding that the prospect of war is more invigorating than the prospect of peace.

Size and Cost Constraints: When Is Self-Sacrificing Behavior Worth the Price?

Many explanations for apparently altruistic behavior show how, at a different level of analysis (typically the gene instead of the organism), the behavior is ultimately beneficial. In fact, this must ultimately be true (on average) for any costly phenotypic characteristic to be selected. The sensitivity of evolved communitarianism to group size and to relative costs and benefits suggests a similar explanation. Although an upstanding communitarian will be at a disadvantage relative to fellow group members who are less devoted to the group, the increase in baseline fertility due to one's own actions could be enough to provide a reproductive advantage compared with the whole population of humans, as long as other groups benefited from less communitarianism overall and hence reproduced at a slower rate. Because the increase in baseline group fertility in our model is based on the average communitarianism in the group, the relative impact of one's own actions is greater the smaller the group.

The same logic holds for heroism, but to an even greater extent, given the admittedly extreme assumption that all members of the losing group die (complete genocide). If one's own actions are critical to victory, then escaping certain death in defeat should be a powerful incentive regardless of any group-serving motivation, and the likelihood of proving critical should be inversely related to group size. Using a formal mathematical model that varied the genocide parameter and assumed that people were either complete heroes or utter cowards, Smirnov, Arrow, Kennett, and Orbell (2006) demonstrated that an equilibrium population frequency does exist at which the expected value of being heroic or cowardly is the same and the expected frequency of heroes varied inversely with group size. As the genocide parameter was relaxed and a greater proportion of the defeated group survived, the expected frequency of heroes also declined.

If the ultimate average fitness (reproductive success) for those who engage in communitarian or heroic behavior exceeds the average fitness for groups in which few people are heroic or communitarian, does their heroism or communitarianism still count as altruism? Yes and no. The answer is yes from the perspective of the in-group that benefits from the behavior, but no for the broader context, including others whom the person only encounters in war and who decidedly do not benefit from (in fact, are harmed by) the same "altruistic" actions. The discrepancy between the two ways of calculating benefit have implications for evolved psychological mechanisms promoting such behavior. We explain why in the following section, which widens the scope from our particular model's results to speculate on the likely consequences of war as a selective pressure on human cognitive and behavioral evolution.

IMPLICATIONS FOR THE CONFLICT IN AND BETWEEN GROUPS IN THE TWENTY-FIRST CENTURY

Most people, most of the time, are thankfully not engaged in open warfare in the twenty-first century. However, we do continue to live and work in group settings, and whatever shaping of human cognition and behavior that war has wrought is still with us, part of the motivational complex (Gat, 2000) that selects from among a complex repertoire of potential actions. In this section, we go beyond the simulation results to suggest some implications the psychology of war might offer in understanding intergroup and intragroup behavior. For this discussion, we draw broadly on both psychological literature and other material on war.

One reader of an earlier draft of this chapter suggested that opening with the example of emergent warfare on an isolated Polynesian island was inappropriate for an essay "about war in the Pleistocene." We kept the opening because it helps signal that we are not just interested in war in the remote past; we are also interested in how human beings in general behave in groups. We believe that the consequences of selective pressures exerted by war might help us understand not only why the population of an isolated island fragmented and retreated into hilltop fortifications sometime in the fifteenth or sixteenth century (Kennett, Anderson, Prebble, Conte, and Southon, 2006), but also why members of work groups in a Fortune 500 company tend to polarize along faultlines, increasing conflict and damaging group performance and member satisfaction (see chapter 3 in this volume).

In this section, we propose some propensities that might function as adaptations to war. We also suggest some implications of those propensities for understanding conflict more generally.

IRRATIONAL ENTHUSIASM FOR WAR

As we mentioned in the introduction, a form of cultural selection known as equilibrium selection can occur when groups with a culture that promotes group-serving behavior outcompete groups that lack such reward systems (Boyd and Richerson, 1990). Behavior aimed at securing rewards specified by the culture requires little explanation, and clearly many societies actively promote and reward behaviors that, absent such rewards, would be counted as altruistic. For example, if serving in the army was expected to pose a small threat of actual danger and was rewarded handsomely with huge salaries and high societal prestige, it would surprise no one if many people actively sought to enlist. What is harder to understand is why people would flock to recruiting stations when the expected costs of joining the army sharply increase, as they do when a country is openly preparing for war. The logic of multi-level selection may provide a partial answer.

When the average global payoff for actions (assessed across the whole population) is positive but appears to be suboptimal when assessed locally, then rational calculations based on local information will dissuade people from action that may be ultimately beneficial. Cultural reward systems can help to tilt the scales, but getting people to embrace behavior that does not appear to be in their own self-interest should continue to be a hard sell. A motivational system capable of promoting such actions in the absence or insufficiency of culturally determined rewards will therefore need to disable the tendency to rely on rational cost/benefit analyses.

We believe this may help explain how the notable tendency of people to disregard the seemingly obvious dangers of war and get caught up in irrational enthusiasm for military adventures could have developed. LeShan (2002) documents both the human attraction to war and the profoundly unrealistic convictions (he calls this "mythic reality") that take hold of people as a group or society transitions from peacetime to wartime. If groups that included people invigorated by the prospect of bloody battles outcompeted groups that did not, such "irrational" enthusiasms would ultimately be an asset. As Montesquieu (quoted in LeShan, 2002, p. 33) noted, "A rational army would run away," but running away is a sure path to defeat and likely slaughter. Hence, we expect that at least some of the cognitive and behavioral propensities selected by war will prove difficult to square with rational calculations.

How is this relevant to teams in organizations? Once an intergroup conflict is openly labeled as war or develops features that prompt a group to interpret the situation as war, attempts to reason with the parties involved should have little or no effect. This is analogous to the disabling of rational thought that occurs when individuals become highly emotionally aroused—for example, when they are in the grip of panic or rage. In the case of an individual, the most pressing first step is to get the person involved calmed down so he or she is capable of processing information more systematically. Similarly, members of groups who have shifted to a mythic mentality need to be shifted out of that mentality to regain their connection to ordinary sensory reality.

LeShan (2002) suggests that stress and uncertainty increase the tendency to shift to mythic reality and that once the shift is made, the satisfying experience of bonding with the in-group provides a powerful reward. Members of a group that have bonded in the crucible of intense intergroup conflict are likely to discount or ignore anticipated negative outcomes for the group, as evidenced by the tenacity of German fighting units that kept up their resistance in World War II long after eventual defeat had become a virtual certainty. As reported by Shils and Janowitz (1948), the most powerful countervailing force in these strongly bonded units was a soldier's concern for a different primary group—his family. Redirecting group members' attention to other important relationships that might be damaged by the conflict is thus one strategy for spilling wind out of the intergroup conflict's sails. In intractable cases, another solution is to break up the groups involved and reassign people to different units.

Results from a study using the intergroup prisoner's dilemma (IPD) game showed that when people were able to communicate with other in-group members (the typical situation for any team that deserves the name), participants tended to increase their contributions to the group even when this resulted in a worse outcome for everyone—including self, in-group, and out-group. The structure of the game models unhelpful contributions that divert a group away from productive activity and toward intergroup hostility. When intragroup communication was not permitted, people decreased their contributions and achieved the outcome that was best for everyone (Goren and Bornstein, 2000). Separated from their groups, members resort to being individuals again and focus primarily on their own outcomes.

RAISE THE BARRICADES AND CONTAIN THE EMPATHY RESPONSE

Along with the reduced capacity to reason realistically about the conflict, another mechanism that is adjusted in a war situation is a general concern for other human beings. Caring stops abruptly at the in-group boundary. War, unlike peaceful interactions such as trade, does not require the mutual consent of both groups. Any group that lacks members willing to defend the group, with force if necessary, is at a disadvantage. Despite the ample historical evidence that people are quite capable of killing one another, often with disturbing enthusiasm, Grossman (1995) argues that the majority of humans are, like most other mammals, disinclined to kill conspecifics. According to Grossman (1995), soldiers must overcome or disable a natural and intense resistance to killing other human beings. Cognitive strategies and strong emotions triggered by war that help remove this "safety catch" should convey a military advantage. A clear boundary between us and them helps. Consistent with Grossman's perspective, and in line with the extreme moral convictions evoked by the transition to mythic reality, Ernest Becker (1975) asserts that "[m]ost men will not usually kill unless it is under the banner of some kind of fight against evil." The proper response to people defined as evil is not a caring response, but denunciation and attack. Because impulses are cheaper than action, we would expect to see violent emotions expressed toward enemies to be more common than violent action.

If war operates as an agent of group selection, it kills people not because of any individuating characteristics they possess, but simply because of their group membership. Hence cues that trigger war-related schemas should heighten attention to group identity and group boundaries. Evidence from experiments using the minimal group paradigm (Brewer, 1979; Tajfel, Billig, Bundy, and Flament, 1971) show how easy it is to evoke such attention, even in the absence of threat and when group membership is based on obviously trivial criteria.

Reclassifying out-group members as nonhuman and therefore not covered by the prohibition against killing could be functional in this way. Social-identity theorists explain in-group favoritism and out-group derogation as strategies to help one feel good about oneself (for example, Brewer, 1979). However, this explanation does not account for the practical function of such identity enhancement or suggest why people would abruptly experience a sharply increased need for self-enhancement in wartime. Terror management theory (TMT) (Greenberg, Solomon, and Pyszczynski, 1997) does a somewhat better job, suggesting that enhancement of self-esteem and the need to counter threats to the in-group's cultural worldview are driven by defensive motives: They protect us from "deeply rooted fears concerning our vulnerability and mortality" (p. 11). Oddly, however, given the explicit attempt to ground TMT in evolutionary thinking, the eponymous terror of the theory is existential, brought on not by any real-life threat, but by the paralyzing but ultimately abstract *knowledge* that we are mortal. We agree that the management of terror has an adaptive function, but we suggest that the terror that most needs to be managed is that evoked by the real or imagined threat of brutal violence against self and kin. From an evolutionary point of view, mechanisms that help protect one from death are more likely to evolve than mechanisms that help protect one from unwanted *thoughts* of death.

Bonding and heightened empathy for one's in-group, coupled with a sharply reduced concern for denigrated others outside the group boundary, should help frightened people overcome the "freeze response" and effectively counter the threat. A motivational system that rewards us for affirming the value of in-group culture and derogating out-group members, especially when cues indicate a war environment, can clear the way for the unpleasant but functional business of committing violence against fellow human beings.

In a context of enhanced group boundaries evoked by threat, any indicator of divided or suspect loyalties among fellow in-group members should immediately attract attention as a possible danger signal. For most of human evolution, groups did not gallop or sail or fly long distances to fight distant enemies; they fought with their neighbors, the same people they also interacted with in nonviolent ways by trading mates and goods. As LeBlanc and Register (2003) note, "Planning a massacre treacherously disguised as a feast or celebration is an example of such shifting behaviors and is a recurrent theme around the world" (p. 68). If this strategy, like the surprise dawn raid, was a common feature of early human warfare, then paranoia and suspicion of treachery could be selected for as protective mechanisms that might save one's group from disaster.

The tightening of group boundaries in response to intergroup suspicion suggests a potential extension of TMT beyond free-floating anxiety about one's own death. Terror management theory proposes that threats to one's cultural worldview endanger the psychological defense mechanisms constructed to keep existential dread at bay. The self is viewed as individual, isolated. However, if one focuses on the relational or collective self, threats to the group might be the more motivating danger, and intragroup conflict is one of those threats. Worchel's (1994) cyclical theory of group development identifies the period of decay as a time when members pay increasing attention to personal needs and when intragroup conflict and competition increase. Subgroups may form and compete for power, and disaffected members may defect to other groups as the group drifts into discontent, with most members feeling helpless to influence the group. To rescue the group from the danger of disintegration, a precipitating event is called for. Worchel (1994, p. 211) notes that "the incident may be relatively minor and unplanned, such as the rumor of mistreatment of a group member, or it may be more dramatic (a riot), and in some cases staged. In small groups, the incident may be an emotional outburst or attack by a single member." If members become anxious about the survival of the group, directing attention to a real or imagined external threat could trigger increased vigilance about defending the group culture and worldview and could spark renewed commitment and group identification. Projection of conflict outward could be functionally effective in repairing intragroup dynamics.

A RUMOR OF WAR

In our computational model, the path to war leads from overpopulation to resource scarcity, consistent with materialist theories of war (for example, Harris, 1984; Ferguson, 2000). We view this as a simplifying assumption in line with work that finds an association between resource stress and war, not as endorsement of a particular theory about one cause of war being necessarily more important than another. We do expect a perception of resource scarcity and associated suspicions that another group might threaten an important in-group resource to trigger war-adapted responses, both functional (pull the group together) and not so functional.

In his study of deadly ethnic riots, which fit our broad definition of war as coalitional violence, Horowitz (2001) found a consistent pattern of rumors that preceded deadly riots. One common theme was that the target group was planning to poison the in-group's food or water. In an atmosphere of anxiety, rumors circulated quickly and became more exaggerated, and no evidence was required for the rumor to take hold. Another common rumor was that the target group was planning an attack or that one or more members of the in-group had already been attacked. (Again, no evidence whatsoever was required for the rumor to be believed.)

In organizational contexts, analogous rumors of resource threat and impending attack can trigger intergroup war schemas. At the organizational level, the prospect of a merger or disputes between management and labor could prove to be a fertile setting for rumors of mass layoffs, for example, which are analogous to threats of annihilation by an outgroup. At the level of the work group, rumors and suspicions by subgroup members on either side of a faultline could trigger a reframing of group interaction as involving hostile intergroup rather than conflictual intragroup or interpersonal relations.

FAULTLINES AND THE IDENTIFICATION MECHANISM

When intense conflicts develop in organizations (in which people often belong to multiple groups) or within a group, which group or subgroup will they turn to as their primary in-group? If a conflict starts to split a larger group in two, how will people line up? The psychology of war provides some relevant theory.

Shaw and Wong (1989) propose that war and evolution have shaped an identification mechanism that directs people's attention to particular markers that signal shared membership in a kin group. These markers, they propose, guide people to identify with particular groups in a war situation. The markers are common language, shared phenotypic characteristics, common religion, shared homeland, and belief in a common descent.

Shaw and Wong's (1989) emphasis on the importance of kin markers suggests a testable hypothesis for the relative impact of faultlines (Lau and Murnighan, 1998): More severe and disruptive conflict among subgroups should develop when the faultlines match more of the markers that signal shared membership in a kin group. Faultlines based on characteristics such as age, gender, or status (which routinely vary among close kin) should have a less powerful impact than faultlines based on language, religion, or belief in a common descent. Phenotypic similarity is a more questionable category, based on the finding that attention to visible differences that signal coalition membership (for example, the color of a sports uniform) can dramatically reduce the tendency to notice and encode more stable phenotypic features such as skin color (Cosmides, Tooby, and Kurzban, 2003).

THE BEST DEFENSE AND WINNING AT ALL COSTS

Horowitz noted that although initial rumors of impending attack or atrocities are often unfounded, they provide a reliable predictor of what the threatened group will do once it launches its own, typically "preemptive," attack. Recall that in the surprise raid or ambush, which is likely the most ancient (and still a highly effective) war tactic, the advantage is with the attacker. If behavioral propensities related to intergroup conflict are sufficiently integrated that they tend to be coactivated, the motivations triggered by intergroup schemas should include not only defensive solidarity but also the impulse to attack. Certainly this was true of the two groups of boys (the Rattlers and the Eagles) who participated in an early study of intergroup relations conducted at Robbers Cave State Park in Oklahoma (Sherif et al., 1961). When the presence of another group was announced, "the Rattlers immediately wanted to challenge them, and to be the *first* to challenge" (Sherif et al., 1961, p. 94, emphasis in original). One Eagles member issued a challenge to the Rattlers through the staff (p. 95) before having actually met any of the other campers.

Just as means must be found to disable any sympathy for out-group members, the immoral nature of an unprovoked attack must be somehow justified. This suggests an alternate interpretation of the rumors that precede an attack. Rather than viewing these as a cause of hostilities, Horowitz (2001) suggests that the inflammatory rumors are a projection of hostile intent on the chosen target that helps rally people to the cause and justify the forthcoming attack in the guise of defense.

Unlike social identity and in-group favoritism, analysis of attack motives is not a prominent theme in the social psychological literature. A study in the TMT tradition does provide potentially relevant findings on the acceptability of unprovoked attacks in the form of hate crimes against out-group members. Participants primed to have high mortality salience by answering questions about their own death were less punitive toward hate crime perpetrators (who were clearly attacking a member of a stigmatized group) than were participants in a control condition who answer questions about dental pain (Lieberman, Arndt, Personius, and Cook, 2001). If we reinterpret the mortality salience manipulation as a cue associated with wartime conditions (in which there is a real and present danger of death), then a more lenient view of unprovoked attacks (consistent with militarily advantageous surprise attacks and raids) would make sense.

Whether a group is in the role of attacker or defender, the single most important protection against the threat of death in war is to be on the winning side. Hence, when wartime schemas are activated, a strong motivation to win at any cost may well have developed as an adaptation promoting survival via the survival of one's group. Despite historical efforts to "tame" war and make it more civilized and less lethal, the desire to win creates a constant temptation to break the rules, commit war crimes, and violate agreements to refrain, for example, from strategic bombing of civilian populations. "Total war" represents the ultimate implementation of the motivation to win at any cost. The endorsement of this strategy in team sports, the source of the famous quote "Winning isn't everything, it's the only thing" (usually attributed to Vince Lombardi, but originally coined by UCLA football coach Henry "Red" Sanders in the 1930s [Overman, 1999]), connects war and sports thematically as settings for intergroup conflict—the first lethal, the second tamed (like ritualized battle or dominance contests) to reduce or eliminate mortality.

A QUASIFUNCTIONAL PERSPECTIVE ON
WAR-ADAPTED PROPENSITIES

Many veterans who are honest with themselves will admit, I
believe, that the experiences of communal effort in battle even
under the altered conditions of modern war have been a high point
in their lives . . . which they would not want to have missed.
—J. Glenn Gray, *The Warriors* (1967, p. 124)

The thematic connection between war and sports provides a useful thread to tie together the functional and dysfunctional ways in which the legacy of war may have shaped the human tendency to resolve conflicts of interest in favor of the group. An atmosphere of threat can evoke inspiring acts of group-serving behavior (heroism) that provide an example for others and get members working effectively together. According to Alexander's (1979) balance-of-power theory, the predatory threat of other human groups and the need to combine forces with other small kin groups to create a balance of power provided the necessary and sufficient forces for the emergence of forms of group living and higher-level organization that are the basis of all of our social and economic institutions today. "I am not implying," Alexander clarifies,

> that no other forces influence group sizes and structures, but that balances of power provide the basic sizes and kinds of groups upon which secondary forces like resource distribution, population densities, agricultural and technological developments, and effects of diseases exert their influences. And I am suggesting that all other adaptations associated with group-living, such as cooperation in agriculture, fishing, or industry, are secondary—that is, that they are *responses to* [emphasis in original] group-living and neither its primary causes nor sufficient to maintain it, at least in a world not so densely crowded with humans that there is essentially no way to live alone. (Alexander, 1979, pp. 222–223)

A balance of power may also be the key to taming warlike responses and channeling them into rule-based systems of intergroup engagement, so that groups that have retreated to hilltop fortresses in fear can be coaxed down from the hills to engage in invigorating but nonlethal contests in the valleys. If the rules of competition are kept fair and standards of behavior are rigorously enforced to prevent a reversion to the more vicious forms of conflict natural to war in the wild, the potential of intergroup conflict to enhance both performance and satisfaction within groups is substantial. Recent reviews of the intragroup conflict literature (e.g., De Dreu and Weingart, 2003) provide a sobering view of intragroup conflict as having systematically negative effects on group performance and member satisfaction. Intergroup conflict can provide a powerful—but dangerous—medicine for these ills.

The theory of optimal distinctiveness (Brewer, 1991) suggests that the fundamental tension humans must negotiate in groups is to find the right balance of connection and distinctiveness. LeShan (2002) suggests that there are two ways of providing a profound and deeply satisfying resolution of this tension. The first is meditation. The second is "the way of armed group conflict" (p. 28). As LeShan notes, "What war promises differs from what it delivers." But its enduring attraction for humans, including those with experience of its worst horrors, has not been extinguished, partly because of how well it delivers in terms of a profound group experience. The problems posed by war remain unsolved, but domesticated forms of this powerfully motivating social activity, played out in the more controlled environment of organizations and work groups, may yield at least a strong echo of the intense satisfaction and peak group performance that war evokes.

ACKNOWLEDGMENTS

Thanks go to Kristin Behfar and Leigh Thompson for the invitation to write this chapter and for helpful comments and encouragement. Thanks also for insightful comments and suggestions to an anonymous reviewer, to Frances White and Warren Holmes and other members of the Evolutionary Focus Group of the Institute of Cognitive and Decision Sciences, to members of the Social Personality Brownbag Series, and to the following members of the Small Groups Lab: Ginger Cloud, K. Mullins, David Osborn, Chuck Tate, and James Warmels.

REFERENCES

Alexander, R. 1979. *Darwinism and human affairs.* Seattle: University of Washington Press.

Arrow, H. 2005. Chaos, complexity, and catastrophe: The nonlinear dynamics perspective. In S. A. Wheelan (Ed.), *The handbook of group research and practice* (pp. 201–219). Newbury Park, Calif.: SAGE Publications.

Axelrod, R. 1997. *The complexity of cooperation: Agent-based models of competition and collaboration.* Princeton, N.J.: Princeton University Press.

Becker, E. 1975. *Escape from evil.* New York: The Free Press.

Boone, J. L. (1998). The evolution of magnanimity: When is it better to give than to receive? *Human Nature, 9* (1), 1–21.

Bornstein, G. 1992. The free rider problem in intergroup conflicts over step-level and continuous public goods. *Journal of Personality and Social Psychology, 62,* 597–602.

Bornstein, G. 1994. The enhancing effect of intergroup competition on group performance. *International Journal of Conflict Management, 5*(3), 271–283.

Bornstein, G., Kugler, T., and Zamir, S. 2005. One team must win, the other need only not lose: An experimental study of an asymmetric participation game. *Journal of Behavioral Decision Making, 18,* 111–123.

Boyd, R., and Richerson, P. J. 1990. Group selection among alternative evolutionarily stable strategies. *Journal of Theoretical Biology, 145,* 331–342.

Brewer, M. B. 1991. The social self: On being the same and different at the same time. *Personality and Social Psychology Bulletin, 17,* 475–482.

Brewer, M. B. 1979. In-group bias in the minimal intergroup situation: A cognitive-motivational analysis. *Psychological Bulletin, 86,* 307–324.

Caporael, L. R., and Baron, R. M. 1997. Groups as the mind's natural environment. In J. A. Simpson and D. T. Kenrick (Eds.), *Evolutionary social psychology* (pp. 317–344). Mahwah, N.J.: Lawrence Erlbaum.

Chagnon, N. 1974. *Studying the Yanomamo.* New York: Holt, Rinehart, and Winston.

Chagnon, N. 1988. Life histories, blood revenge, and warfare in a tribal population. *Science, 239,* 985–992.

Cosmides, L., Tooby, J., and Kurzban, R. 2003. Perceptions of race. *Trends in Cognitive Sciences, 7*(4), 173–179.

De Dreu, C. K. W., and Weingart, L. R. 2003. Task versus relationship conflict and team effectiveness: A meta-analysis. *Journal of Applied Psychology, 88,* 741–749.

Dunbar, R. I. M. 1993. Coevolution of neocortical size, group size and language in humans. *Behavioral and Brain Sciences, 16*(4), 681–735.

Eibl-Eibesfeldt, I. 1979. *Biology of peace and war.* New York: Viking Press.

Ferguson, R. B. 2000. On evolved motivations for war. *Anthropological Quarterly, 73*(3), 159–164.

Fry, D. P. 2006. *The human potential for peace: An anthropological challenge to assumptions about war and violence.* New York: Oxford University Press.

Gaertner, L., and Insko, C. A. 2000. Intergroup discrimination in the minimal group paradigm: Categorization, reciprocation, or fear? *Journal of Personality and Social Psychology, 79*(1), 77–94.

Gat, A. 2000. The human motivational complex: Evolutionary theory and the causes of hunter-gatherer fighting. Part II. Proximate, subordinate, and derivative causes. *Anthropological Quarterly, 73*(2), 74–88.

Goren, H. 2001. The effect of out-group competition on individual behavior and out-group perception in the intergroup prisoner's dilemma (IPD) game. *Group Processes and Intergroup Relations, 4*(2), 160–182.

Goren, H., and Bornstein, G. 2000. The effects of intragroup communication on intergroup cooperation in the repeated Intergroup Prisoner's Dilemma (IPD) game. *Journal of Conflict Resolution, 44*(5), 700–719.

Gray, J. G. 1967. *The warriors.* New York: Harper and Row.

Greenberg, J., Solomon, S., and Pyszczynski, T. 1997. Terror management theory of self-esteem and cultural worldviews: Empirical assessments and conceptual refinements. In M. P. Zanna (Ed.), *Advances in experimental social psychology* (pp. 61–139). San Diego, Calif.: Academic Press.

Grossman, D. 1995. *On killing: The psychological cost of learning to kill in war and society.* Boston: Little, Brown.

Harris, M. 1984. A cultural materialist theory of band and village warfare: The Yanomamo test. In R. Ferguson (Ed.), *Warfare, culture, and environment.* Orlando Fla.: Academic Press.

Hays, W. L. 1988. *Statistics,* 4th edition. New York: Holt, Rinehart and Winston.

Hill, K., and Hurtado, A. M. 1991. The evolution of premature reproductive senescence and menopause in human females: An evaluation of the "grandmother" hypothesis. *Human Nature, 2,* 313–350.

Horowitz, D. L. 2001. *The deadly ethnic riot.* Berkeley: University of California Press.

Howell, N. 1979. *Demography of the Dobe !Kung.* New York: Academic Press.

Junker, L. L. 1999. *Raiding, trading, and feasting: The political economy of Philippine chiefdoms.* Honolulu: University of Hawai'i Press.

Keegan, J. 1976. *The face of battle.* New York: Penguin Group.

Keeley, L. H. 1997. *War before civilization: The myth of the peaceful savage.* New York: Oxford University Press.

Kennett, D., Anderson, A., and Winterhalder, B. 2006. The ideal free distribution, food production, and the colonization of Oceania. In D. Kennett and B. Winterhalder (Eds.), *Behavioral ecology and the transition to agriculture.* Berkeley: University of California Press.

Kennett, D. J., Anderson, A., Prebble, M., Conte, E., and Southon, J. 2006. Human impacts on Rapa, French Polynesia. *Antiquity, 80*(308), 1–15.

Kerr, N. L., and Bruun, S. E. 1983. Dispensability of member effort and group motivation losses: Free-rider effects. *Journal of Personality and Social Psychology, 44*(1), 78–94.

Kirch, P. V. 1984. *The evolution of Polynesian chiefdoms.* Cambridge, UK: Cambridge University Press.

Knauft, B. 1985. *Good company and violence.* Berkeley: University of California Press.

Latané, B., Williams, K., and Harkins, S. 1979. Many hands make light the work: The causes and consequences of social loafing. *Journal of Personality and Social Psychology, 37,* 822–832.

Lau, D. C., and Murnighan, J. K. 1998. Demographic diversity and faultlines: The compositional dynamics of organizational groups. *Academy of Management Review, 23,* 325–340.

LeBlanc, S., and Register, K. E. 2003. *Constant battles: The myth of the peaceful, noble savage.* London: St. Martin's Press.

LeShan, L. 2002. *The psychology of war: Comprehending its mystique and its madness.* New York: Helios Press.

Lieberman, J. D., Arndt, J., Personius, J., and Cook, A. 2001. Vicarious annihilation: The effect of mortality salience on perceptions of hate crimes. *Law and Human Behavior, 25*(60), 547–566.

Loehlin, J. C., Willerman, L., and Hom, J. M. 1988. Human behavior genetics. *Annual Review of Psychology, 39,* 101–133.

Mayr, E. 2001. *What evolution is.* New York: Basic Books.

Meier, B. P., and Hinsz, V. B. 2004. A comparison of human aggression committed by groups and individuals: An interindividual–intergroup discontinuity. *Journal of Experimental Social Psychology, 40,* 551–559.

Miller, G. 2000. *The mating mind.* New York: Anchor Books.

Overman, S. J. 1999. "Winning isn't everything. It's the only thing": The origin, attributions and influence of a famous football quote. *Football Studies, 2*(2).

Patton, J. Q. 2000. Reciprocal altruism and warfare: A case from the Ecuadorian Amazon. In L. Cronk, N. Chagnon, and W. Irons (Eds.), *Adaptation and human behavior: An anthropological perspective* (pp. 417–436). Hawthorne, N.Y.: Aldine de Gruyter.

Pelley, Scott. 2005. Witnessing genocide in Sudan. CBS *60 Minutes,* August 28, www.cbsnews .com/stories/2004/10/08/60minutes/main648277_page2.shtml.

Pemberton, M. B., Insko, C. A., and Schopler, J. 1996. Memory for and experience of differential competitive behavior of individuals and groups. *Journal of Personality and Social Psychology, 71,* 953–966.

Reeve, H. K. 2000. Multi-level selection and human cooperation [review of the book *Unto others: The evolution and psychology of unselfish behavior*]. *Evolution and Human Behavior, 21,* 65–72.

Ross, J. 1984. Effects of contact on revenge hostilities among the Achuara Jivaro. In R. Ferguson (Ed.), *Warfare, culture, and environment* (pp. 83–110). Orlando, Fla.: Academic Press.

Schaller, M., and Conway, L. G. 2001. From cognition to culture: The origins of stereotypes that really matter. In G. B. Moscowitz (Ed.), *Cognitive social psychology: The Princeton symposium on the legacy and future of social cognition* (pp. 163–176). Mahwah, N.J.: Lawrence Erlbaum.

Schelling, T. C. 1960. *The strategy of conflict.* Oxford, UK: Oxford University Press.

Seijts, G. H., and Latham, G. P. 2000. The effects of goal setting and group size on performance in a social dilemma. *Canadian Journal of Behavioural Science, 32*(2), 104–116.

Shaw, R. P., and Wong, Y. 1989. *Genetic seeds of warfare: Evolution, nationalism, and patriotism.* Boston: Unwin Hyman.

Sherif, M., Harvey, O. J., White, B. J., Hood, W. R., and Sherif, C. W. 1961. *Intergroup conflict and cooperation: The Robbers Cave experiment.* Norman, Okla.: Institute of Social Relations.

Shils, E. A., and Janowitz, M. 1948. Cohesion and disintegration in the Wehrmacht in World War II. *Public Opinion Quarterly, 12*(2), 280–315.

Smirnov, O., Arrow, H., Kennett, D., and Orbell, J. M. 2006. *"Heroism" in warfare as a functionally specific form of altruism.* Unpublished paper, University of Oregon, Eugene.

Sober, E., and Wilson, D. S. 1998. *Unto others: The evolution and psychology of unselfish behavior.* Cambridge, Mass.: Harvard University Press.

Stangor, C., Lynch, L., Duan, C., and Glass, B. 1992. Categorization of individuals on the basis of multiple social features. *Journal of Personality and Social Psychology, 62,* 207–218.

Tajfel, H., Billig, M., Bundy, R., and Flament, C. 1971. Social categorization and intergroup behavior. *European Journal of Social Psychology, 1,* 149–178.

Tooby, J., and Cosmides, L. 1988. The evolution of war and its cognitive foundations. Institute for Evolutionary Studies Technical Report 88–1. Cambridge, Mass.: Harvard University Department of Anthropology.

Tooby, J., and Cosmides, L. 1996. Friendship and the banker's paradox: Other pathways to the evolution of adaptations for altruism. *Proceedings of the British Academy, 88,* 119–143.

Turner, J. C. 1987. *Rediscovering the social group: A self-categorization theory.* Oxford, UK: Blackwell.

Van Vugt, Mark, De Cremer, David, and Janssen, Dirk. In press. Gender differences in cooperation and competition: The male warrior hypothesis. *Psychological Science.*

Walker, P. L. 2001. A bioarchaeological perspective on the history of violence. *Annual Review of Anthropology, 30,* 573–596.

Weber, J. M., Kopelman, S., and Messick, D. M. 2004. A conceptual review of decision making in social dilemmas: Applying a logic of appropriateness. *Personality and Social Psychology Review, 8*(3), 281–307.

Wilder, D. A. 1986. Cognitive factors affecting the success of intergroup contact. In S. Worchel and W. G. Austin (Eds.), *Psychology of intergroup relations,* 2nd edition (pp. 49–66). Chicago: Nelson-Hall.

Wildschut, T., Pinter, B., Vevea, J. L., Insko, C. A., and Schopler, J. 2003. Beyond the group mind: A quantitative review of the interindividual-intergroup discontinuity effect. *Psychological Bulletin, 129*(5), 698–722.

Williams, G. C. 1966. *Adaptation and natural selection.* Princeton, N.J.: Princeton University Press.

Wilson, M. L., and Wrangham, R. W. 2003. Intergroup relations in chimpanzees. *Annual Review of Anthropology, 32,* 363–392.

Worchel, S. 1994. You can go home again: Returning group research to the group context with an eye on developmental issues. *Small Group Research, 25,* 205–223.

Wrangham, R. W., and Peterson, D. 1996. *Demonic males: Apes and the origin of human violence.* Boston: Houghton Mifflin.

Wynne-Edwards, V. C. 1962. *Animal dispersion in relation to social behavior.* Edinburgh, UK: Oliver and Boyd.

APPENDIX 5.A: DETAILS OF THE FORMAL MODEL AND EXPLANATION OF SETTINGS FOR DIFFERENT FACTOR LEVELS

The world in the simulation consists of several territories with fixed boundaries. A territory $g = 1,2,\ldots$ is endowed with R_g natural resources. A number of individuals who populate this territory, n_g, form a group consuming its resources. Survival of the group's members is secured if resources per capita do not fall below an exogenous survival threshold, T: $R_g/n_g > T$; otherwise, the group attacks another group.

In the simulation runs reported, the number of territories was fixed at four, and each of the four territories had the same level of natural resources, R_g, fixed at 10, 25, 50, or 75 for the four "sustainable group size" conditions. T was fixed at 1.

Members of all groups have the same baseline fertility, $P_b \in [0,1]$, a natural probability of having offspring in a generation. Baseline fertility can be adjusted for each group depending on its members' average communitarianism. With the latter incorporated, the resulting baseline for the group g becomes $P_b + P_c A_g$, where $P_c > 0$ is the fertility difference between purely communitarian and noncommunitarian groups, and

$$A_g = \frac{1}{n} \sum_{i=1}^{n_g} c_i$$

is the group's average communitarianism, with $c_i \in [0,1]$ being the propensity of member i for this form of altruism. Individual communitarianism is costly to fertility, decreasing the probability of having an offspring by $x < 0$; the cost (set exogenously) is assessed proportional to c_i. The cost was varied in the runs reported in the text as described below.

In all of the simulation runs reported, baseline fertility absent communitarianism (P_b) was set at 0.1. P_c was varied by setting the maximum fertility for complete communitarianism (all members at the maximum level of 1) at .75 for the low-cost/high-benefit setting, at .5 for the medium-cost/medium-benefit setting, and at .25 for the high-cost/low-benefit setting. Cost was varied by setting x (the multiplier for reductions in fertility based on communitarianism) at .05 for low cost, .075 for medium cost, and .1 for high cost.

When population growth causes a group's resources per capita to fall below the survival threshold, that group attacks another group chosen at random. Groups must fight if attacked. Each member of a group can increase the group's fighting strength by altruistic actions in war—which we call heroism. Heroism is a continuous variable, $h_i \in [0,1]$. As with communitarianism, we assume that war fighting decreases the probability of having an offspring by $y > 0$. The group with the greater fighting strength, defined as

$$\sum_{i-1}^{n_g} h_i$$

wins. Members of the losing group die or otherwise vacate the territory; the winning group fissions, dividing its members between its original territory and the vacated territory so that resources per capita are equal in the two territories. Combining the factors above, the probability of member i of a surviving group having an offspring is

$$P_b + P_c A_g - c_i x - h_i y w$$

where $w = 0, 1, \ldots$ is the number of wars. Thus, within a single group, more communitarian individuals always have a lower probability of reproducing. The same is true for more heroic individuals if $w \neq 0$. However, groups whose members are more communitarian and heroic grow faster and are more likely to win wars. For the cost/benefit variations, we constrained y to equal x for all runs, making the cost of heroism and communitarianism equal. Because the benefits of heroism (increased probability of one's group winning a war) depend on the relative group sizes and heroism levels of other members for each encounter, it is emergent and endogenous, and hence not subject to experimental manipulation.

In each generation, an individual i may reproduce depending on its probability of having an offspring. Reproduction is asexual and stochastic. Offspring attributes are copied from the parent subject to a uniform shock with zero mean and an exogenous variance (for all runs reported, the variance was set at .02), which represents the sort of variation that sexual reproduction generates—offspring tend to resemble each parent within a range of variability. In addition, with a very small exogenous probability (set at .001 for all runs reported), offspring attributes can be drawn from a uniform distribution [0,1], which represents completely random mutation, in which an offspring's resulting trait value has no relation to the parent's value.

PART 2

CONFLICT AND GROUP PROCESSES

Chapter 6

GROUP CONFLICT AS AN EMERGENT STATE: TEMPORAL ISSUES IN THE CONCEPTUALIZATION AND MEASUREMENT OF DISAGREEMENT

Gerardo A. Okhuysen and Hettie A. Richardson

ABSTRACT

In this chapter, we suggest conflict in groups can be usefully examined as an emergent state, a construct that is dynamic in nature and varies as a function of members' interactions. Using the literature on emergent social processes, conflict, and groups as dynamic systems, we propose that emergent constructs must possess four characteristics: stability of meaning, variability over time, variability among groups that differ on other meaningful variables, and variation in consensus. Using data from 52 four-person student groups, we perform a series of tests to conclude that conceptualizing conflict as an emergent state is appropriate, and we consider the implications of such distinctions.

INTRODUCTION

The study of conflict in groups has advanced considerably over the past decade, driven by a desire to understand groups in a more fundamental manner and by a practical interest in helping groups become more effective. Although interest in and research on conflict in groups has advanced, there are many outstanding debates. For example, some findings and conclusions regarding conflict in groups are contradictory (De Dreu and Weingart, 2003), while other findings are complex and difficult to understand (Mannix and Jehn, 2004). These difficulties have been attributed to a variety of shortcomings. For instance, the psychometric properties of scales used to measure conflict have been subject to debate, leading to their refinement (Pearson, Ensley, and Amason, 2002). Theoretical distinctions, such as those between task conflict and process conflict or between conflict and emotion (Jehn and Bendersky, 2003), have also been noted as difficulties in the study of conflict.

An important—yet less remarked on—obstacle to pursuing a deeper understanding of the role conflict plays in groups is the gap that exists concerning how conflict is experienced by members of a group, how it is conceptualized theoretically, and how it is operationalized in our research. Specifically, although conflict is widely acknowledged as a dynamic element of groups, and although it is understood to be the result of the ongoing interactions among group members, most studies that examine it have used a single-point measure of the phenomenon, implicitly treating conflict as a stable and static property of groups.[1] Take, for example, examinations of the link between task conflict and performance in a problem-solving or decision-making team. Jehn (1995) suggested that task conflict and performance have a positive relationship because groups with task conflict air their differences of opinion on their work openly. This open discussion, in turn, is supposed to result in better performance as members find better ways to execute their work. Subsequent work has sometimes supported, sometimes contradicted, and sometimes rejected this hypothesis (De Dreu and Weingart, 2003). These findings, though, are largely based on single-point measures of conflict.

In this chapter, we propose two related and complementary ideas. First, we suggest that single-point measures of dynamic elements such as conflict may present a host of difficulties. Consider a straightforward example using task conflict and performance, a case in which a group is unsure of what its task is at the outset of its activities, leading to an active discussion of the task among members. As the task is defined by members, suppose consensus develops, decreasing disagreement and the need for additional discussion, and that this move toward consensus is reflected in a linear decrease in the reported amount of task conflict. Assume, furthermore, that this group performs well. If conflict is measured a single time at the beginning of this group's work, higher task conflict will be related to good performance. However, if conflict is measured at the midpoint in the group's life, a moderate level of task conflict will be related to good performance. As should be evident, if conflict is measured at the end of the group's activities, low task conflict will be related to good performance. Thus, the timing of measurement in any single study might influence the relationship found between a dynamic variable (such as conflict) and a final outcome (such as group performance). Not surprisingly, this type of finding also will be difficult to replicate, as other data sets may incorporate their own (and different) timing properties. As a possible example of the difficulty of replication, De Dreu and

Weingart (2003), in a meta-analysis examining the associations among relationship conflict, task conflict, performance, and satisfaction, conclude that no positive relationship exists between task conflict and performance.

We recognize the difficulty of examining dynamic constructs using single-point measures, and in examining these dynamic properties we rely in this chapter on recent theoretical treatments of groups as dynamic systems. This literature suggests our understanding of groups would be strengthened by an incorporation of dynamic conceptualizations, language, and constructs into our work (Arrow, McGrath, and Berdahl, 2000). However, little work has attempted to translate this theoretical understanding into empirical practice. We suggest that an appropriate strategy for investigating conflict is to conceptualize it as an emergent state, a property of a group that results from interactions among group members and that can provide the group both with structure (Morgeson and Hofmann, 1999) and with dynamic properties that vary depending on members' activities (Marks, Mathieu, and Zaccaro, 2001). We first present a brief literature background on conflict in groups and on groups as complex systems. We then articulate four conceptual and empirical properties of emergent constructs and examine conflict from the perspective of these properties. In particular, we focus on four characteristics of dynamic constructs. These include *stability of meaning*, or a consistency in interpretation; *variability over time*, or an ability to capture differences; variability among groups that differ on other meaningful variables, or a *predictive ability*; and *variation in consensus*, or an ability to capture emergent concurrence. Using data from 52 student groups working on a semester-long project, we use our analyses to explore the properties of relationship, task, and process conflict as emergent states. Finally, we consider the implications of our findings.

BACKGROUND

THE ROOTS OF CONFLICT

Conflict is typically defined as a discrepancy in perceptions or understandings among group members that can be related to several issues in the group (De Dreu and Weingart, 2003; Jehn, 1997; Jehn and Mannix, 2001). Relationship conflict, for example, comes from interpersonal difficulties, whether these derive from differences in political values or simply a general dislike of one another. Relationship conflict at high levels can be reflected in emotional displays, such as anger or frustration. Task conflict is a difference in perspectives related to the work of the group, about what is to be done, and is a discrepancy of ideas and opinions. Finally, process conflict is related to issues of coordination, about how the work is to be done. It is important to note the literature considers conflict to be the expression of these discrepancies. In other words, if individuals subsume their differences, either in the

interest of a relationship or task or because the differences are not considered important, then conflict is understood to be lessened, even if the discrepancies in perspectives remain.

Over time, research has changed its perspective on the value of conflict (Jehn
and Bendersky, 2003) from having a consistently negative evaluation of the role of
conflict in groups (e.g., Hackman and Morris, 1975) to current perspectives that suggest conflict can have some positive outcomes (for example, Amason, 1996; Jehn,
1995). In particular, research that examines the expression of authentic conflict
(Nemeth, Connell, Rogers, and Brown, 2001) and the introduction of task conflict
into groups through the use of a devil's advocate has suggested that conflict may
improve the quality of decision making (Amason, 1996; Eisenhardt, 1989). The
exploration of the potentially positive outcomes of conflict is rooted in a belief that
passive, accommodating, and consensus-driven teams do not always engage in careful analysis of alternatives for decisions (Eisenhardt, 1989; Nemeth et al., 2001).

DYNAMIC ELEMENTS IN GROUPS

Conceptualizations of conflict have always had at their core a characterization of
conflict as a dynamic variable in the group. As such, attention to conflict has
responded to a consistent drumbeat calling for a focus on process as an explanatory element of group activity (Hackman and Morris, 1975; Marks et al., 2001) that
goes hand in hand with calls for longitudinal explorations of group phenomena
(Marks et al., 2001; McGrath, 1984). This focus on dynamic elements, however,
has been restricted by the use of cross-sectional designs that reflect an input/
output perspective, albeit with process measures taking the role of inputs into the
group. As such, constructs reflecting group dynamics often have been operationalized as static properties (Jehn and Mannix, 2001). Although this approach has
been beneficial and has substantially advanced our thinking about various group
processes, it is also problematic because it cannot always reflect the real-life group
phenomena that it attempts to characterize. Although there is still considerable
room for the exploration of groups using cross-sectional methods that assume some
degree of stability in the group, it is also clear that researchers must begin to engage
groups as they are—that is, as entities with dynamic elements. Recent advances in
our thinking on the dynamic nature of groups (and other social systems) are useful in suggesting how we might proceed in such an examination from a theoretical
point of view.

DYNAMIC APPROACHES TO UNDERSTANDING GROUPS

The focus on groups as dynamic systems is not new. For example, a research team led
by Joseph McGrath (1993) collected voluminous data from student groups working
on a variety of tasks during two semesters. These studies (labeled JEMCO 1 and

JEMCO 2) were quite ambitious and insightful, but they also pointed to the problems that appear when using dynamic perspectives to study groups. These difficulties
are best described by some of the researchers themselves; for example, Arrow et al.,
(2000, p. 276) suggest that consideration of groups as dynamic systems provides
results that are "too complicated for definitive analysis." These researchers similarly
note the difficulty with standard study designs for these groups, because "[n]o one
design is satisfactory in all respects." As the authors explain, the JEMCO studies suffered from their ambition, with perhaps an excessive number of objectives for phenomena they tried to explain (which ranged from the effects of communication
media and membership change to the effects of different tasks on the group).

Although these early examinations of groups as dynamic systems pointed to difficulties, recent developments in our conceptualization of social processes may be
helpful in guiding us to more general theoretical approaches, while also providing
specificity for operationalizing research. In particular, recent progress in how we conceptualize social systems can help us simplify a dynamic approach and, at the same
time, allow us to gain a more complete understanding of the elements that make up
a dynamic system. One useful perspective is the elaboration of collective constructs
(Morgeson and Hofmann, 1999) that reflect phenomena emerging from the interactions of lower-level entities and that can provide structure for subsequent interactions. In addition, a recent emphasis on time and temporal issues has provided
important insights and tools for examining dynamic social systems. Zaheer, Albert,
and Zaheer (1999) describe how the use of timescales (time intervals of different
lengths) forces us to clearly specify the time period over which phenomena take
place, helping us advance our understanding of organizational processes through better theory development and specification. Timescales help us understand dynamic
systems by providing us with a means to distinguish between variables that change at
different rates, such as group norms and group emotion. Similarly, Marks et al.
(2001) propose a taxonomy of group process that uses the episodic nature of group
activity as a centerpiece. These episodes of activity can simultaneously account for
the multitasking nature of the group and for the changing nature of group elements
through growth or decay. Finally, Arrow et al. (2000), learning from the JEMCO
studies, propose a complete framework for examining groups as complex systems.
Their detailed treatment of different pressures (internal and external, individual and
group, task and process) highlights how elements within groups can be differentiated when they are examined through a lens that accounts for their dynamic properties.

A particularly useful contribution from the work on dynamic social systems has
come from characterizations of different types of dynamic elements and the properties they possess. For example, authors have attempted to characterize processes,
attractors, and emergent states in a detailed manner. Marks et al. (2001, p. 357), for
instance, reserve the label of group "process" for "members' interdependent acts . . .
to achieve collective goals." Thus, the focus is principally on process as task-oriented
interdependent action. Arrow et al. (2000, p. 41) define "attractors" as regions where

variables "settle into certain values." These attractors can "affect the overall trajecto-ry" of groups and include properties of groups that are stable across longer timescales. Examples might include norms such as "group value consensus," the extent to which members agree on underlying organizing values (Jehn and Mannix, 2001). A third type of dynamic property is an "emergent state," a property of the group that is "typ-ically dynamic in nature and [varies] as a function of team context, inputs, process-es, and outcomes" (Marks et al., 2001, p. 357). Emergent states have "mutable qual-ities" that are "fluid and more easily influenced by context" (Marks et al., 2001, p. 358).

This theoretical differentiation between types of dynamic elements in groups is valuable because it gives us the tools to explicitly consider questions of timescales and stability. However, these advances in our theoretical understanding also have created a need for empirical specification of the different types of dynamic elements. In the next section, we attempt to characterize the empirical properties of emergent states in general and of conflict as an emergent state in particular.

EMERGENCE AS A PROPERTY OF GROUPS

Emergence is typically understood as a property that smaller or simpler entities gen-erate when they are aggregated into a collective (Holland, 1998). Some typical exam-ples are neurons aggregated into the brain, transactions aggregated into markets, and so on. A central characteristic of emergence is that the aggregation of the activities of the lower-level (and simpler) units forms a more complex entity at a higher level (Holland, 1998). For groups, emergence results from the interactions among indi-viduals, and it is from these interactions that group-level phenomena arise.

Although groups themselves can be characterized by emergence, not all proper-ties of groups (as studied in the literature) are the result of emergence. Thus, for example, the demographic characteristics of a group do not rely on the interactions among members, but rather depend on the pre-existing characteristics of members. However, other elements of group life are amenable to being viewed through an emergence lens. For example, those studying the broad field of diversity rely on argu-ments of emergence to understand how group members' differences affect the processes and outcomes of groups. The appearance of faultlines (Lau and Murnighan, 1998), for instance, is a good example of emergence in groups. The composition of the group sets the initial condition for the faultlines, but it is the interactions among members that create the consequences from the initial condi-tions. A similar example comes from work on deep-level diversity (Harrison, Price, Gavin, and Florey, 2002; Harrison, Price, and Bell, 1998), which shows that as inter-actions take place, visible demographic characteristics become less important. Instead, underlying similarities among group members (in attitudes toward work, for example) become more important to those attempting to understand their behavior.

The examples of faultlines and deep-level diversity in groups point to another element that is critical to understanding emergence in groups: the relevance of timescales. In groups, multiple phenomena coexist in a wide variety of temporal arrangements. Some of the phenomena, such as the impact of visible diversity on interactions, can appear immediately upon formation of a group. However, the impact of other elements in the group, such as deep-level similarity or diversity, may have longer gestation periods due to the need to uncover and decipher the individual-level characteristics that constitute it. The differences between timescales become important in our thinking because, as research advances to explain group behavior, the temporal arrangements between phenomena will need to be explored.

Although the emphasis so far in the literature about this topic has been on the internal dynamics of the group, the notion of emergence can also account for influences from the environment on the group and for outputs from the group to the environment. This ability to account for interactions with the environment is important for us because groups are open systems (Gladstein, 1984), and they draw resources and experiences from the environments in which they operate. The environment can cause shocks to groups as well, through the provision of feedback, for example. In addition, groups also influence their environments through their actions and outputs.

As we noted earlier, characterizing dynamic elements in groups is problematic. Many of the instruments used to measure group phenomena—such as conflict—typically are designed to capture a snapshot of a given phenomenon at a single point or on average across a temporal period. For this reason, they are conceptually incongruent with capturing phenomena that are dynamic over varying time intervals. Although existing literature suggests what the properties of an emergent construct might be from a theoretical perspective, the properties of emergence from an empirical perspective are vague. In the following section, we describe four conceptual properties of constructs that attempt to capture emergent states and begin to address some of the empirical implications of those properties.

PROPERTIES OF AN EMERGENT STATE

One way researchers can use the concept of emergence to understand groups is to characterize elements in the group according to their emergent characteristics. We suggest that constructs that attempt to capture emergent states have four properties that are relevant for the constructs' conceptual and empirical meaning. Specifically, the properties are (1) stability of meaning across time, individuals (within and between groups), and contextual influences; (2) true variability in level or intensity over time; (3) differences in patterns of variability among groups that differ on other meaningful variables; and (4) variation among group members in consensus regarding assessments of level or intensity.

Stability of meaning across time. First, an emergent state must be understood or comprehended in the same way over time such that there is "stability of meaning" in the construct being measured. Though emergent states are, by definition, dynamic and mutable, the underlying domain of a given emergent state should not be. Instead, the underlying conceptual domain of the emergent state—as understood by group members and the researcher alike—should remain constant over time. Conceptually, consistency is desirable because it pushes us toward parsimony. As we attempt to understand group phenomena, one challenge we face is trying to characterize similar—yet varied—incidents of social life. A desire for conceptual consistency forces us to carefully aggregate these incidents into an abstract construct while simultaneously fending off a tendency to consider phenomena together that might be distinct. Thus, though levels of the construct may change depending on when a measure is taken (for example, group members may experience high conflict today but low conflict tomorrow), actual understanding among group members and others about what conflict is should remain constant. Otherwise, there is the possibility that supposed assessments of a single proposed emergent state are in reality capturing two or more conceptually distinct group properties—even if, for instance, the same measurement instrument is used at both times.

Consider the example of relationship conflict. If the *understanding* of relationship conflict is mutable, rather than the perceptions about the presence or absence of relationship conflict in the group, then existing measurement techniques are not equipped to capture it as a dynamic construct. However, a consistent understanding of relationship conflict does not mean that group members necessarily agree with one another in their assessments of the presence, absence, or level of such conflict. Rather, consistent understanding implies that people conceptually think about relationship conflict in the same way (for example, as interpersonal difficulties)—regardless of time, group membership, individual differences, or other contextual influences. Such consistency ensures that, as scientists, we have successfully developed meaningful constructs that simplify group life while simultaneously acknowledging its complexity.

Variability over time. Morgeson and Hofmann (1999) argue that emergent properties appear and change as a function of social interaction. As group members develop recognition of the properties that characterize their group over time, emergent states appear. This developed recognition also implies that emergent states are not static but can change in intensity based on the nature and extent of member interaction. Thus, emergent states have the ability to change in level or value over an appropriate time scale, and we suggest that this variability is the second characteristic of an emergent construct. For groups, appropriate time scales can include a single performance episode, multiple performance episodes, or even the life of the group. More specifically, we argue that although a construct does not *have* to change in intensity over the life of a group, it must have the *ability* to do so within that timescale if it is to be considered an emergent state. As such, measures of an emergent construct must be able to capture differences in actual levels of the construct rather than, for example, differences in respondents' conceptualization of the construct (as noted earlier). The latter also means that, necessarily, an emergent construct cannot be adequately captured through single-point estimates.

Difference in patterns of variability. Morgeson and Hofmann (1999, p. 254) also argued that emergent properties can be understood through their function, where function is defined as the causal outputs or effects of a given construct. If an emergent construct is to be useful in increasing understanding about groups, then we would expect patterns of emergence to vary among groups that also differ in other meaningful ways—such as among groups that have achieved different levels of performance on the same task. In other words, differences in patterns of emergent states across groups should be related to other meaningful differences across those groups. As such, we suggest that emergent states should be associated with certain outcomes. Although there should be consistency in how the emergent construct is understood across those outcomes (as per our first property of an emergent state), there also should be variability in the true levels and intensity of the construct across relevant outcomes. To illustrate, the theoretical function of relationship conflict suggests that different levels and rates of change in relationship conflict are likely to be associated with different levels of performance, even though low performers must understand relationship conflict in the same way as high performers do.

Variation in consensus across time. Finally, within the appropriate timescale, members are likely to exhibit varying degrees of within-group consensus regarding their assessments of the level or intensity of an emergent construct. For example, when a group is newly formed, when members have no prior experience with one another, and when members have interacted very little, it is less likely they will report similar levels of task conflict—for they have little common experience and interaction on which to base their assessments. On the other hand, as group members work together for longer periods of time, the group may develop characteristic levels of conflict, and members may become more consistent in their assessment of whether they are experiencing low or high levels of conflict. In addition, environmental shocks to the group—a change in membership, a change in task, or reassessment due to an approaching deadline—may cause group members to temporarily disagree regarding the experienced level of task conflict, until further group interactions allow new, consistent perceptions of task conflict to reemerge.

These changing levels of consensus are important because researchers typically rely on indices of rater consensus as criteria for justifying the aggregation of individual responses to the group level (Bliese, 2000). We suggest that the concept of emergent states implies that, depending on when a measure is taken, researchers should not necessarily expect group members to exhibit consensus about the level or intensity of a construct that is perceived. However, there should always be times at which group members exhibit strong consensus about the perceived intensity of an emergent state. In some instances, it also might be reasonable to expect a pattern of consensus and disagreement to develop across performance episodes or in the face of recurring environmental shocks.

In the next section, we first describe the sample we used to examine the emergent properties of relationship conflict, task conflict, and process conflict. We follow this with descriptions of the analytical procedures and results.

Sample and Methods

Sample

The study was part of a 15-week-long introductory organizational behavior course in a public university in the southwestern United States. During the first week of class, the instructor randomly assigned four individuals to each of 52 groups. The average age of participants was 21 years, and the sample was 32 percent female. The task for the groups was an open-ended project in which the students conducted research on a specific organization to examine it through any one of the analytical frameworks learned in class. The final outcome of each group's work was a written report. Typical reports discussed chief executive officer (CEO) succession, financial fraud, employee selection practices, and so on. For the vast majority of the projects, this report entailed library archival research about a particular focal company. A few reports relied on interviews in addition to archival materials if students had access to individuals who worked or had worked for the focal company.

Data Collection

In the first week, individuals completed questionnaires regarding conflict in their groups immediately after their first in-class meeting. The questionnaire used Jehn's (1995) Intragroup Conflict Scale. This scale includes nine items and characterizes conflict as having three components: task conflict, relationship conflict, and process conflict. Individuals also completed this questionnaire in weeks 5, 9, and 13 of the 15-week semester. Response rates were relatively constant (around 95 percent) across all four data collection moments (see Table 6.1).

Table 6.1
Response Rates per Week (n = 208)

	Week 1	Week 5	Week 9	Week 13
Percent respondents	94%	95%	94%	94%

In addition to the data collected through questionnaires, we also collected performance data as the average grade awarded by two independent raters on the final written report. Each rater could award a maximum of 20 points for each report, and every group member received the same score. The two performance ratings were highly correlated, .73 (p = .001). In no report was the difference in the number of points awarded greater than 2. (In 63 percent of the cases, there was only a 1-point difference, or no difference, in the scores awarded by the two raters.)

ANALYTICAL PROCEDURES

In this section, we describe the analytical procedures we used to test the three types of group conflict to determine the extent to which they exhibit the characteristics of an emergent state. For clarity of presentation, we divide the following discussion into four sections, with each representing the tests conducted for each characteristic of an emergent state: (1) consistent interpretation over time, or stability of meaning, (2) ability to change over time, or variability, (3) differences in patterns of variability among groups that differ on other meaningful variables, or predictive validity, and (4) variation in within-group consensus over time.

Testing for Stability of Meaning across Time

Following the procedure described by Chan (1998), we first examined the extent to which each conflict variable (that is, relationship conflict, task conflict, and process conflict) exhibited measurement invariance over time. In other words, we examined whether the three types of conflict exhibited evidence that respondents conceptualized conflict and the scales used to measure conflict differently across the four measurement occasions. These analyses specifically tested for the presence of beta and gamma change in the conflict constructs (Riordan, Richardson, Schaffer, and Vandenberg, 2001). Beta change occurs when respondents recalibrate the rating scale on which items comprising a given construct are measured such that differences in the construct scores actually represent altered interpretations of the rating-scale anchors. Gamma change occurs when respondents reconceptualize the domain of a construct between measurement occasions; this change essentially indicates that the construct being measured over time is not the same. If either beta or gamma change was present, we concluded group members did not have a consistent understanding of a given type of conflict between the beginning and end of the task activities. As such, the first criterion for an emergent state would not be met, and it would be impossible to examine that construct for true variability over time.

To establish measurement invariance over the four measurement occasions, we estimated a hierarchical series of five nested models (Chan, 1998) separately for each of the three types of conflict. Each model comprised four latent constructs, each representing a given conflict measure at times 1, 2, 3, and 4. Likewise, each of the four constructs was measured using the three associated items from the appropriate time period. The five models varied, however, in that each imposed increasing restrictions (i.e., equal factor loadings, error variances, factor means, and factor variances) on the estimated parameters across time. Support for equal factor loadings would be sufficient to establish measurement invariance over time. Support for equal error variances over time would provide a stricter test of measurement invariance. Nonetheless, when there are true changes in a construct over time, it is not unreasonable to expect error variances to differ as well—even for a truly invariant construct (Chan, 1998). Support for unequal factor means and variances would provide initial support for the following phase of analyses. Details regarding each model estimated can be found in appendix 6.A.

Testing for Variability over Time

Theoretically, relationship conflict, task conflict, and process conflict do have the ability to change over time. In this phase of analyses, however, we empirically tested whether they did change over time in our data. If they did, we examined their patterns of change. Specifically, we used latent growth modeling (LGM), again in a series of nested models for each construct separately. In this latter phase, three models were estimated for each construct: a no-growth model, a linear growth model, and a curvilinear or quadratic model. Detailed descriptions of these models also are found in appendix 6.A. Poor fit for the no-growth model combined with support for either the linear or quadratic models would provide evidence of the existence and nature of variability in level or intensity over time.

Testing for Differences in Patterns of Variability

The third property of an emergent state is that it exhibits differing patterns of emergence among groups that differ in some other meaningful way. In other words, all groups should not exhibit identical levels and rates of variability. Because researchers have proposed that conflict might be experienced differently by those who achieve differing levels of performance (Jehn and Mannix, 2001)—or that patterns of variability in conflict may be predictive of performance—we chose to examine the extent to which patterns of change in conflict across time varied between high performers and low performers.[2] The median level of average performance (as rated by the two raters) was 16.00. Thus, we defined high-performing groups as those that earned an average performance score of 16.00 or better ($n = 94$) and low-performing groups as those that earned an average performance score of less than 16.00 ($n = 71$), after accounting for individuals with missing data. Individuals were assigned to the high- and low-performance designations based on their particular group's average performance.

For this phase of analyses, we estimated models that were similar to those in the previous step, but we modeled variability over time simultaneously for both high and low levels of performance. The purpose of these multigroup models was to fully determine if any significant differences existed in the patterns of change in the three types of conflict between the high and low performers and, if so, what the nature of the differences was. Prior to estimating multigroup LGM models, however, LGM models identical to those estimated for the entire sample were analyzed for high and low performers separately. The purpose of these models was to establish the shape of change for each group of respondents. Provided the same shape was found for both groups for a given type of conflict, it was appropriate to estimate the multigroup LGM models for that type of conflict in order to test for subtler differences in rates of and variance in change. If different shapes were found (for example, one linear, one curvilinear), there was evidence that the pattern of change was fully different between the groups and that multigroup analyses could not be estimated.

When multigroup LGM analyses were appropriate, seven additional models were estimated in which intercept, slope, and quadratic factor means and variances were successively constrained to be equal between high and low performers. If constraining a certain parameter to be equal between the groups produced significantly worse fit in the data, then there was evidence that parameter was significantly different for high and low performers. Again, details of the final seven models tested are presented in appendix 6.A.

Testing for Variation in Consensus across Time

Intraclass correlation coefficient (ICC) values were used to examine the level of within-group consensus of ratings for each type of conflict at each time period. ICC(1) is a measure of the internal consistency, or interrelatedness, of ratings among raters (Shrout and Fleiss, 1979). As such, it can be conceptualized as the extent to which raters are substitutable for one another. It has also been suggested that ICC(1) represents the proportion of total variance that can be explained by group membership (Bryk and Raudenbush, 1992). ICC(2) indicates the degree of agreement of group members' ratings for each type of conflict. Once a construct has fully emerged within a group and/or has reemerged following an environmental shock, we would expect that group members' ratings of conflict would be substitutable for one another and also that the ratings would more likely be a function of group membership than of individual perceptions or differences. In this situation, we also would expect group members to agree about the levels of conflict experienced within their groups.

RESULTS

Testing for Stability of Meaning across Time

Table 6.2 shows fit statistics and model comparison results for all five models estimated in order to examine the first property of emergent states: consistent conceptualization across the entire sample, over time. All three types of conflict show evidence of measurement invariance as indicated by a nonsignificant change in fit between the unconstrained model and model 2. Further, because these analyses are at the individual level, the results not only indicate invariance over time but regardless of group

Table 6.2
Model Fit and Comparison for Determining Stability of Meaning across Time for the Entire Sample

	χ^2 (d.f.)	RMSEA	NNFI	CFI	Model Comparison	$\Delta\chi^2$ (Δd.f.)
Relationship conflict						
Model 1: Unconstrained	47.45 (48)	.00	1.00	1.00		
Model 2: Equal factor loadings	48.80 (54)	.00	1.00	1.00	1 versus 2	1.35 (6)
Model 3: Equal error variances	115.83* (63)	.07	.97	.97	2 versus 3	67.03* (9)
Model 4: Equal factor means	235.71* (57)	.11	.88	.90	2 versus 4	186.91* (3)
Model 5: Equal factor variances	181.72* (57)	.10	.92	.93	2 versus 5	132.92* (3)
Task conflict						
Model 1: Unconstrained	62.49 (48)	.05	.99	.99		
Model 2: Equal factor loadings	68.37 (54)	.05	.99	.99	1 versus 2	5.88 (6)
Model 3: Equal error variances	228.88* (63)	.13	.92	.92	2 versus 3	160.51* (9)
Model 4: Equal factor means	170.81* (57)	.10	.94	.95	2 versus 4	102.44* (3)
Model 5: Equal factor variances	124.70* (57)	.08	.96	.97	2 versus 5	56.33* (3)
Process conflict						
Model 1: Unconstrained	53.73 (48)	.02	1.00	1.00		
Model 2: Equal factor loadings	57.98 (54)	.02	1.00	1.00	1 versus 2	4.25 (6)
Model 3: Equal error variances	131.70* (63)	.09	.96	.97	2 versus 3	73.72* (9)
Model 4: Equal factor means	136.39* (57)	.09	.95	.96	2 versus 4	78.41* (3)
Model 5: Equal factor variances	133.83* (57)	.08	.96	.96	2 versus 5	75.85* (3)

* $p \leq .05$

membership as well. Due to its superior fit, the second model was retained for comparison with model 3 in all cases. Likewise, across all three types of conflict, the second model fit significantly better than models 3, 4, and 5. The significant decrease in fit between the second and third models suggests that the error variances within type of conflict are not equal across time and, according to Chan (1998), differences in true variance across time exist. The significant decrease in fit between the second and fourth models indicates that factor means for each type of conflict are not equal over time. As such, there is further evidence that significant true intraindividual change occurs within the data, and it is appropriate to model latent growth for each type of conflict.

Before considering the differences between models 2 and 5, it is first worthwhile to examine the latent factor means for each type of conflict as established in model 2. Changes in latent factor means are presented in graphic form in Figure 6.1, and the actual factor means at each measurement occasion are shown in Table 6.3. Note that, for the changes in means shown in Figure 6.1, time 1 means are set to a value of 0, such that the mean value at each of the remaining measurement occasions represents the difference in value between that time period and time 1. As illustrated, the general trend among all three types of conflict is for possible quadratic, rather than simply linear, change. For both relationship conflict and process conflict, responses exhibit a positive linear trend in the earlier measurement periods before decreasing in conflict by time 4. For process conflict, responses decrease to a level similar to their initial level by time 4, whereas for relationship conflict the final level remains greater than the initial level reported. Unlike with relationship conflict and process conflict, task conflict responses decrease in magnitude across all four measurement periods—although the rate of decrease appears to lessen slightly between times 3 and 4.

Finally, the significant difference between the second and fifth models across all three types of conflict indicates that factor variances for each are not equal across time. According to Chan (1998), factor variances reflect interindividual differences in true scores over time. For relationship conflict, factor variances are .40, 1.22, 1.57, and 3.17 for times 1 through 4, respectively. Task conflict variances are .89, 2.13, 2.55, and 2.30. Process conflict variances are 1.01, 2.06, 3.26, and 4.43. Factor covariances for all three types of conflict are positive and statistically significant at p = .05. These patterns of variances generally suggest that, at time 1, individuals have similar origins (as might be expected, given that they were all members of newly formed groups) but experience all three types of conflict differently over time. Change over time is confirmed and the precise nature of the growth curves established, however, in the following analyses.

Testing for Variability over Time

Table 6.4 shows fit statistics and model comparison results for the three latent growth models estimated for each type of conflict. The table also presents some key param-

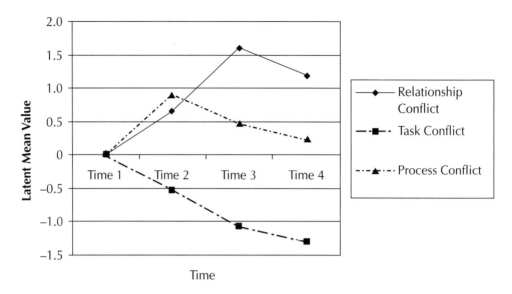

Figure 6.1
Change in Latent Means across Time for the Entire Sample

eters estimated in models 2 and 3 for each of the three conflict variables. For all three types of conflict, model 2 fit significantly better than model 1, indicating that some form of growth is likely and that it is appropriate to examine models 2 and 3. In all cases, the third model also fit significantly better than the second model, indicating that the growth is not simply linear in nature but is, in fact, quadratic. Quadratic growth implies that the growth changes direction at some point in time—that there are paths of both acceleration and deceleration for each type of conflict. This finding largely confirms the pattern of factor means graphed in Figure 6.1.

Given that model 3 is always the superior-fitting model in our data, it is useful to specifically consider the factor means and variances of the second-order intercept, slope, and quadratic factors (also shown in Table 6.4) for each type of conflict. In all cases, the intercept mean value represents the average intercept as estimated from the individual intercepts across the entire sample, and the intercept variance represents variability in individual intercepts about the average estimated intercept. Similarly, the slope mean value is the average estimated slope (or growth trajectory) for a given type of conflict across time, and the slope variance is the average variability in slope. Finally, the quadratic mean value represents the average decelerating component of the growth trajectory for relationship conflict and process conflict and the average accelerating trajectory for task conflict. Again, the quadratic variance indicates variability in the quadratic component.

Table 6.3
Actual Latent Factor Means for the Entire Sample and for High and Low Performers Separately

Conflict Type	Time 1			Time 2			Time 3			Time 4		
	All	High	Low	All	High	Low	All	High	Low	All	High	Low
Relationship	1.95	1.96	1.94	2.56	2.26	2.89	3.43	3.17	3.73	3.07	2.63	3.58
Task	3.96	4.06	3.86	3.37	3.31	3.44	2.85	2.67	3.05	2.57	2.54	2.61
Process	3.14	3.14	3.14	3.90	3.97	3.82	3.45	3.32	3.58	3.27	2.94	3.63

Table 6.4
LGM Model Fit and Comparison for the Entire Sample

	χ^2(d.f.)	RMSEA	NNFI	CFI	Model Comparison	$\Delta\chi^2$(Δd.f.)	Intercept Mean (variance)	Slope Mean (variance)	Quadratic Mean (variance)
Relationship conflict									
Model 1: No growth	439.47* (52)	.20	.72	.78					
Model 2: Linear	163.72* (49)	.12	.91	.94	1 versus 2	275.75* (3)	1.90* (.15*)	.68* (.15*)	
Model 3: Quadratic	105.85* (45)	.10	.95	.97	2 versus 3	57.87* (4)	1.76* (−.10)	1.32* (.04)	−.26* (−.06)
Task Conflict									
Model 1: No growth	379.66* (52)	.20	.81	.85					
Model 2: Linear	93.63* (49)	.08	.97	.98	1 versus 2	286.03* (3)	3.89* (.94*)	−.40* (.22*)	
Model 3: Quadratic	66.61* (45)	.06	.99	.99	2 versus 3	27.02* (4)	3.89* (1.35*)	−.67* (1.18*)	.08* (.05*)
Process conflict									
Model 1: No growth	337.61* (52)	.18	.82	.86					
Model 2: Linear	181.74* (49)	.14	.90	.93	1 versus 2	155.87* (3)	3.11* (.94*)	.10 (.35*)	
Model 3: Quadratic	111.91* (45)	.09	.95	.97	2 versus 3	69.83* (4)	3.04* (.80*)	.74* (.88*)	−.19* (.20*)

Note: Unstandardized values shown for intercept, slope, and quadratic means and variances.

* $p \le .05$

LGM = Latent growth modeling

Beginning with relationship conflict, the nonsignificant variance parameters from the superior-fitting model 3 indicate that there is no significant variability in respondents' initial status for this construct and that respondents increase and decrease at very similar rates. The means values of 1.32 and −.26 for the slope and quadratic factors, respectively, suggest that once deceleration begins, the rate of increase for relationship conflict is greater than its rate of decrease. Like those for relationship conflict, the parameters for process conflict suggest that it is characterized by significant positive growth in earlier measurement occasions and significant negative growth in latter measurement occasions, with acceleration occurring at a greater rate than deceleration. Unlike for relationship conflict, however, variances for the intercept, slope, and quadratic factors of process conflict are all significant. The latter indicates that there is significant variability in the initial status of individuals on this construct and that there is significant variability in respondents' rates of positive and negative change across time. Although not shown in Table 6.4, the covariances between the initial status factor and the slope and quadratic factors for process conflict are .28 (nonsignificant [ns]) and −.06 (ns), respectively. This indicates that there is not a significant relationship between the level of process conflict reported by respondents at time 1 and the rate at which process conflict increases or decreases at later time periods. For example, respondents reporting high initial levels of process conflict do not necessarily experience increased process conflict at greater rates than those reporting low initial levels, or vice versa. The significant covariance of −.34 (p = .05) between the slope and quadratic factors suggests that respondents exhibiting higher rates of acceleration in process conflict are likely to also exhibit lower rates of deceleration.

Task conflict is the only variable for which LGM results indicate negative growth during the earlier measurement occasions and possible positive growth during the later ones. Significant variances for the intercept, slope, and quadratic factors indicate that there is variability in the initial status of individuals on this construct and that there is significant variability in rates of positive and negative change for task conflict across time. Note that the rate of acceleration, as indicated by the quadratic mean value, is very small (even though it is statistically significant). This very small rate of acceleration is likely one reason why no clear acceleration for task conflict can be seen in Figure 6.1. As with process conflict, the covariances between the initial status factor and the slope (−.39; ns) and quadratic factors (.07; ns) for task conflict are not significant, indicating that there is no relationship between the level of task conflict reported by respondents at time 1 and the rate at which it decreases or increases at later time periods. Significant covariance of −.23 (p = .05) between the slope and quadratic factors suggests that respondents exhibiting higher rates of deceleration in task conflict are likely also to exhibit lower rates of acceleration—as might be expected as respondents near completion of the task. Overall, these results suggest that true variability over time does exist for all three types of conflict, and they provide an indication of the nature of intra- and interindividual patterns of variability for each.

Testing for Differences in Patterns of Variability

Results for the multigroup analyses are presented in Table 6.5. Recall that prior to estimating multigroup LGM models, however, LGM models identical to those estimated for the entire sample were analyzed separately for high and low performers. For high performers, the final model obtained for all types of conflict specifies quadratic growth. For low performers, the quadratic model was obtained for relationship conflict and process conflict, but not for task conflict. As is suggested by Figure 6.3, only linear negative growth appears to occur for low performers on task conflict. Because the nature of growth in task conflict is so different for high performers and low performers, it is not appropriate to estimate the multigroup LGM models for this variable. Nonetheless, this difference does confirm substantial variation in patterns of change for task conflict that are associated with high versus low performance.

As is shown in Table 6.5, the second LGM model does not fit significantly differently from the first model for both relationship conflict and process conflict. For all remaining model comparisons, the only significant difference in fit is between models 3 and 4. The fact that model 4 fits significantly worse than model 3 for both relationship and process conflict suggests that the quadratic slopes differ significantly between the high and low performers. Thus, the final LGM model that best represents both relationship conflict and process conflict is one in which intercept and slope means and intercept, slope, and quadratic variances are constrained to be equal across high and low performers. Because they are significantly different, quadratic means should be allowed to freely vary across the two groups in the final models for relationship conflict and process conflict. In other words, for both types of conflict, high and low performers do not significantly differ in their mean initial status or mean rate of increase, nor do they differ significantly in their interindividual variance in initial status, rate of increase, and rate of decrease. High and low performers only significantly differ in their mean rate of decrease. These findings also confirm—albeit more subtly than for task conflict—variation in patterns of change between high and low performers for relationship and process conflict.

To further understand the nature of differences in latent growth between high and low performers, it is necessary to examine the intercept and slope and (where appropriate) quadratic means, variances, and covariances across both groups. These findings are presented in Table 6.6. Note that the parameters presented in Table 6.6 for relationship and process conflict are taken from model 7 of the simultaneous multigroup analyses described previously. The results for task conflict are taken from the separate analyses for high and low performers conducted prior to the multigroup analyses.

As is suggested by Figures 6.2 and 6.3 and Table 6.6, the observed intercept, slope, and quadratic mean and variance parameters for relationship conflict and process conflict follow the same basic patterns of direction and significance for both high and low performers. Nonetheless, model comparison results indicate that the quadratic means are significantly different. The quadratic means shown in Table 6.6

Table 6.5
Multigroup LGM Model Fit and Comparison for High and Low Performers

	χ^2 (d.f.)		RMSEA	NNFI	CFI	Model Comparison	$\Delta\chi^2$ ($\Delta d.f.$)	
Relationship conflict								
Model 1: Unconstrained	224.62*	(126)	.09	.95	.95			
Model 2: Equal intercept means	224.84*	(127)	.09	.95	.95	1 versus 2	.22	(1)
Model 3: Equal slope means	226.06*	(128)	.09	.95	.95	2 versus 3	1.22	(1)
Model 4: Equal quadratic means	234.42*	(129)	.09	.95	.95	3 versus 4	8.36*	(1)
Model 5: Equal intercept variances	226.47*	(129)	.09	.95	.95	3 versus 5	.41	(1)
Model 6: Equal slope variances	226.64*	(130)	.09	.95	.95	5 versus 6	.17	(1)
Model 7: Equal quadratic variances	226.96*	(131)	.08	.95	.95	6 versus 7	.32	(1)
Process conflict								
Model 1: Unconstrained	194.23*	(126)	.07	.97	.97			
Model 2: Equal intercept means	194.46*	(127)	.07	.97	.97	1 versus 2	.23	(1)
Model 3: Equal slope means	196.21*	(128)	.07	.97	.97	2 versus 3	.25	(1)
Model 4: Equal quadratic means	204.10*	(129)	.07	.97	.97	3 versus 4	7.89*	(1)
Model 5: Equal intercept variances	196.23*	(129)	.07	.97	.97	3 versus 5	.02	(1)
Model 6: Equal slope variances	199.73*	(130)	.07	.97	.97	5 versus 6	3.50	(1)
Model 7: Equal quadratic variances	200.41*	(131)	.07	.97	.97	6 versus 7	.68	(1)

* $p \leq .05$
LGM = Latent growth modeling

Table 6.6
Intercept, Slope, and Quadratic Parameter Estimates and Covariances for High and Low Performers

	Intercept Mean (variance)		Slope Mean (variance)		Quadratic Mean (variance)			Covariances	
								Intercept	Slope
Relationship conflict									
High performance	1.77*	(–.01)	1.33*	(.23)	–.30*	(–.04)	Slope	.28	
							Quadratic	–.06	.03
Low performance	1.77*	(–.01)	1.33*	(.23)	–.22*	(–.04)	Slope	.44*	
							Quadratic	–.10*	.02
Task conflict†									
High performance	3.85*	(1.48*)	.84*	(1.33*)	.14*	(.06*)	Slope	–.50	
							Quadratic	.09	–.27*
Low performance	3.88*	(1.00*)	–.44*	(.23*)			Slope	–.08	
Process conflict									
High performance	3.16*	(.72*)	.69*	(.77*)	–.21•	(.19*)	Slope	.17	
							Quadratic	–.03	–.32*
Low performance	3.16*	(.72*)	.69*	(.77*)	–.13*	(.19*)	Slope	.60	
							Quadratic	–.18*	–.29*

Note: Unstandardized values shown.

* $p \le .05$

† Values for task conflict are taken from separate analyses of high and low performers rather than from simultaneous multigroup analyses. The latter analyses were precluded by the fact that the quadratic model fit for high performers, whereas the linear model fit for low performers.

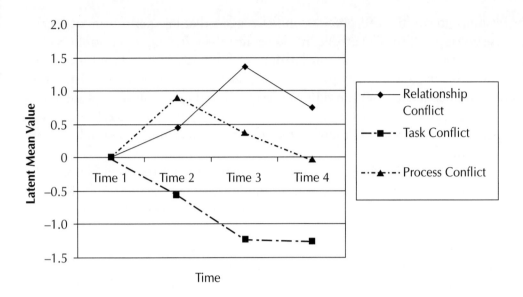

Figure 6.2
Change in Latent Means across Time for High Performers Only

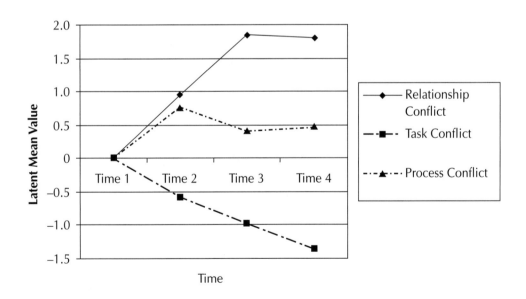

Figure 6.3
Change in Latent Means across Time for Low Performers Only

for relationship conflict and process conflict suggest that low performers decelerate in these two types of conflict at a slightly lower rate than their high-performing counterparts. Combining results from the latent growth models and the latent means, we generally can conclude that low performers accelerate to higher levels of relationship conflict and decelerate from those higher levels more slowly than do high performers. Regarding process conflict, low performers and high performers accelerate at similar speeds to similar levels, but low performers appear to exhibit less overall deceleration over time.

The factor covariances in Table 6.6 indicate that the relationships between the intercept factor and both the slope and quadratic factors are significant for low performers on relationship conflict but are not significant among high performers. These results suggest that for low performers, high levels of relationship conflict at time 1 are associated with greater increases in relationship conflict over the earlier measurement periods and with smaller decreases in relationship conflict between times 3 and 4. The lack of significant covariances for relationship conflict among the high performers indicates that their initial levels on this type of conflict are not associated with later rates of increase or decrease and that the rate of increase is not associated with the rate of decrease. High and low performers also show different patterns of covariance for process conflict. In this case, the slope factor and quadratic factor significantly covary for high and low performers, suggesting that, for both, a higher rate of increase on process conflict is associated with lower rates of decrease. This similarity notwithstanding, the process conflict intercept factor significantly covaries with the quadratic factor for low performers only. Thus, for low performers, it seems that higher initial process conflict is associated with lower rates of decrease in process conflict later on.

Task conflict is the one measure for which quadratic growth does not hold for both high performers and low performers. Nonetheless, it is instructive to consider the intercept, slope, and (for high performers) quadratic parameters for this construct as well. Though high performers show a general decrease in task performance across all four measurement periods, the rate of decrease levels off between times 3 and 4 (Figure 6.2), which produces support for the quadratic model. For low performers, however, there is only evidence of linear decrease in task conflict. The significant covariance between the slope and quadratic factors for high performers on task conflict implies that greater rates of decrease on task conflict are associated with lower rates of increase. For low performers, the intercept and slope factors are not significantly associated, suggesting that their initial status on task conflict is not associated with their ultimate rates of deceleration.

Testing for Variation in Within-Group Consensus across Time
ICC(1) and ICC(2) values are presented in Table 6.7. For relationship conflict, consensus increases and decreases through the four measurement points in the performance episode but shows an overall pattern of increase over time. Both types of ICC

values start at a moderate level for relationship conflict, increase at time 2, and then decrease slightly before increasing again at time 4—perhaps suggesting a reassessment of relationship conflict at time 3 in light of the approaching project deadline. Within-group consensus for process conflict is essentially nonexistent at time 1, but it steadily increases substantially, for both ICC(1) and ICC(2), across the remaining three time periods. Finally, groups exhibit very little agreement in rating task conflict at times 1, 2, and 4, but they show low to moderate levels of agreement on task conflict at time 3. Overall, these results suggest that group members may go through differing episodes or periods of agreement and disagreement as the different types of conflict emerge. It is also interesting to note that although the pattern of consensus over time is consistent for both high and low performers, the high performers generally exhibit higher levels of consensus (Table 6.7).

DISCUSSION

Although researchers have suggested that efforts to conceptualize groups as dynamic systems have been problematic (for example, Arrow et al., 2000), in this work we explicitly suggest that advances in our conceptualization of time and temporal characteristics (Zaheer et al., 1999), of collective constructs (Morgeson and Hofmann, 1999), and of groups (Marks et al., 2001; Arrow et al., 2000) give us an opportunity to revisit such a conceptualization. Furthermore, we suggest that this extant research, combined with advances in the empirical tools available to researchers, gives us the means to advance in a structured and incremental manner our understanding of groups as dynamic systems. As one step, we have suggested a way to establish whether a construct can appropriately be described as an emergent state for analytical and conceptual purposes through analyses that reflect concerns with stability of meaning, variability, and variation in patterns of change across groups and concerns about within-group consensus. In our examination of conflict, we have found evidence to suggest that conflict in groups is amenable to conceptualization as an emergent state. In this section, we discuss the implications of our work.

IMPLICATIONS

The work required to pursue a conceptualization of groups as dynamic systems can benefit from an incremental perspective that relies on current cross-sectional work as a starting point. An important implication of our work is that conceptualizing groups as dynamic systems does not require us to abandon current tools and perspectives. In fact, a proper research agenda should rely on cross-sectional studies to provide us with the means to initially characterize relationships between constructs that are of interest, such as task conflict and performance. We suggest that a useful way

Table 6.7
ICC Values at Each Time Period for the Entire Sample, High Performers, and Low Performers

Conflict Type	Time 1			Time 2			Time 3			Time 4		
	All	High	Low	All	High	Low	All	High	Low	All	High	Low
ICC (1)												
Relationship	.10	.21	.03	.25	.24	.15	.14	.16	.06	.46	.45	.41
Task	-.03	-.06	-.01	-.06	-.05	-.08	.13	.06	.19	-.04	-.05	.00
Process	-.11	-.12	-.10	.05	.02	.10	.30	.30	.30	.43	.39	.46
ICC (2)												
Relationship	.32	.51	.12	.57	.56	.42	.40	.43	.19	.78	.77	.73
Task	-.14	-.28	-.05	-.31	-.22	-.39	.37	.20	.48	-.16	-.25	-.02
Process	-.70	-.75	-.58	.19	.08	.31	.63	.63	.64	.75	.72	.77

ICC = Intraclass correlation coefficient

to bring together existing cross-sectional research with dynamic explanations of group phenomena is to build a bridge between them. Such a bridge would allow us to see the points of contact between the two perspectives, allowing us to advance both.

For us, the cross-sectional work on conflict conducted in the last decade was a solid starting point in our thinking. In particular, the discrepancies in the literature documented by De Dreu and Weingart (2003) were invaluable in framing the need for the exploration of a dynamic characterization of conflict. Their summary of differences in correlations among conflict constructs and the conflicting findings in the relationship between conflict and performance suggested the need for a more detailed examination. For us, these findings suggested that cross-sectional designs might be introducing some difficulties of their own and that these challenges may be overcome with a dynamic perspective. Our use of extant literature as a starting point highlights the tremendous value of meta-analytic procedures in the study of groups. When summaries of research point to inconclusive or contradictory evidence, we may find questions and contradictions that are amenable to examination using a dynamic perspective.

Cross-sectional work is also important because it allows us to tease out potential relationships between constructs. For example, Simons and Peterson (2000) examined the relationship between task conflict and relationship conflict and found that trust in the group is an important factor that allows members to separate the two. In chapter 8, exploration is continued of the interplay of trust and conflict through the addition of another variable—respect—as influencing the relationship. These findings raise several questions from a dynamic perspective. One important question is whether trust and respect are dynamic elements in the group. For instance, it seems reasonable that trust is dynamic, since interactions among members can affect how they perceive one another's reliability, which influences trust. A second question is how stable trust and respect might be over a particular timescale, whether they share a timescale with conflict, or whether they are more stable or more unstable than conflict. After characterizing the dynamic (or static) properties of trust and respect, further examinations could focus on the dynamic interplay of trust, respect, and conflict.

Our findings also point to some potential avenues to strengthen cross-sectional research design. In particular, our results suggest that it is critical to pay increased attention to the timing in the measurement of dynamic constructs. Timing in measurement matters in two different ways. First, ensuring common timing in data collection across groups in a sample ensures comparability across those groups. Dynamic constructs exhibit different characteristics across a single performance episode. Particularly in a group that exists for a single performance episode, the choice to collect data at the beginning, middle, or end of the performance episode should be carefully deliberated.

In addition to highlighting empirical concerns, our work also points to challenges to consider dynamic elements in groups from a theoretical standpoint. Our work suggests that as we develop causal explanations involving dynamic phenomena in groups, we will need to consider temporal aspects (such as when things happen) more explicitly. For example, chapter 4 focuses on the initial composition of groups and how that influences conflict. In this instance, a critical part of their study design is the passage of time, which allows for the emergence of conflict within the group.

As we move forward in our work, we will also need to account for patterns of emergence in dynamic properties and how they might be related to other emergent elements. For example, in our findings we noted a difference in the rate of change of task conflict between high- and low-performing groups. The differences in the slopes (identifying decreases in task conflict) may be indicative of differences in the development of effective conflict resolution. Groups that develop effective conflict resolution approaches may be in a better position to capitalize on differences of opinion precisely because they are more effective at bridging those differences. To the extent that successful groups are developing idiosyncratic approaches to conflict resolution, this may be a reflection of the emergence of norms around conflict.

Also, to the extent that we use single-point measures to characterize dynamic phenomena, it will be necessary to explain the single-point measure in the context of emergence in the group. As we suggested earlier, it is possible that some of the contradictory evidence currently present in the literature might be due to such problems. In the earlier part of this chapter, we noted that the difficulties in linking task conflict and performance (De Dreu and Weingart, 2003) could be caused by differences in measurement timing. Here, we suggest that these differences in measurement timing might also reflect differences across studies in the dynamic characteristics of conflict (such as their starting characteristics, their duration, and so on).

An important point to highlight is that much of the research on conflict is conducted using groups that have a definite beginning and end to their activities. Previous research has shown that such timing patterns can influence the work of groups (Gersick, 1988, 1989; Okhuysen and Waller, 2002). For temporary groups, some elements are likely to follow their existence or life term strongly, with patterns that closely match the groups' starting and ending points. However, other temporal patterns are also possible. As part of their analysis, Jehn and Mannix (2001, pp. 242 and 243) used "group value consensus" to describe "central values" that are held by members, and they measured the "degree of consensus" on those values. Jehn and Mannix (2001) use these group values and the degree of consensus among members as stable underpinnings on which the student groups interact and on which they rely to express and resolve conflict.

Ongoing groups such as university departments, manufacturing teams, or government agency groups are more likely to possess these longer-term, changeable, but relatively stable, characteristics. These differences in temporal dynamics may require slightly different approaches for study. For example, longer-term groups are less like-ly to have task beginnings and endings, and they may be more likely to have group norms (Feldman, 1984) that persist for longer periods of time. Elements such as norms, though, may have temporal dynamics of their own, encapsulated in process-es to create, maintain, and enforce them, and may have particular growth and decay dynamics. In addition, longer-term groups may be affected by task performance dynamics of their own. For example, sales groups may be entrained (Ancona and Chong, 1996) in fiscal reporting cycles, driving higher performance toward the end of three-month or one-year intervals, potentially affecting other group elements such as conflict over those cycles.

FROM STATIC AND DYNAMIC TO A FOCUS ON INERTIAL INFLUENCES

One area that deserves greater attention to help us further our understanding of groups as dynamic systems is the difference in rates of change among constructs. As Zaheer et al. (1999) point out, when we consider a phenomenon we must also con-sider its time scale—that is, the right duration of time to see its evident effects. Thus, at the simplest level we need to characterize elements as having slower or faster rates of change.

As we expand our understanding of groups to include phenomena such as membership change, however, we are likely to find few purely static constructs. Thus, conceptualizations that discuss group elements as subject to different levels of iner-tial influences might be more helpful than ones that focus on strict differences between static and dynamic properties. In addition, a focus on the relative rate of change of constructs would also be useful to help specify where cross-sectional and longitudinal study designs might be appropriate. In particular, cross-sectional designs are most likely to be informative when the likelihood or potential for change over a unit of time is similar across constructs.

In the same way, though, it may be necessary to focus on the development of measurements for phenomena that are similar in the content they capture but that occur at different time scales. Continuing with the study of conflict, for example, might require developing an understanding of conflict in the very short term, such as when conflict causes emotional displays (like anger or frustration). A medium-term analysis such as the one we have presented here might account for conflict as it affects and is affected by other group processes. Finally, a longer-term perspective, in which constructs such as hostility in groups or psychological safety (Edmondson, 1999) are studied, might give us insight into conflict spirals. The need for this research comes from a desire to understand when, for example, conflict becomes a norm that group members operate under, reflecting a more stable situation than the one we describe here. At such a stable state, conflict may cease to act as an emergent state and may instead become an attractor, a global variable that influences other ele-ments in the group (Arrow et al., 2000).

CROSS-LEVEL ISSUES

Our work raises questions related to the aggregation of members' individual-level interpretations of their interactions to group-level emergent states, particularly on the role of intermember consensus in group research. Recent research has used within-group agreement as a test (and a justification) for the aggregation of individual-level data into groups (Bliese, 2000). Chapter 3 explores some of the difficulties involved in aggregating conflict measures. In particular, chapter 3 usefully explains many of the challenges of measurement when multiple interpretations of conflict exist. However, if we are to characterize some group elements as emergent states, theory must account for the possibility that, at certain times during the emergence process, different individuals may see the situation in their group differently and that their perspectives may not converge at those times. Our results suggest that group members can vary in their levels of consensus across a performance episode. Although our data were unable to fully address this issue, it is possible that similar patterns of consensus repeat over performance episodes, provided that membership and other contextual characteristics remain fairly stable. It is also possible that, for ongoing groups, group members ultimately reach a relatively stable level of consensus about levels of all three types of conflict.

Another area that deserves attention is the role of recalibration of variables over time. Further work is required to understand under what conditions individual-level interpretations (or emergent states at the group level) can undergo a significant, steplike change. For example, consider an individual who possesses a low tolerance for conflict. This individual might initially judge the level of conflict in a group as quite high, although over time the individual can recalibrate for this specific group. Similarly, when a group loses a member, it is possible that informal coordination networks are disrupted and perceptions of what constitutes high or low task conflict and/or process conflict could change. An even more intriguing possibility is raised in chapter 10, which explores how interventions from an external party can modify intrateam conflict dynamics. Such interventions are interesting because of the control they afford to managers and leaders in the recalibration of conflict. Although recalibrations such as these are typically considered problematic from an empirical perspective, we should explore whether they might be reconceptualized as a "normal" part of the group process consistent with conceptions of emergent states.

Using emergence as an analogy to understand groups also raises a question regarding the predictability of group behavior. In many computer simulations of emergent systems, end states emerge that reflect stability of some form. Three types of stability, for example, include extinction (the death of the system), hyperstability (a state with no movement), and oscillation (in which the system repeatedly shifts from one arrangement to another in an alternating manner). It is unlikely that individual elements of groups (such as group conflict) will predictably follow one of these patterns of behavior. It may be the case, however, that the group as a whole might follow such a pattern. Behavior that is destructive to groups is relatively common (Hackman, 1990), and hyperstability has been documented in at least some instances (Katz, 1982). In the absence of external influences on a group (in the form of feedback or changes in membership, for example), groups may achieve these stable arrangements. Further exploration on whether an incorporation of these ideas is desirable would be worthwhile.

Naturally, there are also limits to the use of an emergence perspective to explain groups. Perhaps most importantly, emergence typically discusses systems or higher-level entities made up of very simple components with simple interaction rules (Holland, 1998). In addition, the component elements in emergent systems are typically presumed to have simple (or no) intent. Each of these assumptions is difficult to support in the case of individuals interacting in a group situation. However, there are still benefits to considering groups as having emergent elements. In particular, such a conceptualization forces us to more completely characterize the interconnections between individuals and their collective behavior.

A final implication of our work comes from the nature of group processes, in which the aggregation of characteristics of individuals, combined with the interactions between members, gives rise to group-level variables. As with any situation where cross-level influences exist, the examination of groups as dynamic systems is likely to increase in complexity as necessary to account for those cross-level influences. For example, consider an individual with a relatively stable psychological characteristic—for example, a tolerance to conflict. Examining group conflict and tolerance to conflict simultaneously requires accounting for two forms of complexity. On one hand, it is important to account for the interactions between individuals that become group behavior. However, this aggregation must also account for two properties (for example, a personality variable and an emergent state) with different time-scales. These types of cross-level and cross-temporal interactions are likely to be some of the most challenging ones.

CONCLUSION

Our examination of conflict is a very modest step in the path to conceptualizing groups as dynamic systems. However, we believe that such a conceptualization is, in fact, the next step in scholars' examinations of groups. These examinations will be made of small steps such as the two we have outlined—that is, the detailed description of emergent states as one example of a dynamic element and the application of this description to conflict in groups.

NOTES

1. For an exception that treats conflict as dependent on timing, see Jehn and Mannix (2001).

2. Of course, performance is only one of many possible variables that might be associated with groups that are experiencing differing levels of conflict. For instance, we might also expect groups experiencing high initial levels of task conflict to exhibit different patterns of relationship conflict from those experiencing low initial levels of task conflict.

REFERENCES

Amason, A. C. 1996. Distinguishing the effects of functional and dysfunctional conflict on strategic decision making: Resolving a paradox for top management teams. *Academy of Management Journal, 39,* 123–148.

Ancona, D., and Chong, C. 1996. Entrainment: Pace, cycle, and rhythm in organizational behavior. In B. Staw and L. Cummings (Eds.), *Research in organizational behavior, 18,* 251–284.

Arrow, H., McGrath, J. E., and Berdahl, J. L. 2000. *Small groups as complex systems: Formation, coordination, development, and adaptation.* Newbury Park, Calif.: SAGE Publications.

Bliese, P. D. 2000. Within-group agreement, non-independence, and reliability: Implications for data aggregation and analysis. In K. J. Klein and S. W. J. Kozlowski (Eds.), *Multilevel theory, research, and methods in organizations.* San Francisco: Jossey-Bass.

Bryk, A. S., and Raudenbush, S. W. 1992. *Hierarchical linear models.* Newbury Park, Calif.: SAGE Publications.

Chan, D. 1998. The conceptualization and analysis of change over time: An integrative approach incorporating longitudinal mean and covariance structures analysis (LMACS) and multiple indicator latent growth modeling (MLGM). *Organizational Research Methods, 1,* 421–483.

De Dreu, C. K. W., and Weingart, L. R. 2003. Task versus relationship conflict and team effectiveness: A meta-analysis. *Journal of Applied Psychology, 88,* 741–749.

Edmondson, A. 1999. Psychological safety and learning behavior in work teams. *Administrative Science Quarterly, 44,* 350–83.

Eisenhardt, K. M. 1989. Making fast strategic decisions in high-velocity environments. *Academy of Management Journal, 32,* 543–576.

Feldman, D. C. 1984. The development and enforcement of group norms. *Academy of Management Review, 9,* 47.

Gersick, C. J. G. 1988. Time and transition in work teams: Toward a new model of group development. *Academy of Management Journal, 31,* 9–41.

Gersick, C. J. G. 1989. Marking time: Predictable transitions in task groups. *Academy of Management Journal, 32,* 274–309.

Gladstein, D. L. 1984. A model of task group effectiveness. *Administrative Science Quarterly, 29,* 99–517.

Hackman, J. R. 1990. *Groups that work and those that don't.* San Francisco: Jossey-Bass.

Hackman, J. R., & Morris, C. G. 1975. Group tasks, group interaction process, and group performance effectiveness: A review and proposed integration. In L. Berkowitz (Ed.), *Advances in experimental social psychology* (pp. 45–99). New York: Academic Press.

Harrison, D. A., Price, K. H., and Bell, M. P. 1998. Beyond relational demography: Time and the effect of surface- versus deep-level diversity on group cohesiveness. *Academy of Management Journal, 41,* 96–107.

Harrison, D. A., Price, K. H., Gavin, J. H., and Florey, A. T. 2002. Time, teams, and task performance: Changing effects of diversity on group functioning. *Academy of Management Journal, 45,* 1029–1045.

Holland, J. H. 1998. *Emergence from chaos to order.* Oxford, UK: Oxford University Press.

Jehn, K. A. 1995. A multimethod examination of the benefits and detriments of intragroup conflict. *Administrative Science Quarterly, 40,* 256–282.

Jehn, K. A. 1997. A qualitative analysis of types and dimensions in organizational groups. *Administrative Science Quarterly, 42,* 530–557.

Jehn, K. A., and Bendersky, C. 2003. Intragroup conflict in organizations: A contingency perspective on the conflict-outcome relationship. *Research in Organizational Behavior, 25,* 187–242.

Jehn, K. A., and Mannix, E. A. 2001. The dynamic nature of conflict: A longitudinal study of intragroup conflict and group performance. *Academy of Management Journal, 44,* 238–251.

Katz, R. 1982. The effects of group longevity on project communication and performance. *Administrative Science Quarterly, 27,* 81.

Lau, D., and Murnighan, J. K. 1998. Demographic diversity and faultlines: The compositional dynamics of organizational groups. *Academy of Management Review, 23,* 325–340.

Mannix, E. A., & Jehn, K. A. 2004. Let's norm and storm, but not right now: Integrating models of group development and performance. In E. A. Mannix & M. A. Neale (Eds.), *Research on managing groups and teams* (vol. 6, pp. 11–38). Greenwich, Conn.: JAI Press.

Marks, M. A., Mathieu, J. E., and Zaccaro, S. J. 2001. A temporally based framework and taxonomy of team processes. *Academy of Management Review, 26,* 355–376.

McGrath, J. E. 1984. *Groups: Interaction and performance.* Englewood Cliffs, N.J.: Prentice Hall.

McGrath, J. E. 1993. The JEMCO workshop: Description of a longitudinal study. *Small Group Research, 24,* 285–306.

Morgeson, F. P., and Hofmann, D. A. 1999. The structure and function of collective constructs: Implications for multilevel research and theory development. *Academy of Management Review, 24,* 249–265.

Nemeth, C. J., Connell, J. B., Rogers, J. D., and Brown, K. S. 2001. Improving decision making by means of dissent. *Journal of Applied Social Psychology, 31,* 48–58.

Okhuysen, G. A., and Waller, M. J. 2002. Focusing on midpoint transitions: An analysis of boundary conditions. *Academy of Management Journal, 45,* 1056–1065.

Pearson, A. W., Ensley, M. D., and Amason, A. C. 2002. An assessment and refinement of Jehn's (1995) Intragroup Conflict Scale (ICS). *International Journal of Conflict Management, 13,* 110–127.

Riordan, C. M., Richardson, H. A., Schaffer, B. S., and Vandenberg, R. J. 2001. Alpha, beta, and gamma change: A review of past research with recommendations for new directions. In C. A. Schriesheim and L. L. Neider (Eds.), *Equivalence in measurement* (vol. 1, pp. 51–97). Greenwich, Conn.: Information Age Publishing.

Shrout, P. E., and Fleiss, J. L. 1979. Intraclass correlations: Uses in assessing rater reliability. *Psychological Bulletin, 86,* 420–428.

Simons, T. L., and Peterson, R. S. 2000. Task conflict and relationship conflict in top management teams: The pivotal role of intragroup trust. *Journal of Applied Psychology, 85,* 102–111.

Zaheer, S., Albert, S., and Zaheer, A. 1999. Time scales and organizational theory. *Academy of Management Review, 24,* 725–741.

Appendix 6.A:
Detailed Description of Analytical Procedures

Testing for Stability of Meaning across Time

In the unconstrained first model, factor loadings, factor means, and factor variances were all freely estimated. The second model was identical to the first, but identical indicators were constrained to be equal over time. If the chi-square value between these two models did not significantly worsen, then there was evidence of measurement invariance, and, following the logic of parsimony, the second model was retained over the first for further analyses. The third model was identical to the second, but it added the constraint of equal error variances for identical indicators over time. A nonsignificant change in fit between models 2 and 3 would provide additional evidence of measurement invariance, and the better-fitting model would be retained for comparison with the fourth model. Chan (1998) points out, however, that even if factor loadings remain constant across time, "the error variances . . . associated with identical indicators need not be equal across time. In fact, if reliability of an indicator remains constant across time and there are differences in true variance across time, we would actually expect error variances to differ across time because observed variances would differ across time" (p. 449). The fourth model was identical to the superior-fitting, most parsimonious, previously tested model with the addition of all factor means being constrained to be equal over time. If this model exhibited a nonsignificant change in fit from the previously retained model, then there was evidence that no growth occurred in respondents across time. Alternatively, if model 4 was rejected, then it was reasonable to examine the given construct for latent growth over time in the next phase of analyses, and it was also reasonable to estimate the fifth and final model of the present phase of analyses. The final model was identical to the previously retained, superior-fitting model, but all factor variances were also constrained to be equal across time. Comparing the fifth model to the previously retained model gave an initial indication of the nature of interindividual differences in intraindividual change. As such, assuming the initial model comparisons provided evidence of measurement invariance, models 4 and 5 provided preliminary evidence regarding the second characteristic of an emergent state.

Testing for Variability over Time

The first model was a no-growth model that specified a single second-order factor (onto which loaded the four first-order factors defining a given construct as measured at each of the four time periods) representing the intercept, or initial status, of the given conflict construct. Poor fit for the no-growth model indicated that some form of growth model may be appropriate. The second model was identical to the first but specified a linear growth trajectory by adding a second-order slope factor. Factor loadings between the slope factor and the four first-order construct factors were fixed to the values of 0, 1, 2, and 3, respectively, to represent the four equally spaced time periods across which each conflict construct was measured. If the second model fit the data significantly better then the first, there was support for linear growth across time and there was justification for estimating the final latent growth model. The last model was identical to the second, but it also included a second-order quadratic factor. Factor loadings between the quadratic factor and the first-order conflict factors were respectively fixed to the values of 0, 1, 4, and 9 (that is, the slope-factor-loading values squared). If this third model fit the data better than the second, there was evidence of nonlinear change for the given construct.

TESTING FOR PREDICTIVE ABILITY AMONG HIGH AND LOW PERFORMERS

The first latent growth modeling multigroup model that was estimated was, again, an unconstrained model. That is, none of the parameters associated with the second-order intercept, slope, and quadratic factors were constrained to be equal between the two groups. However, on the basis of results from the single-group analyses, factor loadings for identical indicators were constrained to be equal across time in all models. Further, on the basis of results from the first set of multigroup analyses (see Results), factor loadings, error variances, and factor variances were constrained to be equal across the two groups in all models. Acceptable fit for the unconstrained model would offer further confirmation that the same shape of growth was applicable to both groups. The second model was identical to the first but constrained the intercept factor means to be equal across the two groups. If model 2 did not fit significantly worse than model 1, there was evidence that the initial status for both groups was similar, and model 2 was retained for the next comparison. Model 3 was identical to model 2 but added the constraint of equal slope factor means across the two groups. If the difference in fit between models 2 and 3 was not significantly different, there was evidence of no significant difference in slopes between groups, and model 3 was retained for the next comparison. This pattern of model comparison continued for the remaining four models. Thus, model 4 was identical to the previously best-fitting model, but the quadratic means were constrained to be equal across groups. Models 5–7 successively added the additional constraints of equal intercept, slope, and quadratic variances to the previously estimated superior-fitting models.

Chapter 7

CONFLICT AND AUTONOMY IN TEAMS: INTEGRATION AND NEW DIRECTIONS FOR RESEARCH

Claus Langfred

ABSTRACT

The increased adoption of new organizational forms and team designs involving self-management and autonomy has important implications for conflict research. Autonomy can affect many of the variables that are important to conflict research, at both the individual and team levels of analysis. This includes variables that have not been extensively explored in the conflict literature—particularly those related to team design and structure. This chapter illustrates how many of the issues raised by autonomy research may be particularly relevant from a conflict perspective, and it encourages a closer integration of the two fields and suggests specific research opportunities.

INTRODUCTION

Increases in employee autonomy over the past several decades have led to new organizational forms in which both the discretion and the freedom of employees have increased drastically. Combined with a greater reliance on teams in modern organizations (Cohen and Bailey, 1997; Ilgen, Hollenbeck, Johnson, and Jundt, 2005), this has led to increased adoption of and reliance on self-managing teams (Lawler, Mohrman, and Ledford, 1995; Langfred and Shanley, 2001). The research on team conflict, however, has continued to largely focus on more traditional team designs, and many questions about conflict and conflict management in self-managing teams remain unanswered. For instance, what processes and dynamics are different when there is a lot of autonomy in a team, and what are the implications for conflict management? How does autonomy itself affect different types of conflict? How does conflict affect autonomy (and other aspects of team structure and design) as self-managing teams try to manage their own conflict? This further raises questions about how such mechanisms might unfold over time. The purpose of this chapter is not to answer these questions directly, but rather to take a closer look at how conflict research in teams might be expanded by integrating it more with the existing research on autonomy in teams. The specific research questions and opportunities generated by such integration are what will ultimately allow us to understand and manage conflict better in these relatively new organizational forms.

Research on conflict management has provided valuable insights and discoveries for managing teams (Wall and Callister, 1995; De Dreu and Weingart, 2003) and has already spanned a wide variety of contexts and topics (for example, Jehn, Northcraft, and Neale, 1999; Amason and Mooney, 1999; Von Glinow, Shapiro, and Brett, 2004; Hinds and Bailey, 2003; Garcia-Prieto, Bellard, and Schneider, 2003). By expanding the scope of conflict research to include teams with autonomy, important issues and opportunities for the area of conflict research can be uncovered. An increased integration of the two research areas would yield many important avenues for research related not only to the exploration of new processes but also to understanding how structural aspects of team design can influence (and be influenced by) intrateam conflict.

Autonomy is a topic of particular importance to conflict research for several reasons. Autonomy is usually defined as the degree of freedom and discretion in carrying out tasks (Langfred, 2005). When autonomy is manifested at the individual level, it has implications for how members of a team interact, communicate, and work together, all of which can affect (and be affected by) conflict. At the team level, when manifested in the form of self-managing teams, autonomy has completely different implications, raising questions about how teams handle their own conflict in the absence of direct supervisors to manage it for them. This aspect of autonomous teams has not been studied widely, and it is an area ripe with opportunity. In addition, the research on autonomy has revealed several variables of particular value to the study of conflict in teams. Finally, the importance of autonomy to conflict research is highlighted by the fact that autonomy is an aspect of team design and structure that is often neglected in process-based models of conflict.

By exploring autonomy and other variables (both process-based and structure-based) related to team design in the context of conflict management, conflict researchers can find interesting new directions for investigation. Some variables already exist in both literatures and can thus provide a bridge enabling them to be linked further. An example is intrateam trust, which has been studied extensively over the past decade (Kramer and Tyler, 1996). Trust is an important variable in conflict research (Sitkin, Rousseau, Burt, and Camerer, 1998; Korsgaard, Brodt, and Whitener, 2002; Simons and Peterson, 2000; McAllister, 1995; Peterson and Behfar, 2003; Dirks and Ferrin, 2001; Kim, Ferrin, Cooper, and Dirks, 2004), but it has also been explored with respect to its interaction with autonomy (Langfred, 2004). Another important variable is task interdependence, a critical aspect of team design (Saavedra, Earley, and Van Dyne, 1993; Wageman, 1995; Stewart and Barrick, 2000). Task interdependence has been integral to many studies of autonomy (Liden, Wayne, and Bradway, 1997; Langfred, 2000b, 2005; Janz, Colquitt, and Noe, 1997) but has rarely been explicitly integrated into the conflict literature. Nonetheless, it is often discussed in terms related to conflict (Saavedra et al., 1993; Wageman, 1995; Kiggundu, 1983), and there are recent examples of empirical work (Janssen, Van de Vliert, and Veenstra, 1999; Bishop and Dow, 2000).

Autonomy is particularly salient to the conflict literature, since it relates very closely to the concept of process conflict (Behfar, Peterson, Mannix, and Trochim, 2004; Jehn, 1997; Jehn and Chatman, 2000)—which is commonly defined as disagreement about how task accomplishment should proceed, how to delegate work assignments, and who has responsibility for different tasks within the team. Given that autonomy is defined as freedom and discretion (granted either to the team as a whole or to individuals within it) for carrying out tasks, process conflict appears to be the most relevant form of conflict. An increased focus on autonomy in the conflict literature may therefore also revive interest in the somewhat neglected topic of process conflict.

To explore these new directions for conflict research in teams, this chapter will review the current research on autonomy both at the individual level and the team level and will discuss the relevance of autonomy research to current conflict research. It will examine the various ways in which the two fields have natural bridges between them. Furthermore, this chapter will explore ways that research on conflict can move forward by integrating specific variables from autonomy research. Although very little research has incorporated autonomy variables into conflict investigations (in part due to a general dearth of team design variables in conflict research), there are many opportunities to do so related to both process and structure. This chapter will explore some of these variables, drawing attention to specific examples from the autonomy literature and elaborating on how they might enrich conflict research. These opportunities can be revealed by exploring the effects of autonomy (both individual and team) on conflict, including direct, indirect, and interactive effects, as well as by exploring the effects of conflict on autonomy.

AUTONOMY RESEARCH FRAMEWORK AND RELEVANCE TO CONFLICT

The general notion of autonomy has been around for a very long time and has been discussed by thinkers such as Emile Durkheim, Karl Marx, Thomas Hobbes, John Locke, Adam Smith, Amitai Etzioni, and Jean-Jacques Rousseau (to mention a few). However, researchers in organizational behavior have only started to seriously study individual autonomy in the past few decades. The widespread and organized use of task autonomy in organizations is a relatively recent phenomenon. Rarely used systematically before 1980, task autonomy and related forms of employee participation were used in more than 90 percent of Fortune 1000 companies by the mid-1990s (Lawler et al., 1995). Giving task autonomy to employees is generally expected to result in higher motivation, satisfaction, and performance (Argote and McGrath, 1993; Dwyer, Schwartz, and Fox, 1992; Loher, Noe, Moeller, and Fitzgerald, 1985; Spector, 1986).

By its very nature and definition, the notion of autonomy raises questions about the potential for conflict. Increases in the amount of freedom and discretion an individual has in her job will almost invariably influence how and when she interacts with other individuals in ways that include communication, information sharing, dependencies, and coordination. Such factors can have implications for conflict, especially in a team setting where multiple individuals are working interdependently. Often, teams with considerable autonomy fall into the category of the self-managing team, but little is known about how conflict dynamics in such teams may differ from conflict dynamics in more traditional teams.

Given this volume's focus on team conflict, summarized in chapter 1, it is critical to highlight the team-level implications of autonomy. There has been considerable research on both individual autonomy and team autonomy, but there has been relatively little integration across levels in the literature. To be able to link conflict and autonomy research and to explore synergistic research opportunities, a more integrated framework is necessary. Langfred (2000a) provides such a framework by describing various types of self-managing teams. This is a useful starting point to begin our discussion of the implications for conflict research of these new types of teams in organizations. This simple 2x2 framework captures the different team types that become possible when individual-level autonomy and team-level autonomy intersect.[1]

The typology illustrated in Figure 7.1 is particularly relevant for understanding dynamics of self-managing teams—given that the label "self-managing" has typically been applied to team types 1, 2, and 3 without differentiation, despite the fact that they are very different types of teams with different designs and dynamics. It is also important to note that Langfred (2000a) advocated treating both individual and team autonomy as continuous variables, so the types in Figure 7.1 are just a useful convention to help frame the importance of a cross-level approach. In reality, it should be possible to plot any team in the two-dimensional graph, not just the four types illustrated. Thus, the study of autonomy in teams should not be limited to an arbitrary categorical distinction between teams that are self-managing and those that are not—rather, all teams can be quantified in terms of how much autonomy they have (at both levels), even if that quantity is zero. This is especially useful when considering how conflict may operate differently in the team types illustrated.

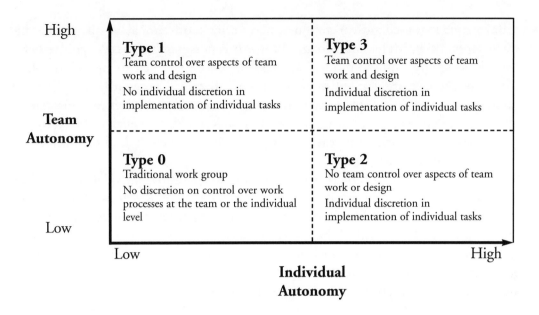

Figure 7.1
Types of Self-Managing Teams (adapted from Langfred, 2000a)

Before discussing possible implications for conflict research for each team type, it is useful to briefly review the literature on autonomy. Much of the research and theory has grown out of the literature on individual-level autonomy and explores how best to design individual jobs (Hackman and Oldham, 1976) as well as teams (Cohen and Ledford, 1994; Cordery, Mueller, and Smith, 1991; Langfred, 2000a; Druskat and Kayes, 1999). Much of this work followed Hackman and Oldham's (1976) Job Characteristics Model, which describes autonomy as one of the "core" job characteristics. The notion that autonomy increases motivation is generally accepted, and some have even suggested that humans have an innate need for autonomy (Deci and Ryan, 1987). Unfortunately, despite numerous empirical studies, little to no theoretical development took place in the decades following Hackman and Oldham's (1976) original work. In terms of possible opportunities for conflict research, several issues immediately suggest themselves. One is the possibility that individual workers will desire (or prefer) more autonomy and may become resentful of or develop negative affect (that is, relationship conflict) toward supervisors who do not grant it but instead rely on tight controls and strict supervision. Thus, some might expect a direct (or indirect, moderated by disposition) link between individual autonomy and conflict with supervisors.

In the related field of employee participation, researchers have suggested that the benefits of increased involvement in (or control over) job decisions are primarily informational (or cognitive) and not necessarily motivational at all (Locke and Schweiger, 1979; Miller and Monge, 1986). It is possible that these cognitive benefits of autonomy will lead to increased task or process conflict. As more individuals in a work setting are granted more autonomy, there will necessarily be differences among preferred task implementation strategies or choices. Given routinization or formalization pressures in the organization, or task interdependencies (driven by task technology, for instance), increased individual autonomy could lead to considerable task or process conflict.

It was not until recently that Langfred and Moye (2004) provided a more comprehensive theoretical model of the various mechanisms by which individual autonomy affects performance—including multiple motivational, cognitive, and structural mechanisms. They clarified those mechanisms, describing how autonomy can have a variety of effects on performance, many of them contingent on various factors ranging from individual disposition and preferences to task complexity to job formalization and task interdependencies. Langfred and Moye (2004) also pointed out that autonomy did not invariably have to have positive effects on motivation and performance, and they described several mechanisms by which granting autonomy to an individual might have no effect, or even negative effects, on motivation and performance. In a team setting, such negative effects could likely lead to frustration and resentment, which can easily result in either relationship conflict with other workers or task or process conflict as the affected individual attempts to correct his or her methods for carrying out tasks. This new comprehensive theory on the effects of individual autonomy will, it is hoped, provide more opportunity for specific and theory-driven empirical research. The various factors and contingencies also raise exciting possibilities for research on conflict, including a greater focus on incorporating models into a traditional input-process-output (IPO) framework or even a more sophisticated input-mediator-output-input (IMOI) recursive model (Ilgen et al., 2005).

When researchers became increasingly interested in autonomy at the team level in the late 1980s, little theory about team-level autonomy existed, and many underlying assumptions were simply "ported" from the individual-level work done in 1976 by Hackman and Oldham, with corresponding (but relatively atheoretical) assumptions about motivational benefits at the team level. It is worth noting that researchers in the field of sociotechnical systems theory (Trist and Bamforth, 1951) had earlier studied autonomous work groups in a variety of case-study settings. In studies about these settings, which included, among others, coal mines in Durham, England (Trist, Higgins, Murray, and Pollock, 1963) and textile mills in Ahmedabad, India (Rice, 1958), researchers explored the benefits of both autonomy and teamwork. However, although they often incorporated autonomous groups into the research, no clear theory about particular dynamics or processes of such groups emerged, and much of the sociotechnical work often lacked a focus on individual psychology and job design. Thus, while the principles underlying the sociotechnical approach are entirely valid, much of the research suffered from the confounds and causal limitations of case-study research. In addition, it suffered from a lack of theory surrounding autonomy itself, as well as the linkage between individual work and motivations on the one hand and team process and outcomes on the other. This line of research may have stagnated in part because the individual-level factors were not integrated with team-level factors and processes, and the lack of specificity of autonomy at both levels clearly limited the conclusions that could be drawn.

With the growing interest in self-management and autonomy in teams over the past two decades, more recent studies have been conducted (Adler and Cole, 1993; Barker, 1993; Cohen and Ledford, 1994; Cohen, Ledford, and Spreitzer, 1996; Cotton, 1993; Macy and Izumi, 1993). However, many of these studies treated autonomy as a categorical variable (teams were either self-managed or they were not) and did not differentiate among types of teams with autonomy but instead considered that a wide range of team designs were "self-managing." The framework (or typology) in Figure 7.1 highlights the different types of teams that can result from various combinations of individual-level and team-level autonomy, illustrating the importance of such a distinction. Due to the broad and vague definition of self-management that is often employed, little attention had historically been given to the potential interplay between team-level autonomy and individual-level autonomy. This lack of specificity has also severely limited any attempts to develop models of conflict in self-managing teams.

Some writers had speculated that there might be a tension between the amount of team-level autonomy and the amount of individual-level autonomy within the team and that team performance might be dependent on the correct "balance" between them (Neck, Stewart, and Manz, 1996; Markham and Markham, 1995; Uhl-Bien and Graen, 1998). The suggestion that teams can be described in terms of their amounts of both individual-level and team-level autonomy, and the idea that there may be an interaction or tension between the two, suggest that research involving autonomy in teams inherently should strive to be cross-level in nature. Until recently, there had been little or no theory underlying the predictions of tension between the individual and group level, and no empirical work to support them. If one were to study only one level in a team, the effects of the other level on performance would be omitted, potentially leading to erroneous conclusions. More importantly, from a conflict perspective, this very notion of tension between levels implies considerable potential for conflict in self-managing teams. Task conflict and process conflict could arise from poor alignment of the two levels of autonomy and resultant inefficiencies or coordination problems. Alternatively, relationship conflict could result from disagreements as to who is granted autonomy and who is not.

Recent studies that have examined individual-level and team-level autonomy together have found evidence of a connection, indicating the importance of studying both together. In the autonomy literature, Langfred (2000a, 2005) has conducted several studies and tested multiple models showing how individual-level autonomy and team-level autonomy can have countervailing effects on team performance. One model illustrated how the two forms of autonomy had opposite effects on team performance when mediated through team cohesiveness, and another illustrated how performance depended on the interactions with task interdependence at both individual and team levels of autonomy. The countervailing effects of the two levels of autonomy in teams highlighted the importance of (1) separating the individual and team levels when studying autonomy in teams and (2) studying both simultaneously in cross-level settings.

These studies are particularly important, not only because they illustrate the cross-level nature of the performance effects of autonomy in teams, but also because they illustrate how these effects can operate through both process-based mechanisms (such as cohesiveness) and structure-based ones (such as task interdependence). While researchers had in the past explored the effect of task interdependence on the relationship between team autonomy and performance (Liden et al., 1997; Janz et al., 1997; Langfred, 2000b), none had explored the effect at the individual level, nor had any studies explored task interdependence in a cross-level setting—which once again illustrated the importance of studying both individual and team levels of analysis simultaneously in order to understand the true nature of team performance (Klein, Danserau, and Hall, 1994; Rousseau, 1985). The importance of incorporating multiple levels of analysis into models and analysis in the study of teams and autonomy strongly suggests the importance of doing the same in studies of conflict.

Thus, looking back at recent research on autonomy, it is important not only to conceptualize and operationalize autonomy as a continuous variable, but also to take both individual and team levels of analysis into account, as the effects at one level may interact with effects at the other level. (In other words, there is likely to be an interaction effect from individual and team autonomy, in addition to main effects for each.) More importantly to the conflict research, however, there are also numerous implications for conflict research evident in the literature on autonomy—with opportunities at the specific level, as well as an important lesson at the general level. At the specific level, the autonomy research provides several variables that can be both the antecedents to and the outcomes of conflict in teams. Specifically, we can explore some of the implications for the four types of teams with autonomy illustrated in Figure 7.1, summarized briefly here.

Type 0: Traditional team—no autonomy. From the perspective of the conflict literature, this is the benchmark type of team that much of the existing conflict research (reviewed in other chapters of this volume) applies to. In the specific example of particularly low individual and team autonomy, relationship conflict would be more likely than other types of conflict—since there is less possibility of process or task conflict, given tasks constrained by rules, procedures, and direct supervision (the opposite of discretion and freedom). This is not to imply that there would not be task or process conflict in such teams. Obviously, the conflict literature is replete with examples of conflict of all types in such teams. The point is merely that teams with high constraints on individual and team autonomy may be somewhat more susceptible to relationship conflict than to other types of conflict.

Type 1: Team autonomy, no individual autonomy. A lack of individual autonomy implies that individuals have little or no discretion in the implementation of their individual tasks within the team, and a high level of team autonomy means that the team as a whole has the freedom and discretion to decide how to carry out its tasks. For individual team members, this means that some mechanism needs to be in place by which the team makes decisions about how to exercise this autonomy. Some teams might conduct a vote to make decisions about job allocations, scheduling, pace, coordination, and so on. Others might begin with one team member identified as the leader and rotate the leadership position. Such decision procedures, the processes involved, and the resulting outcomes can have potential for considerable task and process conflict.

However, on the other side of the coin, teams that have more team-level autonomy also have more options available for effective conflict management, including job redesign and even changing the structure of the team itself. By granting significant autonomy to a team, the organization is often either implicitly or explicitly making that team responsible for managing its conflicts, communication, coordination, information sharing, and so on. Thus, teams very high in autonomy should be particularly fertile grounds for research on conflict management. For example, Barker's (1993) famous, and often misunderstood, study of concertive control in self-managing teams is a study of conflict in the context of high team autonomy. Conflict researchers should thus be particularly interested in studying how the fundamental approach to conflict management in teams may become very different when the team has more discretion in deciding how to manage such conflict. In particular, the possibility that teams might change the team design and structure as a response to conflict is an entirely novel idea that is specific to teams with greater team-level autonomy.

Type 2: Individual autonomy, no team autonomy. In the case of very high levels of individual autonomy but little team autonomy, one might expect more process conflict as individuals decide how to carry out their own tasks but potentially run into problems coordinating their individual efforts with one another to achieve - team-level goals. The more discretion individuals have over the scheduling and sequencing of their work, the more potential there is for process conflict— particularly in the case of high task interdependencies. This is just one of several ways in which conflict might result from team structure, or from the intersection of structure and process, and gradually emerge in the team over time (see chapter 6) as coordination difficulties or task disagreements mount.

When granted autonomy within the team, individuals also assume much more individual responsibility for managing interactions, information sharing, and communicating and coordinating with other team members. One would expect autonomy to be related to conflict and to conflict management style, likely moderated by individual differences in knowledge, skills, and abilities (KSA) at conflict management. Left to their own devices when granted a lot of autonomy, individuals with strong conflict-management KSAs might be expected to experience less conflict, and individuals with poor KSAs would likely experience more conflict as they become a source of disruption and tension in an interdependent team. In addition, several researchers have pointed out the potential for conflict resulting from individual personality difference, particularly in self-managing teams (Armstrong and Priola, 2001; Thoms, Pinto, Parente, and Druskat, 2002). Molleman, Nauta, and Jehn (2004) also found that autonomy can moderate the relationship between individual personality traits and job satisfaction, consistent with Langfred and Moye's (2004) general theoretical model.

Just as individual members' differences exert a powerful force on team dynamics, so too do the social effects of autonomy. One particularly salient example of this is the effect of the combination of trust and autonomy in teams. Langfred (2004) found that individual team members were often reluctant to sufficiently monitor other autonomous team members if trust within the team was high. This reluctance harmed the team's ability to coordinate effectively and ultimately lowered its performance. Specifically, the study found that team performance depended on the interaction of individual autonomy and trust within the team. Counterintuitively, in teams with high levels of individual autonomy, higher trust actually harmed team performance.

The reluctance of members of self-managing teams to actually manage themselves is a particularly interesting aspect of such teams, and it may make them especially vulnerable to conflict. The reluctance of members of self-managing teams to properly deal with emerging conflict was noted by deLeon (2001), who found that when team members were faced with conflict, a common response among them was to ignore it instead of resolving it. Vardi and Weitz (2004) also noted that there is greater potential for misbehavior in self-managing teams—another sign, perhaps, of a lack of management in self-management? This all points to the critical importance of conflict research in the context of high-autonomy teams.

Type 3: Team and individual autonomy. Since this team type includes both high individual autonomy and high team autonomy, the potential for conflict is very high, in that all the reasons to expect either task conflict or process conflict in types 1 and 2 would also manifest themselves in this combined team design. Thus, all of the various possible effects and relationships described for types 1 and 2 would be likely to occur in this type of team as well. In addition, the tensions and inefficiencies inherent in this design described by Langfred (2000a, 2005) will significantly add to the potential for task conflict and process conflict as well. Furthermore, the inefficiencies and performance losses associated with this dysfunctional design could very possibly result in additional relationship conflict as individual team members experience frustration and try to assign blame.

INTEGRATION OF AUTONOMY AND CONFLICT RESEARCH

Our initial review of the relevant portions of the autonomy literature revealed several variables that can be important for conflict and conflict management. That the effect of autonomy on performance can depend on levels of trust, for example, indicates how crucially important *process variables* from the conflict literature can be in helping us to understand the effects of *team design variables*. Conversely, it also illustrates how important team design variables like autonomy can be to the conflict literature. Trust is a central variable in conflict research, and it has been widely studied (Kramer, 1999; Lewicki, McAllister, and Bies, 1998; Kramer and Tyler, 1996; Sitkin et al., 1998; Korsgaard et al., 2002; Simons and Peterson, 2000; McAllister, 1995; Peterson and Behfar, 2003). In addition to having potential interactive effects with conflict, trust is potentially both causally antecedent to, and dependent on, conflict in teams. Chapter 8 explores how trust and respect are different but interrelated predictors of conflict in teams. Langfred's 2004 study is one example of a crossover study that uses variables from both the conflict literature and the literature on team design and self-management.

The mere conceptualization/categorization of teams into types 0 through 3 has important implications for how to think about conflict management and conflict research. In addition, specific variables may be particularly relevant to conflict research in connection with one type of team but not another. Many variables provide the opportunity for combining autonomy and conflict research and may be particularly relevant to certain types of teams. Some of these variables may be more relevant to individual-level processes and effects, and thus team types 2 and 3, while other variables may be more relevant to the team level and team types 1 and 3. Other variables may relate to both individual and team levels and may thus be relevant across all team types.

Cohesiveness is one such variable. The autonomy research has found links between both individual-level and team-level autonomy and cohesiveness. Although a few researchers have begun to study the relationship between conflict and cohesiveness (Jehn and Chatman, 2000; Farmer and Roth, 1998; Barnard, Baird, Greenwalt, and Karl, 1992), many opportunities remain in exploring cohesiveness as a possible moderator or mediator linking autonomy and conflict to performance and, potentially, even to one another. Thus, exploring the link between cohesiveness and conflict would be particularly relevant in the type 3 teams, but also potentially important for both type 2 and type 1, albeit at different levels of analysis.

Information sharing, which has received considerable attention in the conflict literature recently, is another variable that is likely to be strongly related to individual autonomy in teams. As team members have more discretion and freedom in their own work—in type 2 and type 3 teams—the amount of information sharing will likely drop in teams. As with trust and monitoring, increased individual autonomy within teams may have several dysfunctional effects on information sharing and communication. Subsequent misunderstandings and coordination losses may invariably lead to increased task (and possibly relationship) conflict. Although information sharing has received increasing attention in the conflict literature (Amason and Schweiger, 1997; Moye and Langfred, 2005), it has not been addressed in the autonomy literature at all. As such, it is another potential variable that could be very relevant to both literatures.

The very notion of autonomous individuals in teams not being able to coordinate well also goes to the heart of another team design variable that has become central to the autonomy literature, namely task interdependence—defined as the degree of interaction and coordination required of team members if they are to complete tasks (Guzzo and Shea, 1992). The contingencies that task interdependence imposes on relationships between autonomy (both individual-level and team-level) and team performance have been demonstrated (Liden et al., 1997; Janz et al., 1997; Langfred, 2000b, 2005), reaffirming the central importance of task interdependence to team process and performance (Saavedra et al., 1993). In practice, individual autonomy is often associated with low task interdependence and might appear to be at odds with high task interdependence, but it is worth noting that individual autonomy and task interdependence are independent and conceptually distinct. Langfred (2005) demonstrated that, just as high team autonomy fits best with high task interdependence, high individual autonomy fits best with low task interdependence. Thus, in teams where task interdependence is exogenous or driven by task technology (Thompson, 1967), performance is dependent on the process of the team being organized around its interdependencies.

While a few studies in the conflict literature have included task interdependence in their models (Janssen et al., 1999; Bishop and Dow, 2000), it has remained largely unexplored, as have many other team design variables. Task interdependence, however, would seem to be highly relevant to conflict in teams—both as a possible moderator of the effect of conflict on outcomes like trust, communication, and ultimately performance, and also as an antecedent or even an outcome of conflict. In fact, since conflict is inherently based on interactions between people, task interdependence should be a critical variable involved in the study of conflict in teams. Task interdependence is likely to moderate the effect of conflict (both task and relationship) on many measures of outcome, including the effect of conflict on team performance. If work must be highly coordinated among team members for team tasks to be accomplished, the effect of serious task or process conflict in a team is likely to be far more severe than if work can be accomplished by individuals working relatively independently of one another. By the same token, a team characterized by low task interdependence (and low levels of coordination requirements between members) may still be quite effective, even with high levels of relationship conflict, which would likely not be possible if team members had to frequently interact and coordinate. In this way, lower task interdependence might serve as a buffer against some of the negative effect of conflict in teams.

It may also be possible for task interdependence to both be a cause and an effect of conflict in teams. For example, task interdependence might be causally antecedent to relationship conflict. Following the logic just outlined, in a team characterized by very low task interdependence and coordination requirements, it may be possible to incorporate members who have relatively incompatible individual dispositions or personalities. In a team characterized by higher interdependence, with its greater need for interaction and coordination, these people would be unable to avoid conflict. Thus, the interaction of personality disposition and task interdependence is a likely determinant of relationship conflict. It is also possible for task interdependence to be an outcome of conflict in self-managing teams in which task interdependence is not exogenous but can be adapted and modified by the team members (Wageman, 1995; also see chapter 10 in this volume). In such instances, increases in conflict could bring about a redesign of work processes and structures in the team to reduce task interdependencies and coordination requirements such that individual team members minimize their interaction and contact with one another.

Ultimately, many of the studies in the autonomy literature illustrate why it is important to examine team design and structural variables together with process variables in order to truly understand the determinants of team performance. By the same token, integrating more team design and structural variables into the conflict literature can only improve the explanatory power of our models and expand the scope of our understanding. To explore process variables such as conflict, communication, and information sharing together with such team design variables as autonomy (at both levels of analysis) and structural variables like task interdependence would not only provide a multitude of new research opportunities and new directions, but would almost certainly result in much more accurate and better-specified models of conflict and conflict management.

It seems plausible that both the team-level autonomy and individual-level autonomy that can occur in various types of self-managing teams can have significant implications for research on conflict and conflict management. In fact, examples in the literature describe studies in which the mere presence of autonomy had effects on conflict management. For instance, in the study of autonomy and trust (Langfred, 2004), team members were responsible for their own conflict management within the team, but they failed to properly manage the team because they were reluctant to monitor one another sufficiently. This is similar to what Barker (1993) described when there was an influx of new members into self-managing teams and the teams ended up being unable to manage themselves effectively. The dysfunctional outcomes in these teams in part resulted from the freedom of the team and of individuals within the team to manage team process themselves. The two studies pose an interesting contrast, since the granting of autonomy appears to have led to opposing problems. In the first case (Langfred, 2004), team performance was harmed because its members were unwilling (or unaware of the need) to take responsibility for monitoring other team members. In other words, they were too lax in their conflict management responsibilities. In the other case (Barker, 1993), team members very much took responsibility for managing the team process, but in an overly draconian and ultimately harmful manner. Granting autonomy to teams and to individuals within teams thus appears to create unique and largely unexplored questions about conflict management in teams and the still undetermined contingencies and causes that are associated with it. Focusing on autonomy in teams with a conflict management lens is likely to reveal significant challenges for the future design of effective self-managing teams.

The previous exploration suggests that it may be fruitful to explore several issues and variables, both generally for bridging the gap between the autonomy and conflict literatures, and also specifically for exploring the different types of teams that incorporate autonomy into their design. Figure 7.2 illustrates some of these variables and possibilities. In each cell of the three types of self-managing teams is an estimate of the type of conflict expected to be most salient and a list of variables and factors that may be particularly valuable to explore in terms of conflict and conflict management research implications.

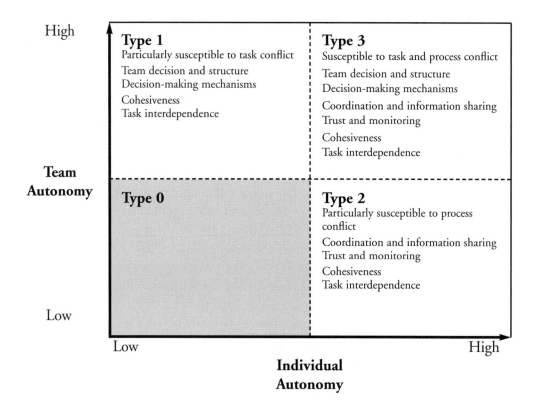

Figure 7.2
Different Conflict-Related Features and New Variables for Conflict Research

FUTURE RESEARCH DIRECTIONS

By incorporating constructs and concepts related to autonomy research in particular and team design in general, new opportunities and directions for research become evident. In addition to the overall managerial/design issue of how to enable various types of self-managing teams to better manage their processes and conflicts, the introduction of new variables also points to many specific research possibilities. In this section, some examples of research possibilities are presented that illustrate a variety of ways to enrich existing models.

One approach is to look at team design variables such as autonomy as outcomes determined by conflict. With such an approach, one can explore the relationship between conflict and trust and the extent to which this might influence design decisions in self-managing teams. For instance, what effects will increased conflict have on team members' desire for autonomy and their willingness to grant autonomy to other team members? In fact, Wageman (1995) suggested that individuals' preference for autonomy could change on the basis of their team experiences, but no empirical research has followed up on her initial work.

The relationship between conflict and trust is also one that has already received some attention (Lewicki et al., 1998; McKnight, Cummings, and Chevarny, 1998). While many process variables might still be explored—such as information sharing or communication style—the basic relationship appears to be a negative one, especially with respect to relationship conflict. Higher conflict is generally associated with lower levels of trust. The interesting question is what effect lower levels of trust might have on autonomy in a team. On one hand, a reduction in trust would likely increase the desire for autonomy on the part of individuals within the team. (This is consistent with new theory suggesting that individual preference for autonomy is both dispositional and situational.) If one does not trust fellow team members, it would make sense to try to get as much control over one's own work as possible. Thus, on the basis of peoples' desire for autonomy and control, one expectation might be that reduced trust would lead to increased individual autonomy. On the other hand, however, if team members do not trust each other, they are not likely to agree to give each other *more* freedom and discretion over individual work. So while each individual might prefer more autonomy and freedom over his or her own work, it is unlikely that the individual would want others—whom he or she does not trust—to have the same discretion. A lack of trust implies a need for increased monitoring (Creed and Miles, 1996; Bromiley and Cummings, 1995; Langfred, 2004), and if individuals feel a need to monitor one another more closely, then individual autonomy will be as curtailed as possible.

Therefore, it seems that there are several interesting potential effects to consider if we explore the effect conflict can have on individual autonomy mediated through trust. People will want more individual autonomy, but they are paradoxically likely to end up imposing more restrictions on and limiting autonomy in the team, similar to what Barker (1993) observed. The issue of individual preferences and reactions also raises the importance of diversity as a design feature of a team and has significant implications for conflict (see chapters 2 and 3). As Langfred and Moye (2004) pointed out, individual differences in preference for autonomy can moderate relationships between autonomy and various outcomes variables and is likely to moderate relationships like the ones described previously. Furthermore, in addition to its mediating role, trust is also likely to have a possible moderating role in a variety of relationships in a team context, since many interactions are dependent on how much people trust one another. In fact, Simons and Peterson (2000) demonstrated how trust moderated the relationship between task conflict and relationship conflict. As such, considering autonomy as an outcome (at both the individual level and the team level) of conflict, not an antecedent, has relevance for all the different team designs in our typology.

An entirely different construct that is again very relevant in this context is that of task interdependence. If a self-managing team has control over work processes and can alter the task interdependence of its work, what effect might increased conflict have on task interdependence? If people are experiencing a lot of task conflict or process conflict in a team, they might want to reduce interdependencies in the team so they will be more insulated from other members' task implementation (an implementation they might not agree with). If task and process conflict are considerable, a simple solution is the "you do your thing, I'll do mine" approach, which can be accomplished if the team has control over task interdependence and can reduce it substantially.

If relationship conflict is high in a team, one would also expect team members to reduce task interdependencies (if possible) simply to minimize the amount of necessary interaction with other team members. The more relationship conflict a team has, the more team members will likely want to avoid contact with one another, and a reduction in task interdependence would help accomplish that. Thus, it seems that increases in any type of conflict—task, process, or relationship—are likely to result in reductions in task interdependence (in teams that have control over task interdependence). Again, these are untested propositions unique to the context of teams with high team autonomy (self-managing or self-designing teams).

If both of the aforementioned effects of increased conflict were to occur—(1) less trust and less individual autonomy and (2) lower task interdependence—this would present a potentially dysfunctional outcome that is another interesting area of potential study (and another illustration of the value of trying to integrate autonomy literature into the mainstream of conflict research). The dysfunction arises from the fact that there is an established interaction between individual autonomy and task interdependence in teams (Langfred, 2005) indicating that when task interdependence is low, teams perform best if individual autonomy is high (to best take advantage of the benefits of cognitive and motivational benefits of autonomy without incurring coordination costs). So, ideally, if team members decide they want to lower task interdependence, they should increase individual autonomy to maximize team effectiveness and performance. The combination of low task interdependence and low individual autonomy might not be directly harmful to team performance, but it is less desirable than the combination of low task interdependence and high individual autonomy—so the team will not perform as well as it could. In other words, conflict in a self-managing or self-designing team will not only result in traditional process losses, but it can result in a dysfunctional and ineffective team design. Thus, by exploring the effects of conflict on team design and structural variables, it is very likely that new mechanisms by which conflict negatively affects performance can be uncovered.

Such relationships may in fact be even more complicated. For instance, it is entirely plausible that the relationship between task conflict and task interdependence—predicted to be negative previously—might be moderated by another variable, such as trust. The logic might be as follows: If task or process conflict is high, it means there is disagreement on how to carry out a particular task or process. If team members do not trust one another, this disagreement might make them wary of being interdependent; they might worry that their performance could be harmed by other people attempting to carry out the task in incorrect or dysfunctional ways. Thus, when trust is low, task conflict is likely to result in lower task interdependence. If trust is high, however, team members may believe that, although they disagree, other team members would not deliberately jeopardize performance, and they may be willing to take the risk (which is the definition of trust) and retain higher task interdependence despite the task conflict. Thus, one might expect trust to moderate the relationship between task or process conflict and task interdependence.

When exploring the possible expanded role of task interdependence in conflict research, we consider that task interdependence may itself also moderate the effects of conflict on other process-based outcomes. In fact, in the team literature in general, task interdependence often is found to moderate critical relationships (Saavedra et al., 1993). In the specific context of conflict and trust, it is possible that task interdependence might moderate the relationship between them. Although in general, increased conflict would be expected to result in reduced trust, the reduction might depend on the degree of task interdependence in the team. Since trust is defined as the willingness to incur risk (Mayer, Davis, and Schoorman, 1995), the extent to which an individual believes the task conflict might actually harm him or her, or harm the team's effectiveness, should affect the extent to which trust is reduced. If task interdependence is lower, team members are somewhat insulated from the effects of task conflict; conversely, when task interdependence is higher, they are highly dependent on one another. Thus, it is not implausible to expect that the negative effect of task conflict on trust would be stronger when task interdependence (and subsequent perceived risk) is higher, and it would be less strong when task interdependence is lower.

Such an interaction might also provide additional insights into the differential effects of task conflict and relationship conflict. Although they might have a similar effect on trust (and on performance: De Dreu and Weingart, 2003), the mechanisms by which those effects are transmitted may be quite different, and structural variables like task interdependence might be a large part of understanding those differences. Many other possible relationships in the conflict literature might be moderated by task interdependence (or other design or structural variables).

In highlighting some of the possible avenues for new research in this chapter, we acknowledge the importance of methodological rigor. Many of the research questions or directions we suggest involve complicated interactive (moderated) relationships among multiple variables or describe dynamic or recursive processes that occur over time (such as those discussed in chapter 6, for example). Add to that the team-level nature of the constructs, and the methodological and analytical challenges are manifold. It is particularly important for the conflict research to rise to the challenge. This includes seeking research settings and sources of data that allow for strong causal inference, large samples of intact teams, the use of established measures, independent respondents for independent and dependent measures, and, ideally, repeated measures over time. From an analytical perspective, issues of aggregation, repeated/ longitudinal data, mediation, and moderation (to just name a few elements) are critical to successful research.

Finally, the examples of research ideas presented here are just that—examples. These specific cases would obviously have to be developed into more sophisticated models and ultimately tested empirically. They are intended to be representative examples of what is possible, not definitive directions for specific research. There are many other possibilities, and this chapter has merely drawn attention to some of the opportunities available.

SUMMARY AND CONCLUSION

There is great variety in the opportunities for new research based on integrating the literatures on conflict and autonomy in teams. When considering autonomy in teams, Langfred's (2000a) typology for self-managing teams is a useful starting point for exploring various new research directions. Building on that, further contingencies and variables (such as information sharing, task interdependence, trust and monitoring, and many other variables) provide additional directions for possible new research on conflict and conflict management. Figure 7.2 illustrates how many of these variables are relevant at different levels of analysis, some of them even across levels.

Using the typology allows us to be much more specific in exploring the potential bridges between autonomy research and conflict research. For example, it reveals that while one might expect both task conflict and process conflict in type 3 teams, type 1 teams may be more susceptible to task conflict, whereas type 2 teams may be somewhat more predisposed toward process conflict. Similarly, while the importance of process variables (for example, decision rules and mechanisms) and the team's ability to restructure its own design may be shared for both type 1 and type 3 teams, factors like information sharing, coordination, and issues of trust and monitoring may be particularly salient for type 2 and type 3 teams. However, some factors (for example, process-related cohesiveness and structure-related task interdependence) remain relevant to all three team types but may operate very differently at the individual and team levels of analysis. Thus, by separating the concept of self-management into more sophisticated distinctions that are relevant to conflict research (that is, the team and individual distinctions that create four types of teams instead of one generic label), we are faced with a variety of research questions that are directly relevant to conflict and conflict management.

Furthermore, by considering new models of conflict—exploring conflict as an antecedent of a team's structural design characteristics (like autonomy or task interdependence), or investigating possible recursive causal loops by which conflict affects trust, which in turn affects conflict, for example—a host of additional potential research directions is revealed. Issues of causality and recursiveness highlight the shortcomings of the traditional IPO model and suggest that more complex approaches may be fruitful—whether the IMOI model of Ilgen et al. (2005) or an alternative Input-Structure-Process-Output (ISPO) model, which would incorporate a team's structural design features into classic process models of conflict in teams. Since the focus of this chapter is the interplay between autonomy and conflict, obvious candidates for structure variables are constructs like autonomy and task interdependence. Such a model would inherently be general in nature and could incorporate many aspects of team design and structure unrelated to autonomy research. Nevertheless, it is important to further develop holistic models of conflict and conflict management.

At a more general level, the increased specificity of the typology used in this chapter will not only serve as a starting point for developing novel research directions in conflict research, but it will also strengthen the development of more effective conflict management techniques. Instead of more general approaches to addressing conflict in vaguely defined "self-managing" teams, it will be possible to specifically tailor conflict management to the particular characteristics of a team type. This capability will not be limited to specifying the continuous variables of individual-level and team-level autonomy, but it will also be applicable to design features such as task interdependence and to process variables such as information sharing, trust, and cohesiveness. By focusing more directly on both design and process features, conflict research will eventually be able to diagnose and manage conflict much more effectively in a variety of team types. One particularly important finding in the literature studying the merging of conflict and autonomy appears to be that self-managing teams run the risk of not actually managing themselves well when it comes to conflict. This has crucial implications for organizations that choose to rely on various types of self-managing teams, suggesting either the necessity of more formal training in conflict management for team members, more rules or procedures (as substitutes for direct managerial intervention or supervision), or perhaps other innovative solutions such as roving internal conflict managers in the organization that can help teams either avoid conflict in the first place or manage it when it arises. As these new types of teams become part of the organizational landscape, perhaps entirely new methods of conflict management will emerge.

Because of the many possible complex relationships among autonomy, conflict, and numerous other variables—both process-related and structural—it is also particularly important to pursue longitudinal empirical studies in this type of conflict research in order to clarify causal directions (as is the case in the recent study by Peterson and Behfar, 2003). Finally, exploring the opportunities for integrating autonomy and conflict research has also highlighted the larger issue of incorporating more team design variables into the conflict literature. Task interdependence and autonomy are the obvious examples discussed in this chapter, but many other potential aspects of team design hold promise for conflict researchers. Not only does a focus on team-level design characteristics provide greater opportunity for researchers in the conflict field, but it will also make the conflict field more interesting and accessible to those outside it.

This chapter posed questions about how conflict operates in teams characterized by high levels of autonomy and how effects and mechanisms may differ from those observed in more traditional teams. It also raised questions about how autonomy itself affects conflict and how conflict affects autonomy and other aspects of team structure. Although this chapter has not provided empirical answers to those questions, it has highlighted the reasons that they are important and has mapped out a framework for exploring them via various new research directions. These suggestions will not only help to integrate the closely related research literatures of autonomy and conflict, but will more importantly contribute to more specific and accurate models of conflict and conflict management in a wider variety of teams.

NOTE

1. It is important to note that team autonomy is conceptually distinct from the aggregation of individual autonomy to the team level. The aggregation of individual autonomy to the team level describes the average level of autonomy of individual team members, whereas team-level autonomy describes the level of autonomy that the team as a unit has (that is, its freedom and discretion in carrying out team tasks). Team-level autonomy still has implications for individual team members, not only since decisions have to be made among team members regarding the implementation of that autonomy, but also since those decisions will affect individual team members.

REFERENCES

Adler, P. S., and Cole, R. E. 1993. Designed for learning: A tale of two auto plants. *Sloan Management Review* (Spring).

Amason, A. C., and Mooney, A. C. 1999. The effects of past performance on top management team conflict in strategic decision making. *International Journal of Conflict Management, 10*(4), 340–359.

Amason, A. C., and Schweiger, D. M. 1997. The effects of conflict on strategic decision making effectiveness and organizational performance. In C. K. W. De Dreu and E. Van de Vliert (Eds.), *Using conflict in organizations* (pp. 101–115). Newbury Park, Calif.: SAGE Publications.

Argote, L., and McGrath, J. E. 1993. Group process in organizations. In C. L. Cooper and I. T. Robertson (Eds.) *International review of organizational psychology* (pp. 333–389). New York: John Wiley and Sons.

Armstrong, S. J., and Priola, V. 2001. Individual differences in cognitive style and their effects on task and social orientations of self-managed work teams. *Small Group Research, 32*(3), 283–312.

Barker, J. R. 1993. Tightening the iron cage: Concertive control in self-managing teams. *Administrative Science Quarterly, 38*(3), 408–437.

Barnard, W. A., Baird, C., Greenwalt, M., and Karl, R. 1992. Intragroup cohesiveness and reciprocal social influence in male and female discussion groups. *Journal of Social Psychology, 132*(2), 179–188.

Behfar, K. J., Peterson, R. S., Mannix, E. A., and Trochim, W. M. K. 2004. *Exploring conflict resolution strategies in autonomous work groups: An example of adaptive structuration in teams.* Working paper, Northwestern University.

Bishop, J. W., and Dow, S. K. 2000. An examination of organizational and team commitment in a self-directed team environment. *Journal of Applied Psychology, 85*(3), 439–450.

Bromiley, P., and Cummings, L. L. 1995. Transactions costs in organizations with trust. In R. Bies, B. Shappard, and R. Lewicki (Eds.), *Research on negotiations in organizations* (vol. 5, pp. 219–247). Greenwich, Conn.: JAI.

Cohen, S. G., and Bailey, D. E. 1997. What makes teams work: Group effectiveness research from the shop floor to the executive suite. *Journal of Management, 23*(3), 239–290.

Cohen, S. G., and Ledford, G. E. 1994. The effectiveness of self-managing teams: A quasi-experiment. *Human Relations, 47*(1), 13–43.

Cohen, S. G., Ledford, G. E., and Spreitzer, G. M. 1996. A predictive model of self-managing work team effectiveness. *Human Relations, 49*(5), 643–676.

Cordery, J. L., Mueller, W. S., and Smith, L. M. 1991. Attitudinal and behavioral effects of autonomous group working: A longitudinal field study. *Academy of Management Journal, 34.*

Cotton, J. L. 1993. *Employee involvement.* Newbury Park, Calif.: SAGE Publications.

Creed, W. E., and Miles, R. E. 1996. Trust in organizations: A conceptual framework linking organizational forms, managerial philosophies, and the opportunity costs of control. In R. M. Kramer and T. R. Tyler (Eds.), *Trust in organizations: Frontiers of theory and research* (pp. 16–39). Newbury Park, Calif.: SAGE Publications.

Deci, E. L., and Ryan, R. M. 1987. The support of autonomy and the control of behavior. *Journal of Personality and Social Psychology, 53.*

De Dreu, C. K. W., and Weingart, L. R. 2003. Task versus relationship conflict, team performance, and team member satisfaction: A meta-analysis. *Journal of Applied Psychology, 88*(4), 741–749.

deLeon, L. (2001). Accountability for individuating behaviors in self-managing teams. *Organization Development Journal, 19*(4), 7–19.

Dirks, K. T., and Ferrin, D. L. 2001. The role of trust in organizational settings. *Organization Science, 12*(4), 450–467.

Druskat, V. U., and Kayes, D. C. 1999. The antecedents of team competence: Toward a fine-grained model of self-managing team effectiveness. In R. Wageman (Ed.), *Research on managing groups and teams: Groups in context* (vol. 2, pp. 201–231). Greenwich, Conn.: JAI Press.

Dwyer, D. J., Schwartz, R. H., and Fox, M. L. 1992. Decision-making autonomy in nursing. *Journal of Nursing Administration, 22.*

Farmer, S. M., and Roth, J. 1998. Conflict-handling behavior in work groups: Effects of group structure, decision processes, and time. *Small Group Research, 29*(6), 669–713.

Garcia-Prieto, P., Bellard, E., and Schneider, S. C. 2003. Experiencing diversity, conflict, and emotions in teams. *Applied Psychology: An International Review, 52*(3), 413–440.

Guzzo, R. A., and Shea, G. P. 1992. Group performance and intergroup relations in organizations. In M. D. Dunnette and L. M. Hough (Eds.), *Handbook of industrial and organizational psychology* (vol. 3, pp. 269–313). Palo Alto, Calif.: Psychological Press.

Hackman, J. R., and Oldham, G. R. 1976. Motivation through the design of work: Test of a theory. *Organizational Behavior and Human Performance, 16.*

Hinds, P. J., and Bailey, D. E. 2003. Out of sight, out of sync: Understanding conflict in distributed teams. *Organization Science, 14*(6), 615–632.

Ilgen, D. R., Hollenbeck, J. R., Johnson, M., and Jundt, D. 2005. Teams in organizations: From input-process-output models to IMOI models. *Annual Review of Psychology, 56,* 517–543.

Janssen, O., Van de Vliert, E., and Veenstra, C. 1999. How task and person conflict shape the role of positive interdependence in management teams. *Journal of Management, 25*(2), 117–141.

Janz, B. D., Colquitt, J. A., and Noe, R. A. 1997. Knowledge worker team effectiveness: The role of autonomy, interdependence, team development, and contextual support variables. *Personnel Psychology, 50,* 877–904.

Jehn, K. A. 1997. A qualitative analysis of conflict types and dimensions in organizational groups. *Administrative Science Quarterly, 42,* 530–557.

Jehn, K. A., and Chatman, J. A. 2000. The influence of proportional and perceptual conflict composition on team performance. *International Journal of Conflict Management, 11*(1), 56–73.

Jehn, K. A., Northcraft, G. B., and Neale, M. A. 1999. Why difference makes a difference: A field study of diversity, conflict and performance in workgroups. *Administrative Science Quarterly, 44*(4), 741–763.

Kiggundu, M. N. 1983. Task interdependence and job design: Test of a theory. *Organizational Behavior and Human Decision Processes, 31*(2), 145–172.

Kim, P. H., Ferrin, D. L., Cooper, C. D., and Dirks, K. T. 2004. Removing the shadow of suspicion: The effects of apology versus denial for repairing competence versus integrity based trust violations. *Journal of Applied Psychology, 89*(1), 104–118.

Klein, K. J., Dansereau, F., and Hall, R. J. 1994. Levels issues in theory development, data collection, and analysis. *Academy of Management Review, 19*(2), 195–229.

Korsgaard, M. A., Brodt, S. E., and Whitener, E. M. 2002. Trust in the face of conflict: The role of managerial trustworthy behavior and organizational context. *Journal of Applied Psychology, 87*(2), 312–319.

Kramer, R. M. 1999. Trust and distrust in organizations: Emerging perspectives, enduring questions. *Annual Review of Psychology, 50,* 569–598.

Kramer, R. M., and Tyler, T. R. 1996. *Trust in organizations: Frontiers of theory and research.* Newbury Park, Calif.: SAGE Publications.

Langfred, C. W. 2000a. The paradox of self-management: Individual and group autonomy in work groups. *Journal of Organizational Behavior, 21,* 563–585.

Langfred, C. W. 2000b. Work group design and autonomy: A field study of the interaction between task interdependence and group autonomy. *Small Group Research, 31*, 54–70.

Langfred, C. W. 2004. Too much of a good thing? The negative effects of high trust and autonomy in self-managing teams. *Academy of Management Journal. 47*(3), 385–399.

Langfred, C. W. 2005. Autonomy and performance in teams: The multi-level moderating effect of task interdependence. *Journal of Management, 31*(4) 513–529.

Langfred, C. W., and Moye, N. A. 2004. Effects of task autonomy on performance: An extended model considering motivational, informational and structural mechanisms. *Journal of Applied Psychology, 89*(6), 934–945.

Langfred, C. W., and Shanley, M. T. 2001. Small group research: Autonomous teams and progress on issues of context and levels of analysis. In R. Golembiewski (Ed.), *Handbook of organizational behavior* (vol. 2, pp. 81–111). New York: Marcel Dekker.

Lawler, E. E., Mohrman, S. A., and Ledford, G. E. 1995. *Creating high performance organizations: Practices and results of employee involvement and total quality management in Fortune 1000 companies.* San Francisco: Jossey-Bass.

Lewicki, R. J., McAllister, D. J., and Bies, R. J. 1998. Trust and distrust: New relationships and realities. *Academy of Management Review, 23,* 438–458.

Liden, R. C., Wayne, S. J., and Bradway, L. K. 1997. Task interdependence as a moderator of the relation between group control and performance. *Human Relations, 50*(2), 169–181.

Locke, E. A., and Schweiger, D. M. 1979. Participation in decision-making: One more look. In B. Staw (Ed.), *Research in organizational behavior* (vol. 1, pp. 265–340). Greenwich, Conn.: JAI Press.

Loher, B. T., Noe, R. A., Moeller, N. L., and Fitzgerald, M. P. 1985. A meta-analysis of the relation of job characteristics to job satisfaction. *Journal of Applied Psychology, 70*(2), 280–289.

Macy, B. A., and Izumi, H. 1993. Organizational change, design, and work innovation: A meta-analysis of 131 North American field studies 1961–1991. *Research in Organizational Change and Development, 7,* 235–313.

Markham, S. E., and Markham, I. S. 1995. Self-management and self-leadership re-examined: A level of analysis perspective. *Leadership Quarterly, 6,* 343–359.

Mayer, R. C., Davis, J. H., and Schoorman, F. D. 1995. An integrative model of organizational trust. *Academy of Management Review, 20*(3), 709–734.

McAllister, D. J. 1995. Affect and cognition-based trust as foundations for interpersonal cooperation in organizations. *Academy of Management Journal, 38,* 24–59.

McKnight, D. H., Cummings, L. L., and Chevarny, N. L. 1998. Initial trust formation in new organizational relationships. *Academy of Management Review, 23,* 473–490.

Miller, K. I., and Monge, P. R. 1986. Participation, satisfaction and productivity: A meta-analytic review. *Academy of Management Journal, 29,* 727–753.

Molleman, E., Nauta, A., and Jehn, K. A. 2004. Person-job fit applied to teamwork: A multilevel approach. *Small Group Research, 35*(5), 515–539.

Moye, N. A., and Langfred, C. W. 2005. Information sharing and group conflict: Going beyond decision making to understand the effects of information sharing on group performance. *International Journal of Conflict Management, 15*(4), 381–410.

Neck, C. P., Stewart, G. L., and Manz, C. C. 1996. Self-leaders within self-leading teams: Toward an optimal equilibrium. *Advances in Interdisciplinary Studies of Work Teams, 3,* 43–65.

Peterson, R. S., and Behfar, K. J. 2003. The dynamic relationship between performance feedback, trust and conflict in groups: A longitudinal study. *Organizational Behavior and Human Decision Processes, 92*(1–2), 102–112.

Rice, A. K. 1958. *Productivity and social organization.* London: Tavistock.

Rousseau, D. M. 1985. Issues of level in organizational research: Multi-level and cross-level perspectives. *Research in Organizational Behavior, 7*, 1–37.

Saavedra, R. P., Earley, P. C., and Van Dyne, L. 1993. Complex interdependence in task-performing groups. *Journal of Applied Psychology, 78*, 61–72.

Simons, T. L., and Peterson, R. S. 2000. Task conflict and relationship conflict in top management teams: The pivotal role of intragroup trust. *Journal of Applied Psychology, 85*(1), 102–111.

Sitkin, S. B., Rousseau, D. M, Burt, R. S., and Camerer, C. (Eds.) 1998. Special topic forum on trust in and between organizations. *Academy of Management Review, 23* (entire issue).

Spector, P. E. 1986. Perceived control by employees: A meta-analysis of studies concerning autonomy and participation at work. *Human Relations, 39.*

Stewart, G. L., and Barrick, M. R. 2000. Team structure and performance: Assessing the mediating role of intrateam process and the moderating role of task type. *Academy of Management Journal, 43*(2), 135–148.

Thompson, J. D. 1967. *Organizations in action.* New York: McGraw-Hill.

Thoms, P., Pinto, J. K., Parente, D. H., and Druskat, V. U. 2002. Adaptation to self-managing work teams. *Small Group Research, 33*(1), 3–31.

Trist, E. L., and Bamforth, K. 1951. Some social and psychological consequences of the long-wall method of goal getting. *Human Relations, 4*, 3–39.

Trist, E. L., Higgin, G., Murray, H., and Pollock, A. B. 1963. *Organisational choice.* London: Tavistock.

Uhl-Bien, M., and Graen, G. B. 1998. Individual self-management: Analysis of professionals' self-managing activities in functional and cross-functional teams. *Academy of Management Journal, 41*, 340–350.

Vardi, Y., and Weitz, E. 2004. *Misbehavior in organizations: Theory, research and management.* Mahwah, N.J.: Lawrence Erlbaum.

Von Glinow, M. A., Shapiro, D. L., and Brett, J. M. 2004. Can we talk, and should we? Managing emotional conflict in multicultural teams. *Academy of Management Review Special Issue: Language and Organization, 29*(4), 578–592.

Wageman, R. 1995. Interdependence and group effectiveness. *Administrative Science Quarterly, 40*, 145–180.

Wall, J. A., and Callister, R. R. 1995. Conflict and its management. *Journal of Management, 21*(3), 515–558.

Chapter 8

THE DIFFERENTIAL EFFECTS OF TRUST AND RESPECT ON TEAM CONFLICT

Matthew A. Cronin and Laurie R. Weingart

ABSTRACT

This chapter examines the effects of trust and respect on task, process, and relationship conflict in simulated management teams. We argue that trust and respect have distinct but related effects on the degree and type of conflict in teams and that therefore they need to be studied in concert to improve our understanding of conflict and conflict management. Respect is the level of esteem a person has for another; trust is the willingness to rely on another in the absence of monitoring. We find that respect increases task conflict and this relationship is even stronger when trust is low. In contrast, respect decreases relationship conflict whereas trust decreases process conflict. Our results imply that respect and trust are different but that measuring one without the other is misleading. We also discuss implications for managing conflict through increasing trust and respect.

INTRODUCTION

Teams are becoming increasingly common as the basic work unit in organizations (Cohen and Bailey, 1997; McGrath and Argote, 2001), so understanding the core processes regarding how teams work becomes more vital. To this end, we seek to understand how interpersonal relationships among team members, in particular trust and respect, affect conflict—one of the core team processes identified by McGrath and Argote (2001). Whether conflict is functional or dysfunctional to a team depends on the type of conflict and how it is managed (see chapter 1). We argue that understanding how trust and respect affect conflict can provide insight on how to manage conflict, which will ultimately lead to improved group performance (De Dreu, 1997).

Before laying out our arguments, we provide basic definitions of trust, respect, and conflict. Although we will develop these definitions later in the chapter, fundamentally we define respect as the level of esteem a person has for another and trust as one's willingness to rely on another in the absence of monitoring (Mayer, Davis, and Schoorman, 1995; Rousseau, Sitkin, Burt, and Camerer, 1998). Regarding conflict, we rely on the commonly used distinctions among task conflict, process conflict, and relationship conflict (Amason, 1996; Jehn and Chatman, 2000; Jehn and Mannix, 2001; Pinkley, 1990). Task conflict centers on what is to be done to achieve the desired objectives and is devoid of interpersonal negative emotions. Relationship conflict, on the other hand, centers on the people involved in the conflict, in particular their interpersonal incompatibilities; it tends to have negative affective components such as tension or friction. Process conflict centers on how the task will be performed, including who should do what and who is responsible for what.

A simplistic approach to studying interpersonal attitudes (like trust and respect) within teams would be to assume that people either feel good about one another or they do not. In that case, a single good/bad dimension would be sufficient to capture the range of teammates' attitudes toward each other. We take a more nuanced approach, that attitudes toward another team member are not necessarily universally positive or negative and that understanding the differential effects of particular attitudes like trust and respect can help us better understand the experience of conflict in a team.

For example, consider a cross-functional product development team we observed in our field research in the auto industry. Members of this team believed their fellow members from other functional areas were valuable to the team (that is, they were respected). For example, the engineers knew the designers would develop a concept that would be aesthetically pleasing and ergonomically correct. However, the engineers questioned whether the designers ever considered that their frequent requests for last-minute changes made the engineers' task more difficult. Thus, the engineers were loathe to rely on the designers (that is, they did not trust them). As a result, this team experienced a high level of conflict over delegation (that is, process conflict).

In another team, we observed evidence of the opposite—high trust but low respect. In that team, engineers thought that many of the changes the designers wanted were frivolous. Although the engineers believed the designers were acting in good faith (high trust), they were dismissive of the designers' needs (low respect). The conflicts in this team were more personal (that is, relationship conflict).

We recognize, then, that trust and respect do not always co-occur. Our research, reviewed in this chapter, explores how trust and respect differentially affect conflict within teams.

Trust and respect are examples of interpersonal factors that can influence the perception of and behavior toward others and therefore affect conflict (Wall and Callister, 1995). Thus, our research contributes to a growing body of literature on how interpersonal relationships affect the experience of conflict (Greenhalgh and Chapman, 1995, 1997; Jehn et al., 2001; Jehn and Shah, 1997; chapter 4 of this volume). In particular, we hope to add to the discourse on how specific facets of interpersonal relationships such as anger (Allred, Mallozzi, Matsui, and Raia, 1997; Van Kleef, De Dreu, and Manstead, 2004) or trust (Butler, 1999; Kimmel, Pruitt, Magenau, Konar-Goldband, and Carnevale, 1980; Simons and Peterson, 2000) affect conflict.

We chose to focus on trust and respect because each influences interpersonal behavior that is important to team functioning. Trust is important in reducing conflict (Jehn, 1995), encouraging cooperative behavior (Gambetta, 1988) and deference to others (Tyler, Degoey, and Smith, 1996), developing network ties (Miles and Snow, 1992), decreasing transaction costs (Uzzi, 1996, 1997; Williamson and Craswell, 1993), and facilitating rapid formulation of ad hoc work groups (Meyerson, Weick, and Kramer, 1996). Respect relates to perceptions of fair treatment (Tyler et al., 1996; Tyler and Lind, 1992), prejudice toward others (Glick and Fiske, 1991, 2001), leader/member exchange (Liden and Maslyn, 1998), decision making (Thompson, Kray, and Lind, 1998), and conflict reduction (Jehn, 1995; Jehn et al., 2001). We expect trust and respect to affect the conflict that occurs in teams as well.

While there is evidence for the effects of trust on conflict (Ross and LaCroix, 1996), there has been little direct examination of respect. For example, Simons and Peterson (2000) showed how trust moderates the effect of task conflict on relationship conflict. When trust was high, task conflict was less strongly related to relationship conflict, suggesting that the task conflict was less likely to be taken personally. In contrast, with the exception of our current line of research, no one has considered respect independently. Another study in our stream of research (Cronin and Weingart, 2005) began to distinguish independent effects of respect and trust on the strategies used to approach a conflict and the climate perceived between parties involved in that conflict. In most research, trust and respect have either been examined in the aggregate, have been confounded, or have been measured in isolation. We believe each approach is problematic.

Researchers who have discussed trust and respect as having an influence on conflict in teams have aggregated these attitudes toward others rather than empirically examining their independent effects. Jehn and Mannix (2001) measured trust and respect along with liking, cohesiveness, and conflict communication norms as a part of *group atmosphere.* They used this aggregate variable as a control variable in their study of task conflict, relationship conflict, and process conflict over time. Unfortunately, the group atmosphere variable was not focal to their arguments, nor were trust and respect disaggregated to observe their individual effects on conflict.

Cronin, Bezrukova, Weingart, and Tinsley (2004) examined how *affective integration,* the aggregate level of trust, respect, and liking, affected the satisfaction and effectiveness of simulated management teams. Again, affective integration was a single aggregate variable that allowed for no detection of each aspect's particular influence on group processes and outcomes.

In other research, trust and respect have been empirically confounded, probably because trust has been confused with its correlates. As Mayer et al. (1995) pointed out, trust often has been defined and measured too broadly. For example, Butler (1991) has 11 factors in his trust inventory, including value congruence, a factor that we will argue is more appropriately attributable to respect. Similarly, McAllister's (1995) measure of trust includes questions about respect. Thus, characteristics that may be correlated with trust (for example, respect) are absorbed (inappropriately) into what is defined as trust.

Finally, some research tends to examine trust in isolation (for example, McAllister, 1995) or respect (for example, Huo, Smith, Tyler, and Lind, 1996). If one is measured without controlling for the other, all the shared variance is attributed to the measured variable, resulting in a biased estimate of the effect size for the variable. This also undermines construct development, as one loses any nuanced interaction among relational dimensions by measuring a single variable in absence of others. For example, we will later argue that trusting a person you do not respect is somewhat hollow, because the benefits of trust will be in relation to something of little value to you. We would not be able to capture this dynamic without independent measures of trust and respect.

In this chapter, we differentiate trust and respect and then argue why each should differentially affect task, process, and relationship conflict. Given the voluminous literature on trust and conflict and the centrality of trust's role in negotiation (for example, Butler, 1999; De Dreu, Giebels, and Van de Vliert, 1998; Kimmel et al., 1980; Moore, Oesch, and Kostal, 1997; Naquin, 2000), we feel we should first clarify how differentiating respect from trust adds value to our thinking about conflict in order to motivate our inquiry. We turn to this issue next.

DEFINING AND DIFFERENTIATING RESPECT AND TRUST

A simple way to distinguish respect and trust is that respect is about esteem while trust is about reliability. Questions relating to trust might be "Are you telling the truth?" "Are you trying to harm me?" Questions related to respect are "How much consideration do you deserve?" "Do your ideas have any value?" These are both important issues, but in practice people are likely to judge them separately. We explore these differences in detail next. Figure 8.1 summarizes the differences and similarities between trust and respect. We argue that these complementary evaluations will affect the amount of conflict in teams.

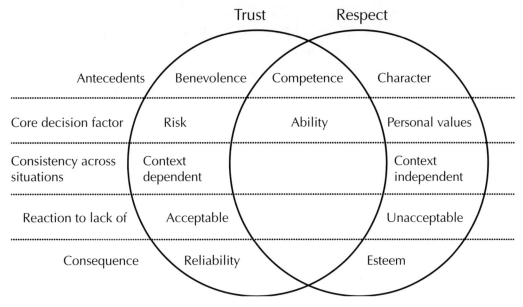

Figure 8.1
A Comparison between Trust and Respect

Trust manifests in the perception that a target (for our purposes, "target" refers to either a person or group) does not intend to deceive or harm the trusting person and is therefore trustworthy (see Mayer and Davis, 1999). As a behavioral inclination, we use the definition that seems to have the most support (Rousseau et al., 1998): Trust is the willingness to be vulnerable to another person in the absence of monitoring (Mayer et al., 1995). People who are trusted can be relied on. This follows from trust's antecedents: benevolence, integrity, competence (Mayer et al., 1995), or a lack of motivation to lie (Hass, 1981). Each of these is a reason to rely on a target, as one would feel the target's actions are done well (competence), done truthfully (integrity), and done without malice (benevolence).

Where trust has been overextended is in the realm of positive evaluation—that is, it may be inaccurate to assume that a trusted target is a valuable one. The inclination to be vulnerable to another implies no fear of harm, not assurance of benefit. Someone or something honest or benign (trustworthy) can still be seen as ineffective (for example, an oversight committee with good intentions and no real power), whereas someone or something malevolent or adversarial (not trustworthy) may still be effective (for example, a highly regarded competitor). Although competence, an antecedent of trust, would lead to the belief that what comes from the competent target is well done in terms of that skill, the skill can be considered of little or no value. We argue that the judgment of value is better assessed from the level of respect.

Respect manifests in the perceived level of esteem one has for a target (Cronin, 2004). As a behavioral inclination, respect is shown by acknowledging the status and dignity of the target (Tyler and Lind, 1992). The determination of value or esteem occurs when an individual appraises a target using his or her own value system (Cronin, 2004). In that values are enduring beliefs about what is good or desirable (Rokeach, 1973), respect implies a "good/bad" judgment of the target. The more a target is judged "good," the more the target is esteemed and believed to deserve consideration. It may be tempting to think of respect as a kind of liking, but a judgment of respect invokes a higher standard than a judgment of liking because it is linked to one's values. There can be times when, although one does not like a person (for example, a brilliant but difficult colleague) or group, one grudgingly respects that person or group.

One can infer from this discussion that respect and trust are correlated because attributes that are esteemed, such as honesty, are also a reason to trust. Yet respect and trust differ importantly in how they arise and change over time. Values are more central to respect than to trust. Respect is the result of an individual using his or her values to make a global assessment of a target's characteristics (Cronin, 2004); the resulting respect is an interaction between what the person values and the target's attributes. Trust can be informed by values (Jones and George, 1998), but the range of values is narrower (generally those related to benevolence and truthfulness), and trust is more a function of the target's values. (For example, being Machiavellian would not make me more trusting of another Machiavellian person, nor would it make me think honesty is less of a reason to trust someone.)

Across contexts, respect is also more constant than trust. The inputs to respect (my values and your attributes) are for the most part traits and should therefore be relatively stable across situations. Trust is much more sensitive to situational factors than respect. For example, an effective colleague who leaves one's corporation to work for a competitor may be less trusted by his former coworkers (the colleague is now a threat), although the coworkers' respect for that person should not change (the colleague is still the same person). Things like the motivation to lie (Hass, 1981) or conflicting goals are reasons for decreased trust; they bear directly on one's judgment of a target's reliability and subsequent willingness to be vulnerable, and these behaviors change across situations because of contextual moderators. Along these lines, we can also note that risk is central to the notion of trust (Gillespie, 2003; Johnson-George and Swap, 1982; Sheppard and Sherman, 1998). This is not true for respect. Respect has little to do with interdependence; it can be (and often is) assessed and demonstrated in the absence of any interdependence between parties (for example, a dismissive comment from a colleague would be disrespectful and produce negative feelings independent of the colleague's interdependence).

We can distinguish differences between trust and respect in terms of how people respond to a lack of either. People can accept, and may even expect, that they may not be trusted, such as when they are on opposite sides of an issue. However, people rarely accept a lack of respect, and violating a person's status and dignity often provokes anger and retaliation (Bies, 1987).

TRUST AND RESPECT IN TEAMS

In teams, trust and respect can exist as a generalized attitude toward other team members, and this should affect the nature of the interaction among team members. With team interaction, when you trust your teammates, you will be willing to rely on them. This logically follows from Mayer et al. (1995), as competence, benevolence, and integrity all imply reliability; you will believe what they say is true and is not intended to manipulate or deceive (Hass, 1981). Thus, trust should reduce a person's need to closely attend to what a target has to say. The person is willing to accept the trusted target's contribution at face value. When you respect people, you feel they deserve to be shown consideration and attention and believe that actions they pursue are likely to be worthwhile and meaningful (Cronin, 2004). This follows logically from the esteem you have for those you respect and your desire to communicate this esteem to them (Lind and Tyler, 1988; Smith and Tyler, 1997; Tyler and Lind, 1992). Thus, respect should increase a person's attention to what a target says or does, even in disagreements, given the desire to always treat a respected person professionally.

For purposes of illustration, let us consider how teams with varying levels of trust and respect might interact. Teams high in both trust and respect should be desirable, as team members would begin with the belief that their fellow teammates have something valuable to add to the team and thus should be listened to. Any information that was shared would then be synthesized by others without their fear of being duped. People's actions would be assumed to be both legitimate (respect) and without malfeasance (trust), and so people would interact seeking to maximize their synergy. Low-trust, low-respect teams would be teams only in name. Members of these teams would want very little to do with one another, both out of self-protection (due to lack of trust) and because interacting with others would be seen as a waste of time (due to lack of respect).

Teams high in respect but low in trust might appear as collections of individualists. One example would be a group of high performers working on a project with the knowledge that only one would get promoted. Although members might respect others on the team, they would be concerned about exposing any vulnerability to their teammates for fear they would be exploited. People would attend to each other's actions more from fear than a desire to collaborate. Teams high in trust but low in respect, on the other hand, are safe but ineffective. Such a team may be overly focused on pleasing its members to the detriment of the mission for which the team was created. The ineffectiveness would mean that members do not see much value in the contributions of their teammates, even if they are well intentioned.

Respect and Conflict

Respect implies that other teammates are esteemed and manifests in the attention and consideration they are shown. When respect is lacking, people may not want to associate with each other, which might limit the amount of experienced conflict. However, when one chooses to dismiss another (showing disrespect), the other will likely react angrily (Cronin, 2004; Miller, 2001) and possibly express aggression back at the person who was disrespectful (Bies, 1987), increasing conflict. Thus, we propose that respect should affect all three types of conflict: task, relationship, and process. We argue that respect will decrease process and relationship conflict but increase task conflict.

Although it may seem counterintuitive at first, we expect the amount of task conflict to increase with increasing respect among team members. If people disagree with their team members but believe that those members' perspectives are likely to have value, then people will be more inclined to take the time to work through the disagreement. The extra time will extend the conflict episode, resulting in the perception of more task conflict. In contrast, in the absence of respect for other teammates, one would not care to bother resolving a disagreement. We therefore hypothesize:

> *Hypothesis 1a (H1a):* **As the level of respect between team members increases, the level of task conflict in the team will increase.**

Respect is based on a value judgment of a target and results in approval or disapproval. Therefore, a person who does not approve of his or her teammates' character is likely to have personality (that is, relationship) conflicts with them. Similarly, since showing respect implies showing consideration for others' status and dignity, when there is little respect for one's teammates, people may feel less inhibited about being disrespectful toward others. That is, teammates may cut each other off, dismiss each other's ideas, or even "dress down" others in front of colleagues—all of which can be disrespectful (Miller, 2001). A person would not do this to those he or she respected because the person would want to demonstrate regard for their status and dignity (Tyler and Lind, 1992). We posit:

> *Hypothesis 1b (H1b):* **As the level of respect between team members increases, the level of relationship conflict in the team will decrease.**

Unlike task conflict, which should be about ideas, process conflict is in part about who should do what. Respect should therefore decrease process conflict because the esteem for others will make teammates want to include those they respect in the activity. One of the ways to show respect is to ask for people's input so that they feel their perspective has been taken into consideration (Tyler et al.,

1996). In addition, one would want to delegate tasks to a person who one thought would bring value to the project, and respect should signal this potential value. Therefore:

> *Hypothesis 1c (H1c):* **As the level of respect between team members increases, the level of process conflict in the team will decrease.**

Trust and Conflict

If trust makes one believe in the truthfulness and good intentions of fellow teammates, then we expect trust to decrease task and process conflict but not affect relationship conflict. We argue that trust should decrease task conflict. One reason is that trust encourages people to leave others alone to do their work and decreases the impulse to monitor (Kruglanski, 1970). This reduces the opportunities for task conflict to occur in the first place. In addition, when people do disagree, the disagreements should not last as long because trust should increase the probability of acceptance of the target's opinion on the disputed issue. Trust should remove some of the worry that the target's claims are wrong or misleading. For example, imagine that a person thinks a target's assignment will take three days to complete. If the target claims it will only take two days, the person can either accept this and stop arguing, or argue more in order to verify the claim. Trust, which should encourage belief in the absence of evidence, would provide the reason to accept the target's claim and thereby cut short the task conflict.

> *Hypothesis 2a (H2a):* **As the level of trust between team members increases, the level of task conflict in the team will decrease.**

We do not expect trust to affect relationship conflict. We argue that as trust decreases, the desire to engage in relationship conflict may increase, but the opportunities to do so will decrease. That is, seeing teammates as untrustworthy may prime a person to argue with the teammates' suggestions because they believe there may be hidden harm in the suggestions. However, at the same time we expect people to avoid interacting with an individual they do not trust (as much as that is possible) in order to reduce any potential vulnerability to that person. These two forces should offset one another, resulting in no relationship between trust and relationship conflict. The reverse is true as well; when trust is high, people will feel safe interacting more but will disagree less. The net result will be no observable relationship between trust and relationship conflict.

> *Hypothesis 2b (H2b):* **Trust between team members will show no effect on relationship conflict.**[1]

We expect that trust will decrease the level of process conflict in a team. It should be easier to come to agreement about delegating work to a competent target, as people will be less likely to fear that the work will be poorly executed. Because trust implies benevolence, a lack of trust may cause people to fear that the result of delegation will harm the other teammates (see chapter 7), leading to process conflict.

> **Hypothesis 2c (H2c):** As the level of trust between team members increases, the level of process conflict in the team will decrease.

The Interaction of Trust and Respect on Conflict

We believe that trust and respect should only interact with regard to task conflict. High respect makes one assume that one's teammates have notions worth pursuing. However, when trust is low, there is little point in pursuing these perspectives because one will be suspicious of the people and their motives. This will mute the effect of respect on task conflict. When trust is high, people will have an easier time incorporating and integrating the perspectives of their teammates because they need not fear malice or lies. We therefore expect the highest level of task conflict in high-trust/high-respect teams.

> **Hypothesis 3 (H3):** The increase in task conflict in teams due to respect will be greater when trust is high.

We do not expect trust and respect to interact to affect relationship conflict; trust adds nothing to provoke people into fighting beyond what respect already covers. That is, the negative character assessment that is related to trust (for example, dishonesty, treachery) is already subsumed in the respect judgment. For process conflict, we also expect no interaction, as the reasons each characteristic affects process conflict (trust is about malfeasance, respect is about showing someone you think they matter) are independent judgments. The shared component between trust and respect that we expect to affect process conflict, competence, could operate through either trust or respect.

METHOD

PARTICIPANTS

Participants were 299 master's of business administration (MBA) students who were in five- to six-person simulated top management teams. After eliminating teams that had fewer than three respondents, we were left with 211 participants in 60 teams.

Students ranged in age from 22 to 54 (M = 30.2 years, SD = 4.4 yrs), and approximately one quarter were women. The teams were engaged in a realistic business simulation called Management Game (Cohen, Dill, Kuehn, and Winters, 1964). Participation in the study earned teams a chance to win six prizes ranging from $250 to $550.

SETTING

The MBA teams act as the top management team of a wristwatch company. The simulated companies operate in a virtual world for a virtual three-year period over 14 weeks. Sixty-seven parameters in the simulation (for example, demand, competition, cost of labor, stock price) interactively determine the dynamics of the world, and the worlds evolve over time in partial response to the organizational decisions made by the teams. The teams make decisions about issues such as product positioning, production method, distribution channels, research and development (R&D) spending, and organizational financing. These decisions are put into the simulation twice a week as moves. Teams also have to deal with exogenous shocks and opportunities that arise in the world such as a class-action lawsuit, a labor negotiation, and purchase of a new factory. At the end of each simulated year, the teams present a report to their board of directors, local business executives who volunteer to act in the simulation. The presentations last about three hours. During this time, teams justify their decisions, summarize their market position, and present their strategy for the coming year.

The simulation begins in March. The students select the team presidents by popular vote. The presidents then pick the rest of the teams in a round-robin draft. The first simulation year ends with a board meeting in April. The simulation is inactive over the summer break. After summer break, the simulation intensifies. The second board meeting is held after the second simulation year ends during the third week in September. It was after this meeting that participants completed the first survey. The third year and final board meeting took place in mid-October. Participants filled out a second survey after the third board meeting.

The Management Game simulation is an attractive hybrid of an experiment and a survey of real top-management teams. As in an experiment, the teams are evenly matched because of the round-robin draft for the team members and the similarity in terms of participants' age and work experience. In addition, all companies start from essentially the same place. As is the case with real top-management teams, the task assigned to teams is exceedingly complex, and participants take it seriously. Management Game has been Carnegie Mellon's flagship MBA course since the 1960s. Because of the complexity, realism, and competitive nature of game, the students are highly motivated and put tremendous effort into the course.

MEASUREMENTS

The data used in the analysis came from surveys administered to team members after the second and third board meetings and from board members' evaluations. The group survey assessed individuals' perceptions of team dynamics—in particular, the levels of respect, trust, and conflict within the team. This survey was given twice so that variables at time 1 (trust, respect) could be used to predict levels of other variables (task conflict, process conflict, relationship conflict) at time 2.

Scales

All items were measured on 5-point scales. The scale items are provided in appendix 8.A. Respect was measured using a 13-item scale (α = .95) developed in Cronin (2004). The trust scale consisted of three items: one general trust item, an item on vulnerability, and an item on truthfulness (α = .81). Task conflict, process conflict, and relationship conflict scales were each adapted from prior work on these three types of conflict (Jehn and Mannix, 2001). Task conflict consisted of five items (α =.85). Relationship conflict consisted of three items (α = .91). Process conflict consisted of six items (α = .80).

Board Ratings

Peterson and Behfar (2003) argued that in ongoing teams, feedback can have an effect on the amount of subsequent conflict. Therefore, it is possible that people's responses to the conflict items at time 2 were influenced by how positive or negative their board of directors' feedback was at their most recent board meeting. To control for this influence, we included each team's board of directors rating of the team's performance at time 2. The rating was the aggregate rating across 12 dimensions (each rated on a 7-point scale ranging from unacceptable to outstanding). These ratings were discussed and agreed on by all members of a board of directors at the time of the board meeting, and the ratings counted toward students' grades.

Scale Development

An issue of paramount importance was whether respect and trust actually reflected distinct latent factors. We compared a two-latent-factor versus one-latent-factor model using structural equation modeling. As predicted, the two-factor model (trust and respect) had an acceptable fit (CFI = .923) and was significantly better than the one-factor model ($\chi^2_{(1)}$ = 24.40, p < .0001). This was critical evidence than trust and respect are naturally distinguishable. This discounts the alternative explanation that the trust and respect items represented a single latent "relationship" factor.

We determined that group-level effects existed for all the variables using analysis of variance (ANOVA) where group is the single independent variable that predicts each of the scale variables used in the analyses. This is equivalent to using an intraclass correlation (Bliese and Halverson, 1996). We found group effects for all variables at $p < .05$. We aggregated the individual responses to the group level by averaging the variable scores for each scale across team members.

The number of people who filled out a particular survey at a given time period varied from one[2] to six (M = 2.4). To guard against biased estimates, we tested whether the number of people on a team who filled out a survey affected the score for each of the different variables, but we found no relationship. After aggregating the scales to the team level, the variables were scaled and centered (Myers, 1990). This was particularly important because when one is calculating an interaction term, uncentered data biases the estimates of the term's beta weights (Aiken and West, 1991).

Model Analyses

The basic framework used for analysis was a regression equation in which the independent variables (trust and respect) measured at time 1 were used to predict dependent variables (conflict) at time 2. We used a weighted least squares regression because the data had several outliers or the errors were heteroscedastic. Observations were therefore weighted by the magnitude of predicted residual.[3] This corrects for any undue influence of a particular observation and reduces heteroscedasticity.

We ran regression equations to test the hypotheses. For each dependent variable, we used our measures of trust and respect and their interaction at time 1 as predictors. Although we only predicted one interaction, we tested for them for all the dependent variables to explore the possibility that it is the combination of trust and respect that influences team conflict rather than either one independently. We used a hierarchical approach in running the analysis, entering trust first, then respect, then their interaction. We used this approach to determine the effect of respect over and above the effect of trust and the effect of the interaction over and above the direct effects of trust and respect. To ensure that our prediction for each type of conflict (for example, task conflict) was not contaminated by covariation with the other two types (for example, relationship conflict and process conflict), we controlled for the other two types in each equation. We also controlled for the board rating at time 2 in accordance with the recommendations of Peterson and Behfar (2003).

RESULTS

Table 8.1 presents correlations among the variables of interest. Note that trust and respect are highly correlated. To judge whether the level of multicolinearity was too high, the R^2 when respect predicted trust was examined ($R^2 = .58$) and was

Table 8.1
Correlation Matrix

	Respect	Trust	Task Conflict	Relationship Conflict	Process Conflict
Respect	—				
Trust	0.79‡	—			
Task conflict	0.31*	0.25*	—		
Relationship conflict	−0.47‡	−0.32†	0.05	—	
Process conflict	−0.45‡	−0.45‡	−0.03	0.70‡	—

* $p < .05$
† $p < .01$
‡ $p < .001$

— = not relevant

acceptable (Myers, 1990). Nonetheless, for all regression equations, the colinearity diagnostics were examined and always fell within acceptable parameters (Norusis, 2004). Examining Table 8.1, it appears that trust and respect tend to have similar correlations across the different types of conflict. Although this may seem to imply that trust and respect are substitutable, using trust and respect as predictors in the regression analyses shows that these bivariate correlations mask a different underlying story. Table 8.2 presents the results of regression analyses using trust and respect to predict the levels of relationship, task, and process conflict. The addition of the trust x respect interaction (T×R) significantly improved the R^2 only in the case of task conflict.

Regression results in Table 8.2 show that respect had a significant effect over and above the effect of trust on relationship conflict (equation 2: F for R^2 change = 10.53, $p < .01$) and task conflict (equation 5: F for R^2 change = 4.48, $p < .05$), but not on process conflict (equation 8). As shown in Table 8.2, equation 2, respect at time 1 was negatively related to relationship conflict at time 2 ($\beta = -.53$, $p < .01$), supporting H1b. As expected, trust was not a significant predictor of relationship conflict (H2b). For task conflict, respect had a positive effect (Table 8.2, equation 5: $\beta = .48$, $p < .05$), supporting H1a, but trust did not have the negative effect predicted in H2a. The T×R interaction revealed a significant effect on task conflict (Table 8.2, equation 6: $\beta = -.35$, $p < .05$), and no other interactions were significant. As shown in the graph of the interaction in Figure 8.2, trust moderated the positive effect of respect. Contrary to the form of the interaction predicted in H3, the positive relationship between respect and task conflict was stronger when trust was low. Finally, trust reduced process conflict (Table 8.2, equation 8: $\beta = -.40$, $p < .05$), supporting H2c, while respect did not (disconfirming H1c).

Table 8.2
The Effect of Respect and Trust on Conflict Management

	Relationship Conflict			Task Conflict			Process Conflict		
	Equation 1	Equation 2	Equation 3	Equation 4	Equation 5	Equation 6	Equation 7	Equation 8	Equation 9
Trust	−0.10	0.27†	0.24	0.31*	−0.04	−0.13	−0.29‡	−0.40*	−0.42*
Respect		−0.53‡	−0.55‡		0.48*	0.34		0.15	0.04
T × R			−0.12			−0.35*			−0.04
Control variables									
Board evaluation	−0.08	0.03	0.03	0.10	0.02	0.02	−0.03	−0.05	−0.06
Relationship conflict				0.12	0.26	0.17	0.64§	0.67§	0.66§
Task conflict	0.13	0.17†	0.14				−0.01	−0.03	−0.04
Process conflict	0.65§	0.59§	0.59§	0.00	−0.06	−0.04			
R^2	0.509	0.585	0.594	0.100	0.165	0.245	0.582	0.587	0.587
F or R^2 change	15.32§	10.53‡	1.33	1.64	4.48*	6.09*	20.54§	0.64	0.09
df	59, 4	58, 5	57, 6	59, 4	58, 5	57, 6	59, 4	58, 5	57, 6

Note: Standardized beta coefficients given.
* $p < .05$
† $p < .10$
‡ $p < .01$
§ $p < .001$

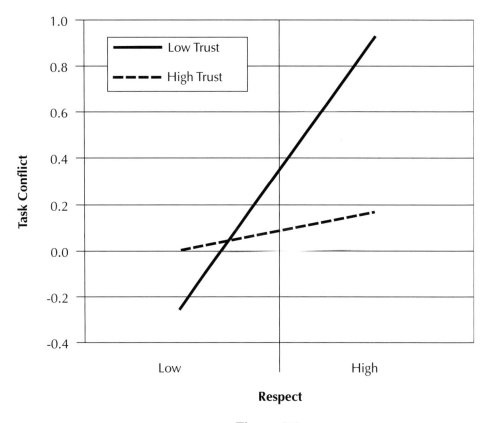

Figure 8.2
Interaction between Trust and Respect on Task Conflict

Discussion

A main objective of this study was to empirically demonstrate that trust and respect have distinct effects on conflict. In that regard, we believe this study has succeeded. In fact, the differential effects of trust and respect were even more extreme than predicted. Rather than both trust and respect independently influencing conflict, they influenced different forms of conflict altogether. Respect and trust did show interdependence as trust moderated the strength of the effect of respect on task conflict, but not in the way we expected. Respect was more strongly related to task conflict when trust was low.

It is not surprising that trust was predictive of process conflict whereas respect was predictive of relationship conflict, since process conflict relates to the distribution and coordination of work whereas relationship conflict is more personal. Effective teamwork requires people to work both independently and interdependently, and team members must rely on others to complete their assignments. Trust is the mechanism of reliance without monitoring and thus reduces process conflict. In that relationship conflict is driven by interpersonal incompatibilities and respect signals compatibility of values, it is not surprising that respect is the primary (if not dominant) driver of relationship conflict.

The interaction between trust and respect on task conflict is also an important and interesting finding. Team members experienced the most task conflict when trust was low and respect was high. We suggest that respect motivates people to heed what teammates have to say; but the lack of trust may make them suspicious of the target's underlying motives and thereby prompts them to seek further clarification and/or assurance. This might extend the amount of time it takes to resolve task conflicts. The combination of high respect and low trust might also increase the frequency of task conflict (that is, more task conflict events rather than longer task conflict events). Lower trust might motivate people to question their respected teammates more often, rather than take what they have to say at face value. Additional research is needed to determine the mechanisms through which the combined effects of trust and respect increase task conflict.

The fact that trust's effect on conflict changed with the addition of respect as a predictor lends credence to the idea that, in prior research, trust was subject to omitted variable bias. That is, trust's effect was bolstered by other unmeasured variables, of which respect was probably one. There is further evidence of this statement in the large differences between the zero order correlations and the resulting beta coefficients found in the regression equations. It is important to note that trust's subdued effects in this context should *not* diminish the importance of trust for conflict. Rather, the point is that along with sharpening the theoretical definition (e.g., Mayer, et al., 1995) and the measurement (e.g., Gillespie, 2003) of trust, we must also sharpen our understanding of its empirical effects by measuring it along with other related but distinct concepts. Trust is *an* important interpersonal factor, not *the* important interpersonal factor.

In distinguishing respect from trust, we explicitly included competence/expertise in our definition and measure of respect (e.g., "I think my teammates have useful perspectives"), but not trust. However, in the past others have tapped into competence/expertise when measuring trust. Thus, one could argue an alternative explanation; that competence and expertise rather than trust or respect are what drives our results. We ran additional analyses separating respect into two subscales, one relating to esteem for principles, the other relating to useful knowledge, which could be construed as expertise or competence. Results did not support this alternative explanation. Whereas the significance of the esteem component decreased to marginal, it was still dominant, and adding knowledge did not add significant predictive power to any of the equations. To some degree, however, trying to separate competence from respect misses the point. Respect is an evaluative judgment that goes beyond competence, but competence is an integral part of respect. Moreover, since attitudes are not partially decomposable (Eagly and Chaiken, 1998), one cannot simply remove competence from the construct and expect it to retain its original character.

IMPLICATIONS

The differential effects of trust and respect imply alternative strategies for conflict management. In the case of relationship conflict, recognized as having few redeeming qualities, one should increase respect among teammates, not trust. If, as others have found (Jehn, Northcraft, and Neale, 1999), process conflict has little benefit for teams, then trust is what should be bolstered to keep process conflict down, increasing respect will not be helpful.

The situation is not as straightforward when it comes to task conflict. While increasing respect appears to raise the level of task conflict, it's usually the case that increasing task conflict is bad for a team. Task conflict has been shown to be more likely to have negative or neutral than positive effects on team performance (De Dreu and Weingart, 2003). On par, increasing task conflict is more likely to hinder than help team performance. However, there may be factors that alter the character of task conflict and thereby increase its usefulness. If task conflict can occur in a collaborative communication context, and perhaps be accompanied by training in effective conflict management, it could positively influence team performance (De Dreu, 1997; De Dreu and Weingart, 2003; Lovelace, Shapiro, and Weingart, 2001). The level of trust becomes especially relevant in this context, in that low trust should reduce the likelihood that teams will be able to develop a collaborative communication context because of the negative attributions teammates may make about each other (Simons and Peterson, 2000). Thus, it is likely that in teams characterized by high respect but low trust the level of task conflict will be high and maladaptive. If a person views a teammate as valuable but also as a person who cannot be trusted, the person will be especially resistant to the teammate's positions and arguments for fear they contain malicious intent that is cunningly disguised. This resistance should stimulate and prolong task conflict.

Another factor related to the level of collaboration among teammates is the approach that the team takes to conflict management. Conflict management, and thus the experience of conflict, can take the form of *interests*-based (problem-solving) discussions; discussions of norms of fairness, standards, and *rights;* or *power* struggles (Ury, Brett, and Goldberg, 1988). Interests-based approaches improve quality of agreements (Pruitt and Carnevale, 1993) whereas more contentious rights-based and power-based approaches decrease quality of agreements (Brett, Shapiro, and Lytle, 1998). We conjecture that the approach to resolving task conflict (interests, rights, or power) may be influenced by the levels of respect and trust within the team, which in turn will influence (that is, moderate) whether task conflict helps or hinders team performance. For example, if as a result of low trust a person does not believe what a target says, will that person be more likely to engage in rights-based discussions (because external standards rely less on belief in the target)? If respect is high and I esteem your values, will it make me more motivated to try to satisfy your interests, hence increasing the effectiveness of interest-based bargaining? If the approach to conflict management influences the effectiveness of task conflict (Fisher, Ury, and Patton, 1991; Weingart, Cronin, Houser, Cagan, and Vogel, 2005), then knowing how trust and respect affect conflict management is of additional value.

LIMITATIONS

We have looked at a snapshot effect of trust and respect on conflict, yet conflict can ebb and flow over a group's life span (see chapter 6 in this volume; Peterson et al., 2003), and there is some evidence that the different types of conflict can have different effects depending on when the conflict occurs (Jehn et al., 2001). As we have theorized, respect and trust may develop differentially over time as well. All of these issues point to taking a more longitudinal approach to the study of trust and respect in groups. Yet our purpose here was simply to test our belief that respect (as well as trust) contributes to the experience of conflict in a group. Our results suggest that additional research in this area would be fruitful.

We also recognize that the teams we examined were very interdependent, as they were specialized and highly pressed for time. Interdependence may moderate some of the effects we found. For example, in the current study, team members had to work together; they were unable to avoid others in their group, even if they don't trust one another. In such a case, team members will probably experience more arguments, perhaps of a more personal strain, so respect may have a larger influence. Alternatively, when people are free to choose who they can work with, which is the case in a more market-driven environment, low trust and low respect may behave more similarly (both would cause withdrawal). Again, these are questions that can only be answered by further research, and our purpose here has been to stimulate interest in that research.

NOTES

1. This is a null hypothesis. We present it for symmetry.

2. Teams had at least three people who filled out the survey, but in some cases there was a single respondent for a team for a time period (i.e., three teams at time 1 and one team at time 2).

3. The actual procedure was to run ordinary least squares (OLS) on the equation and then save the residuals. Calculate the log of the squared residuals, and use these as the dependent variable in the same OLS equation. Save the predicted values of this second regression. Then use $1/\sqrt{\varepsilon}$ raised to the predicted value as the weight.

References

Aiken, L. S., and West, S. 1991. *Multiple regression: Testing and interpreting interactions.* Newbury Park, Calif.: SAGE Publications.

Allred, K. G., Mallozzi, J. S., Matsui, F., and Raia, C. P. 1997. The influence of anger and compassion on negotiation performance. *Organizational Behavior and Human Decision Processes, 70*(3), 175–187.

Amason, A. C. 1996. Distinguishing the effects of functional and dysfunctional conflict on strategic decision making: Resolving a paradox for top management teams. *Academy of Management Journal, 39*(1), 123–148.

Bies, R. J. 1987. The predicament of injustice: The management of moral outrage. *Research in Organizational Behavior, 9,* 289–319.

Bliese, P. D., and Halverson, R. R. 1996. *Group size, group process effects and ICC values.* Paper presented at the Academy of Management.

Brett, J. M., Shapiro, D. L., and Lytle, A. L. 1998. Breaking the bonds of reciprocity in negotiations. *Academy of Management Journal, 41,* 410–424.

Butler, J. K. Jr. 1991. Toward understanding and measuring conditions of trust: Evolution of a condition of trust inventory. *Journal of Management, 17*(3), 643–663.

Butler, J. K. Jr. 1999. Trust expectations, information sharing, climate of trust, and negotiation effectiveness and efficacy. *Group and Organization Management, 24*(2), 217–238.

Cohen, K. J., Dill, W. R., Kuehn, A. A., and Winters, P. R. 1964. *The Carnegie Tech Management Game: An experiment in business education.* Unpublished manuscript, Carnegie Mellon University.

Cohen, S. G., and Bailey, D. E. 1997. What makes teams work: Group effectiveness research from the shop floor to the executive suite. *Journal of Management, 23,* 239–290.

Cronin, M. A. 2004. *The effect of respect on interdependent work.* Unpublished Doctoral dissertation, Carnegie Mellon University.

Cronin, M. A., and Weingart, L. R. 2005. *The differential roles of respect and trust on negotiation.* Paper presented at the International Association for Conflict Management Conference, Seville, Spain.

Cronin, M. A., Bezrukova, K., Weingart, L. R., and Tinsley, C. 2004. *Agree or not agree? The role of cognitive and affective processes in group disagreements.* Paper presented at the International Association for Conflict Management Conference, Pittsburgh, Pa.

De Dreu, C. K. W. 1997. Productive conflict: The importance of conflict management and conflict issue. In C. K. W. De Dreu and E. Van de Vliert (Eds.), *Using conflict in organizations.* London: SAGE Publications.

De Dreu, C. K. W., and Weingart, L. R. 2003. Task versus relationship conflict, team performance, and team member satisfaction: A meta-analysis. *Journal of Applied Psychology, 88,* 741–749.

De Dreu, C. K. W., Giebels, E., and Van de Vliert, E. 1998. Social motives and trust in integrative negotiation: The disruptive effects of punitive capacity. *Journal of Applied Psychology, 83*(3), 408–422.

Eagly, A. H., and Chaiken, S. 1998. Attitude structure and function. In D. T. Gilbert, S. T. Fiske, and G. Lindzey (Eds.), *The handbook of social psychology,* 4th edition (vol. 1, pp. 269–322). New York: McGraw-Hill.

Fisher, W., Ury, W., and Patton, B. 1991. *Getting to yes.* New York: Penguin Books.

Gambetta, D. 1988. *Trust: Making and breaking cooperative relations.* New York: Basil Blackwell.

Gillespie, N. 2003. *Measuring trust in relationships: The behavioral trust inventory.* Paper presented at the Academy of Management Conference, Seattle, Wash.

Glick, P., and Fiske, S. T. 1991. Sexism and other "isms": Interdependence, status, and the ambivalent content of stereotypes. In W. B. Swann, J. H. Langlois, and L. A. Gilbert (Eds.), *Sexism and stereotypes in modern society: The gender science of Janet Taylor Spence* (pp. 193–221). Washington, D.C.: American Psychological Association.

Glick, P., and Fiske, S. T. 2001. Ambivalent stereotypes as legitimizing ideologies: Differentiating paternalistic and envious prejudice. In J. Jost and B. Major (Eds.), *The psychology of legitimacy* (pp. 278–306). Cambridge, UK: Cambridge University Press.

Greenhalgh, L., and Chapman, D. I. 1995. Joint decision making: The inseparability of relationships and negotiation. In R. M. Kramer and D. M. Messick (Eds.), *Negotiation as a social process* (pp. 160–185). Newbury Park, Calif.: SAGE Publications.

Greenhalgh, L., and Chapman, D. I. 1997. Relationships between disputants: An analysis of their characteristics and impact. In S. A. Gleason (Ed.), *Frontiers in dispute resolution and human resources* (pp. 203–229). East Lansing: Michigan State University.

Hass, R. G. 1981. Effects of source characteristics on cognitive responses in persuasion. In R. E. Petty, T. M. Ostrom, and T. C. Brock (Eds.), *Cognitive responses in persuasion* (pp. 141–172). Hillsdale, N.J.: Lawrence Erlbaum.

Huo, Y. J., Smith, H. J., Tyler, T. R., and Lind, E. A. 1996. Superordinate identification, subgroup identification, and justice concerns: Is separatism the problem—is assimilation the answer? *Psychological Science, 7,* 40–45.

Jehn, K. A. 1995. A multimethod examination of the benefits and detriments of intragroup conflict. *Administrative Science Quarterly, 40,* 256–282.

Jehn, K. A., and Chatman, J. A. 2000. The influence of proportional and perceptual conflict composition on team performance. *International Journal of Conflict Management, 11*(1), 56–73.

Jehn, K. A., and Mannix, E. A. 2001. The dynamic nature of conflict: A longitudinal study of intragroup conflict. *Academy of Management Journal, 44,* 238–251.

Jehn, K. A., and Shah, P. P. 1997. Interpersonal relationships and task performance: An examination of the mediating processes in friendships on task performance. *Journal of Personality and Social Psychology, 72,* 775–790.

Jehn, K. A., Northcraft, G., and Neale, M. 1999. Why differences make a difference. *Administrative Science Quarterly, 44,* 741–763.

Johnson-George, C., and Swap, W. C. 1982. Measurement of specific interpersonal trust: Construction and validation of a scale to assess trust in a specific other. *Journal of Personality and Social Psychology, 43*(6), 1306–1317.

Jones, G. R., and George, J. M. 1998. The experience and evolution of trust: Implications for cooperation and teamwork. *Academy of Management Review, 23*(3), 531–547.

Kimmel, M. J., Pruitt, D. G., Magenau, M. H., Konar-Goldband, E., and Carnevale, P. J. D. 1980. Effects of trust, aspiration and gender on negotiation tactics. *Journal of Personality and Social Psychology, 38*(1), 9–22.

Kruglanski, A. W. 1970. Attributing trustworthiness in supervisor-worker relations. *Journal of Experimental Social Psychology, 6,* 214–232.

Liden, R. C., and Maslyn, J. M. 1998. Multidimensionality of leader-member exchange: An empirical assessment through scale development. *Journal of Management, 24,* 43–72.

Lind, E. A., and Tyler, T. R. 1988. *The social psychology of procedural justice.* New York: Plenum.

Lovelace, K., Shapiro, D., and Weingart, L. R. 2001. Maximizing crossfunctional new product teams' innovativeness and constraint adherence: A conflict communications perspective. *Academy of Management Journal, 44*(4), 779–783.

Mayer, R. C., and Davis, J. H. 1999. The effect of performance appraisal systems on trust for management: A field quasi-experiment. *Journal of Applied Psychology, 84,* 123–137.

Mayer, R. C., Davis, J. H., and Schoorman, F. D. 1995. An integrative model of organizational trust. *Academy of Management Review, 20,* 709–724.

McAllister, D. J. 1995. Affect- and cognition-based trust as foundations for interpersonal cooperation in organizations. *Academy of Management Journal, 38,* 24–59.

McGrath, J. E., and Argote, L. 2001. Group processes in organizational contexts. In M. A. Hogg and R. S. Tindale (Eds.), *Blackwell handbook of social psychology* (vol. 3, pp. 603–627). Oxford, UK: Blackwell.

Meyerson, D., Weick, K. E., and Kramer, R. M. (Eds.). 1996. *Swift trust and temporary groups.* Newbury Park, Calif.: SAGE Publications.

Miles, R. E., and Snow, C. C. 1992. Causes of failure in network organizations. *California Management Review* (Summer), 72–93.

Miller, D. T. 2001. Disrespect and the experience of injustice. *Annual Review of Psychology, 52,* 527–553.

Moore, D. A., Oesch, J. M., and Kostal, G. 1997. *Trust in negotiations: The good news and the bad news.* Evanston, Ill.: Northwestern University.

Myers, R. H. 1990. *Classical and modern regression with applications,* 2nd ed. Boston: PWS-KENT.

Naquin, C. E. Jr. 2000. Trust and distrust in group negotiations. *Dissertation Abstracts International Section A: Humanities and Social Sciences, 60*(12-A), 4509.

Norusis, M. J. 2004. *SPSS 12.0 guide to data analysis.* Upper Saddle River, N.J.: Prentice Hall.

Peterson, R. S., and Behfar, K. J. 2003. The dynamic relationship between performance feedback, trust, and conflict in groups: A longitudinal study. *Organizational Behavior and Human Decision Processes, 92,* 102–112.

Pinkley, R. L. 1990. Dimensions of conflict frame: Disputant interpretations of conflict. *Journal of Applied Psychology, 75,* 117–126.

Pruitt, D. G., and Carnevale, P. J. 1993. *Negotiation in social conflict.* Pacific Grove, Calif.: Brooks/Cole Publishing.

Rokeach, M. 1973. *The nature of human values.* New York: Free Press.

Ross, W., and LaCroix, J. 1996. Multiple meanings of trust in negotiation theory and research: A literature review and integrative model. *International Journal of Conflict Management, 7*(4), 314–360.

Rousseau, D. M., Sitkin, S. B., Burt, R. S., and Camerer, C. 1998. Not so different after all: A cross-discipline view of trust. *Academy of Management Review, 23,* 393–404.

Sheppard, B. H., and Sherman, D. M. 1998. The grammars of trust: A model and general implications. *Academy of Management Review, 23*(3), 422–438.

Simons, T. L., and Peterson, R. S. 2000. Task conflict and relationship conflict in top management teams: The pivotal role of intergroup trust. *Journal of Applied Psychology, 85,* 102–112.

Smith, H., and Tyler, T. 1997. Choosing the right pond: The impact of group membership on self-esteem and group-oriented behavior. *Journal of Experimental Social Psychology, 33,* 146–170.

Thompson, L., Kray, L. J., and Lind, E. A. 1998. Cohesion and respect: An examination of group decision making in social and escalation dilemmas. *Journal of Experimental Social Psychology, 34,* 289–311.

Tyler, T., and Lind, E. 1992. A relational model of authority in groups. In M. Zanna (Ed.), *Advances in experimental social psychology* (vol. 25, pp. 115–191). New York: Academic Press.

Tyler, T., Degoey, P., and Smith, H. 1996. Understanding why the justice of group procedures matters. *Journal of Personality and Social Psychology, 70,* 913–930.

Ury, W. L., Brett, J. M., and Goldberg, S. B. 1988. *Getting disputes resolved: Designing systems to cut the costs of conflict.* San Francisco: Jossey-Bass.

Uzzi, B. 1996. The sources of embeddedness for the economic performance of organizations: The network effect. *American Sociological Review, 61,* 674–698.

Uzzi, B. 1997. Social structure and competition in interfirm networks: The paradox of embeddedness. *Administrative Science Quarterly, 42,* 35–67.

Van Kleef, G. A., De Dreu, C. K. W., and Manstead, A. S. R. 2004. The interpersonal effects of anger and happiness in negotiations. *Journal of Personality and Social Psychology, 86*(1), 510–528.

Wall, R. A. J., and Callister, R. R. 1995. Conflict and its management. *Journal of Management, 21,* 515–538.

Weingart, L. R., Cronin, M. A., Houser, C. J. S., Cagan, J., and Vogel, C. M. 2005. Functional diversity and conflict in cross-functional product development teams: Considering representational gap and task characteristics. In L. L. Neider and C. Schreishman (Eds.), *Research in Management* (vol. 4, pp. 89–110). Greenwich, Conn.: IAP.

Williamson, O. E., and Craswell, R. 1993. Calculativeness, trust, and economic organization. *Journal of Law and Economics, 36,* 453–483.

Appendix 8a: Scale Items

Scale	Time 1 Reliability	Time 2 Reliability
Trust	$\alpha = .81$	N/A

I trust my teammates.

I have little faith that my teammates will consider my needs when making decisions.

I believe my teammates are truthful and honest.

Respect	$\alpha = .95$	N/A

I think highly of my teammates' character.

This team sets a good example.

Our team does things the right way.

This team deserves my consideration.

I admire my teammates.

I am proud to be part of this team.

I think my teammates have useful perspectives.

My teammates usually have good reasons for their beliefs.

People on this team have well-founded ideas.

I hold the team in high regard.

I think highly of my team members.

Our team has a reason to be proud.

I respect my team members.

(continues)

Scale	*Time 1 Reliability*	*Time 2 Reliability*
Relationship Conflict	N/A	$\alpha = .91$

Personality conflicts are evident in your team.
There is a lot of emotional conflict among members of your team.
There is a lot of friction among the members of your team.

Task Conflict	N/A	$\alpha = .85$

How frequently do members of your committee engage in debate about different opinions or ideas?
To what extent does your team debate different ideas when solving a problem?
How often do your team members discuss evidence for alternative viewpoints?
To what extent does your team argue the pros and cons of different opinions?
Team members often challenge each other's viewpoints or opinions.

Process Conflict	N/A	$\alpha = .73$

Members of your team often disagree about the best way to make decisions.
Committee members rarely disagree about the optimal amount of time to spend in meetings.
Team members often dispute the effectiveness of the group's decision-making procedures.
There is a lot of tension in your team caused by one or more members trying to take control of work.
There is a lot of tension in your team caused by member(s) not completing their assignment(s) on time.
There is often tension in your team caused by member(s) not performing as well as expected.

N/A - not applicable

α = Cronbach's alpha (measure of reliability for scales)

Chapter 9

CONFRONTING MEMBERS WHO BREAK NORMS: THE INFLUENCE ON TEAM EFFECTIVENESS

Vanessa Urch Druskat and Steven B. Wolff

ABSTRACT

Problem behavior in teams is often a specific form of process conflict enacted by team members who choose to act out rather than use their voice to register complaints about team processes and operations. An effective way to manage this form of process conflict is to institute a norm called "confronting members who break norms." A norm of confronting problem behavior ensures that disruptive behavior is discussed and understood in a timely manner. This keeps team members from making internal attributions about problem behavior and reduces the emergence of destructive relationship conflict in teams. However, not all confrontation is effective. In this chapter, we explore the benefits and costs of confronting problem behavior. We also present a study that examines whether team members' skills associated with emotional intelligence (empathy, self-control, persuasiveness, and developing others) moderate the link between team effectiveness and confronting members who break norms.

INTRODUCTION

One of the most complicated decisions made by a team is whether to confront or ignore problem behavior. We define problem behavior in teams as member behavior that openly defies implicit or explicit team norms—for example, rudeness, lack of cooperation, skipping meetings, coming to meetings unprepared, and general social loafing. On one hand, confronting a member who breaks a norm may have a negative effect on the member and on the group by taking up valuable time and by prompting hurt, anger, and emotional conflict that escalate out of control. On the other hand, ignoring the problem behavior can result in even greater difficulties if the problem behavior continues and group member resentment and anger continue to fester and snowball. This can explode into even bigger levels of emotional or relational conflict or can lead to perceived inequities and member disengagement from the group. The decision over whether to confront or not to confront problem behavior is a difficult one. Many teams and leaders end up waiting it out in the hopes that the problem behavior will stop (deLeon, 2001; Liden, Wayne, and Kraimer, 2001). This is a decision not to confront.

Problem behavior is usually a form of process conflict—for example, a disagreement about how team members should work together to accomplish their task (Jehn, Northcraft, and Neale, 1999). Problem behavior occurs when at least one team member disagrees with an operating procedure or norm held by the team. For example, a member may dominate conversations because he disagrees with a team norm authorizing that certain members' opinions carry the most weight; a member may not show up for meetings because she feels the team's meetings are a waste of time; or a member may not give full effort to the team (that is, social loafing) because it doesn't appear that his effort is necessary (Hertel, Kerr, and Messe, 2000). Such problem behaviors signal discontent and disagreement with the team's current operating or process norms.

Therefore, we propose that adopting a norm of confronting problem behavior, as opposed to ignoring it, is an effective strategy. When carried out effectively, this strategy ensures that the team, in a timely manner, discusses the problem behavior and decides whether process norms should be altered to better meet members' needs. This can increase team members' willingness and ability to work together effectively and can enhance team effectiveness. Our earlier research (Druskat and Wolff, 1999) revealed that when team members gave feedback in a structured, interactive, face-to-face setting, members who received the most negative feedback about their work and behavior in the team (that is, feedback about their problem behavior) rated themselves as feeling significantly more positive about their team after the feedback and discussion than they had felt before receiving and discussing their feedback. Also, after the feedback session, team members, on average, rated their teams as more task-focused than they had prior to the feedback session. These findings suggest that discussing why team members were breaking norms was helpful for those members who broke norms and for the entire team.

A norm that supports confronting problem behavior when it occurs can also keep process conflict from evolving into a more personal and emotional form of conflict labeled relationship conflict. Relationship conflict is defined as conflict that involves personal issues such as dislike among group members and feelings such as annoyance, frustration, and irritation (Jehn and Mannix, 2001). It has been consistently linked to lower team performance and lower member satisfaction (De Dreu and Weingart, 2003).

Of course, not all feedback is effectively delivered. Not all teams have members with the skills they need to handle confrontation in an interpersonally sensitive way (Molinsky and Margolis, 2005; Von Glinow, Shapiro, and Brett, 2004). Unskilled or ineffective feedback could easily be perceived as a personal attack, which would be likely to bring about defensiveness and relationship conflict. Moreover, the greater the number of team members with the skills to deliver effective feedback, the more likely the feedback will be handled and received well.

Our objective in this chapter is to build on our past theory and research examining emotionally competent team norms (that is, norms that create a productive social and emotional team environment) that support team effectiveness (Druskat, Wolff, Messer, and Stubbs, 2003; Wolff and Druskat, 2005). The norm we focus on here is labeled "confronting members who break norms" and is defined as speaking up (that is, using voice) when another member behaves in a way that defies team expectations of acceptable behavior. As will be discussed throughout this chapter, we argue that honest, respectful, discussion-focused confrontation builds team-level trust and leads to fuller cooperation among team members and team effectiveness. The goal of this norm is to encourage all team members to offer constructive feedback and challenges (see Van Dyne and LePine, 1998) and to use the opportunity to discuss, revisit, and adapt norms and procedures to group members' evolving needs. The goal is not to promote conformity (see Janis, 1982).

In this chapter, we define when and why confronting members who break norms is constructive for a team. We propose that such a norm would be most constructive if team members had the skills necessary for constructive confrontation. We also present a longitudinal study that examines whether team members' skills that are consistent with emotional intelligence—empathy, self-control, persuasiveness, and developing others—moderate the link between team effectiveness and a team norm of confronting members who break norms.

THE CONTEXT FOR CONFRONTING MEMBERS WHO BREAK NORMS

A team is "made up of individuals who see themselves and who are seen by others as a social entity, who are interdependent because of the tasks they perform as members of a group, who are embedded in one or more larger social systems (e.g., community, organization), and who perform tasks that affect others (such as customers or coworkers)" (Guzzo and Dickson, 1996). We use the terms "group" and "team" interchangeably.

Team effectiveness is defined here as a multidimensional construct that includes customer satisfaction and the team's ability to continue working together effectively in the future. In long-term groups, a singular focus on customer satisfaction (that is, performance) would eventually harm member well-being, group viability, and, in due course, customer satisfaction (Hackman, 1987).

THE TRIPARTITE INTRA-GROUP CONFLICT TAXONOMY

In this chapter, our definition of process conflict differs from traditional definitions. The conflict literature traditionally divides intragroup conflict into three types: task conflict (sometimes referred to as cognitive conflict), relationship conflict (sometimes referred to as emotional conflict), and process conflict (see Jehn, 1995; Pelled, 1996). Task conflict is defined as differences in viewpoints and opinions pertaining to a group task (Jehn, 1995). As discussed previously, relationship conflict involves personal issues such as dislike among group members and feelings such as annoyance, frustration, and irritation (Jehn and Mannix, 2001). Process conflict is defined as controversies about aspects of how task accomplishment will proceed, including issues of who should do what and how much responsibility different people should get (Jehn et al., 1999). Yet, as defined, process conflict does not often factor as distinct from task conflict (for a fuller discussion of this issue, see chapter 1). Thus, theorists have begun to redefine process conflict. Behfar and her colleagues (Behfar, Mannix, Peterson, and Trochim, 2005) identified three types of process disagreements in groups: conflicts about the timing or pace of work, scheduling conflicts, and workload distribution conflicts. In this chapter, our definition of process conflict is consistent with that of Behfar et al. (2005)—that is, process conflict involves disagreement about operational procedures and work processes including their timing, scheduling, and workload distributions.

TEAM NORMS

In any group, norms are potent expectations that control members' behavior; they trigger conformity in behavior through a system of positive and negative sanctions (Biddle and Thomas, 1966). Norms do not emerge randomly: Over time, team members' back-and-forth interactions, observations, and sensemaking about common experiences shape their expectations for one another (Giddens, 1984; Poole, 1999). These expectations become norms or informal rules (usually unspoken) that enable the team to regulate and regularize member behavior, interactions, and processes (Feldman, 1984).

Well-crystallized norms (that is, norms around which there is high consensus among members) are considered critical to the effectiveness of teams (Hackman, 1987). They relieve the discomfort of the unknown, free team members from having to continually negotiate procedures, and enable members to focus their time and energy on their task. However, while norms facilitate coordination and efficiency, they suppress members' individuality (Peterson, 1999).

Thus, full membership in a team (as opposed to marginalized membership) requires letting go of parts of one's unique individuality (Smith and Berg, 1987). At the same time, team members' unique needs and personalities are an essential source for team growth, renewal, and innovation (Milliken, Bartel, and Kurtzberg, 2003). Crystallized norms that become rigid can keep a team from adapting to the evolving needs of members, the team, and the broader organization to which the team belongs. Thus, complete cooperation and acquiescence to group norms is not necessary or ideal, and occasional disagreements over group process norms can be effective for group functioning (see Tuckman, 1965). In fact, one study found that process conflict (that is, disagreements over group process norms) in successful teams is initially low, but it continually increases as members get closer to meeting their deadlines (Jehn and Mannix, 2001).

WHY PROBLEM BEHAVIOR OCCURS IN TEAMS

Research detailing the team norm development process reveals that team members frequently implicitly or explicitly challenge team norms. This research shows that challenges to existing norms end in one of two ways: They either (1) provoke discussion and negotiation ending in an altered group norm or (2) are dismissed, thus confirming the team's perception that its current mode of operation is suitable for now (Bettenhausen and Murnighan, 1985).

We propose that problem behavior in teams is most often a challenge to process norms by a member who chooses, consciously or unconsciously, to act out (break a norm) rather than using his or her voice to express dissatisfaction with process norms. It would clearly be optimal for team members to challenge norms verbally by using voice behavior, defined as "nonrequired verbal activity that emphasizes expression of constructive challenge with an intent to improve rather than merely criticize" (Rusbult, Farrell, Rogers, and Mainous, 1988; Van Dyne and LePine, 1998). However, research suggests that voice behavior in teams is more likely to come from team members with high levels of global self-esteem and high levels of satisfaction with the team (LePine and Van Dyne, 1998). This description rarely fits all team members.

There are other reasons a team member might be more likely to break a norm than to use voice to express dissatisfaction with current team processes. Using voice requires the belief that one's voice can make a difference in this team. Not all team members have the status necessary to challenge norms and get attention. Research has long shown that high-status team members have the most influence over the norms adopted by a team (Hollander, 1961; Ridgeway, 1987) and that they are permitted more leeway in voicing dissatisfactions with the team (Bales, 1950). Also, the unhappy team member may not use voice because he or she is not fully conscious of the cause of the dissatisfaction or of his or her actions. This individual may not have the interpersonal skills to voice the dissatisfaction in a more constructive manner.

Recognizing the root cause of one's dissatisfaction in a team environment and constructively voicing that dissatisfaction require self-awareness and interpersonal competence. In summary, breaking a process norm (for example, by acting out or loafing) may be the only way some members believe they can get attention. In some teams, they may be right.

Our previous research lends support to our proposal that problem behavior by a team member is frequently the exhibition of unarticulated process needs. In many cases, if these needs are discussed, they can be managed in a way that improves task focus in the team (Druskat and Wolff, 1999). In that time-series study (Druskat and Wolff, 1999), team members provided face-to-face feedback to one another using a structured feedback process. After the feedback sessions, which gave each team member the opportunity to receive and discuss his or her feedback with the full team, those who reported that they were most satisfied by the feedback process and who subsequently rated themselves as feeling most positive about the team were the team members who had exhibited the most problem behavior during the semester. Also, well after the feedback session, team members on average rated their teams as more task-focused than they had prior to the feedback session. This suggests that discussions about team members' behavior can in some circumstances have a lasting positive influence on team effectiveness.

Of course, a team norm of confronting problem behavior can also incur costs. We next discuss potential benefits and costs of confrontation and propose hypotheses related to the skills required for effective confrontation of problem behavior. The results of the study discussed previously (Druskat and Wolff, 1999) also suggest that conforming to other norms could reduce the frequency with which members break norms. For example, it would likely be effective for a team to adopt a norm of periodically holding structured feedback sessions similar to those used in that study. In our theory of emotionally competent norms, we refer to this norm as team self-evaluation and define it as periodically assessing member satisfaction with team and member operations. We argue that team self-evaluation builds team identity and efficacy (Druskat and Wolff, 2001; Druskat et al., 2003; see also Salas, Sims, and Burke, 2005). Such a norm would help to minimize how often confrontation is necessary.

CAVEATS

It is important to point out that in some cases, establishing a norm of confrontation and discussion may not help with team members who act out or break norms. For example, the individual may be a chronic norm breaker in team settings. Wageman and Hackman (2006) refer to such team members as derailers. Derailers may be effective in many areas of their lives, but for one reason or another they will not cooperate in a team setting and they resist coaching (Wageman and Hackman, 2006). It may be that they don't agree with the team's direction or purpose, or they simply may have little interest in sacrificing their individual needs for the team. One category of team derailers who periodically show up in research studies are those who score high in neuroticism, one of the Big Five personality traits. These individuals are characterized as anxious, depressed, angry, emotional, and insecure (Costa and McCrae, 1994). They receive low peer ratings from teammates (Stewart, Fulmer, and Barrick, 2005) and have a negative influence on team performance (Kichuk and Wiesner, 1998).

Another time when confrontation may do more harm than good is when the team has placed a member in the role of team scapegoat. A scapegoat is a member who is devalued and on whom most, if not all, group problems are blamed (Smith and Berg, 1987). Scapegoat theory comes from the psychodynamic perspective on group behavior (see McLeod and Kettner-Polley, 2004), which argues that nonconformists are often unconsciously placed into the scapegoat role to allow other members to distance themselves from anxiety and threat (Gemmill, 1989).

Once the scapegoated member has been labeled as being the problem, team members tend to ostracize him or her, which understandably causes the scapegoat to behave negatively or act out. In his treatise on prejudice, Gordon Allport argued that only scapegoating could account for extreme forms of prejudice (see Glick, 2005). A fuller discussion of scapegoat theory would take this chapter off track. However, it is pertinent to point out that a norm of confrontation could exacerbate a scapegoated team members' troubles. On the other hand, because of its problem-and-discussion focus, a confrontation norm may provide an opportunity for scapegoated members to be heard—and may even prevent the emergence of a scapegoat.

PROCESS CONFLICT VERSUS RELATIONSHIP CONFLICT

Once problem behavior is framed as process conflict, the potential advantages and disadvantages of confronting the behavior can be identified. Like any other form of conflict, process conflict can have either constructive or destructive results when it is confronted and made public. For example, some research has suggested that moderate levels of task conflict can be beneficial for group performance on certain tasks (Jehn, 1995). However, when task conflict escalates, it gets personal and easily and frequently turns into destructive relationship conflict. Thus, task conflict frequently has a negative effect on team performance (De Dreu and Weingart, 2003).

Indeed, any form of conflict—when it spirals out of control, provokes anger, and becomes personal—can become destructive to a team and its performance (Deutsch, 1973). Decades of research suggest that when conflict becomes personal and turns into relationship conflict, team performance is hurt in three ways (Pelled, 1996): (1) The emotional tension in the team is raised, reducing the ability of members to think and assess new information. (2) The anger and frustration leave members less receptive to the thoughts and ideas of other members. (3) It wastes time. The longer the conflict remains unresolved, the more time gets wasted (Pelled, 1996).

To maximize team effectiveness, a primary goal of teams who engage in the form of process conflict discussed in this chapter should be to confront problem behavior in a way that minimizes relationship conflict and maximizes the potential benefits of conflict. Those benefits include positive change, the reconciliation of team members' legitimate interests, and—by virtue of the first two points—increased team solidarity (Pruitt and Rubin, 1986). Without the capacity for change brought about by conflict, teams can easily stagnate and lose their ability to be effective.

Attribution theory (Heider, 1958; Jones and Davis, 1965; Kelley, 1967) explains one avenue by which task or process conflict can become personal and spiral into negative relationship conflict. Attribution theorists have shown that people frequently seek information that explains why others behave a certain way so they can determine how to best respond to the behavior. A fundamental distinction made by attribution theory is whether the behavior can be attributed to factors within the person (an internal attribution) or factors within the environment (an external attribution) (Heider, 1958). For example, if a group member breaks a norm by not attending a meeting, the action might be attributed to the individual's lazy personality (an internal attribution) or to the group's lack of specificity about the meeting time (an external attribution). There is a discernible difference in how this team member would be treated if her behavior was attributed to her personality rather than to the team's situation or environment (Jackson and LePine, 2003). Team members who attribute the missed meeting to something internal to the person are necessarily making the conflict personal. Thus, they are more likely to respond negatively and are more likely to inflame relationship conflict. As described by Pruitt and Rubin (1986), this type of conflict easily shifts from one's initial interest in defending one's behavior (or defending the team) to an interest in winning the argument and eventually to making sure the other team member is hurt more than oneself. Escalation of conflict happens easily in group settings because as the conflict heats up, more and more members get involved (Pruitt and Rubin, 1986).

A NORM OF CONFRONTING MEMBERS WHO BREAK NORMS

We, therefore, propose that one way to keep problem behavior (that is, process conflict) from turning into relationship conflict is to create a team environment in which internal attributions are not so easily applied to problem behavior. Kelley (1967) found internal attributions more likely applied if the behavior in question is exhibited by the individual consistently. Adopting a team norm of confronting members who break norms would call for addressing problem behavior when it is first exhibited. For example, as soon as the member misses a meeting, the behavior is confronted and discussed. This would help minimize the number of times the person demonstrates problem behavior (for example, misses meetings). It would also help minimize the likelihood that the behavior is attributed to internal causes, thus reducing the probability of negative affect and relationship conflict.

However, our previous field research conducted in six diverse organizations (Druskat et al., 2003) suggests that a norm of confronting members who break norms is *not* always associated with effective team performance. This makes sense because not all teams have members who exhibit problem behavior or break norms. Thus, they are less likely to use, with any frequency, a norm of confronting problem behavior. Team members may not break norms in these teams because the team is flexible enough to continually assess and adapt its norms as the needs of the team and its members evolve. As discussed previously, these teams may have a norm of self-evaluation and continuous improvement (see Druskat and Wolff, 2001). Alternatively, team members may not break norms because their teams are similar to those discussed by LePine and Van Dyne (1998)—that is, members use their voice to express disagreements over process norms rather than acting out.

Another important reason why there may be no direct association between team effectiveness and a norm of confronting members who break norms is that team members may not have the skills to effectively confront members who break norms (Molinsky and Margolis, 2005; Von Glinow et al., 2004). Insensitive confrontation could harm the social identity of the member being confronted and cause the member to lose face. The affective response to losing face is usually anger, and the behavioral response is often revenge (Andersson and Pearson, 1999). Thus, ineffective confrontation could lead to, rather than alleviate, relationship conflict. We are aware of no research that has examined the skills necessary for effectively confronting problem behavior in teams. In the next section, we hypothesize a set of emotional-intelligence skills that may increase a team member's ability to effectively and constructively confront a member who breaks norms.

EMOTIONAL INTELLIGENCE SKILLS RELATED TO EFFECTIVE CONFRONTATION IN GROUPS

Group communication theorists provide several critical points about effective feedback in teams. Keyton and her colleagues have argued that all messages communicated in teams contain relational information (Keyton, 1999). For example, when one member confronts another member's inappropriate behavior, the latter hears both the content of the message and also its underlying relational message. In the case of confrontation, the relational message might convey either support and caring or shame, control, and dominance. Thus, confronters need to have the skills necessary to recognize and acknowledge the positive attributes of the member being confronted and to have the self-control to behave in a supportive rather than controlling manner during the confrontation. Without such skills, the confrontation might easily be perceived as a personal attack.

As such, the skills necessary for effective confrontation would likely require emotional intelligence, which has been defined as the ability to monitor one's own and others' emotions, to discriminate among emotions, and to use information about emotions to improve cognitive thinking, including the quality of actions and decisions (Mayer and Salovey, 1993). Because emotion pervades every human interaction (Kemper, 1978), emotional intelligence is particularly useful when actions and decisions involve others (Salovey, Bedell, Detweiler, and Mayer, 2000).

Work teams are social systems in which interactions among members are fundamental to team outcomes. It is no surprise that emotional intelligence has been labeled a valuable team resource (Elfenbein, 2006). We hypothesize that four skills associated with emotional intelligence will prove an effective team resource by enabling respectful, constructive confrontation that can reduce problem behavior and improve a team's ability to function well. In fact, research suggests that when such respect is conveyed, it not only increases feelings of fair treatment (Tyler, Degoey, and Smith, 1996), but it also decreases the emergence of relationship conflict (see chapter 8).

We begin by hypothesizing the relevance of two prototypical emotional intelligence skills (that is, skills that are included in all models of emotional intelligence; for a review, see Druskat, Sala, and Mount, 2006): empathy and self-control. Empathy is defined as sensing another's feelings or perspectives and taking an active interest in the other's concerns (Boyatzis, 1982). Empathy would enable team members to attend to another member's moods, feelings, and nonverbal behavior and to better understand their cause. It would also help members to effectively interpret how the feedback recipient (for example, the member exhibiting a problem behavior) is emotionally reacting to the feedback. Hence it would allow the feedback to be given in a way that it is respectful, least likely to cause defensiveness and anger, and most likely to be seen as a learning opportunity for the team.

The second emotional-intelligence skill that we propose is important to effective confrontation is self-control, defined as the ability to manage (or keep in check) disruptive emotions and impulses (Boyatzis, 1982). Self-control would allow team members to manage their own emotional reactions to the problem behavior. Managing one's own disappointment or anger over the behavior can help mitigate the escalation of anger during the confrontation and discussion. When the escalation of emotion is stopped, it enables the team to more clearly listen for and seek to understand the situational factors that contributed to the problem behavior.

All of our hypotheses assume that, as discussed earlier, not all teams engage in confrontation. This implies that the relationship between team effectiveness and the level at which confronting members who break norms is demonstrated will not be linear. That is, teams with a low level of this norm may very well be high performing because either they effectively minimize conflict through other norms (for example, a team self-evaluation norm) or they use voice to express disagreements. On the other hand, teams experiencing a degree of conflict not addressed through these other means can choose the norm of confronting members who break norms to help them effectively address the conflict. Thus, when the team has the requisite skills to effectively confront members who break norms, the relation between team effectiveness and such confrontation is expected to be U-shaped. If a team displays very low levels of confronting members who break norms, they may achieve high performance by addressing conflict through other means as discussed previously. If the team displays high levels of confronting members who break norms, they achieve high performance by effectively addressing process conflict. A moderate level of confronting members who break norms may indicate that the team is not consistently and fully addressing its conflicts; thus unresolved issues ultimately reduce performance. Such a U-shaped curve can be represented by a quadratic relationship. If the team does not have the requisite skills to effectively confront members, we expect one of two results: Either (1) the more the group confronts members who break norms, the more negative effects the confrontation will have, thus reducing team effectiveness in a linear relation to the degree of confrontation, or (2) the positive and negative effects of confrontation might cancel each other out, leading to a neutral condition in which the degree of confrontation is unrelated to the level of team effectiveness.

Thus, we hypothesize that mean level of skill (for example, in empathy or self-control) in the team will moderate the relationship between team effectiveness and the level of the norm of confronting members who break norms. For high levels of the required skill, the relationship will be quadratic. For low levels of the required skill, the relationship will be either a negative linear relationship or, if the positive and negative effects of the conflict cancel each other out, no relationship. Our first two hypotheses are the following:

Hypothesis 1: **The effect on team effectiveness of a norm of confronting members who break norms will be moderated by the mean level of team members' skill at empathy.**

- *Hypothesis 1a:* **In teams having high mean levels of empathy, there will be a significant positive quadratic relationship between confronting members and team effectiveness.**

- *Hypothesis 1b:* **In teams having low mean levels of empathy, there will be either no relationship or a significant negative linear relationship between confronting members and team effectiveness.**

Hypothesis 2: **The effect on team effectiveness of a norm of confronting members who break norms will be moderated by the mean level of team members' skill at self-control.**

- *Hypothesis 2a:* **In teams having high mean levels of self-control, there will be a significant positive quadratic relationship between confronting members and team effectiveness.**

- *Hypothesis 2b:* **In teams having low mean levels of self-control, there will be either no relationship or a significant negative linear relationship between confronting members and team effectiveness.**

In their treatise on effective feedback, Ashford and Cummings (1983) raise another set of issues that shed light on the skills required for effective confrontation. They argue that effective feedback requires a shift in thinking and behavior. Consistent with our discussion thus far, this shift requires that both parties approach the feedback as an opportunity for learning and development. Both parties take an active role in seeking information and discussing the feedback (Ashford and Cummings, 1983). In this context, the learning and development would need to flow both ways, with the intent that learning and change occur for both the individual being confronted and for the team.

To facilitate the experience of confrontation as a learning opportunity and not a top-down command, we hypothesize the relevance of two additional emotional-intelligence skills (see Goleman, 2001; Sala, 2006): persuasiveness and developing others. Persuasiveness is defined as using tactics to influence another (Boyatzis, 1982). Persuasiveness enables one to gain the buy-in of the person he or she is working to persuade. Skill at persuading or influencing others would enable the team members doing the confronting to convince the confronted member that their intent is to open a discussion about team process norms, not to mount a personal attack. Persuasiveness skills would be an important resource because feedback recipients often feel criticized (Baumeister and Cairns, 1992). Moreover, skill in persuading or influencing would be useful for convincing both the member exhibiting the problem behavior and all other members that everyone's behavior may need to change after the discussion.

Skill at developing others is defined as the ability to support, stimulate, and engage someone in learning, in developing himself or herself, or in improving his or her performance (Boyatzis, 1982). Such a skill would increase team members' ability to engage the confronted member in a discussion focused on learning and development. We offer the following two hypotheses:

Hypothesis 3: **The effect on team effectiveness of a norm of confronting members who break norms will be moderated by the mean level of team members' skill at persuasiveness.**

- *Hypothesis 3a:* **In teams having high mean levels of persuasiveness, there will be a significant positive quadratic relationship between confronting members and team effectiveness.**

- *Hypothesis 3b:* **In teams having low mean levels of persuasiveness, there will be either no relationship or a significant negative linear relationship between confronting members and team effectiveness.**

Hypothesis 4: **The effect on team effectiveness of a norm of confronting members who break norms will be moderated by the mean level of team members' skill at developing others.**

- *Hypothesis 4a:* **In teams with high mean levels of developing others, there will be a significant positive quadratic relationship between confronting members and team effectiveness.**

- *Hypothesis 4b:* **In teams with low mean levels of developing others, there will be either no relationship or a significant negative linear relationship between confronting members and team effectiveness.**

In the following section, we present the study used to test our hypotheses.

METHOD

SAMPLE

The present study was conducted as part of a larger longitudinal study of 382 full-time master's of business administration (MBA) students comprising 48 self-managing teams. Teams were assembled before the start of the MBA program (during orientation in August) and remained intact, working on small or large projects in each course, until the end of the first academic year (May). For all classes, students took the same courses in the same order using standardized syllabi. Teams were composed by faculty in the organizational behavior department who aimed to maximize the demographic diversity within each team. Participation in the study was voluntary. Students were ensured confidentiality. To ensure that participation would not affect course grades, signed permissions were kept in an envelope until after grades were turned in. Ninety-two percent of students agreed to participate in the study. The percentage of members responding from each team ranged from 50 percent (1 team) to 100 percent (19 teams), with a mean of 84 percent. Missing data were due mostly to random absences from the classes at which data were collected. Teams ranged in size from seven to ten members. Most teams (27) had eight members; only one team had ten members. The sample consisted of 270 males and 112 females who ranged in age from 20 to 52 with a mean age of 27 (SD = 4.11) and a median age of 27.

Throughout the first academic year, student teams were self-managing; that is, they held full responsibility for executing their work and for monitoring and managing their own process (Hackman, 1986). For example, in their organizational behavior course, teams were required to complete a large team project that involved data collection in an organization around a chosen topic and a synthesis of that data with scholarly information. The team project grade (team-level grade) was worth 35 percent of a member's individual grade in the course. The project, which was designed to foster team interdependence, culminated in final written and oral reports that presented recommendations for solving the problem. Written and oral reports were presented to the students' class and to their participating organizations.

INDIVIDUAL SKILLS

To operationalize and measure the four emotional-intelligence (EI) skills, we looked to Boyatzis' (1982, 1995) taxonomy of managerial competencies, which is the basis of Goleman's model of EI competencies (Goleman, 2001) and is arguably the most often cited taxonomy of individual knowledge, skills, and abilities (KSAs). Researchers who have used Boyatzis' coding scheme to code qualitative data have found it to yield reliable and valid indicators of specific skills and abilities (see Spencer and Spencer, 1993). To operationalize the EI skills of empathy, self-control, persuasiveness, and developing others, we used Boyatzis' definitions and coding scheme (Table 9.1).

Critical Incident Interviews

Individual skills were measured during the first two weeks of the MBA program (late August to early September) through the use of one-hour tape-recorded, standardized critical incident interviews (CIIs) (see Flanagan, 1954) that were subsequently coded for exhibition of the skills using Boyatzis' (1995) coding scheme.

We used an adaptation of Flanagan's (1954) CII methodology, which was designed by McClelland and Dailey (1972). It focuses on obtaining highly detailed descriptions of job events rather than on attitudes and attributions. Research has shown this type of CII format to be a reliable, valid, and useful method for obtaining accurate and detailed descriptions of work behavior (Motowidlo, Carter, Dunnett, Tippens, Werner, Burnett, et al., 1992; Ronan and Latham, 1974) and for measuring individual skills and abilities (McClelland, 1976, 1998). A primary reason we chose to use the CII method was because it objectively measures the skills we were interested in (Boyatzis, 1982), and we felt its measurement of skills would be superior to self-report data.

The CII method requires interviewees to alternate between describing job events during which they felt effective and ineffective. The role of the CII interviewer is to obtain detailed information while remaining as unobtrusive as possible. Interviewers are limited to asking the following questions: What led up to the event? Who did and said what to whom? What happened next? What were you thinking or feeling at that moment? What was the outcome? Although the CII method provides a retrospective account of behavior and thoughts, validity and reliability of event descriptions are strong (Motowidlo et al., 1992; Ronan and Latham, 1974) because the interviewer probes for highly detailed responses. Further, because the interviewee

Table 9.1
Boyatzis' Managerial Competencies with Definitions and Clusters Used for the Present Study

Skill/Competency	Definition	Examples
Empathy	The intent is to understand others.	1. Understands the strengths and limitations of others. 2. Listens to others by asking and waiting for their reply or taking the time to allow another person to explain or describe something at his/her own pace and in his/her own manner. 3. Demonstrates an ability to see things from someone else's perspective. 4. Demonstrates the ability to accurately read or interpret the moods, feelings, or nonverbal behavior of others. 5. Understands the underlying causes for someone's feelings, behavior, or concerns.
Self-control	The intent is to inhibit personal needs or desires for the benefit of organizational, family, or group needs. However, self-control is often not visible (i.e., when people have self-control you cannot easily see them controlling themselves.)	1. Remains calm in stressful settings (e.g., when being attacked). 2. Explicitly inhibits aggressive outbursts or impulsive behavior that may hurt others or hurt progress toward goals. 3. Explicitly denies a personal impulse, need, or desire for the good of an organizational or group need.
Persuasiveness	The intent is to wield effective tactics for persuasion.	1. Uses factual arguments to persuade and influence others. 2. Takes symbolic actions to have a specific impact on the audience. 3. Convinces by appealing to people's self-interest. 4. Gains the buy-in of influential parties and enlists their help in convincing others. 5. Gets people to buy into or take ownership of ideas or plans.

(continues)

Table 9.1 (continued)
Boyatzis' Managerial Competencies with Definitions and Clusters Used for the Present Study

Skill/Competency	Definition	Examples
Developing others	The intent is to support and stimulate someone to develop his/her abilities or improve his/her performance toward an objective.	1. Gives someone performance feedback to be used in improving or maintaining effective performance. 2. Provides others with information, tools, other resources, or opportunities to help them get their jobs done or to improve their abilities (e.g., giving a promotion as part of their development.) 3. Invites others to discuss performance problems with the explicit purpose of improving their performance. 4. Explicitly tells another that he/she can accomplish an objective and provides encouragement and support.

Source. Adapted from Boyatzis, 1995.

selects the events to discuss, they are usually salient events about which details are easy to recall. Discussions of both effective and ineffective events were sought because they reveal a range of challenges experienced by the individual.

Ten doctoral assistants who underwent two days of formal interview training with an expert on CII methodology conducted the critical incident interviews. Each interview began with a standardized introduction. Interviews were included as a course requirement, and students were asked for permission to tape-record the interview. Students were informed that the interview would be used to provide them with feedback on their skills. (About six weeks after the interviews, students received individual reports that showed the skills and abilities for which they were coded.) The interviewer then proceeded with the critical incident interview, which consisted of asking the participant to describe events within the past year during which he or she felt either effective or ineffective inside or outside of work. Most events discussed in this study involved work incidents that occurred in the year before the student joined the MBA program. Examples of events discussed include overcoming challenges to complete difficult projects at work, managing problem employees during specific incidents at work, and the process from beginning to end of gaining entrance into MBA programs.

Coding the Interviews

The tape-recorded interviews were coded by doctoral assistants who had undergone a two-week training period that involved coding practice tapes and getting feedback from experts on the code (colleagues of Richard Boyatzis who worked closely with the code) on their level of accuracy in identifying the skills and abilities. To be selected as a coder, doctoral assistants had to achieve a minimum of .70 intercoder reliability with expert coders for all skills—that is, they had to agree with expert coders 70 percent of the time.

Coders who passed the reliability test coded the audiotapes of all student interviews. The result was a frequency count of the number of times each student was coded for each of the four skills used in the study. The codebook definitions used for coding the abilities are listed in Table 9.1. The code was applied to a behavior described in an interview if the behavior met the following two criteria: (1) The interviewee intended to exhibit the behavior and (2) the behavior was consistent with one of the specific examples listed in the codebook. Coders erred on the side of conservatism and coded by the rule of thumb "When in doubt, leave it out."

CONFRONTING MEMBERS WHO BREAK NORMS

A questionnaire measuring group norms was administered in November of the first semester, at which point teams had been working together in all classes for three months. A scale to measure confronting members who break norms (among other norms) was developed and pretested using two sections of MBA students who were not involved in the present study. The final scale for confronting members who break norms included the following five items: (1) "In our team we will inform a member if his or her behavior is unacceptable by team standards," (2) "If someone isn't pulling his or her weight on our team, we ignore it" (reverse scored), (3) "In our team, we figure that if a member is doing something we disagree with, it's best not to bring it up" (reverse scored), (4) "In our team someone will confront you if you aren't performing the way the team expects," and (5) "In our team, members will flat-out tell you if you are doing something considered unacceptable." The scale was measured using 7-point Likert scales ranging from 1 (very inaccurate) to 7 (very accurate). Cronbach's alpha reliability of the scale was .77. The intraclass correlation coefficient (ICC) (James, 1982) indicated the between-group variance was significantly greater ($F_{48,279} > 1.9$, $p < .001$) than the within-group variance, thus allowing us to create a group-level variable by taking the mean of individual responses to the questionnaire items.

TEAM EFFECTIVENESS

Team effectiveness ratings were collected at the end of the first semester (December) and were obtained from course instructors who served as group consultants. Instructors rated effectiveness on four dimensions that assess both customer satisfaction and team viability: group product quality, performance compared to other groups, the group's ability to be self-directed, and the group's ability to continue working together effectively in the future. The item response format ranged from 1 (poor) to 7 (outstanding). A factor analysis of the ratings yielded a single underlying factor, thus, instructor ratings were averaged to form a single score.

RESULTS

Our hypotheses propose that skill level moderates the relationship between team effectiveness and confronting members who break norms. For high levels of skill, the relationship between skill level and team effectiveness is hypothesized to be quadratic, with low and high levels of confronting producing the highest level of team effectiveness. For low levels of a skill, the relationship between confronting and team effectiveness was hypothesized to be either a negative linear relationship or no significant relationship. To test the hypotheses, we first divided the sample into high and low levels of the skill being tested. This was done by dividing the sample into two groups split at the median. For each skill tested, we performed both a linear regression and a quadratic regression. If our hypotheses are supported, we would expect the linear regression to show no significant relationships for the high-skill group and either no relationship or a negative linear relationship for the low-skill group. The quadratic regression would show a significant relationship for the high-skill group and no significant relationship for the low-skill group.

Table 9.2 presents intercorrelations among all the variables studied along with descriptive statistics. Tables 9.3 through 9.6 show the results of the linear and quadratic regressions for the skills of empathy, self-control, persuasion, and developing others, respectively. For all regressions with significant beta coefficients, the overall model was significant at $p < .05$. For all models with nonsignificant beta coefficients,

Table 9.2
Correlations and Descriptive Statistics (n = 347 individuals; n = 48 teams)

	Mean	SD	Team Effectiveness	Confronting	Empathy	Self-control	Persuasion
Team effectiveness	5.18	1.16					
Confronting members	4.22	.59	.157				
Empathy	1.05	.65	.080	.011			
Self-control	.27	.21	.124	.030	.36*		
Persuasion	1.37	.55	−.036	.139	.67†	.43†	
Developing others	.41	.25	−.051	.146	.29*	−.04	.33*

* Correlation is significant at the .05 level (2-tailed).

† Correlation is significant at the .01 level (2-tailed).

Table 9.3
Linear and Quadratic Regression Models of Team Effectiveness on Confronting Members Who Break Norms with Empathy as the Moderating Variable (n = 48)

Model	Empathy	Independent Variable	Standardized Coefficients β	t	Sig.	R^2 of Model
Linear model	Low	Confronting members	−.134	−.651	.522	.018
	High	Confronting members	.343	1.674	.109	.118
Quadratic model	Low	Confronting members	−1.396	−.550	.588	.029
		(Confronting members)^2	1.266	.499	.623	
	High	Confronting members	−5.197	−2.300	.032	.323
		(Confronting members)^2	5.559	2.460	.023	

Table 9.4
Linear and Quadratic Regression Models of Team Effectiveness on Confronting Members Who Break Norms with Self-Control as the Moderating Variable ($n = 48$)

Model	Self-Control	Independent Variable	Standardized Coefficients β	t	Sig.	R^2 of Model
Linear model	Low	Confronting members	.093	.456	.652	.009
	High	Confronting members	.264	1.225	.235	.070
Quadratic model	Low	Confronting members	−2.147	−.888	.384	.045
		(Confronting members)^2	2.248	.930	.362	
	High	Confronting members	−5.718	−2.319	.032	.291
		(Confronting members)^2	6.001	2.433	.025	

Table 9.5
Linear and Quadratic Regression Models of Team Effectiveness on Confronting Members Who Break Norms with Persuasion as the Moderating Variable ($n = 48$)

Model	Persuasion	Independent Variable	Standardized Coefficients β	t	Sig.	R^2 of Model
Linear model	Low	Confronting members	.026	.119	.906	.001
	High	Confronting members	.250	1.237	.229	.062
Quadratic model	Low	Confronting members	−.511	−.222	.827	.003
		(Confronting members)^2	.488	.212	.834	
	High	Confronting members	−6.635	−2.665	.014	.305
		(Confronting members)^2	6.902	2.772	.011	

Table 9.6
Linear and Quadratic Regression Models of Team Effectiveness on Confronting Members Who Break Norms with Developing Others as the Moderating Variable ($n = 48$)

Model	Developing Others	Independent Variable	Standardized Coefficients β	t	Sig.	R^2 of Model
Linear model	Low	Confronting members	.164	.760	.456	.027
	High	Confronting members	.158	.769	.450	.025
Quadratic model	Low	Confronting members	−6.459	−2.348	.029	.246
		(Confronting members)^2	6.639	2.414	.025	
	High	Confronting members	−2.565	−1.119	.275	.084
		(Confronting members)^2	2.734	1.193	.246	

the overall model was not significant. Figures 9.1 through 9.4 plot the results of the regressions.

Hypotheses 1 through 3 state that empathy, self-control, and persuasion, respectively, will moderate the relationship between confronting members and team effectiveness. The linear model does not show a significant relationship between confronting members who break norms and team effectiveness for either level of skill (Tables 9.3 through 9.5). It also shows that the quadratic model is also not significant for the low-skill group. For the high-skill group, there is a significant relationship between confronting members who break norms and team effectiveness. Thus, hypotheses 1 through 3 are supported. Empathy, self-control, and persuasion all moderate the relationship between team effectiveness and confronting members who break norms. Furthermore, the relationship for the high-skill group is quadratic in nature, that is, U-shaped. The low-skill group showed no significant relationships between team effectiveness and confronting members who break norms.

Hypothesis 4 states that developing others will moderate the relationship between confronting members and team effectiveness. The results of the regression are shown in Table 9.6 and plotted in Figure 9.4. Although there is a moderating effect, as with the previously discussed skills, it is not as we hypothesized. Similar to the other skills, there is no linear relationship between team effectiveness and confronting members who break norms. There is a quadratic relationship, but unlike

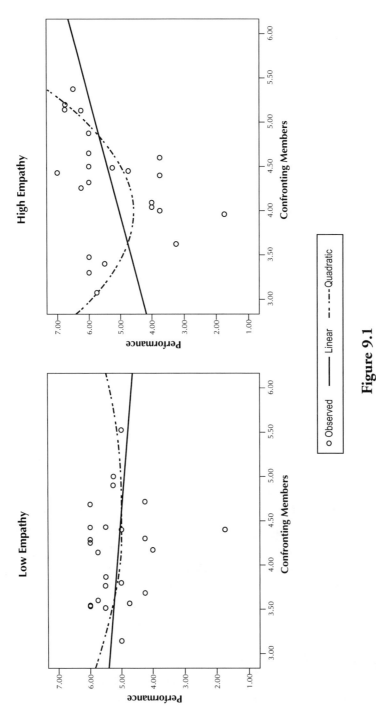

Figure 9.1

Fit of Linear and Quadratic Curves Relating Confronting Members Who Break Norms to Team Effectiveness for Low and High Levels of Empathy

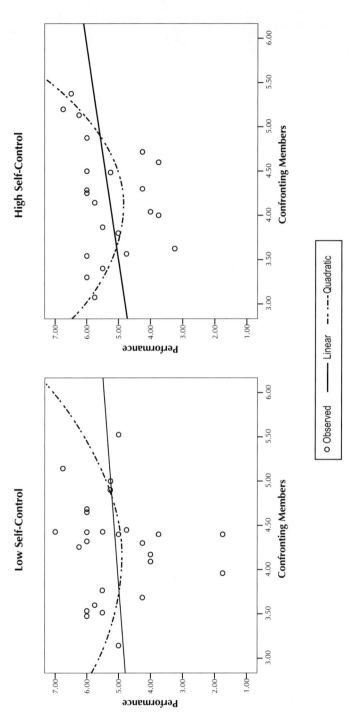

Figure 9.2

Fit of Linear and Quadratic Curves Relating Confronting Members Who Break Norms to Team Effectiveness for Low and High Levels of Self-Control

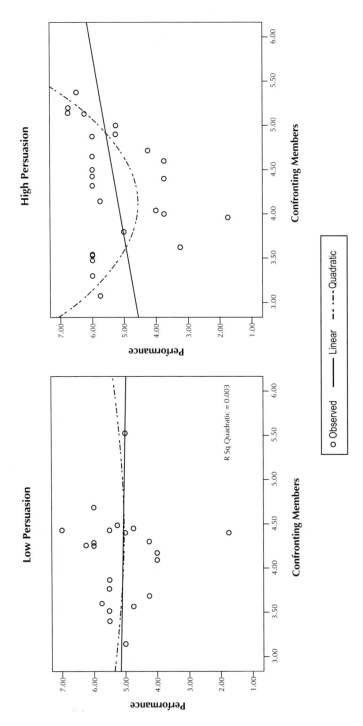

Figure 9.3

Fit of Linear and Quadratic Curves Relating Confronting Members Who Break Norms to Team
Effectiveness for Low and High Levels of Persuasion

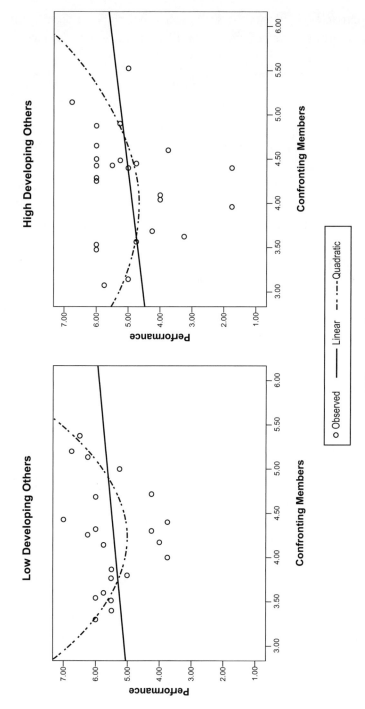

Figure 9.4

Fit of Linear and Quadratic Curves Relating Confronting Members Who Break Norms to Team Effectiveness for Low and High Levels of Developing Others

with the other competencies, it is the low-skill group that shows a significant relationship. The high-skill group does not show a significant relationship between team effectiveness and confronting members who break norms. Although there is a moderating relationship, it is not as we predicted with hypothesis 4; thus, hypothesis 4 is not supported.

DISCUSSION

As demographic and value diversity continue to increase in team settings (Jehn and Mannix, 2001; Jehn et al., 1999), team member process needs are increasingly likely to conflict with emergent process norms. In this study, we found that when disagreement over process norms (that is, process conflict) is enacted in the form of problem behavior (that is, breaking team norms) rather than through using voice, confronting and discussing the problem behavior is an effective tool.

Our study contributes to theory and research on team conflict and team effectiveness by revealing that a team norm of confronting members who break norms is linked to effectiveness when team members have the emotional-intelligence skills that help to make confrontation constructive. Specifically, we found that when members of a team averaged high levels of empathy, self-control, and persuasiveness, a norm of confronting members who break norms was associated with team effectiveness. It is important to emphasize that the relationship between team effectiveness and confronting members who break norms is not linear—it is quadratic. In other words, some teams in our sample were high performing without instituting a norm of confronting members who break norms. These teams were likely similar to the teams discussed by LePine and Van Dyne (1998) in which members easily used voice to convey their needs and differences of opinion. They also may have had other norms in place (for example, team self-evaluation) that made a norm of confronting members who break norms less necessary.

Our hypothesis that average team members' skills at developing others would moderate a link between team effectiveness and confronting members who break norms was not supported. This may be because skill at developing others leads one to think that the most successful route to change encompasses individual adaptation and development. As mentioned, to be constructive rather than destructive, a norm of confronting members who break norms must engender a two-way discussion that considers making changes to process norms to be a reasonable action. Also, it is likely most helpful when confronters treat the problem behavior as a conflict over process norms (that is, process conflict) and seek to attribute the behavior to external causes (see Heider, 1958). Being skillful at developing others may make one more likely to assume that problem behavior signifies the need for individual change.

A UNIQUE PERSPECTIVE ON PROCESS CONFLICT

In this chapter, we defined problem behavior as a form of process conflict. This allowed us to conceptualize problem behavior as potentially constructive rather than destructive for team effectiveness. It is this constructive mind-set that would enable team members to apply an external attribution to problem behavior rather than an internal attribution, so that addressing problem behavior can turn into a conversation over process norms rather than evolving into relationship conflict. Given the fundamental nature of internal attributions, our perspective is optimistic. Is it realistic? Our study results suggest it is, in some circumstances. It appears to be realistic when team members have the emotional/interpersonal skills to facilitate constructive confrontation.

Our findings may also shed light on recent findings about the relationship between task conflict and team performance. In the past decade, researchers and theorists have argued that task conflict, unlike relationship conflict, should be functional for teams because it increases debate and forces the team to confront issues it might otherwise have ignored (see Jehn, 1995; Simons and Peterson, 2000). However, an important meta-analysis recently revealed that task conflict is as negatively associated with team performance as is relationship conflict (De Dreu and Weingart, 2003). This makes sense, given the propensity for any type of conflict to escalate and become emotional and destructive (Deutsch, 1973). The results of our study suggest that a relatively high level of emotional/interpersonal skills among team members might ensure that task conflict is delivered and discussed in such a way that it does not escalate or become emotional. These skills may even enable task conflict to boost team effectiveness; especially if the definition of team effectiveness includes team development and continued viability.

TIME AND CONFRONTATION

Interventions to address conflict are more successful when well timed (see chapter 10). We believe that to be optimally effective, a norm of confronting members who break norms should be instituted early in a team's development. This would make it easier to avoid attributing problem behavior to something internal to the individual (that is, personality or attitude) and to change process norms before they are well crystallized. In fact, Tuckman (1965) argued that conflict in the form of "storming" (in some ways similar to confrontation) was an early, predictable stage in a group's history. He proposed that storming would continue and would prevent a team from becoming fully functional until all members' process needs were sufficiently met.

As we discussed earlier, it would seem optimal for a team to minimize the amount of confrontation required by also instituting a norm of team–self evaluation (Druskat and Wolff, 2001; Druskat et al., 2003). This would necessitate that team members periodically step back and evaluate how effectively the team is performing. It would support the use of voice for constructive change (LePine and Van Dyne, 1998), and it would enable a team to address problems before they escalate and to efficiently adapt to the changing needs of the team and its members (Salas et al., 2005). We propose that confrontation should be used more often in the early stages of a team's tenure and that it would become less necessary once members trust that the norm of team self-evaluation will enable necessary change.

CONCLUSION

Since we first conceptualized the idea of a norm labeled "confronting members who break norms," several colleagues (including some at the Kellogg Team and Group Research Center [KTAG] conference, at which this material was originally presented) have told us that they associate the term "confrontation" with unsympathetic feedback. We have thought about changing the label, but no other term suitably describes the direct feedback we have repeatedly seen enacted by team members in our field research (Druskat, 1996; Druskat et al., 2003). The term has also been used by others to define a problem-solving approach to conflict resolution (Blake and Mouton, 1964; Lawrence and Lorsch, 1967). In fact, Lawrence and Lorsch (1967), who argued about the importance of confrontation norms in organizations, operationalized the term "confrontation" with survey items that included "Come now and let us reason together" and "By digging and digging, the truth is discovered."

Clearly, our study has flaws, and future research is necessary to support the reliability of our findings. It would be useful to get a measure of the degree to which group members perceived problem behavior and the degree to which they perceived that those problems were addressed through the norm of confronting members who break norms. This would enable an examination of team effectiveness through the lens of the perceived degree of problems in the group.

REFERENCES

Andersson, L. M., and Pearson, C. M. 1999. Tit for tat? The spiraling effect of incivility in the workplace. *Academy of Management Review, 24,* 452–471.

Ashford, S. J., and Cummings, L. L. 1983. Feedback as an individual resource: Personal strategies of creating information. *Organizational Behavior and Human Performance, 32,* 370–398.

Bales, R. F. 1950. *Interaction process analysis: A method for the study of small groups.* Chicago: University of Chicago Press.

Baumeister R. F., and Cairns, K. J. 1992. Repression and self-presentation: When audiences interfere with self-deceptive strategies. *Journal of Personality and Social Psychology, 62,* 851–862.

Behar, K., Mannix, E., Peterson, R., and Trochim, W. 2005. *A multi-faceted approach to intra-group conflict: Issues of theory and measurement.* Manuscript submitted for publication.

Bettenhausen, K. L., and Murnighan, J. K. 1985. The emergence of norms in competitive decision-making groups. *Administrative Science Quarterly, 30,* 350–372.

Biddle, B. J., and Thomas, E. J. 1966. *Role theory: Concepts and research.* New York: John Wiley and Sons.

Blake, R., and Mouton, J. 1964. *The managerial grid.* Houston, Texas: Gulf Publishing.

Boyatzis, R. E. 1982. *The competent manager: A model for effective performance.* New York: Wiley-Interscience.

Boyatzis, R. E. 1995. Cornerstones of change, building the path for self-directed learning. In R. E. Boyatzis, S. S. Cowen, and D. A. Kolb (Eds.), *Innovation in professional education* (pp. 50–91). San Francisco: Jossey-Bass.

Costa, P. T. Jr., and McCrae, R. R. 1994. Set like plaster? Evidence for the stability of adult personality. In T. F. Heatherton and J. L. Weinberger (Eds.), *Can personality change?* (pp. 21–40). Washington, D.C.: American Psychological Association.

De Dreu, C. K. W., and Weingart, L. R. 2003. Task versus relationship conflict, team performance, and team member satisfaction. *Journal of Applied Psychology, 88,* 741–749.

DeLeon, L. 2001. Accountability for individuating behaviors in self-managing teams. *Organization Development Journal, 19,* 7–19.

Deutsch, M. 1973. *The resolution of conflict: Constructive and destructive processes.* New Haven, Conn.: Yale University Press.

Druskat, V. U. 1996. *Team-level competencies in superior self-managing manufacturing teams.* Paper presented at the annual meeting of the Academy of Management, Cincinnati, Ohio.

Druskat, V. U., and Wolff, S. B. 1999. Effects and timing of developmental peer appraisals in self-managing work groups. *Journal of Applied Psychology, 84,* 58–74.

Druskat, V. U., and Wolff, S. B. 2001. Building the emotional intelligence of groups. *Harvard Business Review, 79,* 81–90.

Druskat, V. U., Sala, F., and Mount, J. 2006. *Linking emotional intelligence and performance at work.* Mahwah, N.J.: Lawrence Erlbaum Associates.

Druskat, V. U., Wolff, S. B., Messer, T. E., and Stubbs, E. 2003. *Emotionally competent group norms and group effectiveness.* Paper presented at the annual meeting of the Academy of Management, Seattle, Wash.

Elfenbein, H. A. 2006. Team emotional intelligence: What it can mean and how it can impact performance. In V. U. Druskat, F. Sala, and J. Mount (Eds.), *Linking emotional intelligence and performance at work* (pp. 165–184). Mahwah, N.J.: Lawrence Erlbaum Associates.

Feldman, D. C. 1984. The development and enforcement of group norms. *Academy of Management Review, 9,* 47–53.

Flanagan, J. C. 1954. The critical incident technique. *Psychological Bulletin, 51,* 327–358.

Gemmill, G. 1989. The dynamics of scapegoating in small groups. *Small Group Behavior, 20,* 406–418.

Giddens, A. 1984. *The constitution of society: Outline of the theory of structuration.* Berkeley: University of California Press.

Glick, P. 2005. Choice of scapegoats. In J. F. Dovidio, P. Glick, and L. A. Rudman (Eds.), *On the nature of prejudice: Fifty years after Allport* (pp. 244–261). Malden, Mass.: Blackwell Publishing.

Goleman, D. 2001. An EI-based theory of performance. In C. Cherniss and D. Goleman (Eds.), *The emotionally intelligent workplace* (pp. 27–44). San Francisco: Jossey-Bass.

Guzzo, R. A., and Dickson, M. W. 1996. Teams in organizations: Recent research on performance and effectiveness. *Annual Review of Psychology, 47,* 307–338.

Hackman, J. R. 1986. The psychology of self-management in organizations. In M. S. Pallack and R. O. Perloff (Eds.), *Psychology and work: Productivity, change, and employment* (pp. 315–342). Englewood Cliffs, N.J.: Prentice Hall.

Hackman, J. R. 1987. The design of work teams. In J. W. Lorsch (Ed.), *Handbook of organizational behavior* (pp. 315–342). Englewood Cliffs, N.J.: Prentice-Hall.

Heider, F. 1958. *The psychology of interpersonal relations.* New York: Wiley.

Hertel, G., Kerr, N. L., and Messe, L. A. 2000. Motivation gains in performance groups: Paradigmatic and theoretical developments on the Kohler effect. *Journal of Personality and Social Psychology, 79,* 580–601.

Hollander, E. P. 1961. Emergent leadership and social influence. In L. Petrullo and B. Bass (Eds.), *Leadership and interpersonal behavior* (pp. 30–47). New York: Holt Rinehart and Winston.

Jackson, C. L., and LePine, J. A. 2003. Peer responses to a team's weakest link: A test and extension of LePine and Van Dyne's Model. *Journal of Applied Psychology, 28,* 459–475.

James, L. R. 1982. Aggregation bias in estimates of perceptual agreements. *Journal of Applied Psychology, 67,* 219–229.

Janis, I. 1982. *Groupthink.* Boston: Houghton Mifflin.

Jehn, K. A. 1995. A multimethod examination of the benefits and detriments of intragroup conflict. *Administrative Science Quarterly, 40,* 256–282.

Jehn, K. A., and Mannix, E. A. 2001. The dynamic nature of conflict: A longitudinal study of intra-group conflict and group performance. *Academy of Management Journal, 44,* 238–251.

Jehn, K. A., Northcraft, G. B., and Neale, M. A. 1999. Why differences make a difference: A field study of diversity, conflict, and performance in workgroups. *Administrative Science Quarterly, 44,* 741–763.

Jones, E. E., and Davis, K. E. 1965. From acts to dispositions: The attribution process in person perception. In L. Berkowitz (Ed.), *Advances in experimental social psychology* (vol. 2, pp. 220–266). New York: Academic Press.

Kelley, H. H. 1967. Attribution theory in social psychology. In D. Levine (Ed.), *Nebraska symposium on motivation* (vol. 15, pp. 192–240). Lincoln: University of Nebraska Press.

Kemper, T. D. 1978. *A social interactional theory of emotions.* New York: John Wiley and Sons.

Keyton, J. 1999. Relational communication in groups. In L. F. Frey, D. S. Gouran, and M. S. Poole (Eds.), *The handbook of group communication theory and research* (pp. 192–222). Newbury Park, Calif.: SAGE Publications.

Kichuk, S. L., and Wiesner, W. H. 1998. Work team: Selecting members for optimal performance. *Canadian Psychology, 39,* 23–32.

Lawrence, P. R., and Lorsch, J. W. 1967. Differentiation and integration in complex organizations. *Administrative Science Quarterly, 12,* 1–47.

LePine, J. A., and Van Dyne, L. 1998. Predicting voice behavior in work groups. *Journal of Applied Psychology, 83,* 853–868.

Liden, R. C., Wayne, S. J., and Kraimer, M. L. 2001. Managing individual performance in work groups. *Human Resource Management, 40,* 63–72.

Mayer, J. D., and Salovey, P. 1993. The intelligence of emotional intelligence. *Intelligence, 17,* 433–442.

McClelland, D. C. 1976. *A guide to job competency assessment.* Boston: McBer.

McClelland, D. C. 1998. *Assessing competencies: Use of behavioral interviews to assess competencies associated with executive success.* Boston: McBer.

McClelland, D. C., and Dailey, C. 1972. *Improving officer selection for the foreign service.* Boston: McBer.

McLeod, P. L., and Kettner-Polley, R. B. 2004. Contributions of psychodynamic theories to understanding small groups. *Small Group Research, 35,* 333–361.

Milliken, F. J., Bartel, C. A., and Kurtzberg, T. R. 2003. Diversity and creativity in work groups: A dynamic perspective on the affective and cognitive processes that link diversity and performance. In P. B. Paulus and B. A. Nijstad (Eds.), *Group creativity: Innovation through collaboration* (pp. 32–62). New York: Oxford University Press.

Molinsky, A., and Margolis, J. 2005. Necesssary evils and interpersonal sensitivity in organizations. *Academy of Management Review, 30,* 245–268.

Motowidlo, S. J., Carter, G. W., Dunnett, M. D., Tippens, N., Werner, S., Burnett, J. R., et al. 1992. Studies of the structured behavioral interview. *Journal of Applied Psychology, 77,* 571–587.

Pelled, L. H. 1996. Demographic diversity, conflict, and workgroup outcomes: An intervening process theory. *Organization Science, 6,* 615–631.

Peterson, J. B. 1999. *Maps of meaning: The architecture of belief.* New York: Routledge.

Poole, M. S. 1999. Group communication theory. In L. F. Frey, D. S. Gouran, and M. S. Poole (Eds.), *The handbook of group communication theory and research* (pp. 88–165). Newbury Park, Calif.: SAGE Publications.

Pruitt, D. G., and Rubin, J. Z. 1986. *Social conflict: Escalation, stalemate, and settlement.* New York: Random House.

Ridgeway, C. L. 1987. Nonverbal behavior, dominance, and the basis of status in task groups. *American Sociological Review, 52,* 683–694.

Ronan, W. W., and Latham, G. P. 1974. The reliability and validity of the critical incident technique: A closer look. *Studies in Personnel Psychology, 6,* 53–64.

Rusbult, C. E., Farrell, D., Rogers, G., and Mainous, A. G. III. 1988. Impact of exchange variables on exit, voice, loyalty and neglect: An integrative model of responses to declining job satisfaction. *Academy of Management Journal, 31,* 599–627.

Sala, F. 2006. The international business case: Emotional intelligence competencies and important business outcomes. In V. U. Druskat, F. Sala, and J. Mount (Eds.), *Linking emotional intelligence and performance at work* (pp. 125–144). Mahwah, N.J.: Lawrence Erlbaum Associates.

Salas, E., Sims, D. E., and Burke, C. S. 2005. Is there a "big five" in teamwork? *Small Group Research, 36,* 555–599.

Salovey, P., Bedell, B. T., Detweiler, J. B., and Mayer, J. D. 2000. Current directions in emotional intelligence research. In M. Lewis and J. M. Haviland-Jones (Eds.), *Handbook of emotions,* 2nd edition (pp. 504–518). New York: Guilford Press.

Simons, T., and Peterson, R. 2000. Task conflict and relationship conflict in top management teams: The pivotal role of intragroup trust. *Journal of Applied Psychology, 85,* 102–111.

Smith, K. K., and Berg, D. N. 1987. *Paradoxes of group life.* San Francisco: Jossey-Bass.

Spencer, L. M., and Spencer, S. M. 1993. *Competence at work: Models for superior performance.* New York: Wiley.

Stewart, G. L., Fulmer, I. S., and Barrick, M. R. 2005. An exploration of member roles as a multi-level linking mechanism for individual traits and team outcomes. *Personnel Psychology, 58,* 343–365.

Tuckman, B. W. 1965. Developmental sequence in small groups. *Psychological Bulletin, 63,* 384–399.

Tyler, T., Degoey, P., and Smith, H. 1996. Understanding why the justice of group procedures matters. *Journal of Personality and Social Psychology, 70,* 913–930.

Van Dyne, L. L., and LePine, J. A. 1998. Helping and voice extra-role behavior: Evidence of construct and predictive validity. *Academy of Management Journal, 41,* 108–119.

Von Glinow, M. A., Shapiro, D. L., and Brett, J. M. 2004. Can we talk, and should we? Managing emotional conflict in multicultural teams. *Academy of Management Review, 29,* 578–592.

Wageman, R., and Hackman, J. R. 2006. *Top management teams.* Working paper, Dartmouth College.

Wolff, S. B., and Druskat, V. U. 2005. *Toward a socioemotional theory of work group effectiveness.* Unpublished manuscript.

Chapter 10

INTERVENING IN INTRATEAM CONFLICT

Ruth Wageman and Ashley Donnenfeld

ABSTRACT

While intrateam conflict is observed and experienced in the behavioral and affective processes of teams, such processes may not be the ideal point of intervention for improving a team's conflict and its ultimate effectiveness. In this chapter, we compare four kinds of interventions that have been proposed to help teams experience constructive and avoid destructive conflict, we propose a hierarchy of intervention effectiveness, and we explore the implications of our propositions for the kinds of individual capabilities that would allow one to manage conflict well.

INTRODUCTION

Team effectiveness is directly influenced by the kind and amount of conflict that occurs among members (see chapter 1 in this volume). The purpose of this chapter is to address how to best use research knowledge about conflict within teams to enhance the effectiveness of task-performing teams in organizations. We present a framework for intervening in team conflict that (1) draws on existing knowledge of team conflict and team performance effectiveness, (2) proposes a hierarchy of steps organization members can take to address conflicts in their teams, and (3) offers to the research community testable propositions that can spark future research aimed at expanding our collective knowledge about how to intervene in intrateam conflict.

The primary question addressed in this chapter is how any individual can help a team handle conflict in a way that enhances both the performance effectiveness of a team and the ability of members to work together in the future. Many individuals

261

in organizations can mediate conflict, including team leaders, outside consultants, and team members themselves. We are explicitly agnostic about who might intervene to improve conflict processes. Our aspiration is to identify how we can help any of these individuals develop the cognitive and behavioral capabilities that would enable them to intervene successfully and to improve the effectiveness of their teams. We begin this chapter by defining what we mean by team effectiveness. We then explore how organizational scholars account for the relationships found between conflict processes and team performance effectiveness, and we review the implications of these accounts for well-aimed intervention. We next identify the kinds of interventions for improving team conflict processes that exist in the organizations research literature. We specify testable propositions about the relative effectiveness of and the relationships among four distinct intervention strategies for improving intrateam conflict. Finally, we conclude by exploring the kinds of capabilities it takes for individuals to intervene effectively in intrateam conflict and what is involved in developing those capabilities.

TEAM EFFECTIVENESS: OUTCOMES AND PROCESSES

Our definition of team effectiveness is derived from three criteria described by Hackman (1987). Although the salience of the three dimensions varies across time and circumstances for any team, effective teams balance among them, never completely sacrificing any one to achieve the others. These are the characteristics of team effectiveness:

1. The productive output of the team (that is, its product, service, or decision) meets or exceeds the standards of quantity, quality, and timeliness of the team's clients—the people who receive, review, and/or use the output. It is the views of the clients that count, not those of team members, except in those relatively rare cases when the team is the client of its own work.
2. The processes the team uses in carrying out the work enhance members' capability to work together interdependently in the future. Effective teams are more capable as performing units when a piece of work is finished than they were when it was begun.
3. The group experience contributes positively to the learning and well-being of individual team members, rather than frustrating or alienating them.

We posit that a team's ability to achieve these outcomes is a joint function of three performance processes: (1) the level of *effort* group members collectively expend carrying out task work, (2) the appropriateness to the task of the *performance strategies* the group uses in its work, and (3) the amount of *knowledge and skill* members bring to bear on the task. Any team that expends sufficient effort in its work, deploys a task-appropriate performance strategy, and brings ample talent to bear on the work is quite likely to achieve a high standing on the first criterion of effectiveness just specified. By the same token, teams that operate in ways that leave one or more of these functions unfulfilled—that is, by expending effort insufficient for task demands, relying on performance strategies that are poorly aligned with task requirements, and/or bringing inappropriate or inadequate talent to bear on the work—are likely to fall short of client standards of acceptable performance. We refer to these three performance processes as process criteria of effectiveness (Hackman and Morris, 1975).

Both a characteristic "process loss" (Steiner, 1972) and an opportunity for positive synergy, which we refer to as a process gain, are associated with each of the three performance processes. That is, members may interact in ways that depress the team's effort, the appropriateness of its strategy, and/or the use of members' talent. Alternatively, their interaction may enhance collective effort, generate uniquely appropriate strategies, and/or actively develop members' knowledge and skills.

An example of a common process loss around effort is social loafing, or the withdrawing of effort from a task. Such process losses can occur for a variety of reasons, including poorly designed tasks and personal tensions among members (Cohen, Ledford, and Spreitzer, 1996; Jehn and Mannix, 2001). A strategy-related process loss occurs, for example, when team members interact in ways that result in the team choosing ineffectual approaches to work, including engaging in inadequate debate about the processes, instead of relying on inappropriate habitual routines. Process losses in knowledge and skill occur when members discount or underutilize some of the knowledge and skill in the team. A common problem is misweighting, where a team pays more attention to individuals who have higher status in the group and ignores the talents, skills, and viewpoints of individuals with lower status. Process losses thus not only hurt team performance, they represent instances of a negative rather than a positive trajectory over time, and they undermine the well-being of individual team members.

Process gains, in which group performance is enhanced, can also be associated with the key task processes of effort, strategy, and knowledge and skill. Process gains around effort describe interactions in which members energize each other, building greater shared motivation and commitment to the team. Process gains around strategy can be seen when members interact in ways that lead them to develop uniquely suited approaches to the task that individuals could not have generated on their own (synergy). Finally, a typical process gain around knowledge and skill is mutual teaching and learning, in which the capabilities of individual team members are actively built and elevated during the interaction process. These kinds of process gains contribute not only to the ultimate performance of the team, but they also are signs of a positive trajectory over time and contribute substantially to the well-being of members as they learn together and energize each other.

THE RELATIONSHIP OF INTRATEAM CONFLICT LEVELS AND TYPES TO TEAM EFFECTIVENESS

In the following section, we examine the empirical research associating intrateam conflict with both positive and negative team effectiveness outcomes, with a focus on the explanations for the impact of intrateam conflict on team effectiveness generated by scholars in this arena. We show that authors of empirical studies of conflict in teams rely on the previously described three key task processes to draw causal links between conflict and effects on team outcomes. That is, conflict influences team effectiveness in the areas of effort, strategies, and the amount of talent actually brought to bear on the task.

Chapter 1 reviews in depth the three types of conflict that are distinguished in the empirical literature—relational conflict, task conflict, and process conflict—and note that each of the three influences team effectiveness, though in different ways and to differing degrees. In the following paragraphs, we summarize how these three kinds of conflict influence team performance effectiveness and trace those effects through their impact on team effort, strategy, and talent.

RELATIONSHIP CONFLICT AND TEAM EFFECTIVENESS

Emotional or relationship conflict, which is present when friction, tension, and dislike occur among group members, hurts team effectiveness. Dissatisfaction with the group, poor results, and a decreased likelihood that the group will work together in the future all are associated with reported relationship conflict (Jehn, 1995; Roseman, Wiest, and Swartz, 1994; Shah and Jehn, 1993). In addition, problems often associated with relationship conflict in groups include withdrawal and loss of motivation, free-riding, and opinion conformity (Wageman and Mannix, 1998).

What kinds of explanations exist for why relational conflicts undermine team effectiveness? A consistent effort-related theme is noticeable among these accounts. For example, Jehn (1994) argues that relational conflict causes team members to withdraw emotionally from the team as a whole and encumbers their commitment to the task. Amason (1996) posits that relational conflict produces a distraction effect, because a group engaged in attempting to fix the relationships in the team is no longer focusing its efforts on the task. In other words, relationship conflict undermines team effectiveness because it reduces the effort members apply to the task. Most of the explanations we found for the effect of relational conflict on team effectiveness operate through the key task process of team-level effort. An exception is Rahim (2002), who offers the argument that knowledge and skills within a team are underused when a team has relational conflicts. Rahim argues that when individual members of the team are shut out of the group process or when certain team members dominate the discussion as a consequence of relational issues, the team does not draw upon its full complement of talents, and it alienates certain members (also an effort effect).

TASK CONFLICT AND TEAM EFFECTIVENESS

A few past studies suggest that task conflict has beneficial effects on team performance (Amason, 1996; Jehn and Mannix, 2001). Specifically, moderate levels of task conflict with no relationship or process conflict can help group performance in a variety of group tasks (Jehn and Chatman, 2000). Other studies, however, have found no effect or a negative effect of task conflict on team task performance. Regardless of the direction of the observed effect, two explanations for the existence of these effects have been offered. When task conflict has positive influences on team task performance, the reasoning is usually an argument about how task conflict produces better team strategy or knowledge and skill. For example, one line of reasoning is that when members argue and debate different ways of proceeding, they generate better and higher-quality ideas than when there is relatively little debate or disagreement (Mullen and Copper, 1994). Arguments for the benefits of task conflict in the cooperative learning literature typically focus on team knowledge and skill. Johnson, Johnson, and Smith (2000) argue that the exchange of information that happens when task conflict is high actually makes the individual members smarter and results in information being shared that might not otherwise surface, thereby enhancing the degree to which the team uses its full complement of knowledge.

PROCESS CONFLICT AND TEAM EFFECTIVENESS

Process conflict, which is characterized by disagreements about the administrative aspects of the task—who is going to do what, how the work will be subdivided, what roles members will take in the team—hurts team effectiveness (see chapter 1). Two explanations have been offered for the negative effects of process conflict on team effectiveness. Jehn and Mannix (2001) state that process conflict undermines team task performance because it causes the team to use up time and energy arguing about who is going to do what, thereby reducing the effort actually applied to the work itself. It has also been argued that process conflict prevents development of shared perspectives on the task (Jehn and Chatman, 2000). Process conflict, in this view, undermines the quality of the strategy as well as the degree of the coordination team members are able to produce in implementing that strategy, ultimately preventing adaptation and learning as well as high-quality performance.

Despite the diversity of explanations for conflict effects, we find that theories of conflict's effects on team effectiveness operate through the three key task processes we identified earlier. The importance of this point will become evident as we begin to explore intervention strategies in the sections that follow.

INTRATEAM CONFLICT INTERVENTION STRATEGIES

So far, we have established that our collective best understanding of intragroup conflict's effects on team effectiveness occurs through three key task-relevant processes: collective effort, team task strategies, and team use of members' knowledge and skill. In the following section, we describe and characterize four major intervention strategies that have been proposed in the organizations research literature to improve the quality and kinds of conflict that team members experience. The assumption underlying all such proposals is that certain types of conflict that have negative effects on individual and group performance should be reduced, while types of conflict that have positive effects should be enhanced and appropriately managed (Amason, 1996; Jehn, Northcraft, and Neale, 1999; Rahim, 2001).

We distinguish four kinds of interventions that can be used to improve the quality of conflict processes in a team. The most common form of conflict intervention is what we will term "conflict process coaching." Consistent with Hackman and Wageman (2005), we define conflict process coaching as direct intervention in a team to improve the quality of conflict the team is having. Examples in this category include trust-building exercises (to reduce relational conflict) and subgroup structured idea-debates (to increase the degree of task conflict). One virtue of this kind of approach to intervening in conflict is that it theoretically enables group members to learn various behaviors for handling conflict themselves. Consistent with this argument, Rahim (2002) discusses five main styles of handling interpersonal conflict: integrating, obliging, dominating, avoiding, and compromising. Among other common conflict-process coaching techniques are including a devil's advocate in teams or structuring debate so that team members are actively encouraged to disagree with points of view once they are raised. Conflict-process coaching aims to change the behavioral manifestations of conflict directly by eliciting different or countervailing behaviors from team members—but with relatively little success. Innami (1994), for example, shows that devil's advocacy is more effective than other conflict-enhancement techniques for inducing task conflict. However, it can also lead to lower satisfaction and lessened desire to work in the group—creating a trade-off between short-term performance and longer-term team well-being and potentially worsening relational conflicts over time.

A second strategy that is prevalent in the conflict literature is what we refer to as changing the individuals. These interventions predominantly are individual-level training aimed at making the individual team members smarter, more tolerant, or more behaviorally adept when they disagree with others, thereby making the team-level conflict more productive (Baron, 1997; Burke, 1969). Individual-change interventions might include behavioral training in negotiation, cognitive reframing workshops, or attempts to alter members' affective responses to people who hold values or display characteristics that differ from their own. Such interventions operate on two shaky assumptions: (1) that individual characteristics are the underlying cause of conflict, overlooking structural factors altogether, and (2) that changing the individuals outside the context of their teams will address the causes of destructive conflict directly and will transfer readily from the learning setting back into the team process (Argyris and Schon, 1996). Research on the effectiveness of such strategies raises serious doubts about both these assumptions and the ultimate efficacy of individually focused interventions (Lewicki, Weiss, and Lewin, 1992).

The third type of intervention, altering team design, is not widespread in the literature on intrateam conflict. By team design, we mean features of the structure of the team itself and the team's immediate context (Cohen and Ledford, 1994; Hackman, 2002; Wageman, 2001). The use of team design to improve conflict processes has been extensively explored in the cooperative learning and education literatures. For example, a significant number of studies have shown the positive effects of introducing high levels of task and outcome interdependence on constructive conflict in the classroom (Johnson and Johnson, 1989). Not only do they show that teams perform better when these interventions are put in place, but member relationships become more respectful and positive, even in instances of preexisting tension and dislike. In addition, several individuals, most notably Rahim (2002), have argued that structural interventions may be helpful in reducing the level of destructive conflict in organizations because conflicts often are caused by aspects of team structure in the first place. Thus, a team-design intervention, more than conflict-process coaching and individual-level training, may directly alter the causes of intrateam conflict.

The fourth kind of conflict intervention is what we call task process coaching. Task process coaching is coaching that helps the team perform better by improving effort, strategy, and knowledge and skill processes directly. It does not directly address conflict per se. Coaching that addresses effort is motivational in character; its functions are to minimize free-riding or social loafing and to build shared commitment to the group and its work. Coaching that addresses performance strategy is consultative in character; its functions are to minimize mindless adoption or execution of task performance routines and to foster the invention of ways of proceeding with the work that are especially adaptive and well-aligned with task requirements. Coaching that addresses knowledge and skill is educational in character. Its functions are to minimize suboptimal weighting of members' contributions (that is, when the weight given to individual members' contributions is at variance with their actual talents) and to foster the development of members' knowledge and skill (Hackman and Wageman, 2005). The underlying assumption of task-focused coaching as an approach to conflict management is that improving the three key task processes will substantially mitigate the negative effects of conflict on team effectiveness, and where they induce better task debates, they will improve conflict-related processes more directly. Of the four intervention strategies identified here, this approach has been least attempted as a conflict-management approach and least studied for its impact on team effectiveness (Hackman and Wageman, 2005).

Many of the previously described intervention strategies have been employed in the field, but evidence for their effectiveness is thin. Guzzo, Jette, and Katzell's meta-analysis (1985) of psychologically based interventions on performance found that the effects of coaching and individual-change strategies in organizations tend to vary by criterion of performance and contextual factors in organizations, and they often are plagued with problems of research design. We will attempt here to argue for a priority of usefulness of these four different kinds of intervention strategies by combining knowledge of intrateam conflict processes with the research literature on team effectiveness more generally.

PRIORITY AND RELATIONS OF INTRATEAM CONFLICT INTERVENTION STRATEGIES

The following section discusses the priority and interrelations of the four intervention strategies defined previously. The priority we assign to types of interventions is quite different from the priority that they have been assigned in the empirical literature. We argue for the primacy of team design in team conflict intervention, and we outline our propositions consistent with that priority. We argue that (1) design has larger effects on team processes than do coaching the team or changing individuals and (2) process-focused and individual-focused strategies are most effective only when team design is already of good quality. Furthermore, we assert that coaching the task processes directly is more effective for improving team outcomes than is coaching conflict processes per se. Finally, we argue that changing individual attitudes and behavior will have its greatest impact when the context and team processes are first effectively addressed. We pose five propositions about the priority and relationships of intervention strategies in the following list.

> *Proposition 1:* **Team design interventions will have larger positive effects on quality of team processes, including conflict, than will coaching team processes or changing individuals.**
>
> *Proposition 2:* **Process interventions (coaching) and individual strategies are more effective conflict-management strategies when team design is of good quality.**
>
> *Proposition 3:* **Coaching the task processes directly will have more positive effects on team effectiveness than coaching conflict processes.**
>
> *Proposition 4:* **Changing the individuals will have its greatest impact on team conflict and effectiveness when the context and team processes are addressed first.**

Proposition 5: **Individuals will be better at managing intrateam conflict to the degree that they have (1) abstract conceptualization and diagnostic capabilities, (2) a repertoire of intervention practices, and (3) a good sense of timing.**

PROPOSITION 1: DESIGN THE TEAM

The first and most general proposition asserts the primacy of design or structural interventions as the most effective approach to improve processes in a team. Team design establishes the basic process and performance platform for a group, and having a good design increases the quality of all three criteria of effectiveness (Hackman and O'Connor, 2004; Wageman, Hackman, and Lehman, 2005). We draw here on Hackman's (1987, 1990, 2002) proposed conditions for a good-quality design within a group. We define high-quality team design as (1) a real work team with (2) a compelling direction, (3) an enabling structure, and (4) a supportive organizational context (Hackman, 2002). We define each of these features briefly and then explain their impact on team effectiveness.

Real Team
Real work teams are teams with clear boundaries that reliably distinguish members from nonmembers (Alderfer, 1980). They have interdependence for some common purpose (Wageman, 1999; Wageman and Gordon, 2004). Finally, they have at least moderate stability of membership, which gives members time and opportunity to learn how to work together well (Hackman, 2002, pp. 54–59).

Compelling Direction
The direction of a group is the specification of its overall purposes. Good team direction is challenging (which energizes members), it is clear (which orients them to their main purposes), and it is consequential (which engages the full range of their talents).

Enabling Structure
The following three structural features are key in fostering competent teamwork (Hackman and O'Connor, 2004; Wageman et al., 2005).

1. *Task design.* The team task has a high standing on what Hackman and Oldham (1980) call "motivating potential." This means that the team task (1) is a whole and meaningful piece of work (2) for which members have autonomy to exercise judgment about work procedures and that it (3) provides members with regular and trustworthy data about how well the team is doing.

2. *Team composition.* The team is as small as possible given the work to be accomplished, has members with ample task and interpersonal skills, and should consist of a good mix of members—people who are neither so similar to one another that they

duplicate one another's resources nor so different that they are unable to communicate or coordinate well.

3. *Core norms of conduct.* A team should have established early in its life clear and explicit specification of the basic norms of conduct for members' behavior. Shared expectations about behavior—whether imported by members from other group experiences, developed gradually as the team goes about its work, or explicitly specified by the person who creates the team—tend to remain in place until something fairly dramatic occurs to prompt members to reconsider what behaviors are and are not appropriate (Gersick, 1988).

Supportive Organizational Context

In addition to the material resources needed for actually carrying out the work, three features of the organizational context are especially consequential for work performed by teams. First, the reward system should provide positive consequences for excellent team performance. Second, the educational system should make available to the team, at the team's initiative, technical or educational assistance for any aspects of the work for which members are not already knowledgeable, skilled, or experienced—including, if necessary, the honing of members' skills in working together on collective tasks. And third, the information system should provide the team with whatever data and projections members need to select or invent strategies that are fully appropriate for the team's task and situation as it carries out its work.

Collectively, these elements—real team, compelling purpose, enabling structure, supportive context—create a strong platform for the three key task processes of effort, strategy, and use of member knowledge and skill. We propose that altering and improving features of the team's design is the intervention that should be applied first when trying to improve the effectiveness of a team. We suggest this because a high-quality team design establishes powerful and persistent positive influences on the key processes—including conflict processes—that drive performance over time. Effort, strategy, and use of knowledge and skill are strongly established by aspects of the team's purpose or direction, the performing unit itself, and the organizational context (see Figure 10.1).

For example, the level of effort in a team arises out of a consequential purpose (Abramis, 1990; Ginnett, 1993), a motivationally well-designed task (Hackman and Oldham, 1980), and a reward system that provides highly valued rewards for team excellence (Lawler, 2005; Wageman, 1995). When the quality of the direction, the task design, and the rewards are well designed, the energy of team members is predominantly focused on getting the task done well. An engaging task that members care deeply about accomplishing both for intrinsic and extrinsic reasons can propel a level of effort less vulnerable to distracting factors such as value differences, demographic differences, or emotional feelings about each other.

Direction	Structure	Context	➡	Process
Consequential	Motivating team task	Team rewards		Effort
Clear	Core norms	Information system		Strategy
Challenging	Composition	Education system		Talent

Figure 10.1
Impact of Team Design Elements on Key Task Processes

Similarly, a team is able to engage in generating an appropriate approach to the team task when its direction is clear, when it has orienting norms and boundaries around acceptable and unacceptable behavior in the group (Bettenhausen and Murnighan, 1985; Gersick, 1988), and when the information system provides the team members with the data they need to plan their work (Abramis, 1990; Bikson, Cohen, and Mankin, 1999). Under these circumstances, a team is better able to appropriately judge good strategies and to increase the chances that there is lively and intelligent debate about different approaches to the work that results in a genuinely shared mental model for their collaborative work (Mathieu, Heffner, Goodwin, Salas, and Cannon-Bowers, 2000). Finally, when a team is challenged by its purpose to bring its best to the table, when members have a high level of capability for task and team work (Campion, Medsker, and Higgs, 1993; Druskat, 1996; Goodman and Shah, 1992) and when members have access to expert consultation where needed, the team is likely to use well its full range of abilities. It is less likely to suppress or overlook essential knowledge and skill in the team, even in the presence of interpersonal tensions (Guzzo, Wagner, Maguire, Herr, and Hawley, 1986; Johnson and Johnson, 1989).

Thus, the key task processes that are undermined or enhanced by conflict processes in the team and that explain how conflict hurts or helps effectiveness are sturdily established on a positive trajectory by good team design.

Second, intervention in the design of a team will directly address the root causes of most intrateam conflicts (Rahim, 2002). Many empirical studies, particularly the correlational field studies of conflict in organizations, primarily consider the impact, degree, and nature of the conflict on various kinds of affective, behavioral, cognitive, and performance outcomes for teams. However, relatively few such studies look at the antecedents of that conflict.

Nonetheless, there are many examples of conflict being driven by team design, including some from a current study of teams made up of senior executives (Wageman, Nunes, Burruss, and Hackman, in press). We find dysfunctional conflict in senior teams most often when there are flaws in the direction, task design, reward system, and/or composition of the team. For example, when the purpose of a senior management team is unclear, many teams are unable to sustain constructive conflict to the point of reaching a conclusion. Since their ultimate purpose as a team is vague and ill-defined, they have no shared orientation toward a criterion that would allow them to collectively assess different viewpoints—they can only agree to disagree. A common pattern seen in these senior executive teams is the presence of very high scores for challenge and consequentiality of purpose (work considered to be meaningful and important to others) and relatively low scores for clarity of purpose (Wageman et al., in press). When the team purpose is unclear, team members experience stress from their inability to find shared orientations during debates, resulting in interpersonal friction and abandonment of important issues.

Additionally, our findings show that senior executive teams are, to a surprising degree, wasting their meeting time doing relatively trivial and meaningless tasks. For example, many of these teams are meeting for the sole purpose of doing individual presentations to each other about what is going on in the organization, instead of engaging strategic, enterprise-level issues. As a consequence, it may be that some of the relational conflict seen among team members is behavior produced from lack of relevance of others' work to their concerns, and therefore lack of respect for the contributions of others (Pelled, Eisenhardt, and Xin, 1999; Jehn and Mannix, 2001). Better work design could improve relationships in the team by producing a degree of consequentiality and interdependence that contributes to mutual respect (Tyler and Blader, 2003).

A third cause of destructive conflict in senior executive teams is faulty rewards systems. Reward systems that focus on individual rewards and do not reward excellent team performance lead to many recurring disputes about decisions that individuals are motivated to make that optimize their own unit's performance and suboptimize collective outcomes. Clarifying direction, redesigning tasks, and providing meaningful team-level rewards would remove the root causes of dysfunctional relational conflict in these teams and simultaneously allow their task-based disagreements to be resolved in ways that enhance rather than undermine their performance. Even when relationships already are poor, well-focused design interventions can simultaneously improve relationships and refocus task processes to create positive team outcomes. Johnson and Johnson (1989) and their colleagues (for example, Johnson et al., 2000) find that even in schools characterized by a history of intergroup hostility and intolerance among students, task and reward structure interventions in teams enabled collaborative learning and performance and increased liking and respect among team members.

Finally, the third argument for why design should be the starting place for conflict intervention in teams is that team design also directly influences the quality of the relationships that emerge in a team. Donnenfeld and Wageman (2005) conducted a field study on the joint effects of friendship and the quality of design in 54 cooperative learning project teams. The research showed that the quality of the team design had a strong impact on the level of friendships that evolved in the team. Good design led to a well-functioning team on the three key task processes, and these led to the accomplishment of good work. Liking for one another was directly affected by subjects' sense of shared task accomplishment.

Moreover, well designed teams did not have the additional problems that the poorly designed groups had, such as friction among members over free-riding and a decreased ability to get work accomplished because of poor clarity of direction. Thus, the solution to relational conflict is not, we argue, to fix the relationships in the team directly, but rather to improve the quality of the team's design. Good relationships in a team—those that include trust, respect, and high-quality interactions—develop when its members are able to accomplish something significant together, and the predominant influence enabling significant accomplishment is the quality of the team design.

PROPOSITION 2: COACH THE TEAM AFTER DESIGNING IT WELL

Proposition 2 states that coaching interventions and individual strategies are more effective when design is already of good quality. Coaching that focuses on the three key performance processes reinforces the impact on those processes of the structural and contextual features discussed in the previous section. Having a compelling direction, an enabling structure, and a supportive organizational context facilitates good coaching because it permits the team leader to focus mainly on strengthening and reinforcing the impact of the performance-enhancing conditions. When these conditions are not present, however, even well-focused, competently provided coaching is likely to be futile.

In a field study of service teams at the Xerox Corporation, Wageman (2001) found that competent coaching (for example, conducting a problem-solving process) helped well-designed teams exploit their favorable circumstances but made little difference for poorly designed teams. In contrast, poor coaching (for example, identifying a team's problems and telling members how they should solve them) was much more harmful to poorly designed teams than for those that had an enabling team structure and a supportive organizational context. Thus, one cannot coach a poorly designed team to greatness. On the other hand, better-designed teams not only have a higher baseline level of performance, they do even better with effective coaching

(Wageman, 2001). Coaching thus further helps a group realize the benefits of a good basic design.

In addition, structural and contextual features are more important than coaching as influences on team performance processes and outcomes (Cohen et al., 1996). In the Xerox study, Wageman (2001) found that the team design features just described controlled significantly more variance both in the level of team self-management behaviors and in performance effectiveness than did team leaders' coaching behaviors. For team self-management, design features controlled 42 percent of the variance, compared with less than 10 percent for measures that assessed the quality of leaders' coaching activities. For team performance, design controlled 37 percent of the variance, compared with less than 1 percent for coaching. These findings are consistent with other evidence showing that even highly competent process-focused coaching by team leaders or consultants cannot prevail when team processes are controlled or constrained by strong structural or contextual forces (Cohen et al., 1996; Hackman, 1987). It is nearly impossible to coach a team to effectiveness in performance situations that undermine rather than support teamwork.

PROPOSITION 3: COACH ABOUT THE TASK PROCESSES INSTEAD OF CONFLICT PROCESSES

Proposition 3 states that coaching the task processes directly will have a more positive impact than coaching conflict processes. First, relational interventions tend to elicit high degrees of resistance relative to discussions regarding motivation, strategy, and the use of knowledge and skill in the team (Schein, 1988). Relational issues are more personal, fraught, and emotionally threatening than more objective-seeming and impersonal task issues. Therefore, motivational, consultative, and educational interventions are more likely to be enacted and used by a team than are relational interventions.

A second reason that coaching the task process will have greater impact than coaching conflict processes is the effect of coaching on team attention. The teams research literature has pointed out that we all have cognitive limits in our attentional capacities (e.g., Driskell, Salas, and Johnston, 1999). If an individual pays attention to one aspect of team process, he or she is less focused on the other aspects of the team process. Therefore, individuals who focus on reducing relational troubles and conflict in the team are distracted from focus on the task itself. Kaplan's meta-analysis (1979) of the process intervention literature shows that process consultation—direct intervention in the quality of relationships in the team—does not improve team task performance. Coaching relational processes does help teams become more satisfied with relationships and more engaged in the process of working on relationships, but members also become more distracted from the team's work. As a consequence, several of the studies he reviewed showed negative effects of process consultation on performance, as members refocused their energies on relationships and away from doing the actual task of the team.

Third, there is significant evidence in the education literature (Johnson et al., 2000) that constructive controversy—a *task* strategy process intervention—also builds better quality *relationships* in teams. Interventions focused directly on the tasks that help individuals to learn and to generate and evaluate ideas together increase liking, tolerance, and trust in the team. Constructive controversy allows the focus to be on the work itself while good relations among team members are being built at the same time. It is important to note that the phenomenon does not occur in reverse—good-quality relations do not produce constructive controversy. In fact, Woolley (1998) showed that although groups receiving interpersonal process interventions have a subjective experience of functioning better, they do not actually perform better on the task itself. However, improve the process that allows members to accomplish something important together and relationships improve as well.

PROPOSITION 4: WHEN TEAM DESIGN AND TEAM PROCESSES ARE POSITIVE, INDIVIDUALS HAVE A BETTER CHANCE TO BECOME GOOD CONFLICT MANAGERS

Proposition 4 states that changing the individuals will have its greatest impact when the team design and team processes are addressed first. Because individual intervention is more successful when the context and the basic team processes are good, any intervention designed to change the individual should be enacted last in a conflict intervention package. For example, a conflict intervention described by Johnson, Johnson, and Smith (2001) called "Teaching Students to be Peacemakers" had its most positive effects only in the presence of a good team design. Students experiencing high levels of task interdependence with peers, where students were responsible for collectively learning some material and were graded on how well they did so, were better able to learn new conflict-management behaviors. Further, researchers have noted that when members learn new behaviors outside the context of their teams, they lose the learned behavior when they return to the context in which they operate. However, individuals who learn the new behavior within their work teams are much more likely to be able to use it in organizational settings (Lewicki et al., 1992). Thus, the design and process should first be established before addressing any individual interventions.

PROPOSITION 5: WHO CAN INTERVENE EFFECTIVELY IN INTRATEAM CONFLICT?

The following section focuses on some of the key capacities that might enhance the ability of individuals to intervene effectively in intrateam conflict. Proposition 5 asserts that three key capacities enable individuals to develop conflict-intervention skills. These capacities are not intended to represent an exhaustive list of abilities that contribute to conflict-management effectiveness; rather, they are those that derive directly from the prior propositions offered in this chapter.

First are conceptualization and diagnostic skills. Abstract conceptualization and diagnostic skills allow an individual to perceive and interpret, for example, the kinds of design flaws that might be driving conflict processes when too little task conflict or too much emotional conflict in the team is observed. An individual intervener must be able to take an abstract concept, such as clarity of direction, and look at the particular concrete situation within which he or she is working to see what needs to be altered to improve the quality of the team design.

There also are related diagnostic skills that should be developed in an individual who wishes to intervene in his or her team effectively. First, a team member would be helped by learning to be a good observer of team processes, remaining alert and vigilant in detecting behavioral signs of conflict. High-quality observational skills allow an individual to see the magnitude, the focus, and the type of conflict emerging in the team. For example, there may be different behavioral signs when a conflict is driven by a poorly designed reward system than when it is driven by a lack of clarity in the team direction. In addition, at the very minimum, individuals must learn the differences between constructive and destructive types of conflict. This kind of learning can be developed and honed in a traditional classroom setting. Examining, discussing, and comparing cases of team design and behavior helps students to derive diagnoses of underlying causes of conflict and to generate redesign solutions. However, as will be seen, other essential capabilities are less amenable to our traditional means of teaching.

The second capability an individual intervener needs is a repertoire of ways of intervening. If our propositions are correct, an individual almost certainly will need to intervene with people outside the team to improve the quality of a team design. For example, for a team suffering from competitive rewards, a local team leader is unlikely to have the authority to redesign the reward system. As a consequence, individuals should be helped to develop the political skills they need to exercise influence upward and outward in the organization.

Similarly, for task-focused coaching, an individual needs multiple ways of generating high-quality strategy debates, for example, and a repertoire of ways of raising the level of motivation to reengage members' efforts—such as rearticulating the consequentiality and challenge of the purpose, setting goals, and the like. Intervening in conflict thus probably requires high-level improvisatory behavioral skills, in which the individual intervening in the team generates uniquely suited coaching interventions for that team at that particular moment. Thus, the development of programs that teach individual action skills are essential for developing conflict intervention capabilities. Action skills are developed not through lectures and discussions, but through observing, practicing, experiencing feedback, and iterating. This kind of development may demand that we generate novel methods of teaching—for example, allowing small groups to practice and provide feedback, lengthening meeting times to allow iterative practice, and providing individual behavioral coaching by experts.

Finally, we believe that intervening in intrateam conflict requires that individuals develop a good sense of timing. There are times in the life of the group when members are relatively less open to intervention, and at these times an intervention in the team process will not be well received, will not be effective in helping the team, and may actually be detrimental. On the other hand, there are times in the life of the group when a team is especially open to intervention (Fisher, Hackman and Wageman, 2005). A coaching intervention is more effective when the team is ready to address the issues at the time the intervention is made. That readiness varies systematically across the team life cycle. By contrast, even competently administered interventions are unlikely to be helpful if they are provided at a time during the life cycle when the team is not ready for them. Ill-timed interventions may actually do more harm than good by distracting or diverting a team from other issues that require members' attention at that time. Thus, individuals need to develop good timing skills and understand that certain kinds of interventions are most appropriate at the beginning, midpoint, or end of the work team's life cycles (Hackman and Wageman, 2005). In addition, individuals need a degree of emotional stability, because there will be times when for the good of the team it is best to wait and let a conflict get worse, even though the urge to intervene will be strong. Such skill development may require extraordinary creativity on the part of trainers. Techniques for developing timing might include creating experiences that genuinely raise learners' anxieties and provide direct opportunity to practice observation, patience, and behavioral dexterity.

In sum, if our propositions about intervening in team conflict hold, a combination of conceptual knowledge about the kinds of interventions that do and do not stand a chance of helping team conflict processes, behavioral skills, and a fine sense of timing all serve as a good focus for our development activities in helping individuals in organizations successfully intervene in intrateam conflict.

REFERENCES

Abramis, D. J. 1990. Semiconductor manufacturing team. In J. R. Hackman (Ed.), *Groups that work (and those that don't)* (pp. 449–470). San Francisco: Jossey-Bass.

Alderfer, C. P. 1980. Consulting to underbounded systems. In C. P. Alderfer and C. L. Cooper (Eds.), *Advances in experimental social processes* (vol. 2, pp. 267–295). New York: Wiley.

Amason, A. C. 1996. Distinguishing the effects of functional and dysfunctional conflict on strategic decision making: Resolving a paradox for top management teams. *Academy of Management Journal, 39,* 123–148.

Argyris, C., and Schon, D. A. 1996. *Organizational learning II: Theory, method, and practice.* Reading, Mass.: Addison-Wesley.

Baron, R. A. 1997. Positive effects of conflict: Insights from social cognition. In C. K. W. De Dreu and E. Van de Vliert (Eds.), *Using conflict in organizations* (pp. 177–191). London: SAGE Publications.

Bettenhausen, K., and Murnighan, J. K. 1985. The emergence of norms in competitive decision-making groups. *Administrative Science Quarterly, 30,* 350–372.

Bikson, T. K., Cohen, S. G., and Mankin, D. 1999. Information technology and high-performance teams. In E. Sundstrom (Ed.), *Supporting work team effectiveness* (pp. 215–245). San Francisco: Jossey-Bass.

Burke, R. J. 1969. Methods of resolving superior-subordinate conflict: The constructive role of subordinate differences and disagreements. *Organizational Behavior and Human Performance, 5,* 393–411.

Campion, M. A., Medsker, G. J., and Higgs, A. C. 1993. Relations between work group characteristics and effectiveness: Implications for designing effective work groups. *Personnel Psychology, 46,* 823–850.

Cohen, S. G., and Ledford, G. E. Jr. 1994. The effectiveness of self-managing teams: A quasi-experiment. *Human Relations, 47,* 13–43.

Cohen, S. G., Ledford, G. E. Jr., and Spreitzer, G. M. 1996. A predictive model of self-managing work team effectiveness. *Human Relations, 49,* 643–676.

Donnenfeld, A., and Wageman, R. 2005. *The joint effect of group design and friendship on team effectiveness.* Under editorial review.

Driskell, J. E., Salas, E., and Johnston, J. 1999. *Group dynamics: Theory, research and practice.* Mahwah, N.J.: Lawrence Erlbaum Associates.

Druskat, V. U. 1996. *Team-level competencies in superior performing self-managing work teams.* Paper presented at the annual meeting of the Academy of Management, Cincinnati, Ohio.

Fisher, C., Hackman, J. R., and Wageman, R. 2005. *Teaching good timing in team interventions.* Under editorial review.

Gersick, C. J. G. 1988. Time and transition in work teams: Toward a new model of group development. *Academy of Management Journal, 31,* 9–41.

Ginnett, R. C. 1993. Crews as groups: Their formation and their leadership. In E. L. Wiener, B. G. Kanki, and R. L. Helmreich (Eds.), *Cockpit resource management* (pp. 71–98). Orlando, Fla.: Academic Press.

Goodman, P. S., and Shah, S. 1992. Familiarity and work group outcomes. In S. Worchel, W. Wood., and J. Simpson (Eds.), *Group process and productivity* (pp. 276–298). London: SAGE Publications.

Guzzo, R. A., Jette, R. D., and Katzell, R.A. 1985. The effects of psychologically based intervention programs on worker productivity: A meta-analysis. *Personnel Psychology, 38,* 275–291.

Guzzo, R. A., Wagner, D. B., Maguire, E., Herr, B., and Hawley, C. 1986. Implicit theories and the evaluation of group process and performance. *Organizational Behavior and Human Decision Processes, 37,* 279–295.

Hackman, J. R. 1987. The design of work teams. In J. Lorsch (Ed.), *Handbook of organizational behavior* (pp. 315–342). Englewood Cliffs, N.J.: Prentice Hall.

Hackman, J. R. 1990. *Groups that work (and those that don't).* San Francisco: Jossey-Bass.

Hackman, J. R. 2002. *Leading teams: Setting the stage for great performances.* Boston: Harvard Business School Press.

Hackman, J. R., and Oldham, G. R. 1980. *Work redesign.* Reading, Mass.: Addison-Wesley.

Jackman, J. R., and Morris, C. G. 1975. Group tasks, group interaction process, and group performance effectiveness: A review and proposed integration. In L. Berkowitz (Ed.), *Advances in experimental social psychology* (vol. 8, pp. 45–99). New York: Academic Press.

Hackman, J. R., and O'Connor, M. 2004. *What makes for a great analytic team? Individual vs. team approaches to intelligence analysis.* Washington, D.C.: Intelligence Science Board, Office of the Director of Central Intelligence.

Hackman, J. R., and Wageman, R. 2005. A theory of team coaching. *Academy of Management Review, 30,* 269–287.

Innami, I. 1994. The quality of group decisions, group verbal behavior, and intervention. *Organizational Behavior and Human Decision Processes, 60,* 409–430.

Jehn, K. A. 1994. Enhancing effectiveness: An investigation of advantages and disadvantages of value-based intragroup conflict. *International Journal of Conflict Management, 5,* 223–238.

Jehn, K. A. 1995. A multimethod examination of the benefits and detriments of intragroup conflict. *Administrative Science Quarterly, 40,* 256–282.

Jehn, K. A. 1997. A qualitative analysis of conflict types and dimensions of organizational groups. *Administrative Science Quarterly, 44,* 741–763.

Jehn, K. A., and Chatman, J. A. 2000. The influence of proportional and perceptual conflict composition on team performance. *International Journal of Conflict Management, 11,* 56–73.

Jehn, K. A., and Mannix, E. A. 2001. The dynamic nature of conflict: A longitudinal study of intragroup conflict and group performance. *Academy of Management Journal, 44*(2), 238–251.

Jehn, K. A., Northcraft, G. B., and Neale, M. A. 1999. Why differences make a difference: A field study of diversity, conflict, and performance in work groups. *Administrative Science Quarterly, 44,* 741–763.

Johnson, D. W., and Johnson, R. T. 1989. *Cooperation and competition: Theory and research.* Edina, Minn.: Interaction Book Company.

Johnson, D. W., Johnson, R. T., and Smith, K. A. 2000. Constructive controversy. *Change, 32*(1), 28–37.

Kaplan, R. E. 1979. The conspicuous absence of evidence that process consultation enhances task performance. *Journal of Applied Behavioral Science, 15,* 346–360.

Lawler, E. E. 2005. Pay systems for virtual teams. In C. Gibson and S. G. Cohen (Eds.), *Creating conditions for effective virtual teams.* San Francisco: Jossey-Bass.

Lewicki, R. J., Weiss, S. E., and Lewin, D. 1992. Models of conflict, negotiation and third-party intervention: A review and synthesis. *Journal of Organizational Behavior, 13,* 209–252.

Mathieu, J. E., Heffner, T. S., Goodwin, G. F., Salas, E., and Cannon-Bowers, J. A. 2000. The influence of shared mental models on team process and performance. *Journal of Applied Psychology, 85,* 273–283.

Mullen, B., and Copper, C. 1994. The relation between group cohesiveness and performance: An integration. *Psychological Bulletin, 115,* 210–227.

Pelled, L. H., Eisenhardt, K. M., and Xin, K. R. 1999. Exploring the black box: An analysis of work group diversity, conflict, and performance. *Administrative Science Quarterly, 44,* 1–28.

Rahim, M. A. 2001. *Managing conflict in organizations, 3rd ed.* Westport, Conn.: Quorum Books.

Rahim, M. A. 2002. Toward a theory of managing organizational conflict. *International Journal of Conflict Management, 13,* 206–235.

Roseman, I., Wiest, C., and Swartz, T. 1994. Phenomenology, behaviors, and goals differentiate emotions. *Journal of Personality and Social Psychology, 67,* 206–221.

Schein, E. H. 1988. *Process consultation* (vol. 1). Reading, Mass.: Addison-Wesley.

Shah, P., and Jehn, K. A. 1993. Do friends perform better than acquaintances? The interaction of friendship, conflict, and task. *Group Decision and Negotiation, 2,* 149–165.

Steiner, I. D. 1972. *Group process and productivity.* New York: Academic Press.

Tyler, T. R., and Blader, S. L. 2003. The group engagement model: Procedural justice, social identity and cooperative behavior. *Personality and Social Psychology Review, 7,* 349–361.

Wageman, R. 1995. Interdependence and group effectiveness. *Administrative Science Quarterly, 40,* 145–180.

Wageman, R. 1999. The meaning of interdependence. In M. Turner (Ed.), *Groups at work: Advances in theory and research.* Hillsdale, N.J.: Lawrence Erlbaum and Associates.

Wageman, R. 2001. How leaders foster self-managing team effectiveness: Design choices vs. hands-on coaching. *Organization Science, 12,* 559–577.

Wageman, R., and Gordon, F. 2004. As the twig is bent: How group values shape emergent task interdependence in groups. *Organization Science, 16,* 687–700.

Wageman, R., and Mannix, E. A. 1998. The uses and misuses of power in task-performing teams. In R. Kramer and M. Neale (Eds.), *Power, politics and conflict in organizations* (pp. 261–285). Greenwich, Conn.: JAI Press.

Wageman, R., Hackman, J. R., and Lehman, E. V. 2005. *Team diagnostic survey: Development of an instrument.* Under editorial review.

Wageman, R., Nunes, D., Burruss, J., and Hackman, J. R. In press. *Creating executive teams that work.* Boston: HBS Press.

Woolley, A. A. 1998. Effects of intervention content and timing on group task performance. *Journal of Applied Behavioral Science, 34,* 30–46.

INDEX

182, 189, 191; respect and, 205, 219 (table), 222; social skills for, 26; strategies for, 268; style of, 189; task conflict and, 223; team design and, 275; team effectiveness and, 267; team process and, 275; trust and, 205, 219 (table), 222; understanding, 205

conflict process, 271, 277; aggregating, 174; coaching, 268, 274–75; improving 262, 266, 276; team design and, 267; team effectiveness and, 268

conflict research: autonomy and, 182, 191–94, 198, 200; conflict management and, 191; conflict-related features for, 194 (fig.); constructs/concepts of, 195; directions for, 183, 185, 195–98, 199; implication of, 181; new variables for, 194 (fig.); self-managing teams and, 185; trust and, 182, 191

conflict resolution, 11, 102, 256; approaches to, 172; group process/outcomes and, 17

conformity, 42, 65, 68, 264; group, 11, 12; pressure, 11, 15, 43, 59; reducing, 15

confrontation, 236–37, 245–46; constructive, 231, 254, 255; effective, 229, 237–38, 240; EI skills and, 237–41; linear/quadratic curves relating to, 250 (fig.), 251 (fig.), 252 (fig.), 253 (fig.); minimizing, 234, 235; performance and, 239; positive/negative effects of, 239; team effectiveness and, 237, 239, 240, 241, 246, 247 (table), 248 (table), 249, 249 (table), 250 (fig.), 251 (fig.), 252 (fig.), 253 (fig.), 254; time and, 255–56

consensus: group value, 150, 172; intermember, 174; performance and, 154, 169; variation in, 105, 147, 153, 155, 172; within-group, 153, 168–69

constructive conflict, 10, 267, 272, 275, 276

contributions, 49; conflicts over, 16; expectations and, 44

control, 72, 195

cooperation, 9, 103, 233; between-group, 24, 25; encouraging, 207; goals and, 8; in-group, 115; resisting, 234; resource competition and, 8

coordination, 184; norms and, 232; task interdependence and, 193; team type and, 199

correlations, 218 (table), 247 (table); at facet level, 106 (table); at factor level, 106 (table)

cost/benefit structures, 125, 130; communitarianism and, 117; evolution and, 121–22; heroism and, 117

creativity, 15, 94, 277

critical incident interviews (CIIs), 242, 245

cross-level issues, 174–75

death: rates, estimated, 117; selection and, 117; threat of, 135

decision making, 16, 94; biases in, 11, 15; conflict and, 148; racial diversity in, 42; team, 215

decision-making groups, 4, 10, 11, 14, 15, 38, 39, 47, 69

defenders, role of, 135

delayers, 47

demographic studies, 84

derailers, 234

destructive conflict, 267, 272–73, 276

developing others, 229, 231, 242, 249; mean levels of, 241, 253 (fig.); performance and, 240

devil's advocacy, 11, 13, 15, 16, 266

differences, 37, 40, 44, 45, 147, 153, 155, 184; demographic, xvi, 9, 94, 270; intraindividual, 159; personality, xvi, xvii, 9, 96, 108, 212; reducing, 24–25; social-category, 43; status, 48, 49, 50; task-relevant, 42; testing for, patterns of variability, 156–57, 164, 168; value, 270

dignity, 210, 212; violating, 211

direction: clarifying, 272, 273; flaws in, 272; team, 269, 270, 276

disagreements, 65, 233; expressing, 237, 238; mismanagement of, 12; normative and ongoing, 16; performance and, 154; task-related, 10, 11, 154

discouragement, 23, 98, 102, 105

dispersion, 57, 65; alignment versus, 60–61, 63

disruptive personalities, xviii, 9, 229

dissatisfaction, expressing, 233, 234

diversity, 5, 196; age/gender, 104; balance theory and, 41–44; cognitive, 41, 60; compositional, 61; conceptualizing, 84; conflict and, xv, xvi, 37, 63, 81, 93; creating, 38; deep-level, 94, 96, 108, 150, 151; demographic, 241, 254; faultlines and, 84; group, 39, 57–58, 63, 74, 82, 83; group process and, 43, 95; heterogeneity and, 84; informational, 38, 39, 41; insights on, 39–44; management,

ABOUT THE EDITORS

Kristin J. Behfar is an assistant professor of organization and management at the Paul Merage School of Business, University of California, Irvine.

Leigh L. Thompson is J. Jay Gerber Distinguished Professor of Dispute Resolution and Organizations at the Kellogg School of Management, Northwestern University.